CHRISTIANS IN A SECULAR WORLD

McGILL-QUEEN'S STUDIES IN THE HISTORY OF RELIGION

Volumes in this series have been supported by the Jackman Foundation of Toronto.

SERIES TWO In memory of George Rawlyk
Donald Harman Akenson, Editor

#75.00

Christians in a Secular World

The Canadian Experience

KURT BOWEN

McGill-Queen's University Press
Montreal & Kingston · London · Ithaca

BR570 .B69 2004
0134107290402
Bowen, Kurt, 1946-

Christians in a secular
world : the Canadian
c2004.

2004 11 26

ISBN 0-7735-2711-7

Legal deposit second quarter 2004
Bibliothèque nationale du Québec

Printed in Canada on acid-free paper that is 100% ancient forest free
(100% post-consumer recycled), processed chlorine free.

This book has been published with the help of a grant from the Canadian
Federation for the Humanities and Social Sciences, through the Aid to
Scholarly Publications Programme, using funds provided by the Social
Sciences and Humanities Research Council of Canada.

McGill-Queen's University Press acknowledges the support of the
Canada Council for the Arts for our publishing program. We also
acknowledge the financial support of the Government of Canada
through the Book Publishing Industry Development Program (BPIDP) for
our publishing activities.

National Library of Canada Cataloguing in Publication Data

Bowen, Kurt, 1946–
    Christians in a secular world : the Canadian experience / Kurt Bowen.
    (McGill-Queen's studies in the history of religion, ISSN 1181-7445)
    Includes bibliographical references and index.
    ISBN 0-7735-2711-7
    1. Christians – Canada – Social conditions. 2. Christians – Canada –
    Attitudes. 3. Social surveys – Canada. I. Title. II. Series.
    BR570.B69 2004   305.6'771   C2004-900799-8

Typeset in Palatino 10/13
by Caractéra inc., Quebec City

Contents

CHRISTIANS IN A SECULAR WORLD

1

Secularization and Its Discontents: Theoretical and Historical Preliminaries

One central question shapes this book: Does religion really have any impact on the daily lives of people in our modern world? To refine the matter a little further, does religiousness or its lack appreciably affect the beliefs, values, and behaviours of Canadians? Are our overall levels of well-being and our basic outlook on life affected by how religious we are and by what kind of religion we embrace? Does religion have much influence on how we relate to each other in the intimate sphere of family and friends? Does how religious we are have any discernible impact on how involved we are in our local communities, on how much we give to charity, and on our general level of civic mindedness? And does our level and style of religiousness make much of a difference when it comes to how involved we are in political life, the political parties we support at elections, and the kinds of political policies and priorities we endorse and reject? In the current climate, where secular assumptions prevail, these are matters that are commonly ignored.

The preceding questions set the agenda in four of the six substantive chapters that follow. Those four chapters follow chapter 2, in which I chart recent trends in religious involvement and develop a scale of religiosity incorporating public and private expressions of religious commitment. I also assess whether the religious differ much in their social background from the non-religious. Chapter 7, the last substantive chapter, takes up a rather different theme, turning inward

to explore the distinctive religious beliefs of the religiously committed and the diverse ways in which they are involved in their varied
faith communities. My assessment of the state of religion in Canada
at the end of the second millennium then concludes with a review
of the major challenges and controversies that faith communities
today confront.

The questions we ask and the answers we give are invariably
shaped by the quality and type of information we have at our disposal. This book is no exception to that general dictum. Almost all
my conclusions are drawn from eighteen social surveys of Canadians
between 1975 and 1997, conducted by the World Values Survey, Statistics Canada, the Angus Reid polling company, and Reginald Bibby,
who has set a standard for the rest of us by making his treasure trove
of surveys freely available to all scholars on the Internet. Taken
together, these surveys tap the thinking and reported behaviours of
over 100,000 Canadians.

Two general implications stem from my reliance on social surveys.
First, despite the rapid increase in the number of non-Christians in
recent years (described in chapter 2), they remain a tiny minority –
about 5% – of all Canadians. When I refer to the religiously active or
committed, I am therefore speaking of an overwhelmingly Christian
community. Surveys do identify non-Christians, but their numbers
are usually so small in the typical survey of 1,500 that trustworthy
conclusions can rarely be drawn. Since non-Christians range from
Muslims and Jews to Hindus, Rastafarians, and New Agers, to name
but a few, generalizations about them as a group are meaningless. In
short, this is and must be a book about Christians in Canada. Second,
surveys tell us much about the thinking and behaviour of individuals, but surveys by their nature cannot tell us anything about the
travails, successes, and transformations of the social institutions to
which we are all attached. This book is not an account of developments in the life of Canada's churches, though chapter 7 makes a
brief foray in that direction.

Until very recently, sociologists of religion almost invariably took as
axiomatic the secularization thesis that religion is doomed by modernity to ever greater marginality and insignificance. Influenced by the
Enlightenment conviction that religion is a superstition-driven
anachronism, Engels on behalf of the Marxian tradition and Freud
for very different reasons proclaimed the liberating possibilities of
our imminent escape from religious oppression. Weber was much

less sanguine about the growing "disenchantment of the world," but he too believed that the rationalization process at the heart of modernity undermined religion. These early musings were then developed into fully fledged theories of secularization by a variety of European writers in the 1960s and 1970s, of whom the most notable were and are Peter Berger, Thomas Luckmann, David Martin, and Bryan Wilson.[1] For Wilson, who has been the most enduring and articulate spokesman for the secularization thesis, it is "a process whereby religious thinking, practice, and institutions lose social significance."[2] The aforementioned theorists all agree that secularization has been driven by economic development, industrialization, urbanization, and institutional differentiation, which are all components of the broader process of modernization. As a graduate student at this time, I was so persuaded by this broad consensus that I temporarily abandoned the sociology of religion, thinking there was little point in immersing myself in a doomed, dying field.

Yet just as secularization was everywhere being proclaimed as inevitable and indisputable, some began to suggest that the thesis was primarily driven by Enlightenment and socialist antipathies to religion that did not hold up under sustained historical, empirical, and comparative analysis. Particularly telling are the recent, public disavowals by Peter Berger and David Martin, who now say that religious decline is not an inevitable product of modernity[3]. Far more strident are the multiple condemnations by the eminent American sociologist Rodney Stark, who titles a recent article, "Secularization: RIP."[4] It is far beyond the scope of this book to resolve on a global scale these competing claims, but I do need to work out a vocabulary to identify religious trends in Canada, which is certainly a modernized, advanced-industrial, or even postmodern society. The best way forward, as others have observed, is to recognize that the notions of secularization and religiousness both involve a number of different sub-processes that need to be disentangled for us to comprehend the nature and extent of religion's impact today. What follows is my interpretation of these theoretical issues, paying particular heed to the distinctive circumstances of Canada.

SECULARIZATION AS DIFFERENTIATION

Institutional differentiation is the least disputed process associated with secularization. Even Stark at his most tendentious admits, "there would be nothing to argue about,"[5] if the meaning of secularizaton were so confined. Historically, institutional differentiation begins with a growing "separation between church and state." As the process builds momentum, organized religion loses its influence over "justice, ideological legitimation … social control, education, welfare,"[6] and "a range of recreative activities."[7] Each of these newly autonomous social spheres, which shape the lives of all citizens, comes to operate independently of "the originally superordinated"[8] religious domain. For Wilson, "the loss of these functions is the core of the secularization thesis,"[9] a view that Martin also endorses, despite his growing reservations about the secularization thesis as a whole.[10]

Martin is quick to add that he is not proposing some sort of universal, mechanistically inevitable theory. Secularization as differentiation is "centred on the North Atlantic and the West" where "it all began."[11] It is most clearly evident in Europe, where the all-encompassing powers of the church in the medieval period stand as a clear benchmark against which the subsequent separation of church and state may be measured, though there has been considerable variation from country to country in how differentiation has played itself out. That variation is in turn linked to whether the country continued to be predominantly Catholic after the Reformation, the degree to which a religious monopoly was maintained, and whether religious allegiances have been exacerbated by foreign domination and ethnic tensions.[12] As a general rule, Catholic countries with a tradition of religious monopoly have been deeply divided, with Catholics strongly opposed to the modernity that is embraced with equal passion by everyone else. Protestant nations, in contrast, have been much more receptive to modernity. On the other side of the Atlantic, most notably in the United States, the early colonies usually had their established religions. Because of its overwhelmingly Protestant heritage, its principles of democracy and individualism, and the presence of so many dissenters, differentiation – above all the separation of church and state – emerged much earlier and more completely in America than it did in Europe. The result was a competitive pluralism that has given American religion so much of its distinctive vitality.[13] Canada, as we shall see below, has shown characteristics of both the American and the European models. This apparently contradictory state is rooted in and explained by Canada's historic dualism. Thus English-speaking Canada, at least until recently, has had much in common with the American experience. In contrast, French-speaking Quebec closely parallels those European countries in which the Catholic faith of the great majority was reinforced by nationalist tensions brought on by foreign domination.

For Quebec, the British conquest in 1759 was the critical event that defined its subsequent evolution and the role of the Catholic Church in it. After the departure of the French colonial administration, the leadership and institutional organization of "Les Canadiens" was left firmly in Church hands. While Britain's anti-Catholic leanings threatened to disrupt this arrangement, the pragmatism of Quebec's first governor and the subsequent need to keep Quebec on side in the looming struggle with the United States led to the Quebec Act of 1774, which "officially recognized the Catholic religion by allowing the Church to collect tithes."[14] Bishop Briand reciprocated by urging the faithful to accept British rule and by vehemently condemning the short-lived American invasion of Quebec in 1775, which was viewed much more ambivalently by the Canadien rank and file. This "policy of collaboration" was reiterated by fulsome clerical support for the War of 1812 with the United States and was "scrupulously followed … well into the nineteenth century."[15]

Inspired by the French Revolution, the Parti Canadien in Lower Canada grew ever more voluble in their demands for democratic reform and for electoral control over the schools, hospitals, and parish councils under clerical control that integrated Canadien society. Impelled by this direct threat to its power and by deep Catholic animosity towards all Enlightenment ideas, the Church was vociferous in its condemnation of the Parti Canadien and les Patriotes led by Papineau, whose rebellion in 1837 was broken by the British. In the aftermath, "a large number of Catholics" were driven "to break with their church," but the Church's bonds with the laity were soon mended by their embrace of the jailed Patriotes and by their opposition to the British plan to unite Upper and Lower Canada. Now that the lay, anti-clerical leadership of the Patriotes was broken, the power of the Church was greater than it had ever been.[16]

In the nineteenth and into the twentieth century the Church came to play "an ever more prominent role in public education, hospital care, and social services."[17] That institutionally separate world was strengthened by Confederation in 1867, which created the province of Quebec, politically insulated from English-speaking Canada with a wide range of powers to defend the traditions of its overwhelmingly francophone and Catholic population. During these years, the

Church came to present itself and be embraced as "the spiritual and cultural force that defined, with ever greater intensity, the social reality of French Canada [and that] enabled French Canadians to resist assimilation and decline."[18] The majority of Quebecers lived in urban areas by the 1920s, but the Church continued to portray itself as the defender of a rural, Catholic way of life untainted by the corrupting influences of modernity, secularism, and Protestantism. When the provincial government did begin to spend more money on health, education, and welfare after World War II, Premier Duplessis, "the acknowledged boss and master of Quebec," continued to funnel these funds through Catholic agencies, preserving his "political philosophy of anti-statism"[19] and holding Quebec in a state of suspended animation until his death in 1959.

The election of the Liberals to power in 1960 ushered in the era of the Quiet Revolution, when in a few short years the powers of the provincial government were greatly expanded as it took control of health, education, and social welfare as part of its broader agenda of modernizing and invigorating Quebec society. The Catholic school system continued for some years, but the reins of power had shifted decisively to the now dominant state, which quickly became the defender of the Quebecois nation. The "old Catholic ideology" was rapidly replaced by a "new, secular nationalism" rooted in language and state.[20] Overwhelmed by the force of events and prodded by the Second Vatican Council's new (1961–65) openness to an autonomous state and to the legitimacy of a secular, pluralistic world,[21] the Quebec hierarchy acceded to what is a text-book example of differentiation or institutional secularization.

In English-speaking Canada, two quite antithetical forces shaped the founding and early history of its churches. Imperial policy dictated that both Nova Scotia and Upper Canada (the precursor of Ontario), as British colonies, should be Anglican. That logic was reinforced by the desire of officials to define their distinctive identity and forge a bulwark against the much larger American presence to the south. Thus the Church of England became the official, legally established church in Nova Scotia in 1758. Formal establishment was never granted to the Church of England in Upper Canada, but clergy reserves amounting to a seventh of all crown land were set aside for the support of its clergy. The Church of England was also granted monopolies in military chaplaincies and in the issuing of marriage licences.[22] However, that initial privilege was short lived and inevitably doomed by the influx of American Loyalists and later immigrants from Britain whose diverse religious allegiances meant that Anglicans in Upper Canada in 1842 represented only 26% of all Protestants and 22% of the entire population. Similarly, in 1861, Anglicans made up 20% of Protestants and an even smaller 14% of all Nova Scotians.[23]

By the 1840s, reduced grants from the Society for the Propagation of the Gospel (SPG), an Anglican missionary agency in England, caused the Anglican dioceses of the Maritimes to become economically self sufficient, voluntaristic bodies. At around the same time, "the Anglican monopoly of higher education was broken" by the founding of Dalhousie University as a non-denominational institution, though the majority of its board were Presbyterians. When the government subsidy to the Anglican Kings College was then completely removed in 1854, all denominational colleges in Nova Scotia were on the same footing. In the same year, all remaining laws privileging the Church of England were formally repealed by the legislature. Similar trends were evident further west, where Kings College, which was to become the University of Toronto, was secularized in 1854 by prohibiting all religious tests and excluding clergy from high office. In 1868, all remaining grants to denominational colleges were then removed. Prior to this, official Anglican economic privilege had been eradicated by the distribution of the benefits of the clergy reserves to all faiths in 1840 and by the complete elimination of the same reserves in 1854.[24] Thus, well before the Dominion of Canada was created in 1867, the churches in English-speaking Canada were without state support, reliant on the voluntary allegiance of Canadians, and in competition with each other.

After the early and decisive separation of church and state, historians are much divided on when the impact of the churches on politics was further eroded. All are agreed that the Social Gospel movement, described further in chapter 6, led many Protestant churches in the late nineteenth and early twentieth centuries to pursue a wide range of social and moral reforms. For David Marshall, Protestantism's embrace of the Social Gospel unwittingly undermined religious faith by accommodating to the secular agenda and secular leadership that had come to dominate movements of political reform by the end of World War I.[25] Christie and Gauvreau disagree, arguing that the Protestant churches continued to have a marked influence on social policy debates until the middle of the 1930s, though they acknowledge that "the nadir of the Great Depression"

did cause both the clergy and the laity to revert to "traditional evangelicalism."[26] Putting a much more positive spin on the whole matter,
they add that "progressive clergymen had achieved their aim of converting provincial and federal governments to the principle of providing social security" and hence were "sanguine about the
increasing influence" of "social scientists and secular reformers."[27]

Among Catholics, it was the Second Vatican Council in the early
1960s that encouraged a much more open and tolerant attitude to the
secular world. Presumably this is why Grant dates "the unofficial
disestablishment of Christianity" in English-speaking Canada to the
1960s, though he too says it "had virtually come to an end by 1960."[28]
Particularly revealing, says Grant, is the submission of the Roman
Catholic hierarchy in 1966 to federal government proposals to legal-
ize contraceptive use, recommending that "Christian legislators" be
guided by their own conscience and "their own conception of the
common good." No demand was made for adherence to Catholic
teaching. Even more strikingly, the hierarchy publicly endorsed the
legal amendment to decriminalize contraceptives, though they were
not prepared to define contraceptive use "as a moral deed."[29] Two
years later, the Pope issued an encyclical, Humanae Vitae, that firmly
and unambiguously condemned contraceptive use as contrary to
Catholic teaching. Nevertheless, Canada's Catholic hierarchy, in its
Winnipeg Statement, reiterated its advice that Catholics follow their
own conscience.[30] In short, churches across the spectrum in English-
speaking Canada were coming to accept that the state did and should
function according to its own secular agenda. That recognition was
not fully realized until the 1960s, but it was largely in place as early
as the end of World War II.

Beyond politics, in the other social spheres where secularization
theory posits the declining institutional influence of the churches,
there is a significant lack of evidence. In a recent overview of this
issue, Van Die speaks of "the dramatic differentiation between the
sacred and the profane in the last forty years."[31] In much the same
vein, Beyer claims that government after 1945 "took over completely
their (i.e., the churches') erstwhile functions in such areas as education, social welfare, and the like."[32] Yet neither author provides a
scrap of evidence or even a footnote to substantiate these sweeping
claims. I hasten to add my conviction that both Van Die and Beyer
are probably correct, but to date there are still many gaps in the
historical record, especially in the years 1945 to 1970 that lie

neglected between the time periods usually studied by history and sociology respectively.

Three institutional spheres in which religious influence has probably declined and appears to be absent today deserve brief mention. First, in the modern mass media, which so decisively shapes the worldview of Canadians today, Higgins convincingly describes the dominant secular media's ignorance of and disinterest in all but the most bizarre and marginal of religious matters. However, Higgins does not provide any assessment of the degree to which religious news was reported in earlier years.[33] Second, there is widespread agreement that the churches were once major providers of charity and social welfare, and that government largely took over this field after 1945 with the expansion of the "welfare state."[34] Once more, we do not have much information about the former role of the churches; how they were actually displaced; and their current role in providing social assistance, which I suspect is larger than is commonly acknowledged. Finally, there is the vital field of education where more information exists, though an overview is made difficult because each province has its own educational system. The problem is then confounded by the historical convention that accommodated Canada's linguistic divide by creating separate Catholic schools for francophones in English-speaking Canada and Protestant schools for anglophones in Quebec. In fact, the issue of the role of religion in Canadian schools is so important that I address it in chapter 7. It will not, I think, spoil the story if I here note that there is now little or no place for religion in Canada's public educational system.

In short, there is general agreement that by the late 1960s at the very latest Canadian churches had come to have very little impact on the dominant secular institutions that now define our nation. In chapter 6, I explore in greater detail the role of the churches and Christian values in politics in recent years. For the time being, let me simply note that the above, very brief, historical overview provides one reason – though not the only one – why this book is titled *Christians in a Secular World*.

Disengagement or the Decline of Church-Based Religion

Traditional secularization theory argues that the separation of church and state brought on by modernity is usually accompanied by ever-shrinking levels of lay participation in churches. It is on this second level of secularization that recent critics of the secularization model have been far more adamant in voicing their disagreement. Pointing to the revival of Islam around the globe, the resurgence of religious bodies in the old Soviet bloc, and the continued vitality of religion in the United States, they argue that there is simply no connection between modernity and religious decline. They acknowledge that there are very low levels of religious involvement in much of Europe today, but they deny that Europe represents a general or inevitable response to modernity. The secularization thesis, they claim, is founded on an unsubstantiated myth of formerly high religious involvement, which is refuted by historical evidence indicating that only a small fraction of medieval Europeans attended church with any regularity.[35]

I must repeat that the resolution of these conflicting claims is not something I can achieve here. My aim is simply to place Canada within this broader, contested context. The defenders of the traditional secularization thesis argue that the often-fundamentalist expressions of religious effervescence today are sometimes a "rearguard action by an aroused but slowly dwindling minority" facing secularization's dominance in advanced industrial societies. Otherwise, religious movements occur in decidedly non-modern cultures such as the Middle East or in countries experiencing instability and a failed drive to modernize.[36] All such cases are therefore explicable exceptions to the general rule that modernity and religious decline are linked. As for the low levels of church attendance in medieval Europe, defenders of secularization say that this was a time of intense religious faith and conviction that did not involve church attendance. Much evidence can be garnered to support this counter claim,[37] but we are still left with the key qualification that regular church involvement in pre-modern societies was far from universal or normative. On the even trickier matter of high church attendance in the indisputably modern United States, the standard response has been that the churches have accommodated themselves to a massively secular American society and have therefore been secularized from within.[38] I would agree with Martin that this is a less than convincing counter argument,[39] though I would not want to dismiss the growing body of evidence that church attendance levels in the United States are probably exaggerated and may be experiencing some decline.[40] Taken together, secularization's critics convince me that we must move away from any mechanistic notion that modernity inevitably dooms church religion to extinction, while acknowledging that religious involvement often does decline as modernity unfolds in Western nations with an Enlightenment heritage.[41] This is not the kind of categorical conclusion that makes for grand theory, but I think it is the best we can do at such a high level of generality encompassing so many diverse nations. It is also the generalization most consistent with the Canadian experience.

In a young nation expanding constantly over a vast geographical area, Canada's churches were sometimes slow to provide an effective local presence in frontier areas. Thus 17% of present-day Ontario's population was reckoned to be unchurched in 1842, though their number soon dropped to an insignificant 1% not long after 1871. Fuelled by evangelical fervour on the Protestant side and ultramontanism among Catholics, "organized religion was growing faster than society itself" in the last half of the nineteenth century.[42] By 1901, more than 99% of Canadians claimed a religious allegiance and a huge church-building program had created a seating capacity for an impressive 72% of all Canadians at a single service.[43] According to the only two surveys of church attendance that historians have been able to locate for these years, actual head counts in Toronto found weekly attendance rising from 45% in 1882 to 55% in 1896, which may well be a conservative estimate.[44] Forty-five years later, at the end of World War II, the first Gallup poll we have on the issue found that an even higher 67% were claiming that they had attended "a church or synagogue in the last seven days."[45] Ten years later in 1956, weekly attendance was still at a very healthy 61% level. Even when Quebec with its very high 90% rate of attendance is excluded from the calculations, 52% in the nine provinces of English-speaking Canada in 1956 had attended a religious service in the previous week.[46] These are surely striking numbers, indicating that regular church involvement at this time was actually more widespread in Canada than it was in the United States.[47]

The immediate post-war years, with their high birth rates, growing prosperity, and expanding suburbs, seemed to be accompanied by a "boom in religion." Everywhere there were signs of growing membership figures, increased financial giving, much congregational activity, and a building boom that added 1,500 new churches to the United Church alone.[48] However, ever more frequent Gallup polls indicate that Protestant weekly attendance fell from 60% in 1946 to 43% in 1956 and then even further in later years. A similar though delayed decline also became evident among Catholics, beginning in earnest in the 1960s. Bibby, whose massive research and voluminous writings very much define our understanding of religion in Canada today, tells us that weekly church attendance continued its free fall well after the 1960s.[49] By the end of the 1990s, the percentage of Canadians attending religious services weekly was down to a third of the 60% who had been weekly attenders as recently as the 1950s. This is a dramatic decline by any standards. In his most recent book, Bibby advances the provocative thesis that the decades of decline preceding the 1990s were finally being slowed and in some cases reversed by a general "stirring among the country's established churches,"[50] signifying for him, as his subtitle vividly put it, "The Renaissance of Religion in Canada." Chapter 2 outlines in far greater detail my interpretation of recent trends in church involvement. Suffice it to say here, I regard Bibby's interpretation as premature. Secularization in the form of disengagement from organized religion came relatively late to Canada, but it has swept through with a vengeance. In the process, the once marked similarities between the religious situation in the United States and English-speaking Canada quickly evaporated.

Secularization theorists are agreed that secularization is caused by and rooted in the broader process of modernization that led to the churches losing responsibility for many important social functions they had once performed. Secularization theorists further argue that the diminishing institutional power of the churches typically leads to shrinking involvement by the laity or rank and file in organized religion because the churches play an ever less important part in their daily lives. Declining church attendance rates in English-speaking Canada certainly fit nicely, as Beyer has pointed out,[51] with the rise of the welfare state after 1945, though we have seen that Canadian historians are not agreed on the precise nature or timing of the broader process of institutional secularization. There is also a striking logical and temporal connection between the delayed modernization of Quebec and its exceptionally high rates of church attendance that began to fall only in the 1960s. Modernization and the shrinking public powers of the churches clearly help to explain the disengagement of Canadians from organized religion. However, I must confess to a nagging concern that, outside the particular circumstances of Quebec, the long-term process of modernization does not fully explain the later fall in church attendance. I also think that the extensive secularization of Canadian public life by the 1960s cannot adequately explain the continuing decline of church attendance right up to the end of the century that I will document in the next chapter.

Postmodern theories in many hues have emerged in recent years as the majors challengers to the notion of modernization and secularization, though they have not been extensively developed in the sociology of religion. Postmodernists espouse two basic, very different theses. The first is that our postmodern era is receptive to various forms of spirituality that operate outside organized religion. I will take up this idea in the next section. Here I address very briefly the second thesis – that the new dispensation of postmodernity continues to erode allegiance to church-based religion. Three of the most-often repeated postmodern mantras are "the eclipse of grand theory, foundational knowledge, and narrative histories,"[52] all of which may be seen as cultural developments that increasingly disincline the laity to accept the teaching and authority of the churches. There is probably some truth to these sweeping claims, but not much more can be said since postmodernist accounts of religion are so fleeting, ambiguous, and little concerned with systematic exposition or empirical verification. One clear exception to my own sweeping generalization is found in the work of Inglehart, whose ideas I outline below. I must quickly add that Inglehart's reliance on survey research makes him so different in style from the postmodernist mainstream that few in that tradition are likely to embrace him as one of their own.

Religion's primary function in traditional, pre-modern societies, says Inglehart, was to provide the "reassurance" of "an omniscient and benevolent God" in an uncertain world. He acknowledges that modernization in the twentieth century had already led to secularization as governments expanded and displaced religion by taking on "the role of the higher power" for "the general good." Then, the years after 1945 ushered in a new era of prosperity, which combined with the welfare state to create a "sense of existential security" that was completely unprecedented in human history. Prior to this, life in traditional and modernizing societies had been far more uncertain, causing most humans to be centred on "materialist" concerns with "economic and physical security." Now that "survival could be taken for granted," Inglehart sees a new set of "postmaterialist priorities" emerge that are concerned with "self expression and quality of life." Since Inglehart believes that basic values are instilled at a young age, adults who had experienced the depression of the 1930s remained wedded to materialist values, no matter how affluent they became after 1945. Thus the post-war baby boomers are the first generation to embrace postmaterialism. In this postmaterialist world coming to fruition in the 1970s, there is "declining emphasis on all kinds of authority," shrinking confidence in all institutions, and less need for "the security of absolute rigid rules that religious sanctions provide." Thus secularization as evidenced by falling rates of church attendance continues as postmaterialist values spread in what Inglehart now describes as our emerging postmodern world.[53] I will take issue in chapter 6 with the extent to which postmaterialist values are endorsed today, but I think there remains a valuable core of insights into why disengagement from organized religion has continued past the 1960s.

Within the narrower confines of the sociology of religion, the most widely touted alternative to modernization and secularization theories is the rational choice/religious markets theory propounded by Stark and his associates in the United States. They argue that the religious vitality of the United States stems from an unregulated religious market that creates a great variety of faiths catering in a competitive way to all segments of the religious market. They also conclude that Europe's tendency to religious monopoly and low competition explains its low level of religious vitality.[54] This market choice perspective stands in marked contrast to traditional secularization theory. According to Berger, religious diversity or pluralism causes each faith to become a matter of "opinion" rather than a "self-evident reality," plunging "religion into a crisis of credibility" and decline.[55] Others will have to resolve the general merits of these two competing points of view. All I want to stress is that neither assessment of religious competition and pluralism applies very well to Canada.

Outside the singular circumstances of Quebec, we have already seen that English-speaking Canada had an unregulated religious market by the 1850s when a variety of faiths were in competition with each other for the voluntary allegiance of their members. This state of affairs may partially explain the relatively high levels of commitment that prevailed in Canada until the 1940s, but there is no evidence to suggest that religious choices diminished in subsequent years when church attendance rates fell. Bibby is probably correct when he notes that there has traditionally not been much overt competition among Canada's major religious families,[56] but that long-standing state of affairs cannot explain the recent era of decline.

Moreover, Bibby is surely correct when he points out that many denominations in recent years have engaged in "menu diversification" in the face of declining numbers.[57] Thus one can today remain a Catholic or Anglican and yet embrace the charismatic or evangelical movements to be found in both churches. One can also often find congregations in many major denominations that are "gay friendly," that put a strong emphasis on liturgy and music, that stress outreach to the poor and needy, or that cater to a specific ethnic or racial group. This now-institutionalized diversity is nicely portrayed by a radio news report I heard while writing this, which described the activities of a Catholic retreat centre in the province where I live. Listeners were reassured that the busy schedule of week-end retreats offered instruction in forty-three therapeutic techniques from faith traditions all around the world that enable participants to get in touch with God and "to communicate better with Her." Whatever else they may lack, Canada's churches are not short on choice and diversity.[58]

Faith's Decline or "Believing without Belonging"

The traditional secularization model assumed that the declining institutional power of the churches and diminishing lay involvement in them would together lead to "a secularization of consciousness" whereby more and more people would "look upon the world and their own lives without the benefit of religious interpretations."[59] Berger has, of course, repudiated this early view, though it is a useful counterpoint to the evidence from surveys in the 1980s and 1990s that belief in God, an afterlife, heaven, and other religious precepts are endorsed by far more Europeans than the much smaller number who still regularly attend church services.[60] This disjunction between belief and practice is nicely captured in Davie's recent book on Britain, subtitled "Believing without Belonging." She concludes that Britain and Western Europe in general would be better described "as unchurched rather than simply secular."[61] In a similar vein, Inglehart argues that the continuing fall in church attendance in postmodern societies "does not mean that spiritual concerns are vanishing." In fact, he finds "a consistent cross-national tendency for people to spend more time thinking about the meaning and purpose of life." Both trends, he says, are driven by the exceptional security of postmodern times, which frees people from the need for the reassurances traditionally offered by the churches at the same time that it prompts a "growing concern for ultimate ends."[62] "Spiritual concerns," he elsewhere concludes, "will probably always be part of the human outlook."[63]

Bibby has also emphasized that interest in religious matters is far more widespread than the church attendance figures would indicate. He is convinced "that a considerable number of Canadians are failing to associate their interest in mystery and meaning with what religion has historically had to offer." Since interest in religion is high, Bibby employs the market model of Stark and his associates to suggest that "the churches are going broke at a time when the population is going hungry."[64] This conclusion then leads Bibby to an extended, perceptive analysis of why the churches often fail to engage "the spiritual quests of the population."[65] Though I take up a very different set of questions in what follows, I am entirely in agreement that we need to recognize the possibility that there are now two basic ways of expressing religiousness in our modern world. The first consists of those who "believe without belonging;" I call them "Seekers." They may be contrasted with the conventionally church-affiliated, who I shall refer to as the "Committed." This basic distinction is, in turn, the foundation on which I build the religiosity scale that I develop in the next chapter and apply in all others.

I should stress that some observers of unchurched religiousness have a very critical view of it. Grace Davie, in assessing the European situation, has recently admitted that the "nominal attachment" of "believing without belonging" is threatened by "a dramatic generation-by-generation drop in religious knowledge."[66] In America, Bellah and his associates far more acerbically portray the self-described "Sheilaism" of one of their respondents as "significantly representative" of "current American religious life." Sheila Larsen says, "I believe in God. I am not a religious fanatic. I can't remember the last time I went to church. My faith has carried me a long way. It's Sheilaism. Just my own little voice."[67] Bellah et al. argue that Larsen's faith is symptomatic of an extreme "religious individualism" that suffers from "incoherence," self-centredness, and "difficulty with social loyalty and commitment."[68] Wuthnow also draws much the same sort of conclusion. America in the second half of the twentieth century, he says, underwent a transition from "a traditional spirituality of inhabiting sacred places to a new spirituality of seeking." The new "spirituality of seeking" may be better "suited to the complexities of American society," but Wuthnow believes it is a "transient spiritual existence characterized more often by dabbling than depth."[69]

Berger is surely correct when he argues that organized religion is stronger in the United States and that unaffiliated seekers are less common than Bellah and Wuthnow suggest.[70] However, there is good reason to think that this critical view of Seekers might apply more appropriately to Canada, where believers remain numerous, despite a recent and radical drop in church attendance.

In this vein, Peter Emberley, in his book, *Divine Hunger*, perceptively dissects the recent journeys of Canadian baby boomers "on spiritual walkabout," who suffer from a "widespread hostility to traditional Christianity."[71] Boomers, he says have come to a new and growing concern with spirituality, prompted by their now looming mortality, the death of their parents, their sometimes broken lives, and their disillusionment with "the modern project of autonomy and prosperity, and the collective destiny of progress."[72] Like Bellah and Wuthnow, Emberley describes their journeys as "often transitory and ephemeral," pursued in "a community of solitudes," in which they "seem to be escaping commitment and responsibility."[73] Emberley's account is filled with critical insight, but the very nature of his inquiry, which focuses on the journeys of a relatively small number of articulate, highly educated, privileged boomers, leaves one wondering how representative their experiences are of Canadians as a whole. Social surveys are far from the fount of all knowledge, but they can provide some sense of how numerous Seekers really are and the sorts of social backgrounds from which they come. Above all else, I want to know whether and in what ways Seekers differ from both the Committed and the avowedly non-religious. These are some of the major issues addressed in all subsequent chapters.

One final point: some readers may have noticed that an implied distinction between religion and spirituality has crept into the immediately preceding discussion. In everyday language, *religion* is often seen as something done in churches, whereas *spirituality* is the more individualistic pursuit of Seekers who "believe without belonging." Not infrequently, there is also the notion that religion is old, repressive, and bad, while spirituality is new, liberating, and good. These notions are, I think, gaining ever more common currency in public discourse. However, I must point out that there is no scholarly consensus on the precise nature of the imputed distinction. Nor is there any agreement on that second, simplistic, often uninformed, moral evaluation. To further muddy the waters, most people who regard themselves as religious also see themselves as spiritual.[74] I will not be differentiating between religion and spirituality in what follows because I think the distinction is too value laden and fuzzy to be useful. I prefer a broad notion of religion that recognizes that it has both private and institutional dimensions.

Privatization: The Insignificance of Religious Commitment

Privatization is a rich, often-used term in secularization theory with a variety of distinct connotations that help to explain its appeal. Wuthnow has recently pointed out that privatization is sometimes seen as involving the individualization of religion evident in Bellah's portrait of Sheilaism and in the "believing without belonging" syndrome described by Davie, where believers "are left radically alone in their experience of the divine."[75] Conceptions of privatization along these lines are certainly convincing, but this is not the precise emphasis I would make.

A second version of privatization stresses that religious adherents today manufacture their own eclectic version of their religious beliefs and the duties that their faith entails. Since church religion for Luckmann is in irretrievable decline, "the sacred cosmos of modern industrial society no longer represents one obligatory hierarchy." Now there are "assortments of ultimate meaning" that are selected in a "consumer" fashion permitting each of us to "construct" our own "individual system of ultimate significance."[76] In a similar though far more developed vein, Bibby argues that "Canadians are drawing very selectively on religion,"[77] creating their own "religion à la carte," in which they participate in the occasional wedding, funeral, or seasonal ritual and embrace a mishmash of church teachings and otherworldly notions.[78] "Instead of standing over against culture," religion "has become a neatly packaged consumer item – taking its place among consumer commodities that can be bought or bypassed according to one's consumer whims."[79] Though I suspect that selectivity of this sort is not as entirely new as Bibby suggests, his impressively documented theory of "selective consumption" casts much light on Christianity in Canada today. This, again, is not the particular variant of privatization that I would stress.

Berger's take on privatization is, I think, the standard view. He acknowledges the selectivity thesis, but he joins with Luckmann in stressing that religion's influence today is privatized in the sense that it is reduced or confined to "the moral and therapeutic 'needs' of" individuals in the more intimate "spheres of the family and intimate social relationships." Now, in the public domain, "the application of religious perspectives to political and economic problems is widely deemed 'irrelevant.'"[80] When church and state are separated and religious pluralism prevails, as in Canada and most advanced industrial societies, no one faith can define a nation's values and religious prescriptions cannot be state sanctioned or socially obligatory. As involvement in organized religion also declines, there are likely to be fewer people who are infused with religious values that might affect their behaviour. These are both central elements in secularization theory that have already been propounded in preceding pages. However, the aforementioned versions of secularization still leave open the possibility that the values of the shrinking body of religious actives are different from those of other Canadians in the ways they relate to their communities, in the political priorities they cherish, and in their general demeanour in the public realm. These matters are addressed in chapters 5 and 6.

For me, privatization means that the religious values of the religiously active affect fewer and fewer aspects of their daily lives. Here the focus is on the social ramifications of religious commitment and not on the number or percentage that are committed. Fully realized, privatization means that religious commitment has no consequences for the daily life of its adherents. Cast in this way, privatization is not just a synonym for differentiation, the declining social power of the churches, or diminishing levels of religious involvement. Berger, as I have just noted, sees religion's influence as being reduced to the intimate sphere of family and personal relationships, though he and Luckmann fail to advance much, if any, evidence to support their claim that religion actually has any impact in this more intimate realm. Some recent research using the European Values Survey broadly corroborates Berger's thesis.[81] However, it is Bibby's work in Canada that is the most systematic investigation of the privatization thesis as I have just defined it. In fact, Bibby goes much further than Berger in claiming that religion – really Christianity – in Canada is "insignificant to everyday life."[82] Much later, in 1998, summarizing the results of the many surveys he conducted over the years, he concludes that "extensive analyses of religion's impact on everyday life – values, compassion, social attitudes, perceptions of social issues, and personal well-being, for example, reveal that religion, relegated as it is to a specialized commodity, has limited influence."[83] I hasten to add that Bibby in 2002 finally appeared to step back from that long-established position, suggesting very briefly in *Restless Gods* that declining attendance may have negative "implications for civility in Canada."[84]

Given the series of questions with which I began this introductory chapter, readers should not be surprised to learn that I do not embrace the proposition that Christianity today is socially insignificant, though I would quickly add that the percentage of Canadians who are active Christians has declined substantially since the 1950s. My primary concern in all subsequent chapters is to explore the various ways in which the religiously committed differ from other Canadians. Readers should note that the survey data I employ from the 1990s do not allow me to assess whether privatization has grown over the years or whether it is likely to do so in the future. However, by getting some sense of how Christianity affects the lives of those who embrace it, we may be better able to judge the price of its possible demise.

2

Religious Demography of Canadians

How many Canadians today are still involved in a religious group or faith community? Are the religiously involved still shrinking in number, or are there signs of a resurgent spirituality that may save them from future extinction? What kinds of faith group now hold the allegiance of the religiously involved? Are there any religious bodies that are thriving and growing? Which ones are in most serious trouble? Does the amount and form of religious involvement vary across Canada's diverse regions? What kinds of Canadians are most involved in church or faith groups? Is their social background or profile very different from Canadians who have no religious involvement or interest? These are the questions I address in this chapter. They are, I think, intrinsically interesting, but the answers I provide are also the bedrock upon which the remainder of this book is built. My wider aim is to assess the impact of religious faith and community on contemporary Canada. The necessary first step is to identify the number and nature of the religious in Canada.

DEVELOPMENTS SINCE THE 1960S: IS THE DECLINE INEXORABLE?

I have a rich array of survey data for the 1990s, but the quality and quantity of statistical information is much less satisfying for earlier decades. Each of the several sources I examine has its limitations, but

Table 2.1
Number and percentage distribution of the major denominations and religious families in Canada, 1961, 1991, and 2001 census

	1961		1991		2001	
	Number	% of Total	Number	% of Total	Number	% of Total
Roman Catholic	8,342,826	46.8	12,203,620	45.6	12,793,125	43.2
Mainline Protestant	7,573,890	41.5	6,574,375	24.4	5,909,360	19.9
Anglican	2,409,068	13.2	2,188,115	8.1	2,035,500	6.9
United Church	3,664,008	20.1	3,093,120	11.5	2,839,125	9.6
Conservative Protestant	1,171,516	6.4	1,930,820	7.2	1,912,220	5.5
Baptist	593,553	3.3	663,360	2.5	729,475	2.5
Pentecostal	143,877	0.8	436,435	1.6	369,480	1.2
Other Christian	405,562	2.2	1,662,911	6.2	2,093,345	7.1
Non-Christian	271,068	1.5	1,093,680	4.1	1,887,110	6.4
None	94,763	0.5	3,386,365	12.5	4,900,095	16.5
Total	18,238,247	100	26,994,045	100	29,639,030	100

they all give some insight into the extent of the decline in religious involvement since the 1960s.

Readers should note that the census data in table 2.1 record the "specific denomination" of Canadians, "even if they were not necessarily active members of the denomination." The census, we are told, "does not reflect actual membership, nor the degree of affiliation with, or commitment to a given group."[1] With this qualification in mind, one can see that the Roman Catholic Church in 2001 continued to be the largest Christian body by a large margin, claiming the nominal allegiance of 43% of all Canadians, which is not much lower than the 47% who were Roman Catholic in 1961. Mainline Protestants are the second largest group or family, but they saw their market share fall from 42% of Canadians in 1961 to 24% in 1991 and then to 20% in 2001. This is a very considerable contraction in a relatively short period of time. Mainline Protestants are members of the historically dominant Protestant denominations in English-speaking Canada, which are now often portrayed as "liberal" in their outlook. The two largest bodies were and still are the Anglican and United churches of Canada. The much smaller Presbyterian and Lutheran denominations are also placed in the Mainline camp. In contrast, Conservative Protestants come out of an evangelical, non-conformist Protestant tradition that stresses a personal relationship with God and the obligation to evangelize. They are a small but vibrant group, who slightly

Table 2.2
Membership* in selected denominations and percent change 1971–1996**

	Members 1971	Members 1996	% Change 1971–1991	% Change 1991–1996
Anglican	627,346	454,636	−16	−14
United Church	1,016,706	713,195	−20	−12
Lutherans	200,172	200,237	+5	−5
Presbyterians	182,559	143,784	−14	−8
Baptists	128,774	129,055	+1	−1
Mennonites	47,222	75,644	+39	+15
Pentecostals	150,000	218,782	+28	+14
C. & M. Alliance	10,937	31,719	+145	+18
Jehovah's Witnesses	49,204	112,950	+107	+11
Mormons	11,178	130,000	+1027	+3
All Canadians	21,568,310	28,846,760	+25	+7

*Full, Communicant or Confirmed Members
**Yearbook of American and Canadian Churches, 1973–1999

expanded their share of the Canadian population from 6% in 1961 to 7% in 1991. In the 1990s, Conservative Protestants then appear to have lost ground, dropping back to 6%. Though Statistics Canada is widely respected and its massive one-in-five sampling of all Canadians dwarfs all other surveys, I must confess that I have real doubts about these Conservative Protestants numbers. I am particularly troubled by the apparent 15% contraction in Pentecostals in the 1990s, because it is inconsistent with so much anecdotal evidence and with the numbers recorded by its churches (see table 2.2). Historically, Baptists were the dominant force in the Conservative world, but we can see in table 2.1 that Pentecostals – at least until 1991 – were rapidly catching up.[2] The distinction between Mainline and Conservative Protestants is rough and approximate,[3] but it is broadly valid. The collapsed categories are certainly necessary when dealing with the surveys I later use, which never include enough respondents to say anything meaningful about Anglicans, Baptists, Lutherans, or any other specific Protestant denomination. Thus there are three major Christian families: Mainline Protestants, Conservative Protestants, and Catholics, with this last and largest category being subsequently divided into its quite distinctive English-speaking and Quebec branches.

Table 2.1 reveals that there has been a striking growth since 1961 in the percentage of Canadians who claim they do not have a religion, though we should not lose sight of the fact that 83% of Canadians in 2001 still said they were attached to a religious tradition. There has also been very substantial growth among the approximately two million Non-Christians who amounted to 6% of Canadians in 2001. As I noted in the previous chapter, they belong to a great array of very different faiths and share little in common with each other, apart from their tendency to be recent arrivals in Canada. Finally, the expanding body of "Other Christians" are a mixed group, of whom an indeterminate number might be better placed in one of the afore-mentioned religious families. About 60% of "Other Christians" in 1961 and less than a quarter of them in 2001 (23%) were attached to a variety of Eastern Orthodox churches supported by Eastern and Southern European immigrant communities and their descendants. The 154,750 Jehovah's Witnesses and 104,750 Mormons in 2001 are also in the "Other Christian" category. Both the Jehovah's Witnesses and Mormons emerged out of evangelical Protestantism and are similar in many ways to Conservative Protestants, but I have not placed them in the Conservative Protestant fold out of deference to the deeply felt opposition of Conservative Protestants to certain doctrines of the Jehovah's Witnesses and Mormons. Among the approximately 1.4 million remaining "Other Christians," over 98% identified themselves as simply "Christian" or "Protestant." Some were probably once of Mainline Protestant ancestry, while others are certainly Conservative Protestants, though it is impossible to say how many in either case.[4] If we place the Mormons, the Jehovah's Witnesses, and about a quarter of the 1.4 million generic Christians or Protestants in with the Conservative Protestants, then we should revise the Conservative Protestant share of the Canadian population upwards to about 8 or 9%.

Table 2.2 lists the membership figures calculated by a variety of Christian denominations. Since many denominations have not yet made public their membership figures for 2001, I stop at 1996, where I can compare their growth rates with the general population. Because the Catholic Church does not collect its own figures and relies on the census, it has not been included. Non-Christians are also absent, because the annual *Yearbook of American and Canadian Churches* confines its data collections to Christian bodies. Since the denominations all define full membership in different ways, I cannot assess their relative size or share of the religious market, as was done in table 2.1. On the other hand, we get a clearer picture of the number of Canadians who are considered by the religious bodies to be actual members. Since most denominations use similar criteria to define membership over the years, we also get a better fix on which denominations are growing and which are declining. Three major conclusions may be drawn from table 2.2.

First, the actual numbers of members acknowledged by the Mainline Protestant denominations is far lower than the census figures in table 2.1. In part this is because the figures on full or communicant members typically exclude children, but even the Anglican Church's estimate of an "inclusive" membership of 848,256 in 1990 (versus 529,943 full communicant members) is vastly lower than the 1991 census figure of 2,188,115. Similar disparities exist for Presbyterians in 1991 (they estimate an inclusive membership of 245,883 while the census records 636,295), as they do for Lutherans and members of the United Church. No one would suggest that any of these Mainline Protestant groups underestimate their real membership.

Second, denominational figures on full membership in table 2.2 provide further proof of the marked decline in Mainline Protestant churches. By its own account, the United Church experienced a 20% decline in full membership between 1971 and 1991, when the Canadian population as a whole grew by 25%. This decline continued in the first half of the 1990s (−12%) and actually accelerated on a per annum basis. Anglican and Presbyterian records reveal similar declines. Only Lutherans seemed to hold their own, but they experienced a 5% decline in the 1990s and they failed to achieve any growth at all between 1971 and 1999, when the total number of Canadians grew by 34%. Relatively, if not absolutely, Lutherans were also falling behind.

Third, many of the Conservative Protestant denominations in table 2.1 did much better, though the Baptist experience was very similar to that of the Lutherans. In the twenty-year period between 1971 and 1991, Pentecostals, Mennonites, and members of the Christian and Missionary Alliance all experienced significant growth, though only the last two outstripped general population growth by a wide margin. In the 1990s, all three of these bodies, which reflect a real cross-section of Conservative Protestantism, recorded growth rates that were double that of the general population. This is why I have doubts about the official census figures for Protestants in the 1990s. The growth rates of the Jehovah's Witnesses and Mormons were even more impressive in the 1970s and 1980s, but they seem to have lagged in the 1990s, falling behind all but the Baptists in the Conservative Protestant fold. The more striking and crucial contrast is with the dismal record of the Mainline Protestants.

Table 2.3
Percentage attending church or synagogue in the last 7 days:
Gallup polls selected years

	1946*	56	60	65	70	75	80	85	90	91	92	93	94	95	96	97	98
Catholic	83	88	85	83	65	61	51	43	37	41	43	43	41	37	37	32	36
Protestant	60	43	32	32	28	25	26	29	24	27	32	40	33	40	37	33	32
Total	67	61	55	55	44	41	35	32	27	31	33	36	33	31	30	27	29

*Bibby, *Fragmented Gods*, p. 17.

Table 2.3 gives another perspective on the extent of religious decline by summarizing just over fifty years of Gallup polls, which have regularly asked Canadians whether they had attended "a church or synagogue in the last seven days." In recent years the question has been recast to refer simply to "a place of worship." We must treat the figures with some caution since the samples in some years had only about 600 respondents and the art of selecting a nationally representative sample in earlier years was not as well developed as it later became. Nevertheless a number of conclusions emerge. The most notable is surely the overall decline in the percentage of Canadians attending weekly services; by 1990 the 27% attending weekly was much less than half what it had been in 1946. This large and rapid decline suggests that many of those claiming a religious allegiance in the census or listed on the membership rolls of specific denominations have largely become passive adherents.

The Gallup polls did not go deeply into denominational differences, but the distinction between Protestants and Catholics remains revealing. As far back as the 1940s, Protestants were much less likely than Catholics to be weekly attenders. Thereafter Protestant attendance plummeted rapidly to 32% in 1960 and then to about 25% by the mid-1970s. The exceptionally high Catholic rate of attendance stayed above 80% until the middle of the 1960s, when it too nosedived to 37% in 1990, though it was still higher than the Protestant rate of 24% in the same year. I have included the attendance rate for each year of the 1990s to serve as a reminder of the variability in results that arises from a sample that annually contained about 1,000 respondents. In this most recent decade, Protestant and Catholic rates of weekly attendance seem to have finally converged. When we look exclusively at Protestants and Catholics in the 1990s, we might also conclude that the attendance levels were stabilizing and possibly even growing, but this conclusion does not take account of the rising

Table 2.4
Frequency of Canadians 15 years of age or over attending religious services or meetings 1985–2000

	1985*	1990*	1995*	1997**	2000**
Weekly	27	24	23	20	19
Monthly	15	13	11	12	13
Rarely	28	28	24	26	25
Never	19	23	27	17	18
No religion	11	12	15	25	26
Total	100%	100%	100%	100%	100%
(N)	(11,105)	(13,285)	(10,276)	(17,932)	(13,970)

*General Social Surveys (GSS)
**National Surveys of Volunteering, Giving, and Participation (NSVGP)

number of Canadians who were reporting that they had no religion whatsoever. In 1995, Gallup found that the non-religious amounted to 20% of Canadians. Just 14 years earlier, only 7% of Canadians reported having no religion.

Table 2.4 lists findings from the much larger and more methodologically sophisticated surveys done annually by Statistics Canada since 1985. All samples have at least 9,000 respondents with solid 80% response rates. With very minor variations, all the surveys in Table 2.4 asked "Other than on special occasions, such as weddings, funerals, or baptisms, how often did you attend services or meetings connected with your religion in the last 12 months?" The pre-set options given were: at least weekly; at least monthly; a few times a year or less; and not at all. Those who said they did not have a religion were not asked this question. I would not have done it this way, but I can live with the assumption that very few of these professedly non-religious Canadians attend services with any regularity, barring the exceptional circumstances of a funeral, wedding, and the like. I might add that other surveys asking all respondents how frequently they attend services produce very similar estimates of the total rate of weekly attenders.[5]

Note that the estimates by Statistics Canada of weekly attendance are noticeably lower than those by Gallup in every comparable year. The disparity is no doubt caused by Gallup classifying as weekly attenders those Statistics Canada respondents who normally attended rarely or never, but who had attended a service in the preceding seven days. Statistics Canada surveys show that weekly attendance continued to decline throughout the second half of the 1980s and through the 1990s, reaching 19% in 2000. If we take monthly or more frequent attendance as the mark of the religiously involved, then 32% of Canadians in 2000 were "religious" in the sense of being actively involved with their faith tradition. Since 1985, they have shrunk from 44% of Canadians to slightly less than a third. About a quarter of all Canadians say they attend services three or four times a year at most. Such marginal attachment speaks more of a fading historical memory than it does of on-going involvement. The percentage of Canadians who say they never attend does not appear to have grown between 1985 and 2000, but such a conclusion does not take account of the increase from 11% to 26% of Canadians who say they do not have a religion. When these two categories are combined, non-attenders rise from 29% of Canadians in 1985 to 42% in 1995 and 1997, and then to 43% in 2000. Note the highly consistent finding over five years in three large surveys, even when the percentage of the non-religious varies. Over the last 50 years, Canada has been transformed into a predominantly post-Christian, secular society where active adherents of religion have become a clear minority, though a sizable one, of all Canadians.[6]

Table 2.5 allows us to explore further the flight from organized religion by charting church attendance rates by age group between 1985 and 2000. Though I have here used monthly or more frequent attendance as the mark of Canada's religious actives, my conclusions also apply to the more restrictive category of weekly attenders. First, I would note that faith communities as a whole have experienced declines in monthly attendance in every age group over this most recent fifteen-year period. This is particularly true of young (15–24) and middle-aged (35–54) Canadians. To use the youngest Canadians, those between 15 and 24 years as an example, the percentage attending monthly fell from 36% in 1985 to 23% in 2000, which amounts to a 36% contraction over these years. This is shrinkage on a major scale for such a short period of time. Second, Canadians are not returning to church, synagogue, and temple in significant numbers as they age. Take the key example of the first decade of baby boomers born between 1946 and 1955, who were in their thirties in 1985. At that time, 39% professed to be monthly attenders (24% weekly), which was undoubtedly a higher attendance level than in their younger hippie years.[7] Fifteen years later in 2000 when they were between 45 and 54 years of age, their monthly attendance rate had fallen further to 30%; weekly attenders were down to an even skimpier 17%. The

Table 2.5
Percentage of monthly attenders by age group: 1985–2000

	1985*	1990*	1995*	2000**
15–24	36	29	24	23
25–34	32	28	27	25
35–44	43	34	31	27
45–54	47	39	32	30
55–64	59	51	46	41
65+	54	54	52	50
All ages	43	37	34	31
(N)	(11,105)	(13,285)	(10,276)	(13,970)

*GSS   **NSVGP

decline was less marked among late boomers born between 1955 and 1964, but the 30% of them attending monthly in 1985 when they were in their twenties had still fallen fifteen years later to 27%. As for those born after the baby boom who did not begin to leave childhood until 1990 when they were between 15 and 24 years of age, the 29% of them attending monthly had fallen further to 25% when they were 10 years older in 2000. In this same year, only 13% of this post-boomer generation were attending weekly. Predictions of Canadians returning to church as they age or of younger Canadians leading a religious revival are certainly not substantiated here.

Table 2.6 gives weekly attendance trends among the four major families or types of religious tradition in Canada. I would stress four major findings. First the rate of Catholic decline in the 40 years since 1957 has been especially steep, falling from 83% to 23%. Particularly striking is the fall from 88% weekly mass attendance in Quebec in the mid 1950s to 25% in 1990. In the 1990s, the percentage of Quebec Catholics attending mass weekly again fell dramatically from 25% to 15%. I have already alluded in the previous chapter to how the rapid expansion of state power after 1960 and the grinding angst of unrequited nationalism in Quebec undermined the institutional powers and cultural importance of the once mighty Catholic Church. Almost 40 years later, the loyalty of Quebecers to their church still appeared to be fading. The Catholic Church's hold over its adherents was never as strong elsewhere as it was in Quebec, though a still impressive 75% of Catholics in the rest of Canada professed to be weekly attenders in 1957. By 1990, weekly attendance had halved to 36%. Thereafter, the yearly tally by Statistics Canada's big surveys showed a modest decline in the early 1990s, leading to what appeared to be a

Table 2.6
Percent attending religious services weekly by religious family: Selected years

	1957[1]	1975[2]	1990[3]	1995[3]	1997[3]	2000[3]*
Roman Catholics	83	44	31	27	24	23
RCs in Quebec	88	42	25	22	17	15
RCs elsewhere	75	46	36	31	32	31
Mainline Protestants	34	26	16	16	18	18
Anglicans	24	24	14	14	17	18
United Church	40	32	17	17	18	14
Conservative Protestants	49	41	50	50	57	48
All Canadians	54	32	24	22	20	19
(N)	(2,040)	(1,816)	(13,495)	(10,749)	(18,301)	(13,797)

[1]Gallup poll, 1957 ("last Sunday");
[2]Bibby, ("almost every week");
[3]GSS & NSVGP ("other than special occasions- at least weekly"). Note ages range from 21+ for Gallup to 18+ for Bibby to 15+ for GSS & NSVGP.
*Data by religious family is taken from Jones, F., 2002. *Religious Commitment in Canada, 1997–2000*, p. 17. (Draft Manuscript).

temporary stabilization of weekly mass attendance at around 30% by 2000. If the polls are our guide, involvement in the Catholic Church since 1975 has been noticeably stronger outside Quebec than within, though the overall trend everywhere is one of decline.

The polls tell us in table 2.6 that the 34% weekly attendance in 1957 by the Mainline Protestant adherents of the Anglican, Lutheran, Presbyterian, and United churches was already well below the national average of 54%. At that time, the attendance rate in the United Church (40%) was higher than it was for Anglicans (24%) and for Mainline Protestants as a whole, but all converged in a subsequent decline that brought them to a low of 13% weekly attendance in 1994. The low point for Anglicans of 12% was reached in 1993, while the United Church low of 11% occurred between 1994 and 1996. Table 2.6 suggests that Mainline Protestants were reaching a new, if reduced, equilibrium in the 1990s. One might even think that Mainline Protestants were starting a modest revival in the second half of the 1990s, but we shall see in just a moment that this is merely a statistical mirage.

Conservative Protestants, who amounted to about 8% to 10% of Canadians in the 1990s, are the one group of Christians who appear to have been successful at resisting the corrosive effects of secularization. Over the 43-year period after 1957, the weekly attendance rate of their professed adherents showed a temporary decline to about 40% in 1975, thereafter rebounding to 50% in 1990 and 1995

Table 2.7
Number and percent change by various religious categories 1985–2000

	1985 GSS		1990 GSS		2000 NSVGP**
	Number	%	Number	%	Number
Catholics*	4,880,857	−20	4,250,281	−8	3,913,139
RCs in Quebec*	2,265,870	−36	1,749,841	−18	1,440,249
RCs outside Quebec*	2,614,987	−5	2,500,441	−1	2,472,893
Mainline Protestants*	1,924,907	−32	1,645,871	−20	1,315,690
Conservative Protestants*	N/a		1,148,233	+15	1,351,641
Non Christians*	N/a		256,869	+75	448,732
All Monthly Attenders	8,296,618	−15	7,449,203	−6	7,029,202
All weekly attenders	5,296,830	−21	4,923,545	−15	4,199,057
Non religious	2,053,599	+184	2,484,426	+135	5,842,262
All Canadians	19,668,143	+19	20,525,561	+16	24,383,207

*Attend monthly or more frequently

**Data by religious family is taken from Jones, F., 2002. *Religious Commitment in Canada,*
1997–2000, 17 (Draft Manuscript). See note above on Jones data.

and then falling to 48% in 2000. Bibby's 1995 poll put weekly attendance among Conservative Protestants at 64%, though his estimates
for 1990 and 1985 were lower. Various Angus Reid polls over the first
half of the 1990s suggest that about 55% were attending weekly.[8]
These divergent figures are a useful reminder that we should not put
too much weight on a single poll, but the collective body of estimates
makes it clear that there has been no appreciable decline in levels of
Conservative Protestant involvement.

A much clearer picture of recent developments in Canada's major
religious families is provided in tables 2.7 and 2.8. Although table 2.6
tells us a great deal about changing church attendance rates over the
long haul, it does not tell the whole story because it calculates attenders in religious families as a percentage of all nominal adherents, rather
than of all Canadians. In other words, table 2.6 does not take account
of the growing number of Canadians who claim no religion and hence
are not included in the calculus of attendance rates by religious family.
Thus it is that the weekly attendance rate of Mainline Protestants
stayed steady for much of the 1990s and actually seemed to increase
after 1995, at precisely the time when the percentage of Canadians
claiming no religion (see table 2.4) rose dramatically. Presumably,
many of these newly non-religious had formerly been nominal adherents of Mainline Protestantism. Table 2.7 avoids this problem by esti-
mating the actual number of all Canadian attenders within the major

Table 2.8
Religion of weekly attenders, religious actives, and all canadians in 2000 (NSVGP)

	Roman Catholic	Mainline Protestant	Conservative Protestant	Non Christian	No Religion	Total	
Weekly	52	17	25	6	0	100%	(3,435)
Actives*	56	19	19	6	0	100%	(5,464)
All Canadians	43	18	10	4	26	100%	(13,836)

*Attend monthly or more
**Data by religious family is taken from Jones, F., 2002. *Religious Commitment in Canada, 1997–2000*, 17 (Draft Manuscript).

religious families in 1985, 1990, and 2000. I should point out that these are estimates of the total population 15 years of age and over based on projections by Statistics Canada from the survey data – they are not precise enumerations. Note also in table 2.7 that I include all who attend at least monthly because I think this is a fairer demarcation of all who might be regarded as religiously active.

What we see is that the total number of monthly attenders shrank by 1% annually over the last 15 years of the twentieth century. For the inner, active core of weekly attenders, there was an even steeper 21% contraction. Particularly badly hit were Quebec Catholics and Mainline Protestants, who both saw their active membership reduced by about a third over these 15 years. Catholics in the rest of Canada fared far better, losing only 5% of their monthly attenders after 1985 and actually appearing to hold steady at about 2,500,000 in the 1990s. However, the number of weekly attenders, which is a much better indicator of the active, inner core fell by 17% among Catholics outside Quebec after 1985. Over the 1990s, that inner core shrank by 12%. In either case, Catholic trends ought to be compared to the total population of Canada, which grew by a healthy 19% over the same years. Relatively and absolutely Catholics outside and inside Quebec were losing ground. That conclusion is reinforced when we compare the growth rates of any of the above religious categories with the whopping 184% growth of the non-religious between 1985 and 2000.

Conservative Protestants, for whom I have data only since 1990, fared much better, experiencing a 15% increase in weekly as well as monthly attenders. The satisfaction that Conservative Protestants may derive from such numbers must be tempered by the realization that their undeniable growth did no more than keep pace with the expanding Canadian population. Conservative Protestants did not grow as a percentage of the Canadian population, though they did grow within the shrinking ranks of the religiously active. Table 2.8 shows us that by 2000 the Conservative Protestant share of all religious actives (19%) was now on a par with Mainline Protestants. Within the more restrictive – and probably more appropriate – category of weekly attenders, Conservative Protestants had come to outnumber Mainline Protestants by a substantial margin, holding a 25% share of weekly attenders, versus the 17% share of Mainline Protestants. What we are seeing here is a major sea change in the composition of Canadian Protestantism. Traditionally, as we saw in table 2.1, it was the Mainline churches that dominated and defined Canadian Protestantism. Today, Mainline Protestant churches are still the dominant physical presence in Canada's inner cities, towns, and countryside, but the slightly more than one million Conservative Protestant weekly attenders in 2000 exceeded by a considerable margin their Mainline Protestant counterparts, who numbered about 700,000. Of course, Catholics, by any standard, are the largest single group, holding the allegiance of just over half of Canada's religious actives.

Among the religiously active, the diverse body of non-Christians grew more rapidly than any other group, growing from about a quarter of a million to almost half a million during the 1990s. The cause, and I can do no more than speculate here, may be the growing self-confidence and accompanying institution building of the approximately half of all immigrants entering Canada from Asia over the last 25 to 30 years. Now that these communities have become more numerous and established, they have started to build and attend a growing number of mosques, temples, gurdwaras, and other places of worship. However, Bibby's careful analysis of the 1991 General Social Survey found that the 36% of Asian immigrants professing a non-Christian faith was fully matched by the 37% of them claiming to be Christians. Among the Canadian-born of non-European ancestry, only 10% said they were allied to a non-Christian faith.[9] The result, charted in table 2.8, is that non-Christians in 2000 continued to be a tiny minority (6%) of all religious actives and only 4% of all Canadians.

To complete this overview of emerging trends in Canada's faith communities, I want to compare the religious allegiances of Canadians today with those they maintained in childhood. The data are drawn from two surveys done by Angus Reid in 1993, when 3000 respondents were asked what religion they identified with when "you were a child, that is before your teenage years." Table 2.9 charts

Table 2.9
Childhood religion by religion of religious actives* today (Reid 1993)

	RC	Main. Prot.	Con. Prot.	Other	Total
RC	93	7	13	11	52
Main. Prot	5	83	26	16	31
Con. Prot.	1	8	53	20	12
Other	1	2	7	53	6
Total	100%	100%	100%	100%	100%
(N)	(474)	(263)	(135)	(56)	(928)

*Attend monthly or more frequently
P <.001   V = .65

the childhood religious allegiance of those who attend monthly or more often today, differentiating between major religious families. Note that my focus for the moment is on the religious background of those who are religiously active today, since I want to clarify from where faith communities today draw their members. The religious background of the currently marginal or passive does not much illuminate this question.[10]

Table 2.9 indicates that the vast majority (93%) of active Roman Catholics today were raised as Catholics; most of those converting had formerly been Mainline Protestants. A similar situation applies to Mainline Protestants, whose active membership in 1993 had small, roughly equal strands of former Catholics (7%) and Conservative Protestants (8%); 83% of active Mainline Protestants were raised within that tradition, though not necessarily the specific denomination of their birth. However, the inability or unwillingness of these two former groups to recruit from outside their tribal constituency does not apply to Conservative Protestants. Almost half (47%) of active Conservative Protestants surveyed in 1993 were raised in other faith traditions and were subsequently recruited into the Conservative Protestant fold. This impressive capacity for outreach and recruitment is consistent with the great emphasis Conservative Protestants put on evangelism and goes a long way toward explaining the much greater vitality we have already noted among them. Yet table 2.7 reminds us that Conservative Protestant growth has been quite modest, barely keeping up with general population growth. Why this is so is explained in table 2.10.

In table 2.10 we can see how many Canadians have changed their religious allegiances since childhood within each of the major religious

Table 2.10
Religion today by childhood religion (Reid, 1993)

	RC	Main. Prot.	Con. Prot.	Other	No religion	Total
RC	81	4	4	4	5	39
Main. Prot.	5	73	21	5	7	30
Con. Prot.	2	5	54	1	6	7
Other	2	5	7	74	7	7
None	11	14	13	16	75	16
Total	100%	100%	100%	100%	100%	100%
(N)	(1,325)	(1,000)	(231)	(211)	(134)	(2,901)

$P < .001$ $V = .61$

families. Here there is no need to confine ourselves to the religiously active. The great majority (81%) of those who were Catholic in childhood continued in 1993 to profess at least a nominal allegiance to Catholicism. On-going nominal allegiance to the religion of childhood was also characteristic of the majority of Mainline Protestants (73%), others (74%), and religious nones (75%). Let me stress that this apparent stability in religious identification has been accompanied by a huge decline since World War II in the proportion of Catholics and Mainline Protestants who regularly attend religious services. The numbers are summarized in tables 2.3 and 2.6. When Catholics and Mainline Protestants stir themselves to cast off the religious affiliations they inherited from their parents, their favoured option is no religion. About half of the Catholics, Mainline Protestants, and others who switched in Table 2.10 left religion behind. The net result is that the 5% of the Reid survey respondents claiming no religion in their childhood had swollen by 1993 to 16% of all Canadians. It is a mix of declining commitment and some outright flight – not stability – that defines the religious allegiance of Canadians over the last forty to fifty years.

Again, Conservative Protestants are the exception to the general pattern. While three-quarters or more of Catholics, Mainline Protestants, and others by birth continue to profess at least a nominal allegiance to their inherited faith, this is true of only 54% of Conservative Protestants. Switching is far more prevalent among Conservative Protestants than among any other religious families in Reid's survey. The great majority who do switch either renounce religion entirely (13%) or attach themselves to Mainline Protestant churches (21%) where commitment levels are typically much lower. This Conservative

Protestant failure to retain the allegiance of almost half (46%) of their children is the crucial counterpoint to their just noted ability to recruit active members from outside their own Conservative Protestant world. There is therefore a revolving door syndrome among Conservative Protestants that draws in fresh recruits at the same time that it drives out the nominal adherents from childhood who are so common in the Catholic and Mainline Protestant traditions. This revolving door in Conservative Protestantism helps to explain both their distinctively high commitment levels and their diminished capacity to grow and expand.[11]

Leaving aside the small body of non-Christians, all other religious families outside the Conservative Protestant world have been shrinking relative to the general population and in absolute terms, especially when we look at the core group of weekly attenders. The future is far too uncertain to rule out the possibility of future religious revival. But for the time period we have been looking at, including the 1990s, shrinkage and loss are the dominant trends.

Religious Canadians in the 1990s:
Privatized Religion versus Institutional Involvement

My analysis to this point has been exclusively focused on membership rates and the frequency of attendance at religious services and meetings. In part, it is because I can trace this sort of information back a number of years. It is also because I think that the amount of time people put into an activity, organization, or institution – be it politics, sports, or religion – is the best single indicator of the importance of that activity or organization in people's lives. There are, of course, other ways of expressing religious interest and hence of demarcating the religious from the non-religious (or perhaps it would be better to say the more religious from the less religious) in late twentieth century Canada. It is very difficult to reach a definitive conclusion on such an amorphous issue, but I need to draw some sort of working definition to achieve my objective of exploring whether and how the religious in Canada differ from other Canadians.

"Canadians aren't big on organized religion, but that doesn't mean that spirituality isn't important to them." This lead sentence from a recent article in the *Vancouver Sun* reflects the thinking of many Canadians, including public commentators and scholars. Based on a POLLARA poll of 1,410 adults in late 1997, the article reported that only 25% attended services weekly, but "three-quarters ... said religion and spirituality are important to them and 26% say they're becoming increasingly important." The poll also found that about two-thirds pray weekly or more frequently and about half "believe in divine intervention or miracles."[12] What this cross-section of Canadians meant by prayer, spirituality, and divine intervention is less than clear, but these numbers strongly suggest that religious inclinations are far more widespread than the dwindling pool of church-attending faithful might suggest.

Reverend William Kokesch, speaking on behalf of the Canadian Conference of Catholic Bishops (CCCB), whose weekly attenders have been so decimated in recent years, described the poll's findings as "heartening." He added that the widespread belief of Canadians that "spirituality is important in their lives" was "more important than the physical act of going to church." No indication was given in the article whether the CCCB embraced Kokesch's prescription. When asked for his comments, Reverend Bill Phipps, Moderator of the United Church, said "There is a deep spiritual hunger, but a lot of people are no longer finding satisfaction in organized religion." Archbishop Michael Peers, Primate of the Anglican Church of Canada added that "the shift away from regular church attendance in the past few decades, in fact, provides new opportunities for the churches to engage in new ways those now seeking spiritual guidance." One is always left wondering whether newspaper articles do justice to the people they so briefly interview,[13] but these comments suggest that some religious leaders agree that religion and spirituality can and do exist outside organized faith communities. One might, however, wonder how the Anglican Church, or any other church for that matter, intends to engage spiritually those with whom it no longer has any sustained contact.

POLLARA's findings are not the product of a rogue poll, nor is the Vancouver Sun article atypical of the kind of press religion has been recently getting, though the press's attention to religion does tend to be spotty. At the end of 1995, *Maclean's,* our national magazine, proclaimed that "many Canadians are turning inward, to their spiritual selves." Another poll, this time done for *Maclean's* and the CBC found that 82% of Canadians were "somewhat or very spiritual." About half of those polled said that "their lives had become more spiritual in recent years." The article said that some "are experiencing an awakening in established religions," but the examples cited were typically of a "New Age" type, ranging from the popular book *The Celestine Prophecy* to Cara Segger, a 23-year old from Victoria, who "performs the ceremonial magic of Wicca, reads tarot cards and practices elements of Buddhism and Taoism. Says Segger: 'I believe all attempts of mankind and womankind to reach for the divine are valid.'"[14] The American Sheila Larsen, to whom I referred in the first chapter, would no doubt agree.

Heady proclamations of recent growth in privatized, non-institutionalized forms of religiousness must be set against the more critical commentaries of Bellah, Wuthnow, and Emberley discussed in the first chapter, suggesting that interest in the new spirituality tends to be fleeting, superficial, and inconsequential. I will address that possibility in greater detail in subsequent chapters. For the moment all I want to emphasize is that surveys consistently find that very substantial numbers of Canadians continue to insist that religion remains important to them in their daily lives. A variety of slightly different questions from surveys going back to 1975 are summarized in table 2.11. The 65% of Canadians who said they were very or somewhat religious in 1975 falls to about a 60% level throughout much of the 1990s. I do not want to ignore the lower 56% in 2000 who defined themselves as religious, but that slightly downward trend cannot be compared to the much more radical 41% decline in weekly church attendance after 1975 recorded in table 2.6. By the 1990s the 60% of Canadians claiming religion's personal importance was roughly double the percentage of religious actives attending monthly or more frequently. Put slightly differently, about half of all Canadians who see themselves as religious or define religion as personally important to them never or very rarely attend religious services. By these standards, projections about religion's demise seem greatly exaggerated. Could it be that attendance at services is unrelated to being religious?

In 1993, *Maclean's* ran a major cover story proclaiming that "God is alive" and that "most Canadians are committed Christians."[15] The assertion was based on the preliminary results from a set of Angus Reid polls, which I shall explore much more extensively in future chapters. The surveys found that 62% of Canadians in the 1990s still affirmed the traditional Christian doctrine that the "life, death, and resurrection of Jesus ... provided a way for the forgiveness of sins." Two-thirds said Jesus was "the divine son of God," and embraced the belief that Jesus "was resurrected to eternal life." Note that results like this mean that very substantial proportions of Canadians who

Table 2.11
Subjective or privatized religiousness by frequency of attendance at religious services or meetings

	Weekly	Monthly	Rarely	Never	Total	(N)
% Say they are very / somewhat religious (1975)[1]	98	89	56	15	65	(1,859)
% Say religion is very / rather important in their life (1990)[1]	97	84	54	26	61	(1,717)
% Agree my religious faith is very important in my day-to-day life (1993)[3]	99	89	73	38	66	(5,862)
% Agree my religious faith is very important in my day-to-day life (1994)[3]	98	89	64	33	61	(1,489)
% Say religion is very / somewhat important to them (1995)[1]	96	84	48	14	57	(1,688)
% Agree my religious faith is very important to me in my day-to-day life (1996)[3]	96	90	60	31	61	(1,466)
% Consider religion an important part of their life (1996)[3]	98	87	54	26	59	(2,955)
% Who define self as very / somewhat religious (1997)[1]	95	85	59	33	58	(17,058)
% Who define self as very / somewhat religious (2001)[1]	95	86	56	31	56	(13,788)

[1]Bibby [2]WVS [3]Reid [4]NSVGP

rarely or never attend are prepared to embrace these traditional doctrines. An equally impressive 78% rejected the claim that "God is an old superstition … no longer needed … in these modern times." A clear majority (60%) claimed to "have felt God's presence in my life," while 53% rejected the theory of scientific evolution and 49% felt that God always answers their prayers. As for the Bible, two thirds described it as "the inspired word of God" and a third insisted that it be "taken literally word for word." I could go on, but the point is surely clear. If polls like this are our guide, few Canadians in the 1990s were rejecting Christianity or embracing a purely secular worldview.

Interpreting all this is a very tricky business. We will never know whether the survey respondents understood the theological technicalities involved in the questions or whether they had similar understandings of the resurrection, evolution, and the like. The fact that the questions were administered over the telephone makes my unease all the greater. The interpretative problem is then accentuated when we realize that doctrinal orthodoxy is very difficult to identify.

In a recent newspaper interview, Bill Phipps, the Moderator of the United Church said that he had "no idea if there is a hell." He also expressed doubts about heaven and about whether Jesus is the son of God. He added, "I don't believe he [Jesus] rose from the dead as a scientific fact."[16] Much controversy ensued within and outside the United Church. Not a few Christians dismissed Phipps as an extreme liberal atypical of the mainstream, but such labels do not apply to the Pope, who, in 1999, declared that hell has "no physical address," is "not a punishment imposed externally by God," and therefore involves a "self imposed separation from God."[17] Purgatory, fire, and brimstone, it seems, are no longer part of Catholic orthodoxy. In light of such pronouncements by Christian leaders, the pervasive religious traditionalism of Canadians becomes all the more striking.

How are we to interpret such diverse measures of the religiousness of Canadians and hence the number and size of the religious in the 1990s in Canada? If regular participation in a local faith community is our working definition of religiousness, then the religious are confined to the approximately one third of Canadians who attend religious services and meetings monthly or more frequently. If subjective assessment of personal religiousness is the preferred indicator, then our estimate of the number of religious Canadians must be roughly doubled. The standard sociological solution to the conundrum is to recognize that there are a number of interrelated components or dimensions involved in religiousness that must be considered jointly. Religiosity, to employ the favoured technical term, is multidimensional. It cannot be measured adequately by any one dimension, be it attendance at religious services and meetings, doctrinal orthodoxy, personal expressions of piety such as prayer, or subjective evaluations of how religious respondents feel they are.

I think this multidimensional conception of religiosity needs to be qualified in two crucial ways to create a workable and meaningful measure. First, endeavours to measure religious knowledge and orthodoxy are so flawed that they should be abandoned. This applies most obviously to studies involving Christian and non-Christian groups, but there are also substantial variations between Christian denominations in the nature and importance of their defining beliefs.[18] When we add to this the difficulty in identifying orthodoxy within a specific denomination, the exercise dissolves in a sea of ambiguity. Second, I am uncomfortable with indexes that combine

Table 2.12
Religiosity by survey and year

	Bibby 1975	WVS 1990	Reid 1993	Reid 1994	Bibby 1995	Reid 1996	Reid 1996	NSVGP 1997	NSVGP 2000
Very Comitted	30	26	24	22	23	22	20	19	18
Less Committed	11	14	9	13	11	12	17	13	14
Seekers	26	24	35	31	24	29	25	29	27
Non Religious	33	36	32	34	42	37	38	39	41
Total	100%	100%	100%	100%	100%	100%	100%	100%	100%
(N)	(1,859)	(1,717)	(5,904)	(1,489)	(1,689)	(1,466)	(2,955)	(17,058)	(13,798)

several scales such as frequency of attendance, prayer, and reading of religious literature. If each scale has four levels, then a combined, three-item index of religiosity can theoretically range from four to twelve. The methodologically minded are enchanted by this numerical precision and its potential for complex statistical inference, but setting the boundaries between high, medium, and low religiosity on such an index becomes a very arbitrary process. More importantly, 12-point indexes of this sort do not delineate a social category or group that we can recognize in concrete terms. We can, for instance, readily identify weekly attenders and non-attenders, but this clarity is blurred when we talk, for example, of people with more than nine on a 12-point religiosity scale, as opposed to those with four or five points. We are also left wondering how individuals scored on each of the three constituent scales. Individuals with identical nine-point religiosity scores could have very different profiles on the dimension of attendance, prayer, and the like. In brief, simple scales are preferable because their meaning is clearer.

My four-scale religiosity index therefore combines attendance at religious services and meetings with a question that asks survey respondents to assess how religious they are. The precise variations in the questions are summarized in table 2.11. Since I measure both attendance and personal religiosity on four-point scales, I could create an eight-point scale, but it would suffer all the uncertainties just mentioned. For the sake of clarity, I have instead created a four-category index with identifiable social categories. Table 2.12 summarizes the distribution of Canadians in these four categories in nine separate surveys using the slightly different measures of religiosity dictated by the variations in the survey questions on personal religiousness.

Let me clearly define these four categories since I will be discussing them in all succeeding chapters. The Very Committed, who are approximately a fifth of all Canadians, attend religious services or meetings on a weekly basis and define themselves as religious, or say religion is an important part of their lives. I should add that an impressive 91% of the Very Committed say they pray at least weekly; 75% do so daily. Almost two-thirds (63%) also read the Bible or other religious material at least once a week.[19] The Less Committed, who represent about 10 to 12% of Canadians, are largely composed of those who attend religious services or meetings one to three times a month, but not weekly. Also included in the Less Committed are the tiny 1% of Canadians who attend weekly, but say religion is not important to them.[20] The great majority (86%) of the Less Committed say that religion is very important to them in their day-to-day life. Not surprisingly, fewer of the Less Committed pray (57%) or read religious literature (23%) at least weekly, though almost all of them do so (98% and 84% respectively) at least occasionally. Combined, the Committed are about a third of all Canadians. Seekers define themselves as religious or say religion is important in their lives, but they rarely (53%) or never (47%) attend religious services. About 28% of Canadians are Seekers. The remaining 40% or so of Canadians are the Non Religious, who rarely (28%) or never (72%) attend and who say religion in not important to them.

Attentive readers will have noticed that the several surveys and their slightly different ways of defining religiosity yield varying estimates of the relative proportion of Canadians who are in these four religious categories. This is surely predictable given the vagaries of sampling, the fact the surveys were done at different points in time, and the different questions used to tap subjective assessments of religiousness. Since 1975, the ranks of the Very Committed have shrunk noticeably and the Non Religious have grown more numerous; both trends are consistent with earlier data on church attendance. Within the more limited time frame of the middle to the end of the 1990s, I would argue that the estimates of the category sizes are broadly similar, with the notable exception of the 1996 Reid finding that 17% of Canadians are Less Committed; this anomaly is best dealt with in this endnote.[21] This overall similarity in the size of the four categories surely testifies to the validity and robustness of my religiosity scale, since different empirical indicators still produce markedly similar estimates.

CANADA'S COMMITTED, SEEKERS, AND
NON RELIGIOUS: A PROFILE

The following profile is based on the 1997 National Survey of Volunteering, Giving, and Participation by Statistics Canada (NSVGP). I use the NSVGP because it is recent and because its large sample allows me to go into considerable detail on social differences, while retaining enough respondents in each category to retain confidence in the results. I use the slightly earlier 1997 cycle of the NSVGP because the 2000 NSVGP in its public version provides less complete demographic descriptions. There are also technical problems with the religious questions from the 2000 NSVGP that are best dealt with in this footnote.[22] Though all the Statistics Canada surveys have respondents from 15 years of age and up, my analysis here and in all subsequent chapters focuses on Canadians 18 years of age and over. This allows me to compare the results with other surveys, which typically sample Canadians age 18 or older. I also think that the age of 18 better identifies the beginning of young adulthood.

Given the substantial decline in attendance rates at religious services since the 1960s, it seems appropriate to start this social profile by looking at the age distribution of my four religious categories. Rather than using a series of five or ten-year age cohorts, I identify generations who share and have shared certain broad life circumstances in common at roughly the same age as they moved through their life cycle. Encompassing 43% of Canadians over age 17 in 1997, baby boomers were the fruit of the post-war rise in birth rate that then fell dramatically in the 1960s. As Canada's largest generation, their tastes and needs have always had a decisive influence on the cultural ethos of the day. Early boomers grew up in the family-centred culture of the 1950s and entered the labour force when the economy was still booming. They were in their forties and early fifties in 1997. Late boomers came of age in the less dynamic but still expanding economy of the 1970s. Like the early boomers, late boomers embraced the "sixties" culture with its sexual revolution, its questioning of authority, its privileged sense of entitlement, and its conviction that self fulfilment could be and should be the goal of all.[23] The post-boomers, or Generation X as they are sometimes called, were born after 1966. Amounting to about 25% of Canadians, Generation X is clearly outnumbered by the boomers. Raised in the materialistic 1980s, their high economic aspirations have been thwarted

Table 2.13
Religiosity by age group (NSVGP 1997)

	Gen. X Age 18–31	Late Boomers Age 32–41	Early Boomers Age 42–51	Pre-Boomers Age 52–64	Retired Age 65 +
Very Commited	11	13	19	27	35
Less Commited	11	13	12	13	15
Seekers	29	30	31	30	26
Non-Relig.	50	44	39	30	23
Total	100%	100%	100%	100%	100%
(N)	(3,870)	(4,325)	(3,237)	(2,774)	(2,882)

P < .001   Tau-c = −.19

by downsizing, government cutbacks, and a phalanx of already entrenched boomers. I have then divided all who came before the boomers into those aged 52 to 64 in 1997 (born between 1933 and 1945) and those now of retirement age. Together, all born before the boomers outnumber Generation X, but at 32% of the Canadian population they are still exceeded by boomers. The depression of the 1930s and World War II indelibly shaped those of retirement age, while the pre-boomers grew up in WWII, coming of age in the cold war uncertainties of the 1950s. Though we may quibble about the specific year that demarcates any of these generations, each has its distinctive experiences that shape its outlook.

Table 2.13 makes it abundantly clear that the ranks of the Committed shrink and the proportion of the Non Religious expands in each succeeding generation. Among retired Canadians, half are Committed, more than double their counterparts in Generation X (22%). Note that the percentage of Committeds among late boomers (26%) is not that much higher. Only among those born prior to the baby boom do we see a significantly higher percentage of Committeds. Conversely but consistently, the 50% of Generation X describing themselves as Non Religious is more than double the 23% of retirees who do so. The result, laid out in Table 2.14, is that over a quarter of the Very Committed (28%) are retirees, a full 50% are over age 51, and only 15% are in Generation X. Predictably, the Non Religious are far younger with a solid 59% less than 42 years of age.

We should not lose sight of the fact that 22% of Generation X still define themselves as Committed, with all its implications of regular involvement in a religious community and their willingness to say that religion is important to them. Almost half of all the Committed

Table 2.14
Age group by religiosity (NSVGP 1997)

	Very Commited	Less Commited	Seeker	Non Relig.	Total
Generation X Age 18–31	15	22	25	32	25
Late Boomers Age 32–41	16	25	24	27	24
Early Boomers Age 42–51	19	18	21	20	20
Pre Boomers Age 52–64	22	17	16	12	16
Retired Age 65+	28	19	14	9	15
Total	100%	100%	100%	100%	100%
(N)	(4,350)	(2,391)	(4,760)	(5,557)	(17,058)

$P < .001$ Tau-c $= -.19$

(48%) are boomers or the post boomers of Generation X. If Generation X is our guide, then at least a fifth of Canadians will continue to be religiously Committed for the foreseeable future. We should also note that as many early boomers are Committed (31%) as they are Seekers (31%), though both groups are outnumbered by the 39% who are Non Religious. Such numbers provide very little support for stereotyped portraits of boomers as predominantly dissatisfied Seekers fleeing conventional religious involvement. Similarly, among the predecessors of the boomers, a little over a quarter (27%) of Canadians in their fifties, sixties, and retirement years define themselves as not religious and say they rarely or never attend religious services. The Committed are clearly older than other Canadians and the Non Religious are younger, but neither category has an exclusive hold on any one generation. Even in Generation X, the Committed and Seekers together equal in number the Non Religious.

Seekers are slightly more prevalent among early boomers (31%) than other generations, but the differences between generations are really quite minor. Almost as many retirees say they are Seekers (26%), as do Canadians in Generation X (29%). Seekers are therefore remarkably evenly spread across Canada's generations. There are fewer Committeds in Generation X than in any other generation, but the relatively low level of active involvement in religion by Generation X has not resulted in any major expansion of unattached Seekers who continue to regard themselves as religious. Instead, it is the ranks of the Non Religious that have grown in Generation X.

Tables 2.15 and 2.16 chart the religious or denominational affiliation of Committed Canadians broken down by generation. I should

Table 2.15
Religion of committed* by age group (NSVGP 1997)

	Gen. X Age 18–31	Late Boomers Age 32–41	Early Boomers Age 42–51	Pre-Boomers Age 52–64	Retired Age 65 +
RC – Quebec	11	14	17	25	28
RC – RoC	39	37	33	36	28
Main. Prot.	15	20	17	21	30
Con. Prot.	27	22	21	16	11
Non Christ.	8	8	12	3	4
Total	100%	100%	100%	100%	100%
(N)	(990)	(1,410)	(1,178)	(1,338)	(1,712)

*Attend religious services or meetings monthly or more frequently.
P < .001   V = .13

stress that these tables and all subsequent tables dealing with differences by religious family are confined exclusively to the Committed, that is to the 32% of Canadians in the NSVGP who attended religious services at least once a month. This is a departure from normal Canadian practice, which I regard as confused and misleading. Since 75% of Canadians in this 1997 Statistics Canada survey claimed a religious affiliation, I am excluding from my analysis of religious families the 43% of Canadians who identify with a religious tradition, but who attend services very rarely or never. I exclude them from the ranks of the Committed because I think the religious identification of this 43% of Canadians is more a matter of historical memory than one of on-going concern and involvement. According to Bibby's 1995 survey, a full 86% of these nominal adherents attending less than monthly admitted that they were not members of a church, synagogue, or temple.[24] Analysis of Canadians actually attached to religious families is clarified – not muddied – when we restrict membership to the Committed. Subsequently, when I refer to Catholics, Mainline Protestants, and the like, I am referring only to those who are Committed. To further clarify differences between religious families, I have also excluded from table 2.15, 2.16 and all others of their ilk the 2% of the Committed who are "other Christians," because they are too few and internally diverse to allow any meaningful conclusions. Non-Christians will be excluded on the same grounds from the appropriate tables in all future chapters, but I will retain them as a category in this chapter so we can get some general sense of their demographic characteristics. Since non-Christians belong to so many very different faiths, I

Table 2.16
Age group by religion of the committed* (NSVGP 1997)

	RC Quebec	RC Roc.	Main. Prot.	Con. Prot.	Non Christ.
Generation X Age 18–31	10	19	12	24	21
Late Boomers Age 32–41	14	21	19	23	23
Early Boomers Age 42–51	16	18	15	22	34
Pre Boomers Age 52–64	26	21	20	17	9
Retired Age 65+	35	20	34	15	14
Total	100%	100%	100%	100%	100%
(N)	(986)	(2,268)	(1,839)	(1,398)	(137)

*Attend religious services or meetings monthly or more frequently.
$P < .001$ $V = .14$

cannot stress too much that generalizations about them as a whole may well not apply to any particular religion.

Six conclusions may be drawn from tables 2.15 and 2.16. First, the overwhelming majority (93%) of the Committed remain attached to Christianity. Even among boomers and Generation X who are most receptive to other faiths, non-Christians collectively amount to a small 8 to 12% of the Committed. Christianity's difficulties in Canada may be legion, but they are not caused by the intrusion of other faiths. Second, though 50% or more of the Committed in all generations are Catholics, these tables again demonstrate the striking decline of Catholics in Quebec and their much more stable situation in the rest of Canada. Catholics in Quebec plummet from 28% of the Committed in their retirement years to just 11% of Generation X, while the Catholic percentage of the Committed in the rest of Canada actually grows among younger generations. A full 61% of Quebec Catholics are in their fifties or older, which is roughly double the proportion for all Canadians (32%) and all Quebecers (33%). Third, the contraction in younger age cohorts is almost as acute among Mainline Protestants who fall from 30% of the Committed over age 65 to 15% of the Committed born after the baby boom. The result is that over half of Mainline Protestants (54%) are in their fifties or older. Fourth, Catholics in the rest of Canada have a generally younger and more balanced age structure, though the 20% who are over age 65 is still above the national average of 15%. Fifth, Conservative Protestants have far more younger people and far fewer elderly in their ranks than either Catholics or Mainline Protestants. Non-Christians appear almost as youthful, though we should not put too much weight on conclusions

Table 2.17
Religiosity by community size (NSVGP 1997)

	500,000+	100,000– 499,999	15,000– 99,999	14,999 or less	Rural
Very Commited	17	21	20	22	23
Less Commited	12	13	10	13	15
Seekers	28	31	29	33	30
Non-Relig.	43	36	40	33	32
Total	100%	100%	100%	100%	100%
(N)	(3,858)	(4,252)	(2,402)	(2,283)	(4,218)

P < .001   Tau-c = -.07

drawn from such a small sample that represents such widely divergent traditions. If youth is the measure of vitality, then Conservative
Protestantism is the most vital of Canada's four major religious families. Finally, we can see that Conservative Protestantism's 19% share
of the Committed rises to 27% in Generation X, which puts their
market share at almost double the 15% retained by Mainline Protestants in this admittedly shrunken and youngest generation of the
Committed. If we narrow our focus to the Very Committed in Generation X (age 18–31), then Conservatives outnumbered Mainline
Protestants by an even more substantial 42% to 10% margin. In the
years to come, it is the Conservative branch of Protestantism that will
become its ever more dominant force.

The differences between rural and urban areas are summarized in
Tables 2.17 and 2.18. All are as predictable as they are minor. The
Committed are less common in Canada's largest cities (29%) than
they are in rural areas (38%), though the differences are quite small
and the Committed are a clear minority at every point on this rural–
urban continuum. Conversely, the Non Religious are more numerous
in big cities (43%) than in the countryside (32%). In between, in the
smaller cities and town of Canada the proportion of Committed and
Non Religious fall within the narrow range that separates big city
from rural area. There is also very little variation in the relative
number of Seekers in rural and urban areas. What small variation
exists reveals that Seekers are most prevalent in our smaller towns
(33%) and least so in our big cities (28%). As for religious differences
within the Committed, 88% of non-Christians reside in our largest
cities, where they are a noticeable but still small minority (13%) of
the Committed. Elsewhere non-Christians make up insignificant

Table 2.18
Rural-urban distribution of the committed by religious families (NSVGP 1997)

	RC Quebec	RC RoC	Main. Prot.	Con. Prot.	Non Christ.
500,000+	42	45	36	40	88
100,000–499,999	12	22	19	17	6
15,000–99,999	12	9	11	13	3
14,999 or less	11	8	11	9	2
Rural	24	16	23	21	1
Total	100%	100%	100%	100%	100%
(N)	(986)	(2,263)	(1,833)	(1,394)	(137)

*Attend religious services or meetings monthly or more frequently
P < .001   V = .14

minorities of 1 to 2%. Otherwise, Catholics outside Quebec are most likely to be big city dwellers (45%) and least likely to live in a rural setting (16%). Mainline Protestants, on the other hand, are most likely to be rural folk (23%) and slightly less likely to reside in a big city, but I must repeat that all the differences between religious family are really quite small. Barring a slightly greater concentration of the Non Religious in our largest cities, all of the major religious categories in tables 2.17 and 2.18 have broadly similar rural–urban profiles. Stereotypes of the secular city and a religious countryside receive very little support from these data. We must also bear in mind that half (49%) of all Canadians live in cities with over half a million inhabitants and only 16% are now fully rural. Differences in religiosity by community size are of only minor significance.

Gender or sex differences are now recognized to have a pervasive and important impact in Canadian society. A great deal has been written on the links between Christianity and gender in general, but the empirical research in Canada on attendance at religious services indicates that the gender gap is very modest.[25] The 1997 NSVGP confirms this impression, though that conclusion depends on how we cast the data and on whether we consider the compounding effect of age differences. Looking at all age groups, we can see in the right-hand columns of table 2.19 that 35% of females versus 29% of males are Committed. A six-point difference of this sort is very small by the usual standards of survey research, though it is statistically significant. The small size of this overall gender gap is partly caused by the smaller gender gap among Canadians of retirement age and those under age 32 belonging to Generation X. However, the six-point

Table 2.19
Religiosity by sex and age (NSVGP 1997)

	Age 18–31		Age 32–51		Age 52–64		Age 65 +		All Ages	
	Sex		Sex		Sex		Sex		Sex	
	Male	Female	Male	Female	Male	Female	Male	Female	Male	Female
Very Committed	10	12	13	18	23	30	33	37	17	22
Less Committed	11	11	12	13	12	15	16	15	12	13
Seekers	24	33	27	33	29	32	23	29	26	32
Non-Relig.	55	45	48	36	37	23	28	19	45	33
Total	100%	100%	100%	100%	100%	100%	100%	100%	100%	100%
(N)	(1,635)	(2,205)	(3,407)	(4,155)	(1,220)	(1,554)	(1,057)	(1,825)	(7,319)	(9,739)
	P < .001 V = .11		P < .001 V = .12		P < .001 V = .15		P < .001 V = .11		P < .001 V = .12	

Table 2.20
Male-female ratio by religion of committed* (NSVGP 1997)

	RC Quebec	RC RoC	Main. Prot.	Con. Prot.	Non Christian
Male	43	43	43	43	62
Female	57	57	57	57	38
Total	100%	100%	100%	100%	100%
(N)	(986)	(2,268)	(1,839)	(1,398)	(137)

*Attend religious services or meetings monthly or more frequently
P < .001   V = .10

gender difference exists in the large boomer generation and it actually extends to a ten-point gender gap for pre-boomers under age 65. The latter differences, I should add, are also very modest, though they do make it clear that women are generally more likely than men to be Committed. The net result, charted in table 2.20 is that 57% of Committed Christians are females and 43% are males. This generalization applies without exception across all the major religious families of Roman Catholics, Liberal Protestants, and Conservative Protestants. The gender gap is apparently reversed among Non Christians, though we are always left wondering how much faith we can put in such a small sample.

As for the remaining religious categories, more women (32%) than men (26%) are Seekers (31%). In this case, the very modest gender gap applies to all the age categories in table 2.19. It is therefore among the Non Religious that we find the greatest gender gap, with 45% of males and 33% of females reporting they are not religious. As with the Seekers, the gender gap among the Non Religious is much the same in every generation. In short, women are more religious than men in the triple sense that they are more likely to be Committed, more likely to be Seekers, and less likely to be Non Religious.

As is so often the case in Canada, regional differences are varied and complex. Table 2.21 shows us that the Committed are more abundant in the Atlantic provinces than in any other Canadian region, though the 42% who are Committed are still a minority of all Maritimers. At the other end of the country, the 21% of British Columbians who are Committed makes the west coast the least religious region in Canada. However, any notion of a simple east–west gradient of declining religiosity is undermined by the 28% of Quebecers who are Committed – the second lowest level in the country. The Committed

Table 2.21
Religiosity by region (NSVGP 1997)

	Atlantic	Quebec	Ontario	Man-Sask	Alberta	BC
Very Commited	26	17	22	23	18	13
Less Commited	16	12	14	14	12	8
Seekers	30	25	30	34	30	30
Non-Relig.	29	47	34	29	40	48
Total	100%	100%	100%	100%	100%	100%
(N)	(3,429)	(3,074)	(5,158)	(2,557)	(1,370)	(1,470)

P < .001   V = .09

rise to 35% of Ontario's residents and to 37% in Manitoba and
Saskatchewan, falling to 30% in Alberta. Seekers are much more uniformly distributed across Canada's regions, though fewer Seekers are
to be found in Quebec (25%) than anywhere else in Canada. Despite
British Columbia's low percentage of Committeds and its reputation
as Lotus Land, it does not have any more Seekers than does the rest
of Canada, barring, of course, Quebec.

What Quebec and British Columbia do share in common are the
two largest bodies of Non Religious in the country. In British Columbia, the Non Religious are 48% of the population; in Quebec they are
47%. I have already alluded to the dramatic fall in Catholic weekly
mass attendance in Quebec since the 1950s. Old Gallup polls also
allow us to compare weekly attendance by province in 1956 with the
1997 figures from the NSVGP. Using this slightly different base, weekly
attendance at religious services in Quebec fell from 84% in 1956 to
17% in 1997. In British Columbia over the same time period, weekly
attendance dropped from 31% to 15%. The 31% rate for British
Columbia in 1956 was the lowest in the country and well below the
national rate of 61%.[26] Secularism therefore has a much longer tradition in British Columbia than in Quebec, though Quebec has almost
caught up.

When we confine our analysis to the religious or denominational
allegiance of the Committed across Canada's regions, as is done in
table 2.22, a number of patterns stand out. As has always been the
case, the religiously Committed in Quebec continue today to be overwhelmingly Catholic, but Quebec's pre-eminence in Canadian
Catholicism has been shattered by more than a century of Catholic
immigration from Ireland, Europe, Latin America, and even India
and Africa. Today, 64% of Canadian Catholics live outside Quebec.

Table 2.22
Religion of the committed by region (NSVGP 1997)

	Atlantic	Quebec	Outside Quebec	Ontario	Man-Sask	Alberta	BC
RC	54	89	44	48	40	33	23
Main. Prot.	27	3	26	25	32	23	29
Con. Prot.	19	6	22	17	27	38	31
Non Christian	1	2	8	9	1	6	16
Total	100%	100%	100%	100%	100%	100%	100%
(N)	(1,669)	(1,078)	(5,550)	(1,992)	(1,053)	(470)	(366)

*Attends religious services or meetings monthly or more frequently
P < .001 V = .26

Here in these other nine provinces, Catholicism's 44% share of the Committed is greater than that of any other religious family, though the combined Protestant population is slightly greater at 48% of all who are Committed. In both the Atlantic provinces and Ontario, Catholics actually outnumber Protestants. Only in the Prairie provinces and British Columbia do Protestants become the numerically dominant group, though Catholics are still about a third of the Committed in the Prairies and a far from tiny 23% in British Columbia. Anyone familiar with *Alberta Report* and *British Columbia Report* or the federal Alliance Party will not be surprised to learn that Conservative Protestants are the largest religious family in these two provinces. East of Alberta, Mainliners outnumber Conservative Protestants by a modest margin of 20% to 15% among all the Committed, though Conservatives have a larger share of the Very Committed (21% vs. 17%). Non-Christians are most heavily concentrated in Ontario and British Columbia, which have been the two major centres of immigrant settlement in recent years.

A long-standing tradition of recruiting immigrants from abroad, an attendant growing diversity in the ethnic origins of Canadians, and an official government policy of multiculturalism are all thought to be some of the defining characteristics of Canada and Canadians. Here, in tables 2.23 and 2.24, I explore religious differences between those who have ever been landed immigrants and those who are Canadian by birth. Landed immigrant status means that a person from another country has legally entered Canada as a permanent resident with the promise that he or she may take up Canadian citizenship after a period of time that is now set at three years. The 1997

Table 2.23
Religiosity of landed immigrants* and Canadians by birth (NSVGP 1997)

	Landed Immigrants*	Canadians by Birth
Very Commited	26	18
Less Commited	16	12
Seekers	25	30
Non-Religious	32	41
Total	100%	100%
(N)	(1,566)	(15,483)

*All who have ever been landed immigrants
P < .001   V = .11

NSVGP tells us that 19% of Canadians 18 years of age or older are or once were landed immigrants. Almost half of all immigrants (44%) have entered Canada since 1980; another 22% did so in the 1970s.

Table 2.23 shows a consistent though modest tendency for immigrants to be more religious than Canadians born here. The magnitude of the difference should not be overstated; there is a 12-point spread between the 42% of immigrants and the 30% of Canadians by birth who are Committed. At the other end of the spectrum, we find a larger block of Non Religious among Canadians by birth (41%) than immigrants (32%). Seekers are much more evenly distributed among immigrants and Canadians by birth, though the latter are somewhat more likely to portray themselves as Seekers.

Among the Committed, non-Christian faiths attract the allegiance of a solid 22% of immigrants and only 2% of Canadians by birth (see table 2.24). Nevertheless, the great majority of Committed immigrants are Christians (78%). Even among Committed immigrants arriving since 1980, almost two-thirds (61%) are involved in one or another Christian denomination. The NSVGP data therefore confirm Bibby's previously noted conclusion that immigration poses no major threat to the pre-eminence of Christianity among Canada's Committed. I would only add that the number of non-Christians is clearly likely to grow in the future. Overall, Catholics show an impressive ability to reach out to immigrants. Thus the Catholic share of Committed immigrants is substantial (46%) and not much less than their 54% hold on the Committed born in Canada. However, that overall Catholic ability to reach out to new Canadians does not apply to Quebec Catholics, who represent a tiny 3% of Committed immigrants but a much more solid 24% of the Committed born in Canada. In

Table 2.24
Religion of the committed* among landed immigrants** and Canadians by birth
(NSVGP 1997)

	Landed Immigrants	Canadians by Birth
RC – Quebec	3	24
RC – RoC	43	31
Main. Prot.	11	24
Con. Prot.	20	18
Non Christian	22	2
Total	100%	100%
(N)	(663)	(5,961)

*Attends religious services or meetings monthly or more frequently
**All who have ever been landed immigrants
$P < .001$ $V = .42$

marked contrast, Catholics outside Quebec have a larger share of Committed immigrants (43%) that they do of the Committed born in Canada (31%). The success of the Catholic Church outside Quebec in embracing immigrants and its failure to do so within Quebec illuminates further the greater vitality of Catholicism outside Quebec. Conservative Protestants have also been successful in reaching beyond their base among the Canadian-born (18%) to increase slightly their share of Committed immigrants (20%), though their outreach has not been nearly as successful as Catholics have been outside Quebec. On the other hand, Mainline Protestants have seen their 24% share of the Canadian-born fall to only 11% of Committed immigrants. Among Committed immigrants who have arrived since 1980, Mainline Protestant and Quebec Catholic outreach fall to dismal 5% and 2% levels respectively; Conservative Protestants continue to hold their own with 19%; and Catholics outside Quebec retain a sizeable though reduced 35% share of Committed immigrants. This failure to attract immigrants clearly adds to the growing challenges confronted by both Mainline Protestantism and Quebec Catholicism.

Tables 2.25 and 2.26 give us some idea of how ethnicity interacts with religiosity, but I must stress that the measure of ethnicity used by Statistics Canada and the NSVGP is seriously flawed. The methodologically inclined might care to consult this endnote for details.[27] These problems make it impossible to draw any conclusions on the relative size of the ethnic categories, but we can learn something about the degree of religiosity within ethnic categories. Tables 2.25 and 2.26 should be viewed as suggestive and not authoritative.

Table 2.25
Religiosity by ethnicity (NSVGP 1997)

	British	French	European	Visible Minority	Aboriginal
Very Commited	16	19	27	21	7
Less Commited	11	11	16	14	16
Seekers	31	25	32	18	33
Non-Relig.	43	45	25	47	44
Total	100%	100%	100%	100%	100%
(N)	(6,072)	(3,806)	(1,525)	(260)	(111)

P < .001   V = .09

Table 2.26
Religion of the committed by ethnicity (NSVGP 1997)

	British	French	European	Visible Minority	Aboriginal
RC	32	95	61	26	57
Main. Prot.	44	1	13	19	8
Con. Prot.	23	4	26	23	23
Non Christian	2	0	1	32	13
Total	100%	100%	100%	100%	100%
(N)	(2,201)	(1,537)	(722)	(93)	(32)

* Attends religious services or meetings monthly or more frequently
P < .001   V = .43

Like Canadians by birth, those of British and French origin are less religious than Canadians as a whole in that the percentage of Committed in their ranks is below average and the percentage of Non Religious is above average. Aboriginals appear to be the least religious ethnic group in Canada, though the small size of the sample diminishes our confidence in this conclusion. European-origin Canadians have the largest body of Committed (43%) and the smallest proportion of Non Religious (25%). However, I suspect that this is a statistical mirage created by confining Europeans to those of exclusively European ancestry and excluding Canadians of mixed European or European and other ancestries. Visible minorities are also more likely than other Canadians to be Committed (35%). This is then counterbalanced by a higher proportion of visible minorities (47%) describing themselves as Non Religious. While no one ethnic group seems particularly prone to being Seekers, the French and visible minorities are less inclined to embrace this religious option. The one qualifier I would add is that none of these differences is large or substantial. Canadians do vary in the amount and form of their religiousness, but no ethnic group is predominately in one or another religious type; all have a rich mixture of the Committed, Seekers, and Non Religious.

When we turn to the denominational allegiances of the Committed, it comes as no surprise to find that 95% of Canadians of French origin are Catholic. The Catholic Church also has the allegiance of substantial proportion of the Committed who are Aboriginals (53%), Europeans (61%), British (32%), and visible minorities (26%). It is this broad base of support across ethnic groups that makes Catholicism Canada's largest faith. Table 2.26 shows that Committed Canadians of British origin are the strongest supporters of Mainline Protestantism (44%), but this should bring no particular joy to Mainline Protestantism since the British are less religious than other Canadians. Conservative Protestantism, in contrast, holds the allegiance of greater percentages of Europeans (26% vs. 13%), visible minorities (23% vs. 19%), Aboriginals (23% vs. 8%) and even the French (4% vs. 1%) who are Committed. It is this broader ethnic base in Conservative Protestantism that is another of its strengths. The corollary, of course, is that Mainline Protestantism's narrower ethnic base compounds its difficulties. The same table's finding that only 32% of Committed visible minorities are non-Christians reinforces similar earlier findings on immigrants. As for Aboriginals, the minority who are Committed (23%) continue to be overwhelmingly attached to Christian faiths; only 13% profess a non-Christian faith. The low percentage of Committeds among Aboriginals surely testifies to their rejection of their Christian missionary heritage. To date this rejection has caused surprisingly few Aboriginals to seek solace in another religious tradition.

To complete this social profile of the Committed, Seekers, and Non Religious, I trace the impact of income and educational differences, or what might broadly be called class differences. The bottom line of table 2.27 reveals surprisingly little variation by religious category in total household income for Canadians as a whole. The Very Committed earn somewhat less ($44,655) than the average Canadian household ($47,572) and the Non Religious earn a wee bit more ($48,847). The more compelling conclusion is that all religious categories earn about the same amount. We know that income varies considerably by age and we have seen that the Committed tend to be older than other Canadians and the Non Religious younger. In fact, the average

Table 2.27
Average (mean) annual household income by religiosity:
All Canadians and Canadians aged 40–59 (NSVGP 1997)

	Very Commited	Less Commited	Seeker	Non Religious	Total	(N)
Age 40–59	$57,034	$61,638	$53,129	$55,985	$55,983	(5,795)
All Ages	$44,655	$47,990	$47,614	$48,847	$47,572	(17,058)

Table 2.28
Average (mean) annual household income by religion of the committed:*
All Canadians and Canadians aged 40–59 (NSVGP 1997)

	RC Quebec	RC RoC	Main. Prot.	Con. Prot.	Non Christ.	(N)
Age 40–59	$63,074	$60,595	$63,055	$50,316	$55,628	(2,238)
All Ages	$40,708	$49,300	$47,019	$46,476	$48,879	(6,628)

*Attends religious services or meetings monthly or more frequently

age of the Committed (50) in 1997 was 10 years older than that of the Non Religious (40). To sort out the impact of age, I include the top line in table 2.27, which compares Canadians in their top wage-earning years of 40 to 59, thereby excluding the lower income years of retirement and early years in the labour force. Within this more restricted category, average household income rises by almost $8,000 to $55,983 and there is somewhat more variation by religious type. Here the average household income of the Very Committed ($57,034) is a little above the Canadian average ($55,983), which is virtually identical to the household income of the Non Religious ($55,985). Seekers ($53,129) earn just below the national average, which is surpassed rather more noticeably by the Less Committed ($61,638). With the partial exception of the Less Committed, income differences between Committed, Seeker, and Non Religious Canadians are very small. By this measure, class differences have no significant bearing on religiosity. If any reader is uncomfortable with using means to measure average incomes, please be reassured that identical conclusions emerge when we compare median incomes on my religiosity scale. The data are in this endnote.[28]

Income differences between religions are outlined in table 2.28. When we narrow our focus to the peak earning years of 40 to 59, the household incomes of Quebec Catholics ($63,074) and Mainline Protestants ($63,055) are both 13% above the national average for all Canadians in that age bracket ($55,983). The average income of Catholics in the rest of Canada ($60,595) is a more modest 8% greater than the national average, while Conservative Protestants in this age group ($50,316) are 12% below the national average. There are therefore some notable though far from large income differences by religious family among the middle-aged. However, these differences largely disappear when we disregard age and look at the average household income of all Committed Canadians, which is surely the better indicator of the overall class standing of each religion or religious family. Apart from the lower household income of all Committed Quebec Catholics, all the other religious families have highly similar household incomes that hover very closely around the national average of $47,572. Overall, the household incomes of the four Christian families are very similar to each other and to the Canadian average.

When it comes to the educational differences charted in table 2.29, there is a curvilinear relationship, which means that the Committed are most prevalent amongst the least and most educated, though the differences are exceedingly modest. The lower educational levels of older Canadians, who are more likely to be Committed, explains why Canadians with less than completed high school are most likely to be Committed (37%) and least likely to be Non Religious (34%). When we confine our analysis to the much better educated baby boomers (see table 2.30), the Committed rise from 23% of those with less than high school to 34% of Canadians with at least some university education. This apparent link between religiousness and education is then contradicted by Seekers who fall from 31% of high school drop-outs to 22% of those with a university education. Thus higher educational attainment makes Canadians both more likely to be Committed and less likely to be Seekers, though all these differences are really very modest. The result is that Non Religious boomers shrink very slightly from 46% of the least educated to 44% of the most educated. Data of this sort clearly refute any idea that educational advance erodes religious commitment. Let me be clear that it would be equally erroneous to conclude that a lack of education fosters non-religiousness. The most sensible conclusion is that the religious or non-religious tendencies of Canadians are not much affected by their educational level.

Table 2.29
Religiosity by educational attainment, excluding full-time students (NSVGP 1997)

	Less than High School	Completed High School	Post Secondary:	University*
Very Commited	24	16	18	20
Less Commited	13	11	12	13
Seekers	30	30	31	29
Non-Relig.	34	43	38	39
Total	100%	100%	100%	100%
(N)	(4,200)	(2,877)	(6,134)	(2,938)

*Some or Completed
P < .001   Tau-c = -.03

Table 2.30
Religiosity by educational attainment among baby boomers (Ages 32–51), excluding full-time students (NSVGP 1997)

Religiosity	Less than High School	Completed High School	Post Secondary:	University*
Very Commited	13	13	16	21
Less Commited	10	12	13	13
Seekers	31	32	32	22
Non-Relig.	46	43	39	44
Total	100%	100%	100%	100%
(N)	(1,194)	(1,429)	(3,198)	(1,613)

*Some or Completed
P < .001   Tau-c = .04

Educational differences by religious family are charted in tables 2.31 and 2.32. Although Quebec Catholics are notably less likely to have finished high school (47%), this is much less true of Catholics in the rest of Canada. These differences are then further eroded when we confine our analysis to baby boomers. Non-Christians, on the other hand, are more likely than any other religious family to have a university education (29%), though I must add the by-now familiar qualifier that this need not apply to any specific Non-Christian body. Mainline Protestants are slightly more likely than Conservatives to have a university education, but otherwise their educational profiles tend to be highly similar. I should note that stereotyped portraits of Conservative Protestantism as the refuge of the uneducated are not supported by these data, since they have proportionately fewer high school drop-outs (24%) than does Canada as a whole (27%) and the very same percentage with a university education (16%). In short, we

Table 2.31
Education by religion among the committed*, excluding full-time students (NSVGP 1997)

	RC Quebec	RC RoC	Main. Prot.	Con. Prot.	Non Christ.
<High School	47	30	23	24	24
High School	11	17	19	20	15
Post Secondary**	30	36	36	40	23
University**	12	17	21	16	29
Total	100%	100%	100%	100%	100%
(N)	(965)	(2,173)	(1,797)	(1,328)	(125)

*Attends religious services or meetings monthly or more frequently
**Some or Completed
$P < .001$ $V = .12$

Table 2.32
Education by religion among religiously committed* baby boomers (Ages 32–51), excluding full-time students (NSVGP 1997)

	RC Quebec	RC RoC	Main. Prot.	Con. Prot.	Non Christ.
<High School	23	14	10	13	22
High School	17	19	23	21	9
Post Secondary**	47	43	40	45	38
University**	13	25	27	22	31
Total	100%	100%	100%	100%	100%
(N)	(951)	(658)	(594)	(65)	

*Attends religious services or meetings monthly or more frequently
**Some or Completed
$P < .001$ $V = .11$

can discern a variety of small differences between religious families and between the Committed and all other Canadians, but none are particularly noteworthy or important. All five of these religious families have memberships drawn from a great mixture of educational backgrounds that are broadly similar to those of all Canadians.

In concluding this chapter I see no point in summarizing the evidence of declining religious involvement in Canada since the 1960s and my subsequent review of what it means to be religious in Canada today. There is much more to be gained from pulling together the immediately preceding social profile of the Committed, Seekers, and the Non Religious in the second half of the 1990s.

Some readers may have noticed that I have not yet made any reference to the statistical tests that lie below every table. I have avoided commenting on them until now because the statistically knowledgeable can readily draw their own conclusions, while those unfamiliar with such matters are understandably deterred by this technical minutia. I also think it is the actual evidence in the tables – and not the statistical tests – that ought to be our prime concern. However, there is certainly some value to these tests, which are briefly described below for those not versed in statistical matters. Remember that my social profile of Canadians differentiated by religiosity is based on the 1997 NSVGP, which has a huge sample of 17,058 Canadians. The consequence of this large sample is that all the tables in this chapter are very statistically significant (indicated by $p < .001$), which means that we can be pretty certain that the tables' findings are true of Canadians as a whole and are not caused by sampling error.[29] That is reassuring news, but statistical significance, as every textbook in the field attests, should not be equated with substantive significance. The latter refers to whether the differences we have observed between the Committed, Seekers, and the Non Religious are sufficiently large to really matter or have a major impact. Quite small differences may be statistically significant in a large sample, but the differences may well be unimportant in any other sense. In the end it is substantive, not statistical significance that matters most. This substantive significance is measured by Tau-c and Cramer's V using technical criteria too complex to summarize here. The larger the size of Tau-c or V (on a scale from .00 to 1.00), the greater is the substantive significance of the findings under discussion. Since there are no hard and fast rules for specifying precisely when a difference is small or large, assessments of substantive significance are ultimately a subjective call. However, most social statisticians would agree that the differences between the Committed, Seekers, and the Non Religious in this chapter, barring a few exceptions I will note below, are not very large or important. That is the key statistical conclusion.

The clearest finding by far is that the Committed, and above all the Very Committed, are older than other Canadians, while the Non Religious are much younger. Even allowing for some Canadians becoming more religious as they age, the ranks of the Committed are likely to shrink in the future. Since Seekers are no more prevalent among the young than the old, there in no sign of a growing, unquenched religious hunger among younger Canadians that faith communities might hope to tap. Instead, it is the ranks of the avowedly Non Religious that grow among the young.

Second, some differences by religious family or tradition among the Committed are quite strong. Conservative Protestants, Catholics outside Quebec, and non-Christians have age profiles that are broadly similar to all Canadians. It is therefore Quebec Catholics and Mainline Protestants who have the oldest age profiles and who may expect to experience the greatest declines in the future. There are also some notable religious differences between the Committed by region, immigrant status, and ethnicity. Conservative Protestantism and the Catholic Church outside Quebec have been most successful in reaching out from their traditional, Canadian-born base to attract New Canadians and Canadians from a variety of ethnic backgrounds. The singular ability of the Catholic Church to embrace Canadians from across the entire ethnic spectrum is the prime reason for it being the largest single faith community in Canada. The only shadow on the horizon for the Catholic church here is that its share of visible minorities (26%), who are now the great majority of immigrants, is well below its 52% hold on all the Committed. Again it is the Catholic Church in Quebec and Mainline Protestantism which have been least successful in reaching beyond their original ethnic bases and attracting immigrants.

Finally, there are a number of small and predictable differences by sex, community size, migrant status, and ethnicity that set the Committed apart from other Canadians. Thus women, rural folk, and immigrants are more likely to be Committed, while the Non Religious are more common in big cities and among men, the Canadian born, and old-stock, French, British, and Aboriginal ethnic groups. Let me reiterate one last time that none of these differences is very large. When it comes to the household incomes and educational attainments of Canadians, there are insignificant differences between the Committed, Seekers, and the Non Religious. With the just-mentioned, partial exception of certain differences by age and between religious family, all the religious categories enumerated here, including the Non Religious and Seekers, contain Canadians from all walks of life in proportions broadly reflective of all Canadians. In other words, these religious categories are not caused by other, underlying interests rooted in class, ethnicity, region, and the like. Religiosity or religiousness is a non-reducible, all-encompassing way in which Canadians can be classified and distinguished from each other. What remains to be seen is whether religiosity or its lack affects the behaviour and outlook of Canadians in other walks of life.

3

The Religious Individual:
Well-Being and Personal Values

My sociological background inclines me to focus on how people think and behave in their relationships with others. This concern is pursued in all other chapters, but it seems appropriate to start any analysis of religiosity's impact on Canadians by looking at whether the psychological state of Canadians is affected by how religious they are. Let me be clear that the answers to this question depends on what Canadians say is their psychological state – and not on some independent assessment of it. Besides the possibility that some may be lying for a host of obvious reasons, one could reasonably argue that none of us is equipped to asses our own mental health or the priorities that really drive us. This stricture is the too often ignored bane of all survey research, but it surely applies with particular force when people are asked to evaluate something so complex as their own psychological state. Yet, having given the warning, we are left with the reality that these self-reports, no matter how flawed they may be, are the only information we have. We must therefore proceed with a skeptical eye, mindful that we are looking beyond the statistical minutiae for the general patterns that emerge from the surveys summarized in the following tables.

PSYCHOLOGICAL WELL-BEING

In exploring what others have written on the connections between religion and well-being, I quickly discovered that sociologists are not

the only ones interested in them. Psychologists and even epidemiol-
ogists have spilled much ink on the links between health and religion.
They are also devoting more attention to it every day. I have no
intention of imposing on readers anything like a comprehensive
review of this burgeoning literature,[1] but I would like to identify
three broad conclusions I drew from the work of others, particularly
in psychology, which may help readers to assess the survey data I
subsequently examine.

First, there is a long-standing anti-religion tradition in psychology
that certainly has its counterpart in sociological thinking, though I
think the animus is much deeper in psychology. Sociology has tended
to dismiss religion rather condescendingly as the understandable but
futile retreat of the deprived and stupid who are incapable of resolving the real problems in life they confront. Psychology has a much
more virulent tradition, most notably in psychoanalytic thought, that
sees religion as a clear threat to mental health and maturity. Freud
was particularly blunt in his portrait of religion as "the obsessional
neurosis of children," which "comprises a system of wishful illusions
together with a disavowal of reality, such as we find in an isolated
form nowhere else but in … a state of blissful hallucinatory confu-
sion."[2] Many other psychopathologists, including Erich Fromm and
Albert Ellis, were and are of much the same mind. The practical result
is that diagnostic instruments, such as the Minnesota Multiphasic
Personality Inventory (MMPI), "include items that ask about religious
belief, prayer, and experiences of the presence of God, and treat affir-
mative answers as evidence of psychopathology."[3] These are, of
course, extreme examples; there are other psychologists and sociologists who view religion in a much more positive light. Nevertheless,
this critical take on religion in the social sciences is very much part
of the dominant secularization paradigm that so often regards religion's decline as inevitable, progressive, and good.

Second, psychologists are not agreed on what they mean by mental
health. Batson and his colleagues identify seven different conceptions
of mental health that range from the simple absence of a certifiable
mental illness to more debatable versions that focus on freedom from
guilt and worry, personal competence and control, self acceptance
and self-actualization, and open mindedness and flexibility[4]. Resolving these contending views is well beyond my competence and the
concerns of this book, but each conception will undoubtedly have its
doubters. Some conceptions of mental health seem much less likely
to be associated with religiosity than others. As we have just seen, the

MMPI actually defines most basic forms of religious behaviour and belief as pathological. Faced with choosing between the above alternatives and the equally, if not more daunting task of measuring each one, much of the empirical research has asked their survey respondents how happy or satisfied they are with their day-to-day life. Even momentary reflection suggests that there are many circumstances in life where it would be neither sane nor mentally healthy to feel happy or satisfied. Happiness and satisfaction scales also raise the aforementioned question of whether most of us are capable of accurately assessing whether we really are happy or satisfied with life. The only sensible resolution to all this is to recognize that every measure of mental health or psychological state has its flaws. All our answers are no more than approximations to the difficult questions we pose.

Third, despite my two preceding observations, all the recent reviewers of the empirical research in the field agree with Ellison's recent assessment that "various aspects of religious involvement are linked with desirable mental health outcomes."[5] Supporting evidence has been around for several decades, but psychology did not begin to take the issue seriously until quite recently. This may have been caused in part by its anti-religion bias, but the neglect was also compounded by the tendency of early researchers to report their findings without investigating in any systematic way whether the link between religiousness and health held up under sustained analysis. Though there are dissenting studies, reviewers of this recent, more methodologically sophisticated work agree that the relationship still holds. Thus a highly sophisticated study of African-Americans found that: "a composite measure of organizational religious involvement (including frequency of religious attendance) is as strong or stronger a correlate of life satisfaction as is physical health status, a finding that persists even after controlling for effects of other religious dimensions, sociodemographic correlates of health and religiosity, and health status itself."[6] The key qualifier to all this is that these linkages between mental health and religiosity are statistically significant and therefore presumably real, but they have tended to be "modest"[7] or "small."[8] In layman's language, this means that the psychological differences between the highly religious and the non-religious are not terribly large or important. Such distinctions, I should add, have not much concerned academic psychologists.

I should note briefly that there is an equally large body of research indicating that the religiously involved also have better physical health than the non-religious. These epidemiological studies reveal that religiosity is linked to greater life expectancy and lower morbidity stemming from hypertension, cardiovascular disease, cancer, and the like.[9] The survey data I am using do not generate these objective measures of physical health. There is additional research indicating that subjective measures of physical health are also associated with religiousness, though some attach less importance to this conclusion because "subjective health is not an accurate indicator of actual physical health."[10] Some but by no means all of the research on questionnaire-derived measures of health have been further criticized for failing to take account of level of physical activity or capacity. Among the elderly in particular, it may often be that illness prevents them from being religiously involved – and not that religiousness causes them to be healthy. It is precisely for this reason that I have not done a detailed analysis of the NSVGP, which has a question on self-assessed health but nothing on level of physical activity. In the NSVGP, the self-reported health of Canadians under age 65 does not vary much by their degree or type of religiousness. Thereafter, the more religious are significantly less likely to say they have poor health, but we cannot be sure what is cause and what is effect.[11] Nevertheless, all the literature reviews I have already cited are agreed that there is a general, though by no means large relationship between physical health and religiosity.

Almost all of the just summarized research was conducted in the very distinctive circumstances of the United States, where weekly attendance rates are about double those in Canada. There are three major studies with Canadian content. Bibby, in his 1985 Canadian survey found that "those people who are religiously committed are neither more nor less likely than other people to claim to be happy or satisfied."[12] We might bear in mind that Bibby defined as committed the 44% of Canadians who defined themselves as "committed to Christianity."[13] He therefore does not use the behavioural indicator of attendance at religious services to measure religiosity, as I and so many others have done in our definitions of religiousness. This may explain why other Canadian researchers have not corroborated Bibby's conclusions.

Using the 1985 General Social Survey, Gee and Veevers found that weekly attenders were more likely than those without a religion to describe themselves as very satisfied with life in general.[14] The authors add that this overall relationship was much weaker on some dimensions of life satisfaction than others and that the non-religious in British Columbia were sometimes more satisfied than attenders. Gee and Veevers therefore give very qualified support to the thesis that religiosity promotes psychological well-being. On the other hand, a much more sophisticated report based on the 1996 General Social Survey found compelling evidence that the religiously active are more satisfied with life. In this case, Warren Clark noted that any study of satisfaction with life should also take into consideration such factors as "income, family structure, education, age, sex and employ-ment status," which also "contribute to a person's sense of well-being." After controlling for the impact of these alternative influences so that the impact of religiosity alone was being assessed, Clark found that "the odds of feeling very satisfied with their lives were 1.7 times higher for weekly attenders than for those who had not attended during the last 12 months."[15]

In a somewhat different vein, Frankel and Hewitt compared mem-bers of Christian clubs on an Ontario university campus with stu-dents in first and second year sociology courses. They assumed that membership in a Christian club in the secular environment of a Canadian university campus signified real religious commitment, which was confirmed when they found that the affiliated Christian students were much more likely to embrace basic Christian concepts. Otherwise, the two populations were broadly comparable in social background. Hewitt and Frankel found statistically significant evi-dence that the affiliated Christians scored higher on a test of psycho-logical well-being, claimed higher life satisfaction, and registered lower stress levels. No single difference is that large and there are none of the controls that Clarke employed, but the differences together reveal a discernibly higher level of psychological well-being among the affiliated Christians.[16]

Turning to my data, table 3.1 lists a variety of questions from the NSVGP and the Reid surveys that allow us to explore how religiosity affects the psychological well-being of Canadians in the 1990s. I have included two questions on satisfaction with life to demonstrate how slightly different ways of formulating the question and response options produce different sets of numbers, although both yield similar conclusions. In both surveys a higher proportion of the Very Commit-ted say they are very satisfied (52%) or completely satisfied (48%) with their lives than those in any of the other religious categories. Conversely, the Non Religious are least likely to describe themselves

Table 3.1
Personal outlook by religiosity

	N	Very Commited	Less Commited	Seeker	Non Relig.	Total	Tau-c
% Very satisfied with life in general (1 on 4-point scale)[1]	(17,032)	52	43	44	38	43	.11***
% Completely satisfied with your life these days (1–2 on 7-point scale)[2]	(1,484)	48	36	37	35	39	.10**
% Extremely happy with your life (1–2 on 7-point scale)[2]	(1,477)	59	42	46	38	45	.16***
% Very happy[3] (1 on 3-point scale)	(1,650)	28	19	21	21	22	.04
% Have no control or control over few decisions in every-day activities[1]	(17,019)	11	14	13	13	13	.01*
% Strongly agree they have confidence they will carry out their plans[2]	(1,485)	63	52	60	52	57	.08***
% Not worry about not having enough money in the future[1]	(17,027)	41	33	26	28	31	.09***
% Worry a lot about not having enough money in the future[1]	(17,027)	10	18	21	21	18	–.08**

[1]NSVGP 1997 [2]Reid 1994 [3]Bibby 1995 ***P < .001 **P < .01 *P < .05

as highly satisfied. Both surveys reveal a very similar 13 to 14-point spread between the two ends of the religiosity spectrum. As we shall soon see on so many other matters, the Less Committed and Seekers do not have much in common with the Very Committed. Both have satisfaction profiles that are much closer to those of the Non Religious. It is therefore the Very Committed who stand out. This conclusion needs to be qualified in two key ways. First, the great majority of Canadians describe themselves as satisfied with life. In the NSVGP, for instance, a whopping 92% said they were either very satisfied (43%) or somewhat satisfied (49%); only 8% admitted to being dissatisfied in any way. It is difficult to tell whether this reflects how privileged Canadians generally are or whether it is caused by the very human tendency to want to present oneself in a favourable light when confronting others. Presumably, both forces are at work. Secondly and relatedly, none of the differences just mentioned are very large. The Very Committed are more likely to describe themselves as very satisfied than other Canadians, but not by a large margin.

The related issue of how happy Canadians claim to be produces results very similar to the satisfaction scales. The Reid and Bibby surveys from 1994 and 1995 in table 3.1 are another reminder that different questions and samples can be expected to cause variations in response patterns. However, both surveys underline the central finding that the Very Committed are most likely to describe themselves as very happy, though the contrast with the Non Religious is much more striking in Reid's survey than it is in Bibby's, where the difference fades into statistical insignificance. Here too the Less Committed and Seekers tend to have profiles that have much more in common with the Non Religious than with the Very Committed. In this situation where so few Canadians admit to being really unhappy,[17] religiosity has a discernible but quite minor impact.

The next two rows or questions in table 3.1 are the closest approximations I could find in my data to what Batson and his co-authors refer to as the personal competence or control dimension of mental health, which Frankel and Hewitt measure on a mastery scale. Though they argue there is an overall link between religiousness and well-being, both studies fail to find any significant correlation, one way or the other, between religiosity and this specific dimension of competency or mastery.[18] The pertinent data in table 3.1 make a slightly stronger case, though here too the evidence is ambiguous. From the NSVGP, we learn that the great majority of Canadians say they have control over all decisions (32%) or most decisions (55%) that affect their everyday activities; only 12% admit to having control over few decisions, and a minuscule 1% say they have no control. For a change of pace, table 3.1 examines the 13% of Canadians saying they have little or no control. We can see that fractionally fewer of the Very Committed (11%) than the Less Committed, Seekers and Non-Religious (13 to 14%) admit to having little or no control in their lives. Differences of this magnitude are really too small to matter, though the large size of the sample insures that they are statistically significant. On the other hand, rather more of the Very Committed (62%) than the Non Religious (52%) emphasize that they "generally have confidence that when I make plans I will be able to carry them out." Taken together these two questions suggest to me that the Very Committed have a slightly greater sense of control in their lives than do other Canadians. I hasten to add that minor differences of this sort are only noteworthy because they are consistent with the more general trend for religiosity and well-being to be linked.

For Batson et al.'s worry and guilt dimension of mental health, I do not have any measure of guilt,[19] but the last two lines of table 3.1 give us some sense of how religiousness is linked to how much Canadians worry about not having enough money in the future. Unlike their replies on general satisfaction, happiness, and sense of control, far more Canadians are prepared to say they worry financially. In all, 30% admit to worrying a moderate amount and 18% do so "a lot"; 31% say they do not worry. The results are surely predictable. More of the Very Committed (41%) than the Non Religious (28%) say they do not worry, while more than twice as many of the Non Religious (21%) than the Very Committed (10%) worry a great deal. Remember from table 2.27 in chapter 2 that the average household income of the Very Committed is actually a bit lower than that of the Non Religious. Independently of how much money they have, the Very Committed are less anxious about money and the Non Religious more anxious.[20]

Table 3.2 summarizes the extent to which levels of well-being vary by religious family among the Committed, who attend religious services or meetings at least monthly. I will summarize these differences much more briefly because I think the differences here are less striking. Unlike table 3.1, many of the differences here are statistically insignificant, which means that we cannot put much faith in them. In this more uncertain context, I draw three conclusions.

Table 3.2
Personal outlook by religion of the committed

	N	RC Quebec	RC RoC	Main. Prot.	Con. Prot.	V
% Very satisfied with life in general (1 on 4-point scale)[1]	(6,481)	36	49	58	57	.17***
% Completely satisfied with your life these days (1–2 on 7-point scale)[1]	(427)	36	46	51	45	.11
% Extremely happy with your life (1–2 on 7-point scale)[2]	(427)	61	53	51	54	.08
% Very happy[3] (1 on 3-point scale)	(587)	31	25	23	26	.07
% Have no control or control over few decisions in every-day activities[1]	(6,472)	7	15	10	12	.09***
% Strongly agree they have confidence they will carry out their plans[2]	(428)	56	67	61	54	.11
% Not worry about not having enough money in the future[1]	(6,481)	50	30	40	43	.15***
% Worry a lot about not having enough money in the future[1]	(6,481)	14	15	11	9	.08***

[1]NSVGP 1997   [2]Reid 1994   [3]Bibby 1995   ***P < .001   **P < .01   *P < .05

First, among the Committed, Quebec Catholics stand out for having the lowest percentage who claim to be either very or completely satisfied with their lives. The contrast is most striking in the NSVGP, which shows a 20-point spread between the 36% of Quebec Catholics and the 57 to 58% of Protestants who say they are very satisfied with their lives. Though the details vary on the two surveys tapping satisfaction levels, Catholics outside Quebec have consistently higher satisfaction levels than their counterparts in Quebec. Conversely and even more strikingly, the percentage saying they are very or extremely happy with their lives is higher among Quebec Catholics than it is in the other three religious families. I cannot adequately explain these intriguing differences between Quebec Catholics and the rest of the Committed, but I will refer to them again when discussing regional variations.

Second, in the NSVGP, high satisfaction with life is more widespread among Protestants as a whole than it is among Catholics outside and inside Quebec. However, there is no discernible or decisive pattern to the other differences between Protestants and Catholics outside Quebec enumerated in table 3.2. Thus Protestants and Catholics outside Quebec have broadly similar profiles in how happy they claim to be, in their sense of control of their daily lives, and in how much they worry about money matters. Compared to Protestants, Catholics outside Quebec are slightly more likely to claim that they are confident in their future plans and not worried about money, but the differences are really quite small. With the aforementioned exception of Quebec Catholics, generalizations about Protestant–Catholic differences in well-being are hard to make and even harder to sustain. Third the differences in the well-being of Conservative and Mainline Protestants are too small and inconsistent to be interpreted meaningfully. I should note that table 3.2 and all future tables on religious differences by religious family do not include non-Christians because they are too small in number and too internally diverse to allow any meaningful generalizations.

I was once tempted to conclude my examination of religion's role in life satisfaction at this point, but I became mindful of the common criticism in the literature reviews previously cited that researchers often failed to consider other influences on well-being. I am also fully aware that a detailed analysis of each of the measures of well-being in table 3.1 could produce a mountain of overly detailed analysis with little gain in the end. I therefore explore alternative explanations of well-being and the role of religiousness in the whole picture by confining my analysis to the NSVGP survey question that asked Canadians "How satisfied are you with your life in general?" Subjective as it is, this remains the best summary measure we have. It has the added advantage of a very large sample that permits detailed analysis with sufficiently large sub-populations to allow us to draw reliable conclusions. If some find what follows too detailed, I can only ask your forbearance. This further effort produces some interesting conclusions.

I had thought that satisfaction with life would grow as Canadians age, but this expectation is not confirmed by the NSVGP. The results are summarized in table 3.3. The 44% of all post-boomers (ages 18–31) who rate themselves as very satisfied with life is fractionally higher than the 42% of retired Canadians making the same claim. It follows that the tendency of the Very Committed to be older than other Canadians does not explain why the Very Committed are more likely to be satisfied with life in general. In every age group there is hardly any variation in the 52–53% of the Very Committed who are very satisfied. On the other hand, the Less Committed, Seekers, and the Non Religious all become a little less satisfied with life as they age. The magnitude of the decline should not be overstated, but we

Table 3.3
Percentage very satisfied with life in general (4-point scale) by religiosity and age
(NSVGP 1997)

	Generation X (15–31)	Late Boomer (32–41)	Early Boomers (42–51)	Pre Boomer (52 –64)	Pre Boomer (65 plus)
Very Commited	52	52	52	52	53
Less Commited	47	47	37	42	40
Seekers	48	44	42	46	35
Non Religious	40	37	38	35	37
Total	44	43	42	44	42
N	(3,838)	(4,318)	(3,231)	(2,765)	(2,876)
Tau-c	.10***	.12***	.08***	.13***	.15***

***P < .001   **P < .01   *P < .05

can see in table 3.3 that the 48% of post-boomer Seekers very satisfied
with life falls to 35% of Seekers in their retirement years. The gap
between the Very Committed and the Non Religious (measured by
Tau-c) tends to be cumulative, widening as Canadians age. Religiousness and its lack have long-term, growing consequences, though
modest ones. At every age group the Very Committed are more satisfied with life than are other Canadians. As they age, all other Canadians become less satisfied. For all but the Very Committed, life is a
gradual process of disillusionment.

When we look at the effect of household income in table 3.4, we
can immediately see that levels of satisfaction are substantially higher
among the more affluent. Thus the proportion claiming they are very
satisfied with life rises from 30% of those with household incomes
below $20,000 to 59% in households earning $80,000 or more. Nevertheless, the Very Committed in every income category have the highest proportion claiming to be very satisfied with life. At the other end
of the spectrum, the lowest level of satisfaction in all but one income
level occurs among either Seekers or the Non Religious, who are our
two least religious categories. Thus religiosity has an impact on satisfaction levels that is independent of the role played by income. We
can also see in this table that the gap between the Very Committed
and the Non Religious in their satisfaction levels is least pronounced
among those at the bottom and top ends of the income ladder. For
Canadians who are very poor or very rich, religiosity has less of an
impact on satisfaction levels than it does for the 48% of Canadians
with family incomes between $20,000 and $60,000 a year. In the
middle-income bracket of $40,000–59,999, for instance, there is a

Table 3.4
Percentage very satisfied with life in general (4-point scale) by religiosity and family income (NSVGP 1997)

	<$20,000	$20,000–39,999	$40,000–59,999	$60,000–79,999	$80,000 plus
Very Commited	36	49	57	61	70
Less Commited	32	41	45	50	52
Seekers	28	36	46	58	61
Non Religious	28	31	37	45	55
Total	30	38	44	52	59
N	(4,256)	(4,821)	(3,797)	(2,184)	(1,974)
Tau-c	.06 ***	.15***	.14***	.12***	.09***

***P < .001   **P < .01   *P < .05

Table 3.5
Percentage very satisfied with life in general (4-point scale) by religiosity and education (NSVGP 1997)

	Less than High School	Completed High School	Post secondary[1]	University[1]
Very Commited	45	54	51	66
Less Commited	34	46	44	53
Seekers	35	47	42	58
Non Religious	27	37	38	54
Total	36	44	42	57
N	(4,318)	(3,032)	(6,596)	(3,086)
Tau-c	.14***	.14***	.10 ***	.08***

[1]Some or completed
***P < .001   **P < .01   *P < .05

20-point gap between the Very Committed and the Non Religious in the proportion describing themselves as very satisfied with life. In contrast, there is a much smaller eight-point satisfaction gap between the Very Committed and the Non Religious with family incomes below $20,000, though it is the Very Committed who are the most satisfied. Religiousness or its lack therefore has its greatest impact on the satisfaction levels of Canadians from middle-class backgrounds.

Table 3.5's data on the impact of education and religiosity on satisfaction levels parallels in a less pronounced manner the above findings on the influence of family income. Satisfaction levels are greater for the better educated, though the really big jump occurs for those with a university education, of whom 57% say they are very satisfied with life. Note that the highest satisfaction ratings occur among the

Table 3.6
Percentage very satisfied with life in general (4-point scale) by religiosity and region
(NSVGP 1997)

	Quebec	Rest of Canada	Atlantic	Ontario	Man/Sask.	Alberta	BC
Very Commited	37	56	54	54	61	59	64
Less Commited	35	45	47	43	52	56	39
Seekers	32	47	43	46	47	38	57
Non Religious	36	39	38	38	38	42	40
Total	35	46	45	44	48	46	48
N	(3,070)	(13,962)	(3,423)	(5,149)	(2,552)	(1,369)	(1,469)
Tau-c	.00	.13***	.14***	.12***	.19***	.13***	.16***

***P < .001   **P < .01   *P < .05

Very Committed in every age category, while the least satisfied are the Non Religious at every educational level bar university graduates, where the Less Committed are slightly less satisfied. Education makes a difference, but so too does religiosity at every educational level.

More surprising, I think, are the variations in satisfaction levels by region (see table 3.6). Leaving aside momentarily the very special case of Quebec, the overall satisfaction levels in the remaining regions are broadly similar, with Manitoba/Saskatchewan and British Columbia having slightly more people who profess to be very satisfied with life. There is no clear or simple religious reason for these two regions to have more satisfied residents, since B.C. has the lowest block of Very Religious (13%) and Manitoba/Saskatchewan one of the highest (23% – see table 2.21). Outside Quebec, the Very Committed are everywhere most likely to rate themselves very satisfied with life in general, while the Non Religious are least satisfied everywhere but B.C., where they are outdone by the Less Committed. One could speculate about why Seekers have a distinctively high level of satisfaction in B.C. (56%) and a notably lower one on neighbouring Alberta (38%), but these and all other regional peculiarities lead us into too fine a level of detail to merit pursuing. The more general conclusion is that levels of religiousness have a similar and noticeable influence on life satisfaction in all of Canada outside Quebec.

Quebec is different because it is the one region of Canada where the Very Committed profess they are no more satisfied with life in general than the Non Religious. Unlike the rest of Canada, there is very little variation by any religious category in the percentage who are very satisfied with life. Substantially fewer Quebecers are also

Table 3.7
Percentage very satisfied with life in general (4-point scale) by religiosity
and marital status (NSVGP 1997)

	Never Married	Married	Widowed	Separated/ Divorced
Very Commited	43	56	46	31
Less Commited	41	45	36	35
Seekers	41	48	27	26
Non Religious	31	44	29	20
Total	36	48	35	25
N	(3,453)	(10,276)	(1,500)	(1,804)
Tau-c	.11***	.09***	.16***	.11***

***P < .001   **P < .01   *P < .05

satisfied with their lives (36%) than are Canadians in the rest of Canada (46%). Quebecers seem to have a distinctly low and uniform level of dissatisfaction with life that extends to even the Very Committed. To further muddy the waters, Quebec is equally distinctive for being the region with the highest proportion of residents who define themselves as extremely happy with their lives (50%). In the rest of Canada, 44% rate themselves as extremely happy.[21] Thus Quebecers rate themselves both the happiest and the least satisfied residents of Canada. It is not clear to me whether Quebecers are happy with their dissatisfaction or dissatisfied with their happiness. Their potent mix of happiness and dissatisfaction surely tells us quite a bit about why and how Quebecers have endured their gruelling, long-standing debate over their place in Canadian federalism. What remains less clear is why Quebecers of all levels of religiousness voice such similar and relatively low levels of satisfaction with life in general. Despite their pervasive dissatisfaction, many more Very Committed Quebecers rate themselves as extremely happy (71%) than do the Less Committed (42%), Seekers (51%), and the Non Religious (37%). If all Quebecers emulated the Very Committed, the comparatively high level of happiness they now profess would grow by 50%, but they would remain as dissatisfied as ever.

The impact of marital status on life satisfaction is outlined in table 3.7. Despite a rising divorce rate, more married Canadians rate themselves as very satisfied with life (48%) than those in all other marital categories, including the never married (36%). Not surprisingly, the divorced or separated are least likely to be very satisfied (25%). With two quite minor exceptions, the Very Committed across

Table 3.8
Percentage very satisfied with life in general (4-point scale) by religiosity and
comparative health (NSVGP 1997)

	Excellent	Very Good	Good	Fair	Poor
Very Commited	77	57	39	30	25
Less Commited	69	44	33	23	10
Seekers	63	50	32	23	16
Non Religious	61	39	22	23	18
Total	65	46	29	25	18
N	(4,382)	(5,724)	(4,415)	(1,927)	(578)
Tau-c	.12***	.13***	.14***	.05*	.01

***P < .001   **P < .01   *P < .05

marital categories are most likely to say they are very satisfied with
life and the Non Religious are least likely to make the same claim.
The consoling impact of high religious commitment is particularly
evident for the widowed and least so for the married, but the differences are really quite small. The more compelling conclusion is that
religiosity's impact on life satisfaction affects Canadians in all marital
or non-marital situations.

To complete this review of influences on life satisfaction, I explore
in table 3.8 the impact of physical health. The NSVGP asked Canadians
to rate their health "compared to other people your age." The great
majority (85%) rate their health as excellent to good; the remaining
minority rate it as either fair (12%) or poor (3%). The percentage of
Canadians describing themselves as very satisfied with life declines
substantially with deteriorating health, even as the self-assessments
of Canadians move from the apparently very similar categories of
excellent health (65% very satisfied) to very good health (46% very
satisfied) and to good health (29% very satisfied). For those with poor
health, only 18% say they are very satisfied with life. For those with
excellent to good health we see the familiar pattern of the Very Committed being most satisfied and the Non Religious least satisfied.
Here, where the gap between the Very Committed and the Non Religious is greatest, the Tau-c measure of the strength of the relationship
is also greatest, though the relationship is modest by the usual standards of social statistics. Among the 15% of Canadians in fair to poor
health, the Very Committed still say they are more satisfied with their
lives than do all others, but the gap between the Very Committed
and the rest shrinks, except for the Less Committed in poor health,

Table 3.9
Regression of life satisfaction on social forces (NSVGP 1997)

	Correlation (r)	Beta
Health	.349**	.333**
Household income	.207**	.119**
Marital status	.169**	.104**
Religiosity	.111**	.098**
Age	.010	.069**
Education	.157**	.069**
Rural – urban	.054**	.063**
Employment status	.095**	.019*
Sex	.001	.015*

$R^2 = .181$ $p < .001$

whose numbers in the sample are so small that we should not put much faith in this particular result. In other words, being Very Committed certainly helps those in fair and poor health to cope with their plight, but religiosity's impact overall is diminished. Levels of religiousness have their greatest influence on life satisfaction for the 85% of Canadians in excellent to good health.

This review demonstrates that religiosity still has a discernible impact on life satisfaction when we control for or take account of each one of these other factors. This is useful, but we have not yet assessed how much influence religiosity has when we take account of all of these other influences at the same time. This complex statistical task is known as multivariate regression analysis. Table 3.9 lists the beta weights for a variety of possible influences on life satisfaction. All those unfamiliar with statistics need to know is that the beta weight measures the influence or impact of the particular factor on life satisfaction after taking account of or controlling for all the other factors or variables being measured. The larger the beta weight, the bigger is the independent effect. I have also included the original zero-order correlation, which measures how strongly life satisfaction is related to each variable prior to introducing the controls and calculating the beta weights. Besides factors such as health, income, and the like that I have already reviewed, I have included a few more possible influences on life satisfaction that did not merit separate, earlier discussion. Sex identifies the impact of being male or female. Employment status differentiates between those employed in the labour force and those not employed. Rural–urban refers to the community size variable used earlier in table 2.27. Finally, marital status is a simplified version of the original four marital categories that differentiates between those who are married and those who are not.

What we see in table 3.9 is that the physical health of Canadians is the single largest determinant or predictor of life satisfaction. The beta weight of health (.333) towers above all other influences, including religiosity. The next most powerful influence is household income, which has a beta weight of .119. Thus the independent impact of income on life satisfaction is greater than both marital status (.104) and religiosity (.098), which have very similar beta weights that are clearly less pronounced than income's impact, though not by a large margin. A noticeable notch further down in impact are age (.069), education (.069), and rural–urban location (.063). Finally employment status (.019) and sex (.015) have a much more negligible impact. All relationships are statistically significant, but we should not attach much importance to this in such a large survey.

Two technically contradictory conclusions may be drawn from these findings. Both tell us something useful. The first is that the combined impact or explanatory power of all of the factors listed in table 3.9 is very limited. In technical language, the R^2 or amount of the variance explained by the causal factors we have examined is very modest. Technically a 100% complete explanation would produce an R^2 of 1.00, but table 3.9's R^2 is .181. We never get predictive models with 100% explanatory power, but an R^2 of .181 explains less than 20% of the variance or variability in the degree to which Canadians are satisfied with their lives; in other words, 82% remains unexplained. By this standard, I and all the other researchers who have looked at the factors listed in table 3.9 have failed to identify the major determinants of life satisfaction.

The second, more positive conclusion would start with the recognition that analyses of variance typically account for only fraction of the R^2. The world is complex and we should not expect to be able to account for most of the R^2. What matters is the relative standing of the causal forces we examine, which are measured by the beta weights. By this standard, health is clearly the key determinant of life satisfaction. This makes intuitive sense. Income – equally unsurprisingly – has the next largest influence, but it is almost equalled by the impact of marital status and religiosity, which are in turn more important than community size, education, age, employment status, and sex in shaping the satisfaction levels of Canadians. Religiosity is not the prime cause of life satisfaction, but it is an independent influence on life satisfaction that operates even after we have controlled for most of the major social forces at work in Canadian life. In the pantheon of social forces shaping the life satisfaction of Canadians, religiosity is a major player.

PRIORITIES IN LIFE

The central driving force of religion in general and Christianity in particular is the search for meaning and purpose in a world where evil, injustice, sin, suffering, and scarcity abound. There are, of course, many competing meaning systems in the world today including socialism, materialism, nationalism, and hedonism, to name but a few. What makes religion distinctive is that it centres its system of meaning on the supernatural, God, or gods. It therefore seems appropriate to start any assessment of religiosity's impact on the priorities of Canadians by asking them how they rate the pursuit of meaning and spirituality in their lives.

Nationally, the World Values Survey of 1990 found that 43% of Canadians often think about the meaning and purpose of life, while another 38% sometimes do so; only 18% say they do so either rarely (13%) or never (5%). For most Canadians, questions about the meaning of life are not pressing or common concerns, though we should not lose sight of the solid 43% who say such concerns engage them often. Table 3.10 reveals that many more of the Very Committed (52%) than the Non Religious (35%) often think about the meaning of life.

To avoid putting too much weight on a single questionnaire item, I include in the same table three other questions from Angus Reid's surveys that explore the same area. When Canadians are asked whether they live their lives with a sense of purpose, substantially more of the Very Committed (78%) than the Non Religious (51%) strongly agree. The same pattern in a reduced form is also evident when asked if they agree or disagree with the statement "I don't know what life is really all about." The last of the questions asks Canadians whether they agree or disagree with the assertion "It is more important to understand my inner self than to be rich and successful." Here we have a much more pointed test of the relative importance of meaning and mammon in people's lives. Nationally, on a seven-point scale 37% completely agree, while only 6% say they totally disagree. Few Canadians, it seems, are prepared to admit that their inner life is less important than material success. The converse, that understanding one's inner self is the more important priority, is a conviction that is much more widely stressed by the Very Committed (52%) than the Non Religious (29%). Concern with the meaning and purpose of life is far from the exclusive preserve of the Very Committed, but intense concern with such matters is much more prevalent among the Very Committed than the Non Religious.

Three further conclusions may be drawn from the first four questions summarized in tables 3.10 and 3.11. First, and perhaps not so surprisingly, the Less Committed are much less focused on questions of life's purpose than are the Very Committed. Second, the Seekers (who say religion is important to them but are not regularly involved in a faith community) show much more interest in the big questions about life's meaning than do the Non Religious, but their professed concern is consistently less than that of the Very Committed. The difference between the Very Committed and the Seekers is quite small on the first of the questions in table 3.10, but it is much greater on the others. Again it cannot be surprising to learn that regular involvement in a community centred on the meaning of life should enhance such concerns. Finally, some not terribly strong differences by religious family may be discerned. Here and in all subsequent tables on religious differences for the Committed, I cannot use the World Values Survey because it fails to differentiate Mainline from Conservative Protestants. In the first three of the Reid questions in table 3.11, more Conservative Protestants than anyone else consistently express commitment to the pursuit of meaning. There are some striking variations between Catholics inside and outside Quebec that sometimes violate the last generalization, but I cannot see a pattern in these Catholic differences. Mainline Protestants are least likely to be intensely concerned with such matters, though here too the differences are too small and the overall pattern too inconsistent to draw any solid conclusion. Overall, it is the Conservative Protestants who stand out.

The bottom third of tables 3.10 and 3.11 sharpens our focus from a general concern with meaning to the more specifically religious priority of having and seeking meaning through mystical experience and spirituality. On this narrower religious ground, the differences between the religious and non-religious become predictably more acute. When Canadians are asked whether they have ever experienced a moment of sudden religious insight or awakening, 48% of the Very Committed say they have, compared to only 15% of the Non

Table 3.10
The pursuit of meaning and spirituality by religiosity

	N	Very Commited	Less Commited	Seeker	Non Relig.	Total	Tau-c
% Often think about the meaning and purpose of life[1]	(1,704)	52	42	48	35	43	.14***
% Strongly agree beyond everyday demands of my existence, I live my life with a sense of purpose[2]	(1,485)	78	66	66	51	64	.22***
% Strongly disagree deep down I really don't know what life is all about[3]	(2,892)	63	55	48	44	51	.15***
% Agree completely it is more important to understand my inner self than to be rich and successful[2]	(1,478)	52	29	39	29	37	.16***
% Ever had a religious or mystical experience, that is a moment of sudden religious insight and awakening[4]	(1,450)	48	32	34	15	30	.27***
% Strongly agree I want to live a spiritual life more than I want to be rich[4]	(2,834)	63	33	32	15	32	.37***

[1]WVS 1990   [2]Reid 1994   [3]Reid 1993   [4]Reid 1996   ***P < .001   **P < .01   *P < .05

Table 3.11
The pursuit of meaning and spirituality by religion of the committed

	N	RC Quebec	RC RoC	Main. Prot.	Con. Prot.	V
% Strongly agree beyond everyday demands of my existence, I live my life with a sense of purpose[1]	(427)	80	74	63	79	.15*
% Strongly disagree deep down I really don't know what life is all about[2]	(868)	57	58	54	80	.18***
% Agree completely it I more important to understand my inner self than to be rich and successful[2]	(421)	51	34	44	50	.09
% Ever had a religious or mystical experience, that is a moment of sudden religious insight and awakening[3]	(428)	40	38	32	63	.22***
% Strongly agree I want to live a spiritual life more than I want to be rich[3]	(845)	32	42	45	81	.33***

[1]Reid 1994   [2]Reid 1993   [3]Reid 1996   ***P < .001   **P < .01   *P < .05

Religious. This is a large difference, though we should not fail to note that slightly over half of the Very Committed have not had such an experience. Mainline Protestants are least likely to have done so (32%) and Conservative Protestants most likely (63%). Here too it is interesting to note that the born-again religious tradition of Conservative Protestantism does not automatically generate sudden religious awakening among even its most committed members.

The last question in the same two tables asks Canadians whether they agree or disagree with the assertion that "I want to live a spiritual life more than I want to be rich." Nationally, 63% agree, 32% disagree, and 4% say they do not know. Only a minority of Canadians are prepared to deny that spirituality is more important than wealth, but the percentage strongly agreeing is four times greater among the Very Committed (63%) than it is among the Non Religious (15%). In none of the other questions in table 3.10 is the gap between the Very Committed and the Non Religious so large. There is also a very large gap between the 81% of Conservative Protestants and the approximately 40% of Catholics and Mainline Protestants who strongly agree that spirituality is more important than wealth. Support for the same proposition is predictably higher among Seekers and the Less Committed than it is for the Non Religious, but the very similar levels of

Table 3.12
Non religious priorities (% say very or highly important) in life by religiosity

	N	Very Commited	Less Commited	Seeker	Non Relig.	Total	Tau-c
SELF							
Self fulfilment[1]	(1,454)	70	77	77	75	75	.03
Fun and enjoyment[1]	(1,463)	64	70	71	72	70	−.05
Self respect [1]	(1,463)	90	89	91	90	90	.00
Sense of accomplishment[1]	(1,462)	77	84	83	78	80	.00
Freedom[2]	(1,671)	90	86	86	86	87	.02
WORK, MONEY, & PRESTIGE							
Rewarding career[2]	(1,561)	48	61	60	51	54	.00
Security[1]	(1,462)	73	78	81	72	76	−.03
Being well respected[1]	(1,464)	73	72	77	68	73	.05
Success in what you do[2]	(1,661)	64	59	68	53	60	.10**
Recognition	(1,655)	26	31	37	30	31	.02
RELATIONSHIPS							
Sense of belonging[1]	(1,466)	69	65	65	53	61	.14***
Warm relationships[1]	(1,462)	84	81	82	73	79	.10***
Friendliness[2]	(1,684)	80	59	77	63	70	.12***
Honesty[2]	(1,684)	96	90	94	81	89	.13***
Kindness[2]	(1,687)	85	72	88	71	79	.12***
Forgiveness[2]	(1,676)	73	51	67	42	57	.25***
Generosity[2]	(1,679)	71	59	70	42	58	.26***
Concern for others[2]	(1,679)	80	62	77	58	68	.18***

[1]8+ on 10-point scale, Reid 1996 [2]Bibby 1995 ***P < .001 **P < .01 *P < .05

support among the Seekers and the Less Committed are both dwarfed by the far higher level among the Very Committed. When it comes to both the pursuit of meaning in life and the primacy of spirituality over wealth, it is the roughly one in five Very Committed Canadians who really stand out.

Bibby's data and the Reid surveys contained in tables 3.12 and 3.13 allow us to explore whether religiosity has much influence on a large number of non-religious priorities in life. To impose some order on their numerous questions, I have grouped them under the three headings of self and self-fulfilment; worldly priorities of work, money, and prestige; and intimate relationships with others.

Canadians are almost equally united in saying that the cultivation of their own needs, desires, and capacities is a prime priority in their lives. On the 10-point scales from very unimportant (1) to very important (10) used in the Reid surveys, 75% of all Canadians rate self-fulfilment an 8 or higher; only 9% rate it 5 or less. An even more

Table 3.13
Non religious priorities (% say very or highly important) in life by religion among
the committed

	N	RC Quebec	RC RoC	Main. Prot.	Con. Prot.	V
SELF						
Self fulfilment[1]	(415)	73	78	71	70	.07
Fun and enjoyment[1]	(417)	67	71	67	58	.09
%Self Respect[1]	(418)	90	93	91	81	.13
Sense of accomplishment[1]	(417)	83	85	74	74	.12
Freedom[2]	(593)	84	94	87	84	.13
WORK, MONEY, & PRESTIGE						
Rewarding career[2]	(541)	62	59	48	35	.19**
Security[1]	(419)	77	79	71	65	.11
Being well respected[1]	(418)	91	71	64	65	.24***
Success in what you do[2]	(586)	63	65	59	61	.05
Recognition	(582)	24	40	25	16	.20**
RELATIONSHIPS						
Sense of belonging[1]	(412)	65	68	67	68	.03
Warm relationships[1]	(419)	80	83	83	80	.04
Friendliness[2]	(596)	60	75	79	76	.17*
Honesty[2]	(598)	93	94	92	98	.09
Kindness[2]	(600)	76	78	85	86	.10
Forgiveness[2]	(598)	42	66	75	86	.33***
Generosity[2]	(595)	67	67	66	74	.06
Concern for others[2]	(595)	67	73	75	86	.14

[1]8+ on 10-point scale, Reid 1996   [2]Bibby 1995   ***P < .001   **P < .01   *P < .05

striking 90% of Canadians rate self-respect as very important (8+); 87%
rate freedom highly; and 80% give a sense of accomplishment the
same high rating. Fun and enjoyment are slightly less valued by Canadians in this set of questions, though 70% say these are highly important to them and only 10% rate them 5 or less. Moreover, data from
the World Values Survey not listed here tell us that a full 85% of Canadians think a greater emphasis on the development of the individual
would be a good thing; only 3% think it would be a bad thing. Table
3.12 shows us that a slightly smaller percentage of the Very Committed put a high value on self-fulfilment and fun and enjoyment, but
these differences are so small that they are neither substantively nor
statistically significant. On other questions concerning the importance
of the self, the Very Committed are indistinguishable from other Canadians. Among the Committed, Conservative Protestants are a little less

likely to put a high priority on fun, enjoyment, and self-respect, while Catholics are a bit more prone to stress a sense of accomplishment. Here too all of the differences are very small and statistically insignificant. Overall, the cult of individualism in Canada is so deeply rooted and widespread that it is almost universally embraced, regardless of how religious or irreligious we are.

When it comes to matters of work, money, and prestige, the priorities of the Very Committed are much the same as those of other Canadians. Highly similar proportions of the Very Committed and the Non Religious place a high value on security and a rewarding career. Slightly more of the Very Committed than the Non Religious stress the value of success and being well respected, though it is actually Seekers who most consistently and most widely stress these material concerns. As for differences by religious family, Catholics appear to be a little more likely than Protestants to value career, security, and being well respected. These small differences are only noteworthy because they discredit the long cherished notion in sociology of a distinctive Protestant ethic that enabled Protestants to outperform Catholics in the world of work. At the other end of the spectrum, Conservative Protestants, who are most likely to prize religious concerns, tend to place the least value on worldly matters. Taken as a whole, the most compelling conclusion is that the majority (70%) of these many differences by level of religiosity and across religious family are statistically insignificant. Barring a few interesting but small differences by religious family, all are otherwise trivial.

It is only when we come to the realm of personal relationships that noteworthy differences emerge in a consistent fashion. A sense of belonging, warm relationships, friendliness, honesty, and kindness are all valued more frequently by the Very Committed than the Non Religious, though the differences are modest ones in the 11 to 17-point range. That gap then further grows for forgiveness, generosity, and concerns for others. Simply put, caring relationships with others are more widely prized by the Very Committed than the Non Religious. On these matters, Seekers are much more like the Very Committed, which is a notable departure from their usual pattern to emulate the Non Religious. Differences between the Committed in the major religious families are much smaller, with many fading into statistical insignificance. Variation is greatest on the questions tapping friendliness and forgiveness. Bearing these qualifications in mind, we might cautiously conclude that Quebec Catholics are least likely to stress the importance of relationships in their lives and Conservative Protestants are most likely to do so.

Let me repeat that it is the Very Committed in general who really stand out for placing a consistently high value on caring personal relationships. Though the Committed do not much differ from other Canadians in the importance they attach to other, non-religious priorities, we should recall that they are also distinguished by their greater interest in the meaning of life and in wanting to live a spiritual life more than to be rich. I should also add that more detailed calculations of the data in tables 3.10 to 3.13 show that the differences I have stressed between the Very Committed and the Non Religious remain much the same when we control for and hence take account of the potential influence that the older age structure of the Committed might have on the findings. Since the older age structure of the Committed is the one demographic or background social trait that really sets them apart from other Canadians, we can have all the more confidence that the above differences are real. These conclusions tell me that the Very Committed in particular differ from other Canadians in quite fundamental ways. The particular differences I have just noted should come as no surprise to those familiar with basic Christian doctrine.

GOOD AND EVIL:
VIEWS OF HUMAN NATURE

Tables 3.14 and 3.15 allow us to assess whether religiosity affects Canadians' perceptions of how much good and evil there is within us and our surroundings. Once more I have included similar questions from different surveys to reduce the possibility that any single finding is a rogue. The Very Committed are more likely than the Non Religious to regard human nature as "fundamentally perverse and corrupt" (33% vs. 20%) and to believe that "the world is basically filled with sin and evil" (40% vs 18). As is often the case, Seekers are closer to the outlook of the Non Religious than they are to the Very Committed. Among the Committed, it is Conservative Protestants who stand out by a large margin with their dark, evil-filled view of the world. The great majority of Catholics and Mainline Protestants – and hence a substantial majority of the Very Committed as a whole – have a more optimistic view of human nature that has more in common with the views of the Non Religious than it does with those

Table 3.14
Views on human nature (% agree) by religiosity (Reid 1996)

	N	Very Commited	Less Commited	Seeker	Non Relig.	Total	Tau-c
Human nature is fundamentally perverse and corrupt	(1,450)	33	17	22	20	23	.08**
The world is basically filled with sin and evil	(1,457)	40	28	26	18	25	.17***
There is much goodness in the world that hints at God's goodness	(1,417)	97	92	91	52	78	.40***
People can be generally trusted to do what is right	(2,920)	63	68	63	63	64	.02
It just isn't wise to trust people these days	(1,453)	45	51	50	41	46	.05
It is best to trust people, even if they sometimes betray your trust	(1,457)	65	62	54	55	58	.09**

***P < .001   **P < .01   *P < .05

Table 3.15
Views on human nature (% agree) by religion of the committed (Reid 1996)

	N	RC Quebec	RC RoC	Main. Prot.	Con. Prot.	V
Human nature is fundamentally perverse and corrupt	(412)	22	16	16	62	.40***
The world is basically filled with sin and evil	(416)	20	22	26	78	.46***
There is much goodness in the world that hints at God's goodness	(413)	92	95	98	96	.12
People can be generally trusted to do what is right	(857)	59	65	72	52	.15***
It just isn't wise to trust people these days	(417)	60	37	43	43	.18**
It is best to trust people, even if they sometimes betray your trust	(416)	67	60	66	70	.08

***P < .001   **P < .01   *P < .05

of Conservative Protestants. However, this dark side must be counterbalanced by the over 90% of the Committed, including Conservative Protestants, who agree "there is much goodness in the world that hints at God's goodness." The much lower support for this view among the Non Religious is surely caused by the linking of God to goodness in the question. Such a confusing double-barrelled question does not tell us much about the Non Religious, but it does reveal much about the Committed. Among Conservative Protestants, the forces of good and evil are both seen as powerfully present. For everyone else, including Catholics and Mainline Protestants, evil is downplayed and goodness widely affirmed. This mindset may also been seen in the 1995 Gallup poll finding that belief in God (88%) and heaven (71%) are much more prevalent than belief in hell (43%) and the devil (40%).[22]

The same general belief that there is more goodness than evil in the world surely explains why more Canadians trust people to do what is right (64%) than think "it just isn't wise to trust people these days" (46%). On these two questions, there is no discernible difference between the Very Committed and the Non Religious. We do see a clear though far from large difference on the question of whether "it is best to trust people, even if they sometimes betray your trust." On this more principled issue of extending our trust even when it may be betrayed, more of the Very Committed are in agreement (65%) than are the Non Religious (55%). The Less Committed and the Seekers are in their predictable places in between. Conservative Protestants therefore have a distinctively dark view of human nature and the presence of evil in the world, but they – and all the Committed – are more likely than other Canadians to believe that trust should be extended to others, despite our very human failings.[23]

ETHICAL OUTLOOK:
RELATIVISM, VENGEANCE, AND FORGIVENESS

It would be foolish to presume that the small number of questions in tables 3.16 and 3.17 adequately tap the ethical and moral standards of Canadians. Subsequent chapters will deal with a host of specific issues ranging from abortion to treatment of the poor and needy. Here I explore briefly whether the Very Committed differ from other Canadians in their general moral outlook.

The 1990 World Values Survey found that less than a third (31%) of Canadians believe "there are absolutely clear guidelines on what is good and evil" that "always apply to everyone." A full 62% say "what is good and evil depends entirely on the circumstances at the time." The remaining 8% say neither option is valid. These are very stark options, but other questions from the Reid surveys certainly produce much the same results. Thus 63% of Canadians are agreed "there is no absolute right or wrong. It all depends on the situation." In much the same vein, 59% of Canadians concur that "what is right and wrong is a matter of personal opinion." The majority of Canadians might seem to favour a relativistic view of ethics and moral standards, though we should not ignore the substantial majority who disagree. Rather than talking in either/or terms, I would say that most Canadians are inclined to lean more in a relativistic direction than an absolutist one.

Table 3.16 makes it clear that the Very Committed are much more likely than the Non Religious to take an absolutist view of ethics and morality. The great majority of the Non Religious embrace a relativistic view, but the Very Committed are much more divided with half embracing the absolutist option and the other half the relativist one. Again, this implies to me that the Very Committed are much more inclined to consider both relativistic and absolutist standards in defining what is good and evil. Among the Committed Catholics enumerated in table 3.17, a solid majority (66%) rising to 78% in Quebec agree there is no absolute right or wrong. Even in the more

Table 3.16
Ethical views (% agree) by religiosity

	N	Very Committed	Less Committed	Seeker	Non Relig.	Total	Tau-c
There are absolutely clear guidelines on what is good and evil. These always apply to everyone.[1]	(1,653)	44	33	29	22	31	.19***
There is no absolute right or wrong. It all depends on the situation[2]	(1,444)	51	61	65	73	63	-.17***
What is right and wrong is a matter of personal opinion[3]	(1,468)	50	53	62	63	59	-.12***
If someone harms me I try to get even[3]	(1,472)	15	27	21	33	25	-.14***
If the actions of a drunk driver resulted in the death of a member of my family, I would eventually forgive that person[3]	(1,444)	60	32	39	24	38	.26***
If a guest in my house was to steal something from my house, I would forbid that person from entering again[3]	(1,469)	58	68	71	71	67	-.09**

[1]WVS 1990 [2]Reid 1993 [3]Reid 1994 ***P < .001 **P < .01 *P < .05

Table 3.17
Ethical views (% agree) by religion of the committed

	N	RC Quebec	RC RoC	Main. Prot.	Con. Prot.	V
There is no absolute right or wrong. It all depends on the situation[1]	(426)	78	56	49	29	.32***
What is right and wrong is a matter of personal opinion[2]	(424)	69	50	49	33	.23***
If someone harms me I try to get even[2]	(427)	15	26	14	14	.15*
If the actions of a drunk driver resulted in the death of a member of my family, I would eventually forgive that person[2]	(416)	48	46	46	71	.19***
If a guest in my house was to steal something from my house, I would forbid that person from entering again[2]	(425)	65	66	62	46	.14*

[1]Reid 1993   [3] Reid 1994   ***P < .001   **P < .01   *P < .05

restrictive category of Very Committed Catholics, 65% say the same thing. Leaning less strongly in the relativistic direction are Mainline Protestants, who are fairly evenly split. Only among Conservative Protestants do a solid majority reject relativism and lean towards absolutism. Clearly the relativism so widely embraced by the Non Religious and Seekers is also integral to the ethical standards of Catholics and Mainline Protestants. Is this a sign that Catholics and Mainline Protestants who are Very Committed are succumbing to the secular ethics of the Non Religious? That conclusion is easily drawn, though we should not forget that concern with absolute standards is still far more prevalent among Catholics and Mainline Protestants than it is among the Non Religious.

The remaining questions in tables 3.16 and 3.17 ask Canadians how they would respond if someone else caused them harm or grief. Nationally, only 25% admit that "if someone harms me, I try to get even." The great majority of Canadians therefore deny they are driven by the understandable though less than moral urge to seek revenge. Still, far fewer of the Very Committed admit to vengefulness (15%) than do the Non Religious (33%). More Committed Catholics outside Quebec have vengeful feelings (26%) than do either Quebec Catholics (15%) or Protestants (14%), though we should not place too much weight on relatively small differences based a quite a small sample. When asked if they would eventually forgive a drunk driver who killed a member of their family, 38% of all Canadians say they would. The answers undoubtedly tell us more about people's values than their likely future behaviour, but again we see that many more of the Very Committed (60%) than the Non Religious (24%) say they would pursue the path of forgiveness. This is a striking difference that is reinforced by the earlier finding in table 3.12 that forgiveness is much more widely endorsed as a priority in life by the Very Committed (73%) than the Non Religious (42%). I might also note that the responses of the Less Committed and Seekers on the specific question of forgiving a drunk driver have much more in common with the Non Religious than they do with the Very Committed. A similar though less marked tendency for the Very Committed to be more forgiving is evident on the last question asking if Canadians would forbid entry into their homes to a guest who had stolen something from them. Among the Committed on both these questions, it is Conservative Protestants who most stress the ethic of forgiveness. By these standards, forgiveness and the inappropriateness of vengeance are both more widely embraced by the Very Committed than they are by other Canadians.[24]

ACTIVE OR PASSIVE: ATTITUDES TO CHANGE BY RELIGIOSITY

In this last section I want to assess the widely held view that religion fosters a passive, defeatist attitude to all endeavours to change our imperfect world by focusing its adherents' concern on other-worldly rather than this-worldly matters. Is it true, as Marx put it, that "religion is the opium of the masses"? Once again a full answer to this question must await future chapters when I explore how religiosity affects attitudes on a variety of social and political issues. Here we address the more general question of whether there are any signs of a basic passivity among the Committed. Tables 3.18 and 3.19 summarize the pertinent questionnaire items from the Reid surveys and the wvs.

The first two questions in table 3.18 assess the degree to which Canadians feel compelled to convince others of their own convictions. Nationally 41% of Canadians say they rarely or never find themselves "persuading your friends, relatives, or fellow workers to share your strongly held opinions;" 16% say they do so often and 43% do so at times. Most of us therefore are sometimes outgoing in our views, though only a real minority of us are chronic evangelists.

Table 3.18
Active or passive: attitudes to change (% agree) by religiosity

	N	Very Commited	Less Commited	Seeker	Non Relig.	Total	Tau-c
Rarely or never find yourself persuading your friends, relatives, or fellow workers to share your strongly held opinions[1]	(1,708)	44	43	41	39	41	.05
You should keep your idea of what is right or wrong to yourself[2]	(1,454)	23	23	23	24	24	.01
Feel a serious responsibility to make the world a better place so I am constantly trying to change things[3]	(1,484)	59	55	57	46	53	.11***
If an unjust law were passed by the government, I could do nothing about it[1]	(1,668)	38	38	41	40	40	-.02

[1]WVS 1990 [2]Reid 1996 [3]5-7 on 7-point scale, Reid 1994 ***P < .001 **P < .01 *P < .05

Table 3.19
Active or passive: Attitudes to change by religion of the committed

	N	RC Quebec	RC RoC	Main. Prot.	Con. Prot.	V
You should keep your idea of what is right or wrong to yourself.[1]	(413)	34	24	16	18	.14**
Feel a serious responsibility to make the world a better place so I am constantly trying to change things.[2]	(426)	63	64	52	54	.11

[1]Reid 1996   [2]5+ on 7-point scale, Reid 1994   *** $P < .001$ **$P < .01$ * $P < .05$

On the religious front, slightly more of the Very Committed (44%) than the Non Religious (39%) rarely or never try to convince others of their strongly held views, but the difference is so small that it is neither statistically nor substantively noteworthy. The answers to the accompanying Reid question suggests Canadians as a whole are rather more outgoing. More importantly, for our purposes, the Very Committed and the Non Religious are again alike in rejecting by a margin of three to one the proposition that "you should keep your ideas of what is right and wrong to yourself." In this case where differences by religious family can be calculated, Catholics are measurably more reticent than Protestants in thinking that personal convictions should be kept to oneself, though a substantial majority in all religious traditions disagree. When it comes to promulgating their own views, the Very Committed are no more or less outgoing than other Canadians.

The final two questions in table 3.18 address the issue of passivity in an even more direct manner, in asking Canadians if they are prepared to change the world in which they live. More of the Very Committed (59%) than the Non Religious (46%) agree that they "feel a serious responsibility to make the world a better place so I am constantly trying to change things." The difference is statistically significant, but modest. Table 3.19 indicates that Catholics are most active or interventionist in their outlook and Conservative Protestants least so, though the differences are not statistically significant. The findings appear to contradict the preceding question's finding that more Catholics say that ideas of what is right and wrong should be kept to oneself. Given these inconsistencies and the small size of all the differences, I would conclude that no appreciable differences by religious family really exist here. On the second question, slightly fewer of the Very Committed (38%) than the Non Religious (40%) agree that "if an unjust law were passed by the government, I could do nothing about it." In this case, the difference is so small that it is statistically and substantively insignificant. As one final piece of evidence, I would refer readers back to table 3.1, where we saw that the Very Committed are slightly more likely than the Non Religious to express feelings of control over their everyday activities and to have confidence they will be able to carry out their plans.

What are we to make of all these findings? Let me be clear that I am not arguing that the Very Committed have a more activist or self confident attitude to change than others Canadians, though a rather weak case along these lines could be made. What I am arguing is that there is no support for the notion that religiousness fosters passivity, helplessness, and feelings of lack of control in the face of social change. Stereotyped portraits of the Very Committed as tranquillized millennialists listlessly awaiting divine intervention are simply wrong.

In looking back over all that has been covered in this chapter, the key summary issue is whether we can discern a distinctive psychological profile among the Very Committed that distinguishes them from other Canadians. None of the differences are large, but collectively they are striking. Compared to other Canadians, most notably the Non Religious, the Very Committed are more likely to say they are satisfied with life, happy, and confident they will carry out their plans. They are also less worried about money matters, despite having incomes about the same as other Canadians. With very few exceptions, Seekers and the Less Committed have profiles that have much more in common with the Non Religious than with the Very Committed. Less than very active involvement in a faith community and private religious concerns without regular participation in a religious group both have little salutary impact. Few Canadians admit to being really unhappy, unsatisfied, or lacking control over their everyday activities, but the Non Religious are most likely to report distress of this sort. The premise of the psychoanalytic tradition that religion is bad for your mental health is repudiated by the data reviewed here.

The detailed analysis I did on the determinants of psychological well-being, measured by satisfaction with life, make it clear that high religiosity or its lack have an independent impact on satisfaction, even after we take account of other possible influences. Physical health, family income, marital status, education and the like all affect satisfaction levels, but religiosity still has its own independent influence that makes it a major, though not the most important, determinant. The key qualification is that less than a fifth of the variation in life satisfaction is explained by all the factors reviewed here, including religiosity. Psychological well-being remains a largely unexplained mystery.

When it comes to many other aspects of their psychological profile, the Very Committed share much in common with the Non Religious and all other Canadians. Fun and enjoyment, security, success, a rewarding career, and being well respected are all endorsed as important priorities in life by Canadians of all degrees of religiousness. The cult of individualism, a generally activist approach to the possibilities of social change, and a trusting view in the essential goodness of human nature that downplays sin and evil are widely shared traits that do not much differentiate the Very Committed from other Canadians. The key exception to these very sweeping generalizations are the Conservative Protestants who have a much stronger sense of sin and evil, though they, like all the Very Committed, are even more convinced that there is much goodness in the world that derives from God.

Where the Very Committed do notably differ is in the high value they attach to personal relationships and to friendliness, kindness, and generosity. They also tend to think more frequently about the meaning and purpose of life and to place a greater value on spirituality than on money. Unlike the strong moral relativism of the Non Religious, Catholics and Mainline Protestants stress a mix of both absolutist and relativistic considerations, while Conservative Protestants lean much more heavily towards absolute moral standards. The Very Committed are also more inclined to condemn vengeance, to espouse forgiving those who hurt us, and to believe trust should be extended to others, even though it may be betrayed. This last set of differences suggests that the Very Committed are distinguished by their greater concern for the welfare of others.

There remains – at least in my mind – the nagging worry I noted at the beginning of this chapter that Canadians of all religious dispositions are poorly equipped to assess their own psychological state and the general principles that really do guide our lives. If I am right, we should suspend final judgment on the foregoing conclusions until we can get a better fix on how Canadians actually think and act in the more specific contexts of family, community, and public life. To these issues we turn in the next three chapters.

4

Intimate Relations:
Sex, Marriage, Family, and Friends

Our intimate relationships involving sex, marriage, family, and friends play a major role in shaping our identity, our sense of well-being, and our character. The crucial importance of intimate relations is amply demonstrated by survey findings that Canadians place a heavier importance on family than any other priority in our lives. The intimate relationships we so prize are, nonetheless, going through an unprecedented time of stress, challenge, and change. Since the 1960s divorce rates have soared, common-law relationships have grown far more frequent, birth rates have fallen, single-parent families have become much more prevalent, and traditional gender relations have been everywhere questioned, if not overturned. The goal of this chapter is to assess the extent to which religiously committed or active Canadians differ from other Canadians in the ways in which they think and behave in this intimate domain.

Readers should note that this chapter makes quite extensive use of two of the large General Social Surveys (GSS) by Statistics Canada that lack the questionnaire item on self-assessed religiosity on which I have built my religiosity scale of the Very Committed, Less Committed, Seekers, and Non Religious. When using the GSS, I am obliged to use a simpler religiosity scale based solely on frequency of attendance at religious services or meetings. In these cases, I differentiate between weekly attenders; monthly attenders (1–3 times a month); the marginal or rarely attending (once a year to a few times a year);

and non attenders, who do not attend at all. Readers who look back to chapter 2's description of my original religiosity scale will see that the Very and Less Committed overlap extremely closely with weekly and monthly attenders. Conceptualizations of the remaining two categories on both scales are rather more divergent, but readers should rest assured that there is a strikingly high 0.90 correlation between the two scales. In layman's language this means that attendance and commitment have such a high degree of overlap or similarity that they are both tapping the same underlying dimension of religiousness. I prefer for reasons already mentioned my religiosity scale, but I have absolutely no hesitation in using attendance as a suitable measure of religiosity when necessary.

SEXUAL ATTITUDES

Driven by the discovery of the pill and the growing availability of reliable, unobtrusive forms of contraception, the sexual revolution of the 1960s brought a new openness to sexuality, especially to premarital sex. Data on the actual levels of sexual activity by Canadians are always fraught with the problem of knowing how much faith we can put in answers to such intimate questions. Various small surveys of post-secondary students indicate that the percentage claiming to have experienced premarital sexual intercourse rose from about 50% in the late 1960s to about 75% in the late 1980s.[1] For teenagers aged 15 to 19, about 55% of them since the early 1980s have been saying they are sexually involved.[2] As early as 1975, 94% of Canadians were saying that birth control information should be available to teenagers who need it. In the same year, less than a third (32%) of Canadians were prepared to endorse the view that premarital sex was "almost always" or "always wrong."[3] By 1993, the Reid surveys found that 79% of Canadians agreed that "it is ok for unmarried people to have sex;" 8% disagreed moderately and only 13% did so strongly. Opposition was predictably greater among older Canadians, but even a majority (62%) of pre-boomer Canadians over age 55 condoned premarital sex. Among the more critical age group of 18–34, for whom premarital sex is a much more pressing and personal issue, an overwhelming 89% voiced their approval. The actual levels of sexual activity of unmarried teens and young adults may not be as great as they would like to think or as their parents fear, but the belief that premarital sexual activity is acceptable is almost universally affirmed by those who make the final decision.

Overall, religiosity is quite strongly linked to disapproval of premarital sex. In table 4.1 we see that the 93% approval rate by the Non Religious falls to 50% for the Very Committed. The fact still remains that half of the Very Committed in 1993 were prepared to condone premarital sex. These opinions would probably have caused shocked condemnation from earlier generations of the Committed, but we should not lose sight of the marked difference between the Very Committed and the Non Religious in 1993. That 43-point spread is caused in part by the tendency of the Very Committed to be older than the Non Religious. However, a clear majority of the Very Committed aged 18–34 say it is acceptable for unmarried people to have sex, though they are still much more likely to voice their disapproval (39%) than are the Non Religious (5%). Among Canadians in their late 40s and early 50s the gap between the Very Committed and the Non Religious (measured by Tau-c) widens, suggesting that parental opposition is greatest from and most strongly felt by the Very Committed. Note that the Less Committed tend to be much less disapproving than the Very Committed, while the Seekers have much the same point of view as the Non Religious. Table 4.2 demonstrates that permissiveness is least common among Conservative Protestants (31%) and most prevalent among Quebec Catholics (72%). In between are the 66% of Catholics elsewhere in Canada and the 54% of Mainline Protestants who say it is acceptable for unmarried people to have sex. Young Catholics and Mainline Protestants are even more tolerant of premarital sex, but young Conservative Protestants endorse their parents' views. By this standard, Conservative Protestants rightly deserve the "conservative" label they have been given. Catholics, on the other hand, are much less mindful of their church's conservative stance, while the in-between stance of Mainline Protestants suggest that they too do not always heed their denomination's traditional teaching that premarital sexual activity is wrong. In short, in a general climate of sexual permissiveness, religiosity still has a notably conservative influence, which is then refracted through the lens of specific denominational traditions that do not necessarily mirror the formal teaching of their leaders.

The same tables also indicate that Canadians are far less tolerant or approving of extramarital sex than premarital sex. A full 86% say

Table 4.1
Sexual attitudes by religiosity

	N	Very Committed	Less Committed	Seeker	Non Relig.	All Canadians	Tau-c
% Agree it is ok for unmarried people to have sex[1]	(1,440)	50	75	87	93	79	-.34***
% Agree it is ok for unmarried people to have sex (Age 18–34)[1]	(500)	61	94	93	95	89	-.17***
% Agree it is ok for unmarried people to have sex (Age 45–54)[1]	(252)	48	73	83	98	75	-.39***
% Agree extramarital sex is always wrong[2]	(1,659)	81	70	63	43	60	.34***
% Agree extramarital sex is always wrong (Age 30–49)[2]	(612)	80	64	58	37	53	.36***
% Say a happy sexual relationship very important to a successful marriage[3]	1,706	72	74	74	72	73	.00
% Engage in sex weekly (Age 18–49)[2]	(671)	62	67	63	65	64	-.01

[1]Reid 1993 [2]Bibby 1995 [3]WVS 1990   ***P < .001   **P < .01   *P < .05

Table 4.2
sexual attitudes by religion of the committed

	N	RC Quebec	RC RoC	Main. Prot.	Con. Prot.	V
% Agree it is ok for unmarried people to have sex[1]	(425)	72	66	54	31	.28***
% Agree it is ok for unmarried people to have sex (Age 18–34)[1]	(99)	88	92	76	36	.51***
% Agree extramarital sex is always wrong[2]	(587)	75	75	75	92	.15*
% Agree extramarital sex is always wrong (Age 30–49)[2]	(168)	68	66	63	89	.22
% Engage in sex weekly (Age 18–49)[2]	(173)	67	65	71	61	.06

[1]Reid 1993 [2]Bibby 1995 ***P < .001 **P < .01 *P < .05

that extramarital sex is either "always" (60%) or "almost always" (26%) wrong; another 12% say it is "sometimes wrong" and only 12% describe it as "not wrong at all." Within this climate of general disapproval, the 81% of the Very Committed claiming extramarital sex is always wrong is nonetheless about double the 43% of the Non Religious making the same claim. By any standard, this is a major difference. Though Seekers are much like the Non Religious in their attitude towards premarital sexual activity, in this case Seekers are very much in between the divergent views of the Very Committed and the Non Religious. Predictably enough, the almost universal (92%) condemnation by Conservative Protestants sets them apart from the rest of the Committed, though the 75% disapproval levels for Catholics and Mainline Protestants are still well above those for Seekers and the Non Religious. I think it is especially noteworthy that the gap between the Very Committed and Non Religious in their views on extramarital sex is most acute among middle-aged boomers between 30 and 49 years of age. It would seem reasonable to assume that the middle aged are most prone to extramarital behaviour because they are much more likely to be married than younger Canadians and they probably have a stronger sexual drive than those fifty or more years of age. Thus religiosity's impact on extramarital attitudes is most powerful for precisely those Canadians who are most susceptible to extramarital temptations.

Some might conclude that the sexual conservatism of the Very Committed is rooted in a general antipathy to sexuality in any form. Table 4.2 does not support that stereotype. The 72% of the Very

Committed in 1990 who said that a happy sexual relationship is very important to a successful marriage is virtually identical to the 73% of the Non Religious who responded in the same way. The difference is both statistically and substantively insignificant. Though I do not have a great deal of faith in questions that probe so intimate a matter as personal sexual behaviour, Bibby's 1995 survey found that religiousness or its lack had no appreciable impact on the actual sexual behaviour of Canadians. To eliminate the confounding and distorting impact of the older age structure of the Very Committed on the matter, I confined the analysis in tables 4.1 and 4.2 to Canadians under fifty years of age.[4] There we see that the 62% of the Very Committed saying they engage in sex at least weekly is virtually identical to the 63% of Seekers and the 64% of the Non Religious making the same claim. Sexual activity levels also appear to be strikingly similar across the four major religious families, though one might make a very weak and statistically insignificant case that Conservative Protestants are a little less sexually active than other Committed Christians. The Very Committed are therefore more conservative than other Canadians in their approach to premarital and extramarital sexuality, but sexuality in marriage is every bit as important to the Very Committed as it is to other Canadians.

MARRIAGE, DIVORCE, AND COMMON-LAW RELATIONSHIPS

The 1960s are rightly regarded as a "demographic watershed"[5] in the way Canadian families have been constituted. In the baby boom years after World War II, more and more Canadians were getting married, their average age of marriage was falling, and fertility rates reached a peak of 3.9 births per woman in 1959.[6] Thereafter, fertility fell to a 1.6 rate in 1986 and then to 1.5 in 1999,[7] though a much higher fertility rate of 2.1 is needed over the long haul to prevent our population from declining.[8] The average age for first marriages had risen by 1996 to 27 years for brides and 29 years for grooms. In that same year, the crude marriage rate of 5.2 was almost half its 1972 level of 9.2. Accompanying these demographic developments were the divorce and common-law revolutions (to be described later) that further transformed the Canadian family. This picture of dramatic change since the 1960s needs to be tempered by the realization that the average age of marriage and crude marriage rates are "similar to those early in the century."[9] I should add that 69% of Canadians aged 18 to 64 in 1996 had married at some point in their lives; which is not much fewer than the 73% who had done so in 1984.[10] The traditional Canadian family made up of a married couple with children had also fallen from 55% of all families in 1981 to 45% in 1995, but a married couple with children still remained the largest single family type in that later year.[11] Nevertheless, so much has changed over the last 40 years that we are obliged to ask whether marriage and the family as traditionally constructed in Canada have a future.

The first three questions in table 4.3 and 4.4 make it abundantly clear that marriage and family are still highly valued by most Canadians. Only 12% of all Canadians and 15% of people under 30 are prepared to endorse the view that marriage is an outdated institution. We are also widely agreed that family is very important to us (86%); an even higher 93% of us say that we receive a great deal or quite a bit of enjoyment from family life. In every case, more of the Very Committed than the Non Religious make these pro-family claims, but the differences are far from large. The more compelling conclusion is surely the widespread consensus at all levels of religiousness that marriage and family are very important to us. Though I have not here presented all the corroborating evidence, that general conclusion holds across generations, as well as across all the major religious families.

Where disagreement emerges – and it does so quite impressively – is on the related issues of whether it is right or moral for unmarried couples to live together and to raise children. About two-thirds (68%) of all Canadians have no objections to an unmarried couple living together; only 18% say it is always or sometimes wrong. Doubts grow when unmarried couples have children, but only 34% say it is always or almost always wrong; 24% say it is sometimes wrong and 43% have no objections whatsoever. Predictably, this general reluctance to condemn family-like relationships outside of marriage is even more widespread among boomers and those who have come of age since the 1960s. That said, the Very Committed and Non Religious have very different views on these matters – 89% of the latter and only 28% of the former see nothing wrong in unmarried coupes living together. Similarly, the conviction that it is always or almost always wrong for unmarried parents to raise children rises from 14% among the Non Religious to 67% of the Very Committed. Since these large differences (measured by Tau-c) are only slightly reduced for those

Table 4.3
Views on marriage and family by religiosity

	N	Very Commited	Less Commited	Seeker	Non Relig.	All Canadians	Tau-c
% Agree marriage is an out-dated institution[1]	(1,659)	6	9	12	19	12	-.12***
% Say family life is very important to them[2]	(1,674)	89	90	92	79	86	.10***
% Receive a great deal or quite a bit of enjoyment from family life[2]	(1,683)	97	93	92	91	93	.05**
% Say an unmarried couple living together is not wrong at all[2]	(1,657)	28	63	72	89	68	-.49***
% Say an unmarried couple living together is not wrong at all Age 18–49[2]	(723)	32	69	82	93	78	-.41***
% Say an unmarried couple having kids is always or almost always wrong[2]	(1,658)	67	41	33	14	34	.43***
% Say an unmarried couple having kids is always or almost always wrong Age 18–49[2]	(722)	65	34	21	9	24	.39***

[1]WVS 1990 [2]Bibby 1995 ***P < .001 **P < .01 *P < .05

Table 4.4
Views on marriage and family by religion of the committed (Bibby 1995)

	N	RC Quebec	RC RoC	Main. Prot.	Con. Prot.	V
% Say family life is very important to them	(595)	88	95	85	93	.14
% Receive a great deal or quite a bit of enjoyment from family life	(562)	95	96	98	99	.07
% Say an unmarried couple living together is not wrong at all	(584)	62	42	37	9	.34***
% Say an unmarried couple having kids is always or almost always wrong	(586)	28	55	67	88	.41***

***P < .001   **P < .01   *P < .05

under the age of 50, they cannot be explained by the older age structure of the Very Committed. In and of itself, religiosity makes a real
difference. Seekers, as is so often the case, emulate the Non Religious
more than the Very Committed. There is also a consistent tendency
for family-like relationships outside marriage to be most roundly
condemned by Conservative Protestants and most widely endorsed
by Quebec Catholics. Catholics in the rest of Canada and Mainline
Protestants occupy their typical middle ground. In general, and with
Quebec Catholics a clear exception, the Committed stand out from
other Canadians in their conviction that it is immoral for couples to
have children in relationships that are not rooted in the institution of
marriage. Other Canadians say they value family and marriage
highly, but they are not prepared to join the Very Committed in
making this traditional, moral judgment. This judgmental tendency
in the Very Committed is, in turn, rooted in their greater, general
willingness to embrace an absolutist ethical stance, as we saw in
chapter 3.

I have included table 4.5 because I think it is a useful complement
to the marriage questions in tables 4.3 and 4.4. Since the data are
drawn from the General Social Survey, they must be cross-classified
by attendance rather than religiosity. Nationally, 70% of Canadians
say it is important to be married to be happy in life. This is not the
same high level of consensus that we find on the preceding questions
tapping the importance of marriage, but there is still a very solid
majority of Canadians who see happiness as being inextricably linked
to being married. Many more weekly attenders than non-attenders

Table 4.5
Percentage who say it is important to be married to be very happy in life (GSS 1995)

	N	Weekly	Monthly	Rarely	Never	All Canadians	Tau-c
18–29	(2,026)	87	82	70	58	67	.23***
30–39	(2,022)	89	75	63	53	65	.28***
40–49	(1,880)	83	72	66	51	64	.27***
50–64	(1,756)	87	77	79	68	76	.19***
65 plus	(1,470)	90	88	89	83	88	.06**
All ages	(10,041)	87	79	71	59	70	.24***

***P < .001   **P < .01   *P < .05

make the same link (87% vs. 59%) between marriage and happiness. Among weekly attenders at all age levels, there is very little variation in the high percentage that connect marriage with happiness. Younger non-attenders, on the other hand, are notably less likely to make the same connection. Three conclusions therefore emerge. First, since non-attenders have been growing over the last half-century and weekly attenders have been declining, fewer Canadians in the future are likely to make the marriage–happiness link. Second, the highly religious are much more likely to make the same connection and are likely to continue to do so in the future. Third, it would not, I think, be churlish to add that the highly religious are right that there is indeed a link between being married and a sense of well-being. As we saw in table 3.6 and will see again in table 4.7, married Canadians more frequently report high satisfaction with life than do the never-married, the widowed, the separated, and the divorced. Thus the Committed's attachment to marriage is rooted in their conviction that it promotes happiness, as well as being morally preferable.

Recent years have, of course, seen the rapid growth of separated, divorced, and common-law families, which have all emerged as serious competitors to the traditional family. My prime concern is with how religiosity relates to these new family forms, but I first need to provide a brief account of their prevalence and character.

The origins of what has come to be known as the divorce revolution can be dated very precisely to 1968 when Canadian federal law on the matter was dramatically changed. Prior to that date, divorce was expensive, difficult to obtain, socially taboo, and rare. Under the new legislation adultery and mental and physical cruelty were acknowledged as grounds for divorce, but the truly revolutionary element to the 1968 legislation was its recognition that a three-year legal separation of a couple was sufficient grounds for recognizing the "irretrievable breakdown" of the marriage. Thus was ushered in the era of "no-fault divorce." Almost two decades later in 1986, a reduced one-year period of separation for marital breakdown and divorce was introduced. Since then, "the vast majority of people" choose to use one year of separation as grounds for divorce because it is faster and cheaper than proving adultery or abuse. As uncontested divorces are also cheaper, "over 90% of divorces are now granted without a formal court hearing" and less than 5% of divorces are contested in court.[12]

In the year immediately following the 1968 legislation, the divorce rate tripled and then continued its upward spiral throughout the 1970s and into the 1980s, with another large increase in the mid 1980s, when the revised legislation of 1986 was introduced.[13] Unfortunately, divorce rates were initially based on the ratio of divorces to the total population and tell us little about the likelihood that married people might divorce. To remedy this situation, Statistics Canada developed complex projections of "the proportion of people who are expected to divorce before their 30th wedding anniversary," if the duration-specific divorce rates for a given year prevailed or stayed stable over the next 30 years. Leaving aside for the moment the questionable assumption built into the Statistics Canada methodology, their estimates suggest that about 40% of married Canadians in the second half of the 1980s had divorced or would divorce, though that rate briefly peaked at 51% in 1987.[14] With such figures, few could deny that a divorce revolution was well underway.

Since the late 1980s, the divorce rate has actually fallen quite substantially from a projected rate of 41% in 1990 to 35% in 1997.[15] However, there is no reason to believe that marital breakdowns have become any less frequent; it may simply be that more and more separated couples are not following through with a final divorce. Some have linked this development to "cuts in the Ontario Legal Aid Plan in 1996."[16] More broadly, couples may have little motivation to move from formal separation to divorce unless they decide to remarry. Since remarriage has become less frequent and common-law relationships among the separated have grown,[17] the compulsion to divorce has diminished. The divorce rate is therefore a less and less meaningful indicator of the rate of marital dissolution. I prefer to use the simpler and clearer data in table 4.6 that lists the percentage of ever-married

Table 4.6
Percentage separated, divorced, or previously divorced in first marriage of ever
married, by age 18–64; 1984, 1990, and 1995

	1984 FHS*	1990 GSS	1995 GSS
18–29	11	12	14
30–39	18	21	20
40–49	19	27	29
50–64	12	20	24
Total Age 18–64	15	21	23

*Figures for the 1984 Family History Survey are taken from S. MacDaniel and C. Strike, 994.
Family and Friends, Statistics Canada Catalogue No. 11-612E, No. 9.

Canadians at the time of the survey who were separated, divorced, or ever divorced from their first marriage. Here we are dealing with the actual rates of first marriage dissolution that include separation as well as divorce.[18] We also avoid making the less than certain assumption that current age-specific divorce rates will remain stable in the future.

Table 4.6 makes it clear that the combined divorce and separation rate continued to grow in the second half of the 1980s and into the 1990s. It is also surely striking that the overall divorce rates are much lower than the projected estimates by Statistics Canada to which I have just alluded. It may well be that a few more separations and divorces will occur among the 29% of early boomers in their forties whose marriages had broken down in 1995, but their final rate of marital dissolution is unlikely to be anything like the 40% to 50% rates bandied about in the press.

Table 4.6 does not, of course, take account of the parallel growth of common-law relationships, which do not alter the rate of marital break-ups, though they certainly reduce the likelihood of marriage occurring in the first place. By common-law, Statistics Canada and I simply mean "two persons of the opposite sex who are not legally married to each other, but live together as husband and wife in the same dwelling."[19] Common-law couples, who were 12% of all families in 1996, are growing more rapidly than any other family type and are projected to equal the number of couples in marriages by the year 2020.[20] Almost half of all common-law couples in 1996 had children, who were 14% of all children under age six and a tenth of all children under age 10.[21] Though Canadians continue to voice their preference for marriage and two-parent families, few could disagree that the traditional two-parent family based on marriage for life is being eroded by the divorce and common-law revolutions.

Before turning to the impact of religion, I need to assess whether there are any reasons to be concerned about the increase in separations, divorces, and common-law unions. In the 1970s, there was a tendency to see divorce as liberating or emancipating by allowing escape from abusive relationships. That generalization undoubtedly still holds true for some couples today, but the empirical studies since the 1980s on the consequences of divorce consistently draw far bleaker conclusions.

About half of all divorces in the 1980s and 1990s involved children. According to a large survey in 1994/95, 20% of children born in 1987/88 had seen their parents separate by age five. Presumably, the figures are much higher for older children. For children whose parents were in a common-law relationship, 63% had experienced parental separation by age five.[22] Separation, divorce, and common-law relationships therefore affect far more than the adults involved.

The most immediate and clearly negative consequence of separation is economic. Even talking into account support payments, women experience a 23% decline in median family income a year after separating. Men experience a 10% gain, when account is taken of the number of family members.[23] Bear in mind that the great majority of children (86%) experiencing a separation live with their mother after that separation,[24] despite the growth of joint custody arrangements in recent years. Five years after their separation, the adjusted family income of women was only 5% below their pre-separation income. However, that economic recovery was confined to the 45% of separated women after five years who had remarried or entered a common-law relationship. After the same five years of separation, the family income of single mothers and their children was still 21% less than their pre-separation income.[25] Equally telling is another recent study by Statistics Canada that found that "changes in family composition were far more likely than a change in a parent's job to move a child into or out of low income."[26] Separation, divorce, and family composition have a profound impact on family income and the likelihood of poverty in Canada.

The Canadians surveyed in tables 4.7 further tell us that separation and divorce do nothing to foster contentment. An impressive 77% of Canadians rate themselves as very satisfied with their home life, but there is a striking gap between the 87% of married Canadians and the

Table 4.7
Satisfaction with life by marital status

	N	Single	Common Law	Married	Separated/ Divorced	Widowed	V
% Very Satisfied with life[1]	(1,715)	61	66	73	47	70	.16***
%Very Satisfied with home life[1]	(1,712)	66	76	87	55	77	.26***
% Have a very stressful life[2]	(10,344)	14	20	13	25	10	.10***

[1]8–10 on 10-point scale WVS 1990   [2]GSS 1995   ***P < .001   **P < .01   *P < .05

much lower 55% of the separated and divorced who make that same claim. Very much in between are those in common-law relationships (76%). Similar patterns also emerge from the same table when Canadians are asked about their satisfaction with life in general and whether they have very stressful lives. None of these findings should be surprising, but they are worth noting because they make it clear that the trauma of separation and divorce is more than financial.

When it comes to longer term consequences, studies of common-law unions find that they are less stable than marriages; that cohabitation delays marriage when it does occur; and that those who co-habited before marriage are more likely to separate than those who married without first living common-law.[27] Virtually identical findings emerge from a very sophisticated study of young adults aged 25 to 32, whose parents had divorced, widowed, or remained intact when the young adults were teens. The study found that young adults with divorce in their background were more likely than their counterparts from widowed or intact family backgrounds to delay marriage and to experience separation once they married. Interestingly, the marital behaviour of those with a widowed background was the same as those with intact family backgrounds. These initial or first-order differences were still evident when the authors of the study took into account the income and labour market activity of the parents of the young adults. The same study also explored the income levels of the young adults. In this sphere, young adults with divorced parents earned appreciably less than those from intact backgrounds, but this difference either disappeared or shrank into insignificance when account was taken of the parents' social backgrounds.[28] Another briefer study found that Canadians from two-parents families at age

Table 4.8
Percentage separated, divorced, or previously divorced among ever married aged
18–64 by attendance

	N	Weekly	Monthly	Rarely	Never	All Canadians	Tau-c
Reid, 1996	(900)	17	19	30	37	27	−.18***
Bibby, 1995	(995)	11	25	30	29	24	−.15***
GSS, 1995	(5,675)	14	16	22	33	24	−.17***
GSS 1990	(6,740)	10	13	23	31	21	−.18***

***P < .001   **P < .01   *P < .05

15 were more likely to have completed high school (80%) than those from lone parent families (71%) or blended (step-parent) families (70%). In this case, the difference persisted even when the authors considered the differing educational levels of the parents.[29] For the moment we cannot be sure whether childhood experiences of separation and divorce diminish the capacity of adults to prosper in the market place. However, all the data we have show that childhood experience of marital dissolution does weaken their capacity to form lasting relationships.

Table 4.8 brings us back to the impact of religiosity on divorce and separation. Four surveys in the 1990s permit me to make calculations of this sort. The overall rate of marital break-up appeared to grow very slowly from 1990 (21%) to 1995 (23%) and then jumped rather mare markedly to 27% in 1996. However, I would not put too much weight on this last spurt since it is based on a smaller survey and used different questions to measure marital break-up.[30] The more striking finding to my mind is that the spread or gap between weekly attenders and non-attenders (measured by Tau-c) is very similar in all four surveys. This gives us great confidence that differences by religiosity are real and that we are not dealing with a rogue survey. Using the large GSS of 1995 as our guide, the marital breakdown rate of weekly attenders (14%) is less than half the 33% rate for non-attenders. Monthly attenders (16%) in this case are very close to the weekly rate. Those who attend rarely are even more prone to marital disruption (22%), but they are still in a clearly intermediate position. It is therefore the non-attenders who really have a distinctively high rate of divorce and separation. Since their numbers are growing and they already represent 42% of all Canadians, we may expect marital breakdown to become more common in the

Table 4.9
Percentage separated, divorced, or previously divorced among ever married
by religiosity and age

	N	Very Commited	Less Commited	Seeker	Non Relig.	All Canadians	Tau-c
Reid, 1996							
Age 18–64	(885)	18	18	31	35	27	−.15***
Bibby, 1995							
Age 18–64	(1,425)	11	24	39	24	25	−.10**
Reid, 1996							
Age 45- 54	(238)	19	31	48	38	36	−.17*
Bibby, 1995							
Age 45–54	(361)	19	22	57	29	33	−.05
Bibby, 1995							
Age 40–49	(321)	18	18	55	32	33	−.08

***P < .001   **P < .01   *P < .05

future. In short, there is a clear connection between religiousness and
the likelihood of marital breakdown.

Table 4.9 calculates divorce rates for my usual religiosity index that
draws on both church attendance and a subjective measure of religiousness to separate out the Committed, Seekers, and the Non Religious. Though I have greater confidence in the accuracy of the GSS
and its large sample, I would note that its simpler religiosity measure
is broadly consistent with my own religiosity scale using the Reid
and Bibby surveys. However, table 4.9 brings out a noteworthy pattern among Seekers that cannot be revealed in the GSS. With one
exception it is Seekers – and not the Non Religious – who stand out
for having the highest divorce rate. That distinction is particularly
striking among Canadians in their 40s and 50s who are on the leading
edge of the divorce revolution and have higher rates than any other
age group. Thus, in Bibby's 1995 survey, the 55% of Seekers in their
40s who are separated, divorced, or previously divorced towers
above the 32% rate for the Non Religious and the much lower 18%
of the Committed. I cannot explain why this is so, but the evidence
is compelling. The wayward, wandering tendency implicit in being
a religious Seeker also seems to operate quite strongly in marital
matters. Those interested in why the Tau-cs in table 4.9 are much
lower than in table 4.8 might consult this endnote.[31]

Table 4.10 makes it clear that the large difference in divorce rates
between weekly attenders and non-attenders cannot be attributed to

Table 4.10
Percentage separated or divorced in first marriage among ever married by attendance and age (GSS 1995)

	N	Weekly	Monthly	Rarely	Never	All Canadians	Tau-c
18–29	(540)	5	3	11	24	14	−.18***
30–39	(1,863)	12	13	18	27	20	−.13***
40–49	(1,616)	16	23	29	40	30	−.20***
50–64	(1,656)	17	17	23	36	25	−.17***
65+	(1,446)	5	7	10	20	11	−.13***
All ages	(7,121)	12	14	20	31	21	−.18***

***P < .001   **P < .01   *P < .05

the older age structure of the former and hence the greater likelihood that their formative years took place before the divorce revolution was underway. We can see that the gap between weekly attenders and non-attenders exists at every age level. The overall divorce rate for Canadians in their twenties (14%) is predictably lower than the national rate because few have been married very long, but the aforementioned gap (see Tau-c) is as strong as ever. The gap does narrow a little for those in their thirties, but the breakdown rate for weekly attenders (12%) is still less than half that for non-attenders (27%). Most importantly, the gap is greatest among late boomers in their forties in 1995, who had the nation's highest level of marital breakdown. The connection between religiosity and marital dissolution is therefore greatest amongst those who are most at risk of marital breakdown.

Let me be clear – we cannot be certain from the above that religiosity or its lack causes or has an impact on separation and divorce. There is an old methodological maxim that correlation does not prove causality. This is particularly germane here because we are measuring current levels of religiosity for people whose separations and divorces occurred an indeterminate number of years earlier. We do not know how frequently the divorced attended religious services prior to their divorce. All we know is how frequently they attend today. This reservation applies equally to many of the other social forces such as income, community size, and employment status, that might affect marital stability. Thus I cannot pursue here the more detailed sort of analysis done elsewhere on how religiosity ranks in the hierarchy of forces that cause separation and divorce.

I would guess – and I can do no more than this – that divorce prompts some formerly active attenders to feel so rejected that they cease their involvement. I also suspect their numbers are not that large. Of the major Christian denominations, the Catholic Church stands out for its refusal to condone the remarriage of the divorced and for its denial of the sacraments or full membership rights to all divorced members who do remarry, though these restrictions do not apply to the separated and divorced. As one priest told me, "We tell our people a broken marriage is not a sin." Some very Conservative Protestant denominations are still forthright in their condemnation of divorce under any circumstances. However, I suspect that the Pentecostal Assemblies of God are more typical in their acceptance as full members both the divorced and the remarried.[32] Even the rule that their pastors may divorce but not remarry was hotly debated at their annual General Conference in 2000. Though the old rule was upheld, it was agreed that each congregation could decide whether to allow divorced people to serve in lay positions of leadership.[33] Even here, the old taboos are clearly crumbling. As for Mainline Protestants, the United Church places no restrictions whatsoever on divorce or remarriage, while the Anglican Church is almost equally tolerant.[34] All Christian denominations with which I am familiar teach that marriage ought to be a life-long commitment, but broken marriages are now so commonplace that they are simply accepted and no longer evoke the scandal they one did. There is also good reason for believing that the stress, discontent, and deprivations of divorce impel some to seek solace, mutual aid, and hence new or renewed involvement in a faith community. These causal patterns are complex and will not be elucidated until more research is done. My suspicion is that the separated and divorced in the years immediately prior to the breakdown were generally less religiously active than those whose marriages remained and still remain intact. All that can be safely said is that there is an "elective affinity" between high religiousness and marital integrity that is reflected in attitudinal surveys (table 4.3), Christian teaching, and current rates of separation and divorce.

Acceptance of divorce has spread across most of Christianity, but there remain differences by denominational family that are not always what one might expect. The data are summarized in table 4.11. The teaching of the Catholic Church on marriage and sexuality has been particularly unbending, but the overall rate of marital breakdown

Table 4.11
Percentage separated, divorced, or previously divorced by age and religion of the committed (GSS 1995)

	N	RC Quebec	RC RoC	Main Prot.	Con. Prot.	V
18–29	(162)	6	6	0	1	.15
30–39	(560)	21	11	18	10	.12*
40–49	(464)	14	18	24	26	.11
50–64	(678)	13	15	15	30	.16*
65+	(773)	4	6	5	13	.11
All ages	(2,637)	11	12	13	17	.06*

***P < .001   **P < .01   *P < .05

among active Catholics attending at least monthly (12%) is about the same as the 13% rate of far more liberal, mainline Protestants. However, Catholics do have a noticeably lower rate of marital breakdown (16%), when we look at baby boomers in their forties, the age group most prone to divorce. We cannot, of course, be certain whether committed Catholics are less inclined to divorce or whether committed Catholics who divorce and wish to remarry flee their church. I suspect both factors are at work. On the Protestant side, I was surprised to find that marital stability is less common among Conservative than Mainline Protestants. The greater openness of Mainline Protestant churches to the divorced and their desire to remarry has apparently not fostered any great wave of marital instability. As for Conservative Protestants, we cannot again be certain whether they are more inclined to divorce or whether their distinctive evangelistic endeavours have a particular resonance among the victims of divorce. Here too I would guess that both interpretations apply.

Despite my earlier warning that we cannot identify the forces that initially cause divorce, I think a partial exception to this generalization can be made for the educational attainment of Canadians, because divorce typically occurs after formal education is completed. Rates of marital stability or instability for all Canadians are very similar at all educational levels. Thus the 21% rate of marriage breakdown among those with a university education is virtually identical to the 22% rate for those who have not completed high school. However, the lack of a connection here may be caused by the tendency of older Canadians to be less well-educated than others and to divorce less frequently. To diminish the effect of age, table 4.12 confines analysis to those under

Table 4.12
Percentage separated or divorced in first marriage among ever married aged 18–50
by attendance and education (GSS 1995)

	N	Weekly	Monthly	Rarely	Never	All Canadians	Tau-c
University[1]	(1,083)	10	12	21	27	20	−.16***
Post Secondary[1]	(1,554)	14	18	21	32	24	−.16***
High School	(764)	16	10	17	30	21	−.15***
<High School	(706)	19	26	29	43	33	−.20***
Total	(4,173)	14	16	22	33	24	−.17***

[1]Some or Completed   ***P < .001   **P < .01   *P < .05

age 50 who are beneficiaries of the educational boom after World War
II and who came of age during the divorce revolution. They are our
baby boomers and Generation X. Within this more restricted group,
those with less than a completed high school education have more
marital instability (33%) than do the university educated (20%). However, we should not lose sight of the fact that fewer weekly attenders at
all educational levels have marital breakdown than do non-attenders.
More importantly, the gap between those who weekly and never
attend is greater at every educational level than is the gap between
the most and least educated.[35] In other words, religiosity has a greater
impact on the likelihood of divorce and separation than does education. Similar conclusions emerge if we compare the relatively small
impact of current occupation on divorce and separation (22% of pro-
fessional and managers aged 18–50 have divorced versus 29% of the
unskilled). In this case, I have not bothered to compile a table because
I suspect that occupations prior to marital breakdown, especially
among women, were rather different. The general conclusion is surely
clear – religiosity is a major influence on marital stability in Canada
that operates across all age groups and educational levels. If we all
emulated weekly attenders, baby boomers would see their rates of
divorce and separation fall from 30% to 16%. With non-attenders as
the norm, the rate of marital dissolution would rise to 40%. These are
not insignificant differences.

The accompanying growth in common-law relationships is shown
in table 4.13 where we see that the percentage who have ever lived
common-law rises from an insignificant 5% of Canadians over age
65 to a 44% rate for those in their thirties. This is a striking increase
in a relatively short period of time, though I think it worth noting

Table 4.13
Percentage ever lived common-law by attendance and age (GSS 1995)

	N	Weekly	Monthly	Rarely	Never	All Canadians	Tau-c
18–29	(2,063)	11	22	34	41	33	−.20***
30–39	(2,557)	25	29	46	54	44	−.25***
40–49	(1,904)	18	18	31	42	32	−.22***
50–64	(1,795)	9	12	13	26	16	−.16***
65+	(1,541)	2	6	7	9	5	−.06***
All ages	(10,259)	12	18	28	37	27	−.22***

***P < .001   **P < .01   *P < .05

that a majority of Canadians in every age group say they have never lived in a common-law relationship.[36] The practice is increasingly common, but it is not yet the Canadian norm. Barring retired Canadians who missed the common-law revolution, weekly attenders in all other age groups are much less likely than non-attenders to have lived common-law. In the peak age group of thirty-something, the 25% of weekly attenders who have lived common-law demonstrate that they are by no means immune to the practice, but they still represent less than half the 54% of non-attenders who have done so. The wide gap between weekly attenders and non-attenders in younger age groups (measured by Tau-c) makes it clear that religiosity's impact cannot be dismissed as in fact being caused by the religiously active being older than other Canadians. In and of itself religiosity makes a difference. In fact, the strength of that impact, again measured by Tau-c, is almost as great for religiosity (−.22) as it is for age (−.24), which so evidently makes such a big difference.

The overall variation in the rate of common-law relationships by religious family or denomination is not nearly so large as it is for religiosity. Nevertheless, I should briefly note the more acute differences listed in table 4.14 that prevail among younger age groups, where common-law relationships are most frequent. The experience of living common-law is much more common among Quebec Catholics under the age of 40 than it is for anyone else who is religiously active. Since far fewer Catholics elsewhere in Canada have lived common-law, there is no generic Catholic explanation for Quebec's distinctiveness. The widespread popularity of common-law unions in Quebec[37] is surely part of the pervasive overthrow by secular nationalism of Quebec's former religious identity. As for the other

Table 4.14
Percentage ever lived common-law by age and religion of the committed (GSS 1995)

	N	RC Quebec	RC RoC	Main. Prot.	Con. Prot.	V
18–29	(406)	33	17	23	7	.25***
30–39	(673)	53	20	34	21	.26***
40–49	(515)	18	20	20	16	.04
50–64	(717)	6	10	11	13	.08
65+	(829)	5	1	1	7	.14**
All ages	(3,256)	16	13	14	12	.05

***P < .001   **P < .01   *P < .05

differences, Conservative Protestants in their twenties are less likely to have experimented with a common-law union than the rest of the religiously active. For those in their thirties, it is Mainline Protestants who are most likely to have experienced a common-law relationship. Neither finding is particularly surprising. With the conspicuous exception of younger Catholics in Quebec, the more general conclusion is that the religiously active are much less likely to have experienced a common-law union than are non-attenders. Since living common-law increases the likelihood of marital breakdown,[38] the relative infrequency of common-law living among the religiously active helps to explain their lower rates of divorce and separation.

FAMILY DYNAMICS:
RELATIONSHIPS WITH CHILDREN, PARENTS,
AND RELATIVES

The 1990s have often been depicted as an era when the quality of family life has been battered by stressed, dual-income couples with not enough time for each other, their children, and their relatives. In pursuing my focus on how religion affects family dynamics, I start with some evidence of Canadian attitudes to child-raising and the conflicting demands of work and family, but my primary concern is with how these values are concretely expressed in the everyday activities that define our family life. In all this, gender or male–female differences play a major role.

The first question in the top row of tables 4.15 and 4.16 indicates that only a tiny proportion of Canadians today (7%) are prepared to endorse the view that "a man does not have to be very involved in

Table 4.15
Child raising and gender role attitudes within the nuclear family by attendance (GSS 1995)

	N	Weekly	Monthly	Rarely	Never	Total	Tau-c
% Agree a man does not have to be very involved in sharing the everyday tasks of raising children	(9,826)	8	11	7	6	7	.02**
% Agree an employed mother can establish as warm & secure a relationship with her children as a mother who does not work for pay	(9,404)	62	71	76	72	71	-.07***
% Agree a pre-school child is likely to suffer if both parents are employed	(9,411)	71	64	59	58	62	.11***
% Agree a job is all right, but what most women really want is a home and children	(8,917)	65	63	56	47	55	.16***
% Agree a family is all right, but what most men really want is to be successful in their job	(9,178)	56	58	52	53	54	.02*
% Agree a man should refuse a promotion at work if it means spending too little time with his family	(8,506)	61	53	52	50	53	.09***
% Agree a woman should refuse a promotion at work if it means spending too little time with her family	(8,617)	70	63	60	57	61	.11***

***P < .001   **P < .01   *P < .05

Table 4.16
Child raising and gender role attitudes within the nuclear family by age and religion of
the committed (GSS 1995)

	N	RC Quebec	RC RoC	Main. Prot.	Con. Prot.	V
% Agree a man does not have to be very involved in sharing the everyday tasks of raising children	(3,082)	9	8	9	8	.02
% Agree an employed mother can establish as warm & secure a relationship with her children as a mother who does not work for pay	(3,093)	56	69	71	62	.12***
% Agree a pre-school child is likely to suffer if both parents are employed	(2,953)	75	64	61	79	.16***
% Agree a job is all right, but what most women really want is a home and children	(2,831)	74	60	59	60	.12***
% Agree a family is all right, but what most men really want is to be successful in their job	(2,851)	70	56	49	47	.17***
% Agree a man should refuse a promotion at work if it means spending too little time with his family	(2,674)	45	58	57	75	.21***
% Agree a woman should refuse a promotion at work if it means spending too little time with her family	(2,730)	57	67	68	81	.17***

***P < .001   **P < .01   *P < .05

sharing the everyday tasks of raising children; this is not primarily
a man's responsibility." In theory, there is virtual unanimity that the
daily tasks of child rearing are not primarily a woman's job. On this
Canadians are agreed, regardless of how frequently they attend religious services or the type of religious family with which they are
involved. If that were all there were to family life, it would surely be
idyllic, but that impressive consensus is not to be found on any of
the other questions in tables 4.15 and 4.16.

The next two questions in the same tables ask Canadians whether
children are adversely affected when parents work outside the home.
The answers given very much depend on how the question is
phrased. A clear majority of Canadians (71%) say "an employed
mother can establish just as warm and secure a relationship with her
children as a mother who does not work for pay." On the other hand,

almost as many (62%) say "a preschool child is likely to suffer if both parents are employed." The two questions are different, but I think the conclusion to be drawn from them is clear. Though Canadians are generally reluctant to blame working mothers, a majority, though a small one, believe that preschoolers suffer when both parents work outside the home. We are very much divided on the topic. This state of affairs is also likely to persist for some time, as even a slim majority of Canadians under age 30 (55%) say children are harmed when both parents work.

Using as our guide the less ambiguous second question that does not specifically blame mothers, weekly attenders are more likely to stress the ill effects of both parents working (71%) than are non-attenders (58%). The difference between the two is by no means large, but additional calculations I have done too bulky to present here find a similar gap between attenders and non-attenders across all age groups.[39] The difference is therefore caused by religiosity and not the older age profile of religious actives; the same difference is also likely to persist for some time into the future. Active religious involvement therefore has a modest tendency, most notably among Quebec Catholics (75%) and Conservative Protestants (79%), to foster a traditional or conservative view that preschoolers need an at-home parent. Anyone uncomfortable with my use of causal language here should consult this endnote.[40]

The final four questions in tables 4.15 and 4.16 explore whether Canadians think the key priorities of family and work differ for men and women. Once more we see much disagreement with Canadians being roughly equally divided on both sides of each question. More weekly attenders (65%) than non-attenders (47%) are likely to say "What women most want is a home and children," but they do not differ in any noticeable way on the parallel question of whether men prize their work more than their families. When asked separately whether men and women "should refuse a promotion at work if it means spending too little time" with their families, more weekly attenders than non-attenders express their agreement. Again the difference is a modest one extending across most age groups, though there is a slightly higher level of general agreement that it is women who ought to give priority to their families. However, we should not lose sight of the fact that a majority of weekly attenders and non-attenders think men as well as women ought to think of family before a promotion. For reasons I cannot discern, Quebec Catholics are more

Table 4.17
Mean number of children ever-raised by attendance and age (GSS 1995)

	N	Weekly	Monthly	Rarely	Never	All Canadians
18–29	(2,067)	0.5	0.5	0.5	0.4	0.4
30–39	(2,563)	2.1	1.7	1.6	1.4	1.6
40–49	(1,907)	2.4	2.4	2.1	1.9	2.1
50–64	(1,796)	3.2	3.0	2.7	2.5	2.8
65+	(1,543)	3.6	3.3	3.1	2.9	3.2
All Ages	(10,276)	2.4	2.0	1.7	1.4	1.8

likely than other religious actives to embrace the traditionalist view that women be focused on home and children, while men be more concerned with their jobs. When it comes to refusing a promotion that might jeopardize family obligations, Conservative Protestants lead the way. Also note that Conservative Protestants are almost as likely to extend this advice to men (75%) as they are to women (81%).[41] I would conclude from all this that the religiously active are more likely than non-attenders to assign the responsibilities of families and children to women. I hasten to add that the differences are small, that a majority of Canadians are of the same mind, and that weekly attenders also emphasize the responsibilities of men to their families. This is very thin gruel for anyone seeking a distinctively sexist outlook among the religiously active.

The probing of attitudes is often revealing, but I am always inclined to put a greater weight on behavioural indicators. Table 4.17 lists the average or mean number of children ever raised by both males and females, with breakdowns by age and amount of religious involvement. The numbers in table 4.17 are therefore not the same as the completed fertility rate to which I alluded earlier,[42] though the two measures are clearly connected. Overall, the average of 2.4 children raised by weekly attenders is 33% higher than the national rate of 1.8 and a whopping 71% above the 1.4 children raised by non-attenders. These differences are shaped by the higher fertility and church attendance rates of older Canadians, but more than this age factor is involved. The number of children raised by Canadians below the age of 30 is now uniformly low regardless of religious involvement. In every other age group, differences by attendance are apparent. Early boomers in their forties are particularly instructive because their biological reproduction is essentially set, though the total

Table 4.18
Mean number of children ever raised by religion and age of the committed (GSS 1995)

	N	RC Quebec	RC RoC	Main. Prot.	Con. Prot.
18–29	(407)	0.5	0.5	0.6	0.4
30–39	(675)	1.7	1.9	1.9	2.2
40–49	(517)	2.2	2.4	2.3	2.6
50–64	(717)	2.9	3.1	3.2	3.7
65+	(829)	4.1	3.7	2.9	3.5
All Ages	(3,261)	2.7	2.2	2.4	2.0

number of children they raise may grow in our era of blended families. In this age group of 40–49, the average number of children ever raised by weekly attenders (2.4) is 26% higher than the rate for non-attenders (1.9). If we narrow our focus to the more revealing number of children actually in the households of early boomers, then the rate for weekly attenders (1.8) is 50% higher than the non-attending rate of 1.2. This works out to about half a child (0.6) more per household for weekly attending early boomers. Table 4.17 also makes it clear that the differences between the religiously active and inactive are as large or larger for late boomers in their thirties and for all pre boomers, who had much higher fertility levels. Both before and after the "baby bust" of the 1960s and 1970s, the religiously active have cared for more children than have other Canadians.

Table 4.18 shows us that Catholics in Quebec have raised more children than anyone else, but that distinction will soon disappear. In fact, Quebec Catholics under 40 raise fewer children than the religiously active in the other major religious families, though the Quebec Catholic rate is still a bit higher than that of non-attenders. Almost two-thirds of Canada's active Catholics today live outside Quebec (64%). Their baby boomers now have about as many children as do Protestants, though the average number of children they raise (2.1) is higher than the 1.6 rate for non-attending boomers. The much-reduced number of children now raised by Catholics confirms a 1993 Angus Reid poll finding that 91% of active Catholics, despite their church's teaching, believe "it is perfectly acceptable for people to use artificial birth control to prevent unwanted pregnancies." On the Protestant side, we can see that older Conservatives now in their retirement years once raised more children (3.5) than did their Main-line counterparts (2.9). However, declining fertility across the board

Table 4.19
Labour force status by attendance among married women with children less than
6 years of age (NSVGP 1997)

	Weekly	Monthly	Rarely	Never	All Canadians
Employed Full Time	34	48	44	43	43
Employed Part time	23	23	23	19	22
Not in Labour Force	43	29	33	37	36
Total	100%	100%	100%	100%	100%
(N)	(298)	(195)	(356)	(414)	(1,257)

Tau-c = −.02   P > .05

has much reduced that traditional difference, leaving Conservative boomers with only marginally more children (2.3) than Mainline Protestant boomers (2.1). If anyone wonders why the overall number of children raised by Conservatives (2.0) is lower than the Mainline average of 2.4, the answer is to be found in the greater ability of the Conservatives to attract younger Canadians, who have smaller families than their elders. Today the number of children raised by those under 50 varies only slightly across religious families.

According to the NSVGP in 1997, two-thirds (67%) of Canadian women with children under the age of six were in the paid labour force or looking for work. Table 4.19 allows us to assess whether the religiously active implement the greater concern they expressed in table 4.15 that children suffer when both parents work. The data in table 4.19 are confined to married women because they have the option of relying on a male bread winner for financial support. That option is not available to separated, divorced, or never-married women with small children.[43] Compared to the religiously inactive, married female weekly attenders with small children are less likely to be employed full-time, a very tiny bit more likely to be employed part-time, and more likely to be out of the labour force and presumably at home with their children. The differences are really quite small, though there is a nine-point spread between the 34% of weekly attenders and the 43% of non-attenders who are employed full-time. The difference cannot be attributed to greater economic need among the religiously inactive since we have already seen that the religiously active have virtually identical mean and median family incomes. Moreover, further calculations I have done indicate that weekly attending married women with children aged six to twelve are just

Table 4.20
Labour force status by religion among married women with children less than 6 years
of age attending at least monthly (NSVGP 1997)

	RCs All	RC Quebec	RC RoC	Main. Prot.	Con. Prot.
Employed Full Time	49	44	50	26	30
Employed Part time	20	11	22	39	27
Not in Labour Force	32	45	29	35	43
Total	100%	100%	100%	100%	100%
(N)	219	39	178	169	139

V = .18   P < .01

as involved in the labour force, both full-time and part-time, as their
non-attending counterparts. In and of itself, religiosity has a predictable though small impact on whether women work when they have
preschool children.

From the data in table 4.20 I would draw two conclusions. The first
is that married Protestant women with preschoolers are noticeably
less likely to be employed full-time than are either Catholics or non-
attenders, who are both very similar in this regard. Again, economic
necessity cannot explain the striking contrast with Protestants, since
the average incomes of Catholic boomers inside Quebec ($64,023) and
in the rest of Canada ($61,423) are greater than the incomes of both
Mainline Protestant ($58,182) and Conservative Protestant ($52,093)
boomers. Second, Conservative Protestants stand out for having a
combination of relatively few mothers of preschoolers employed full-
time (30%) and more (43%) not working at all. This state of affairs is
made all the more striking by the comparatively low family incomes
of Conservative Protestants. These choices are consistent with the
distinctively high percentage of Conservative Protestants who feel
that preschool children will suffer if both parents are employed. Here
too, it is religious tradition – not economic necessity – that explains
these variations.

One of the great challenges in Canadian family life over the last
30 years has been how to meet the responsibilities of childcare and the
running of a household now that both partners in marriages and
common-law relationships are typically working outside the home.
Tables 4.21 to 4.24 provide some insight into these issues by summarizing some findings from the 1992 General Social Survey, which
explored how Canadians allocate their daily time in our pressure-filled

Table 4.21
Mean weekly hours caring for household and children under age 15 by sex and
attendance among married or common-law canadians aged 20–49 (GSS 1992)

	N	Weekly	Monthly	Rarely	Never	All Canadians
Male	(1,052)	24	24	23	23	23
Female	(1,232)	61	61	55	64	60
Male/Female Ratio		.39	.39	.42	.36	.38

Table 4.22
Mean weekly hours doing housework* by sex and attendance among married or
common-law canadians aged 20–49 (GSS 1992)

	N	Weekly	Monthly	Rarely	Never	All Canadians
Male	(1,639)	11	11	10	11	11
Female	(1,932)	24	22	21	22	22
Male/Female Ratio		.46	.50	.48	.50	.50

*Includes unpaid housework and house maintenance

Table 4.23
Mean weekly hours caring for household children under age 15 by sex and religion of
the committed among married or common-law canadians aged 20–50 (GSS 1992)

	N	RC All	RC Quebec	RC RoC	Main. Prot.	Con. Prot.
Male	(327)	22	15	26	29	25
Female	(512)	55	39	64	71	68
M/F ratio		.40	.38	.41	.41	.37

Table 4.24
Mean weekly hours doing housework* by sex and religion of the committed among
married or common-law canadians aged 20–50 (GSS 1992)

	N	RC All	RC Quebec	RC RoC	Main. Prot.	Con. Prot.
Male	(447)	12	14	11	11	10
Female	(741)	23	25	22	24	23
M/F ratio		.52	.56	.50	.46	.43

*Includes unpaid housework and house maintenance

world. The estimates by survey respondents of how much time they had devoted in the preceding week to childcare and housework are unlikely to be very precise and may well be exaggerated. The analysis is confined to respondents who are married or in common-law relationships because questions about sharing duties with a conjugal partner simply do not apply to single parents, be they separated, divorced, widowed, or never married. I have restricted analysis to those aged 20–50, as they feel most acutely the competing demands on their time from children, work, and housework. Doing so also helps to reduce the confounding influence of the older age structure of the religiously active.

Over a typical week, Canadians with children under the age of 15 say they devote an average of 42 hours to caring for their children. They also say they spend another 17 hours a week doing housework that ranges from cooking, cleaning, and grocery shopping to house repairs. Overall, the 23 hours men spend weekly on childcare is only 38%, or less than half, the 60 hours their spouses and partners devote to their children. When it comes to housework, men do relatively more, but they still put in only half the amount of time (48%) of their female partners. Even when both work full-time, men narrow the gap only fractionally, putting in 52% of the time spent by women with their children and 65% of the female average for housework.[44] Regardless of whether or not women work, they continue to do far more than their male partners in running their homes and caring for their children.

Differences in religious involvement in tables 4.21 to 4.24 do nothing to diminish the foregoing conclusions. Among weekly attenders, the average amount of time males devote to their children is only 39% of the female average. That male/female ratio of .39 falls to .36 among non-attenders, but a decline of this sort is so small that it is unimportant. That pattern is reversed when it comes to housework, where the male/female ratio for hours devoted to housework is .44 for weekly attenders and .50 for non-attenders. Since religious involvement seems to prompt both slightly more and slightly less gender equality in the home, it is difficult to say whether religiosity is intrinsically inclined in either direction.[45] Differences by religious family are also very minor. At best, there are some grounds for concluding that Conservative Protestant males are a little less likely to share household and child-raising responsibilities with their spouses than are men from the other religious families.[46] To me, the one strong conclusion that emerges from all these tables is that females at all levels of religiosity devote far more time than males do to childcare and housework. There is still a marked sexual division of labour in Canadian homes that is largely untouched by how religious or non-religious we are.

Tables 4.25 and 4.26 conclude this section with a summary of questions from different surveys that explore how strongly Canadians are attached to the members of their immediate families and to the wider network of their extended kin. With the divorce revolution and all the talk of how pressured and time-deprived Canadians are today, I was surprised to discover how much contact Canadians do maintain with their immediate family. A striking 71% say they have seen their parents at least once a month over the preceding year; 54% say they do so weekly. Even more telling in our era of so much geographic mobility are the 68% who phone or write their parents at least weekly and the 88% who do so monthly. Only 4% say they have ceased contact with their parents. Not surprisingly, teenagers and young adults maintain the closest ties, but 63% of the middle-aged (30–49) who are busy with their own families also say they see their parents at least monthly; again 87% are in monthly contact by phone or letter. Equally striking are the 70% of Canadians who say they have been in at least monthly communication with one or more of their brothers and sisters who do not live in the same household; 36% say they phone or write on a weekly basis. Even allowing for a measure of exaggeration, it is clear that many Canadians maintain close contacts with their parents and adult brothers and sisters. Hardly any admit to severing all contact.

In this context where Canadians so emphasize preserving links with immediate family, it should come as no surprise to learn that the religiously active are no more family minded than anyone else. Weekly attenders are a little more likely than non-attenders to see their parents on a weekly basis (55% vs. 50%), but their levels of monthly contact with both parents and siblings are virtually identical. Among the religiously active attending at least monthly, Quebec Catholics are noticeably more likely to say they see their parents and siblings on at least a monthly basis. I would attribute this to their being restricted in their opportunities for geographic mobility because 64% of francophone Quebecers cannot speak English.[47] Conservative Protestants, on the other hand, are a little less likely to maintain immediate family ties. This may be caused by the high commitment levels they expect, their

Table 4.25
Family relations by attendance

	N	Weekly	Monthly	Rarely	Never	Total	Tau-c
% Seen parents in last month.[1]	(8,385)	68	77	77	68	71	-.03*
% Phoned / written parents in last month.[1]	(8,531)	87	89	91	88	88	.00
% Seen at least monthly brothers & sisters living outside this household.[1]	(11,662)	59	64	63	55	59	.05***
% Phoned / written at lea st monthly brothers & sisters living outside this household.[1]	(11,655)	71	77	73	66	70	.06***
Mean number of relatives (excluding immediate family, to whom feel close)[2]	(11,154)	8.9	9.5	8.3	5.6	7.4	N/a***
% Very confident have a relative to depend on to spend a lot of time in an emergency.[3]	(1,472)	78	81	80	82	81	-.03
% Very confident could borrow several hundred dollars from a relative in an emergency.[3]	(1,468)	70	75	69	72	71	.01

[1]GSS, 1990 [2]GSS,1996 [3]Reid 1996 ***P < .001 **P < .01 *P < .05

Table 4.26
Family relations by religion of the committed

	N	RC Quebec	RC RoC	Main. Prot.	Con. Prot.	V
% Seen parents in last month.[1]	(2,694)	81	72	74	63	.13***
% Phoned / written parents in last month.[1]	(2,674)	82	89	92	88	.10**
% Seen at least monthly brothers & sisters living outside this household.[1]	(4,372)	71	61	53	55	.14***
% Phoned / written at least monthly brothers & sisters living outside this household.[1]	(4,370)	78	73	71	68	.08***
Mean number of relatives (excluding immediate family, to whom feel close).[2]	(4,259)	5.2	10.6	9.5	10.5	N/a
% Very confident have a relative to depend on to spend a lot of time in an emergency.[3]	(410)	70	88	82	75	.17**
% Very confident could borrow several hundred dollars from a relative in an emergency [3]	(409)	50	83	80	67	.29***

[1]GSS, 1990   [2]GSS,1996   [3]Reid 1996   ***P < .001   **P < .01   * P < .05

above-average levels of apostasy from childhood to adulthood,[48] and the attendant family rifts that undoubtedly arise. However, here too the differences are really quite small. Across all the major religious families, levels of involvement with immediate family are quite high and very similar to those of the religiously uninvolved.

The fifth row in tables 4.25 and 4.26 lists the average number of extended kin (beyond spouse, parents, siblings, and children) to whom Canadians feel close. The active kinship network of weekly attenders (8.9) is more than half as large again as that of non-attenders (5.6). Since weekly, monthly, and infrequent attenders all have about the same number of close kin, it is the non-attenders who really stand out. Non-attenders tend to be younger, but age is not the cause here. In fact, the difference between weekly and non-attenders in the size of their kinship networks is actually greater among boomers (10.4 vs. 6.3) and Generation Xers (9.8 vs. 5.7) than it is for Canadians as a whole. Among the religiously active, Quebec Catholics are alone worth noting with an extended kin network (5.2) about half the size of the other religious families. With the conspicuous exception of Quebec Catholics, the religiously active have an extended kin network about twice as large as that available to non-attenders. This is a major difference that stands in marked contrast to the insignificant differences between weekly attenders and non-attenders in the strength of their immediate family bonds.

That last conclusion does not appear to be supported by the last two rows in table 4.25. Here, there is once more no significant difference between weekly attenders and non-attenders in the percentage who feel confident they could rely on a relative in an emergency with the aid of that relative's time or money. This absence of a difference may be caused by my earlier finding that the Very Committed are more inclined than others to see the world as filled with sin and evil and to say that "it just isn't wise to trust people these days" (see table 3.14). The differences are too small to make much of a case along these lines, though the particularly marked tendency of Conservative Protestants to stress the presence of evil in the world may explain why they are less confident of receiving aid from a relative than are Mainline Catholics or Catholics outside Quebec. The particular tendency of Quebec Catholics to distrust people in general may also explain their lower level of confidence in receiving aid from relatives. There is clearly a danger of weaving too many slender distinctions. The more robust, certain conclusions are that the religiously active share with all Canadians strong links to their immediate families and they have a wider network of extended kin to whom they can presumably turn in time of need.

FRIENDS AND NEIGHBOURS

This last section on friends and neighbours will be brief because it leads us to the periphery of the world of intimate relations and because many of the conclusions coincide with those already drawn. The pertinent data are summarized in tables 4.27 and 4.28.

Besides having more relatives to whom they feel close, weekly attenders also report they have more close friends (9.2) than do the non-religious (6.5), though in this case the gap or spread of 42% between religiously active and inactive is a little bit less than it is for relatives. When the impact of the older age structure of the religiously active is reduced by confining analysis to ages 18 to 49, the gap between weekly attenders and non-attenders (10.0 vs. 5.9) is actually slightly strengthened. There is, of course, a cumulative effect at work in that the intimate network of friends and relatives beyond the

Table 4.27
Relations with friends and neighbours by attendance

	N	Weekly	Monthly	Rarely	Never	Total	Tau-c
Mean number of close friends, excluding family[1]	(11,129)	9.2	9.0	7.4	6.5	7.6	N/a
% Socialise a few times a month or more with friends outside the neighbourhood[2]	(17,133)	71	71	67	71	70	.00
% Have weekly or more frequent contact with neighbours over last 12 months[3]	(1,487)	73	71	65	58	65	.13***
% Very confident have a friend to depend on to spend a lot of time in an emergency[3]	(1,485)	75	68	69	73	71	.01
% Very confident could borrow several hundred dollars from a friend in an emergency[3]	(1,466)	54	47	44	51	49	.00
% in small group meeting regularly & providing support or care for participants[3]	(1,487)	51	37	24	24	31	.22***

[1]GSS, 1996   [2]NSVGP, 1997   [3]Reid, 1996   ***P < .001   **P < .01   *P < .05

Table 4.28
Relations with friends and neighbours by religion among the committed

	N	RC Quebec	RC RoC	Main. Prot.	Con. Prot.	V
Mean number of close friends, excluding[1]	(4,248)	4.6	9.6	9.7	12.7	N/a
% Socialise a few times a month or more with friends outside the neighbourhood[2]	(6,485)	57	74	74	77	.17***
% Have weekly or more frequent contact with neighbours over last 12 months[3]	(419)	69	70	75	76	.06
% Very confident have a friend to depend on to spend a lot of time in an emergency[3]	(419)	57	78	75	78	.18**
% Very confident could borrow several hundred dollars from a friend in an emergency[3]	(412)	37	59	51	54	.17**
% in small group meeting regularly & providing support or care for participants[3]	(419)	25	42	58	53	.26***

[1]GSS, 1996   [2]NSVGP, 1997   [3]Reid, 1996   ***P < .001   **P < .01   *P < .05

immediate family for weekly attenders (18.1) has an average of six more people in it than the comparable mean of 12.1 for non-attenders. I would not put a great deal of faith in the specific numbers, but the overall edge in size of support network is clearly in favour of the religiously active.

A little over a third of Canadians (36%) say they socialize with friends on a very regular weekly basis. Another 36% say they do so a few times a month. Most of us therefore regularly socialize beyond the confines of family. Weekly attenders are no more or less inclined this way than anyone else. Canadians also say they have frequent contact with their neighbours; 65% are in touch at least weekly and an impressive 86% are at least monthly. In this area, weekly attenders are more likely to report frequent weekly contact with their neighbours (73%) than are non-attenders (58%), though the greater neighbourliness of the religiously active is at best a modest difference. Socializing and general neighbourliness are therefore widely practised by Canadians, regardless of their level of religious involvement.

When it comes to feeling confident that a friend can be counted on for help in an emergency, we see, as we did on the related questions concerning relatives, that the religiously active and inactive are equally confident. Note that only 11% of Canadians are prepared to express any doubts.[49] On the related question of borrowing money, overall confidence levels are noticeably lower, and the slightly higher confidence level of weekly attenders is so small that it is statistically insignificant. Levels of religious involvement therefore do not do affect the avowed confidence of Canadians that they will receive support in needy times. I am inclined to think that their reluctance to admit to doubts of this sort[50] is driven by a desire to not speak badly of friends and by extension themselves. Reasoning of this sort is obviously speculative. For me the more critical question is whether Canadians are actually likely to receive support in times of need. That question brings us back to the evidence I have already mentioned indicating that the religiously involved have more friends and relatives to whom they feel close than do the religiously inactive. In much the same vein, table 4.27 indicates that "involvement in a small group that meets regularly and provides support or caring for those who participate" is much more common among the weekly attenders than non-attenders. In fact, the 51% of weekly attenders in a small group is more than twice the 24% rate for non-attenders. This is a major difference. Together these behavioural indicators suggest that the religiously involved do have a larger and more organized support network to be drawn on in times of need than do the religiously uninvolved.

I would draw two main conclusions from table 4.28, which compares friendship patterns across the four major religious families. First, Quebec Catholics have weaker friendship networks than anyone else. Not only do they have fewer relatives to whom they feel close, but their average number of close friends is less than half that of all of the other major religious families. Quebec Catholics also socialize less frequently with friends, are less confident of aid from friends in an emergency, and are much less likely to be members of a small group. Immediate family ties are very important to Quebec Catholics, but their relations beyond that narrow ground are weakly developed and hesitant when compared to the religiously active elsewhere in Canada. Since Catholics in the rest of Canada do not share these traits, the cause must be rooted more in their ethnic than their religious heritage.

Second, I would stress that the similarities between the other three religious families outweigh their differences. It is true, for instance, that Conservative Protestants claim more close friends than anyone else, but that needs to be set against the great popularity of small group involvement among Mainline Protestants. Similarly, Catholics outside Quebec are less likely to be in a small religious group, though their overall participation in small groups is not that much lower than the Protestant rate. Leaving aside Quebec Catholics, the really striking contrast is between the religiously active and inactive. I might add that none of these conclusions is altered by more detailed analysis that takes account of the age differences between weekly attenders and non-attenders.

In concluding this chapter, I want to stress one underlying theme. Despite all the changes that have occurred in family life in recent decades, Canadians from all walks of life continue to attach a great deal of importance to their families. Over 90% say they receive much enjoyment from their families and impressively high percentages of adults keep in touch with their parents. Where the religiously active and inactive part ways is in the greater commitment of the religiously active to the marriage bond, which is manifest in their rejection of sexuality outside – but not inside – marriage and in their lower divorce rates. The religiously active also have a much larger network of relatives and friends to whom they feel close and they are notably more likely to be members of a small group. In short, the religiously active are embedded in a much more stable and extensive network of intimate relationships than are non-attenders. In our contemporary world where family relationships are highly valued but ever more precarious, these are not insignificant differences.

5

Civic Sensibilities:
Volunteering and Charitable Giving

Ever since de Tocqueville's perceptive comments in the early nineteenth century on how America's many voluntary associations were the bedrock for its democracy, scholars have emphasized the importance of local associations in sustaining the quality and vitality of the communities in which we reside.[1] Some have claimed that levels of civic involvement have been falling recently in the United States, though there is enough well argued dissention to make me think the answer is less than clear.[2] As for Canada, the evidence is too skimpy to permit a firm conclusion. In the first large and conclusive national survey, conducted in 1987, 27% of Canadians over the age of 15 said that they had volunteered or freely given their time and labour over the last year to community and charitable organizations ranging from religious congregations to service clubs, sports programs, youth groups, food banks, hospital auxiliaries, parent-teacher associations, Meals on Wheels, seniors groups, and a host of cultural activities.[3] That national volunteering rate then rose to 31% in the second national survey in 1997, only to fall back again in the year 2000 to the 27% level recorded in 1987.[4] The 1997 National Survey of Volunteering, Giving, and Participating (NSVGP), which I use because it has the most detailed set of demographic variables, tells us that the total number of hours volunteered by Canadians in the year prior to the survey were equal to 578,000 full-time, year-round jobs, while total charitable giving exceeded $4.5 billion.[5] Not everyone is agreed that we should be so reliant on voluntary labour and charitable giving, but it is indisputable that they now decisively shape the quality of community life we enjoy.

COMMUNITY INVOLVEMENT

Given the Canadian obsession with self and self-fulfillment described in chapter 3, it should come as no surprise to learn that only 47% of Canadians think that "being part of a group is very important to me."[6] Since the Very Committed are, by definition, communally inclined, it is equally unsurprising to find in table 5.1 that the Very Committed are more group minded (57%) than are the Non Religious (43%). The difference is statistically significant, but it is by no means a large one. What really strikes me is the very substantial minority of the Very Committed (43%), who express varying degrees of reservation over the merits of belonging to a group.

Far more Canadians (81%) say they agree with the statement "I like to work on community projects." There is probably a politically correct thrust to this question that inflates the number of genuinely keen community workers, but the fact still remains that less than a fifth of Canadians are prepared to admit their dislike. In a much more pronounced vein, a whopping 94% of Canadians agree that "It is important to be very involved in the community you live in." On both these questions, more of the Very Committed profess to be more community minded than do the Non Religious, but the differences are really too small for us to attach much substantive significance to them. On the related but reversed question asking Canadians whether they agree that donating time to volunteer organizations is a waste of time, only 9% are willing to make the claim. Rather more Canadians (26%) agree that "volunteer work is the kind of thing you do when you don't have enough going on in your life," though we should not lose sight of the fact that 74% of Canadians disagree. The more important conclusion to be drawn from these last two questions is that the differences by level or type of religiousness are so small that they are both statistically and substantively insignificant. From table 5.2 it can be seen that the Committed in Canada's three major religious families of Catholics, Mainline Protestants, and Conservative Protestants are also in broadly similar agreement on the virtues of community involvement and volunteering. The individualism of Canadians that causes many of us to be wary of belonging to a group is therefore

Table 5.1
View on community participation by religiosity

	N	Very Commited	Less Commited	Seeker	Non Relig.	Total	Tau-c
% Agree being part of a group is very important to me[1]	(1,485)	57	54	42	43	47	.12***
% Like to work on community projects[2]	(1,440)	86	87	82	75	81	.10***
% Agree voluntary and charitable organizations play a major role in making our communities better places[3]	(16,906)	95	95	95	92	94	.03***
% Feel it is important to be very involved in the community you live in[2]	(1,459)	98	95	95	91	94	.05***
% Disagree donating time to volunteer organizations a waste of my time[2]	(1,460)	90	95	88	91	90	.00
% Disagree volunteer work is the kind of thing you do when you don't have enough going on in your life[2]	(1,459)	67	79	75	75	84	-.04

[1]Reid 1994 [2]Reid 1996 [3]NSVGP 1997 ***P < .001 **P < .01 *P < .05

Table 5.2
View on community participation by religion of the committed

	N	RC Quebec	RC RoC	Main. Prot.	Con. Prot.	V
% Agree being part of a group is very important to me[1]	(427)	62	56	55	55	.06
% Like to work on community projects[2]	(412)	87	86	89	85	.05
% Agree voluntary and charitable organizations play a major role in making our communities better places[3]	(6,451)	95	96	96	94	.03
% Feel it is important to be very involved in the community you live in[2]	(418)	97	98	98	93	.11
% Disagree donating time to volunteer organizations a waste of my time[2]	(418)	84	94	96	93	.18*
% Disagree volunteer work is the kind of thing you do when you don't have enough going on in your life[2]	(416)	66	80	73	69	.12

[1]Reid 1994   [2]Reid 1996   [3]NSVGP 1997   ***P < .001   **P < .01   *P < .05

counterbalanced by a wide-reaching consensus that community participation and service are laudable and desirable activities that enhance the social fabric of our communities. On these matters, both religious and non-religious Canadians are in essential agreement.

Instead of asking Canadians what they think of community involvement, tables 5.3 and 5.4 explore the extent to which they actually participate in, volunteer their labour to, and serve on the committees of our many community and voluntary associations. We are still dealing here with self-reports that are not independently substantiated, but there is a refreshing candour in the admission of Canadians that we are much less likely to practise what we so widely preach. As I have done before, I have included very similar questions from two completely different surveys in order to help us assess how much faith we can put in the conclusions we draw from them.

Nationally, 43% of Canadians in the NSVGP and 46% of Canadians in the Reid survey of 1996 say they are members of or participants in one or more of a lengthy list of community organizations covered by both surveys. Such highly similar figures make their accuracy and reliability all the more probable. This makes Canada one of the more associationally active countries in the world,[7] though this participation rate is only about half that of the over 80% of Canadians who

Table 5.3
Community involvement by religiosity and type of organization

	N	Very Commited	Less Commited	Seeker	Non Relig.	Total	Tau-c
PARTICIPATION							
% Member / participant in community organizations[1]	(17,054)	62	48	40	34	43	.22***
% Member / affiliated with community organizations[2]	(2,955)	67	59	36	35	46	.28***
VOLUNTEERING							
% Volunteer in last year[1]	(17,058)	47	35	28	25	31	.16***
% Doing any voluntary work[2]	(2,955)	62	56	30	32	42	.27***
Average (Mean) Number of hours volunteered per year by Volunteers[1]	(5,263)	203	131	135	132	153	N/a
Average (Median) Number of hours volunteered per year by Volunteers[1]	(5,263)	104	67	56	56	70	N/a
% Of all hours volunteered[1]		38	12	23	27	100	N/a
LEADERSHIP							
% Ever served on a committee[2]	(2,955)	47	43	21	23	31	.22***

[1]NSVGP 1997   [2]Reid 1996   ***P < .001   **P < .01   *P < .05

Table 5.4
Community involvement by religion and type of organization among the committed

	N	RC Quebec	RC RoC	Main. Prot.	Con. Prot.	V
PARTICIPATION						
% Member or participant in community organizations[1]	(6,490)	47	52	66	72	.20***
% Member /affiliated with community organizations[2]	(866)	50	56	77	69	.21***
VOLUNTEERING						
% Volunteer in last year[1]	(6,491)	29	38	57	58	.24***
% Doing any voluntary work[2]	(866)	46	53	74	64	.21***
Average (Mean) Number of hours volunteered per year by Volunteers[1]	(2,159)	191	158	162	205	N/a
Average (Median) Number of hours volunteered per year by Volunteers[1]	(2,159)	72	70	96	113	N/a
LEADERSHIP						
% Ever served on a committee[2]	(866)	36	38	57	51	.18***

[1]NSVGP 1997   [2]Reid 1996   ***P < .001   **P < .01   *P < .05

say they like to work on community projects and the over 90% who say doing so is a good thing. Religiosity's impact on participation is substantial. The 62% or 67% (depending on the survey) participation rate of the Very Committed is almost double the 34–35% rate of the Non Religious. In table 5.3 we see once again that Seekers are much more like the Non Religious than the Very Committed, while the Less Committed are noticeably less community minded than the Very Committed. In both surveys, Catholics, most notably in Quebec, are less communally active than Protestants, though not by a large margin. Between Conservative and Mainline Protestants there is no clear difference or pattern.

When it comes to volunteering or giving unpaid labour to any community organization, the national rate of 31% in the NSVGP is noticeably less than the 42% rate from the 1996 Reid survey. The questions are slightly different,[8] but I can think of no plausible reason for the discrepancy other than the unpredictable fluctuations of samples even when they are well designed. I am inclined to put slightly greater faith in the NSVGP, which has a larger sample, was specifically designed to study volunteering in detail, and was conducted by the methodologically sophisticated staff at Statistics Canada. Despite their different numbers, the two surveys are in clear agreement that volunteering is strongly affected by religiosity. Using the lower numbers of the NSVGP, volunteering is much more common for the Very Committed (47%) than the Non Religious (25%). Once again, Seekers have volunteering rates very similar to those of the Non Religious. Volunteering is also much less widely practised by Catholics (35%) than by Protestants (58%). Very similar conclusions pointing once more to the pre-eminent role of the Very Committed, which I see no point in elucidating, may be drawn on the related question of whether Canadians have ever served on the committee of a community organization.

Particularly instructive is the additional NSVGP question asking volunteers how many hours they spent volunteering on a weekly and monthly basis in each of the organizations in which they were involved over the last year. From these replies the NSVGP allows us to calculate the mean and median number of hours in a year that volunteers spend. The results are listed in table 5.3. For those not versed in statistical matters, the mean is calculated by dividing the total number of all hours volunteered by the number of volunteers. The mean is what is normally understood by the concept of average. The median, on the other hand, is the midpoint in the distribution from highest to lowest of the hours volunteered. Nationally, the "typical" Canadian volunteer at the 50% midpoint of hours volunteered spent 70 hours annually; this is the median. In marked contrast, the national mean for volunteers is 153 hours. The mean is so much higher than the median because the number of hours volunteered is a highly skewed distribution. This simply means that a small number of volunteers do far more volunteering than everyone else. In fact only the top 29% of volunteers equal or better the mean number of 153 hours of volunteering. With highly skewed distributions of this sort, the median gives us a much better sense of the typical or average volunteer.

Some may doubt the veracity of the minuscule 0.3% of volunteers who say they spend over 2,000 hours a year volunteering, as this is the equivalent of a full-time, 40-hour-a-week job with only a two-week annual holiday. I should add that only 1% of all volunteers claim to volunteer more than 1,200 hours a year, or 24 hours a week. I lack any conclusive proof, but all the religious bodies and voluntary agencies I have consulted tell me there are a small number of super volunteers who definitely spend 25 or more hours a week volunteering. A very few, who are often retirees, spend far more time in their volunteer activities than most of us do working. Among the 1% top elite, 53% are Very Committed. If they are excluded from our calculations, the national mean for volunteers falls from 153 hours to 135 hours, but the median drops only fractionally from 70 hours to 67 hours.

Using the more revealing median as our measure of hours annually spent by volunteers, we see even more starkly the impact of religiosity. The 104 median hours spent by Very Committed volunteers is 86% higher than the 56-hour annual median of the Non Religious. If the mean is our guide, then the same differential is reduced to 54%, though this is still a striking difference. As we have so often seen before, the median numbers of hours volunteered by the Less Committed (67) and Seekers (56) are much more like the median of the Non Religious than the Very Committed. Among the three major religious families, Conservative Protestant volunteers expend far more hours than anyone else (113 hours). In between are Mainline Protestant volunteers with a median of 96 hours, who are trailed considerably by Catholic volunteers (71). We also need to remember that substantially fewer Catholics volunteer (35%) than do Protestants (58%). Overall, there is a compounding or reinforcing effect that should not be missed. The Very Committed are much more likely than other Canadians to volunteer and those who do so spend much more time at it. The result, charted in table 5.3, is that the 19% of Canadians who are Very Committed are responsible for 38% of all hours volunteered in Canada. They are in a class by themselves.

Volunteering

Here I want to move beyond the basic pattern of volunteering just described to a more detailed analysis of how religiosity mixes with regional, class, and other social differences to influence volunteering patterns. I focus on volunteering becomes it seems to me to be one of the two best indicators we have of our civility, by which I mean our willingness to give of ourselves to the communities in which we reside. The other indicator, which I take up later, is the amount of money we give to charities.

As Canadians move from young adulthood into their forties, volunteering becomes more widely practised, though only a substantial minority of early boomers (37%) do so (see table 5.5). Thereafter, volunteering rates fall to a 23% rate for retirees. There is also a more marked and consistent pattern of volunteers devoting more time to volunteering as they age, reaching their peak levels in their retirement years (see table 5.6). Differences by age are therefore modest, but the

Table 5.5
Percent volunteer by religiosity and age (1997 NSVGP)

	Generation X (18–31)	Late Boomer (32–41)	Early Boomers (42–51)	Pre Boomer (52–64)	Pre Boomer (65 plus)
Very Commited	50	55	57	46	35
Less Commited	34	41	46	34	21
Seekers	26	33	33	25	15
Non Relig.	26	28	28	21	16
Total	29	34	37	31	23
(N)	(3,840)	(4,325)	(3,287)	(2,774)	(2,882)
Tau-c	.12***	.18***	.23***	.22***	.18 ***

***P < .001   **P < .01   *P < .05

Table 5.6
Median number of hours annually volunteered by religiosity and age of volunteers (1997 NSVGP)

	Generation X (18–31)	Late Boomers (32–41)	Early Boomers (42–51)	Pre Boomers (52–64)	Pre-Boomers (65 plus)
Very Commited	101	106	113	98	91
Less Commited	59	61	80	74	71
Seekers	51	58	55	65	53
Non Relig.	49	49	70	69	81
Total	57	65	78	79	80
(N)	(2,210)	(2,877)	(2,147)	(1,705)	(1,480)

Very Committed at every age level have volunteering rates that are roughly double those of the Non Religious. Moreover, the difference in volunteering rates between the Very Committed and the Non Religious actually grows from a 92% differential among Generation X to a 119% difference among pre-boomers. Among volunteers in every age group, it is the Very Committed who devote more hours than anyone else to volunteering, though in this case the differential is most marked among young adults (106%) and shrinks to a far more modest 12% difference among retirees. Over the life cycle, religiosity's already large influence on volunteering rates grows ever more important, but it has a diminishing impact as the years go by on the hours volunteers put in.

Tables 5.7 and 5.8 allow us to explore the combined impact of gender and participation in the labour force on volunteering. The analysis is here confined to those aged 25 to 60 in order to sharpen the impact of labour force participation by excluding the many young who are still students and those in their retirement years. Five

Table 5.7
Percent volunteer by religiosity, sex, and whether in labour force among Canadians
25–60 (1997 NSVGP)

	In Labour Force		Not in Labour Force	
	Female	Male	Female	Male
Very Commited	58	54	47	42
Less Commited	44	37	37	39
Seekers	34	29	26	23
Non Relig.	31	24	25	20
Total	38	31	32	27
(N)	(4,928)	(4,621)	(1,668)	(590)
Tau-c	.19***	.19***	.19***	.18***

***P < .001   **P < .01   *P < .05

Table 5.8
Median number of hours annually volunteered by religiosity, sex, and whether
in labour force among volunteers 25–60 (1997 NSVGP)

	In Labour Force		Not in Labour Force	
	Female	Male	Female	Male
Very Committed	82	109	149	146
Less Commited	48	84	59	68
Seekers	45	77	56	76
Non Relig.	54	59	56	123
Total	56	80	76	100
(N)	(3,398)	(2,829)	(1,032)	(320)

conclusions stand out for me; two of them I find surprising. First, women in and outside the labour force[9] are more likely than men in both sets of circumstances to volunteer, though the differences are by no means large. Second, and more surprisingly, women in the labour force are more likely to volunteer (38%) than are women outside it (32%). These data undermine any notion that volunteering has been adversely affected by the mass entry of women into the labour force. Third, and least surprising, the Very Committed of both sexes inside and outside the labour force are more likely to volunteer than are their Non Religious counterparts. Fourth, both male and female volunteers in the labour force spend less time volunteering than do those outside the labour force. This predictable difference is of roughly the same magnitude for both males and females. Lastly, males inside and outside the labour force who volunteer spend more hours at it than

Table 5.9
Percent volunteer by religiosity and whether have children age 1–18 (1997 NSVGP)

	None	*1*	*2 or more*
Very Commited	42	54	67
Less Commited	31	41	47
Seekers	25	31	35
Non Relig.	23	28	32
Total	28	35	42
(N)	(11,124)	(3,293)	(2,641)
Tau-c	.15***	.18***	.25***

***P < .001   **P < .01   *P < .05

Table 5.10
Median number of hours annually volunteered by religiosity and number of children age 0–18 among volunteers (1997 NSVGP)

	None	*1*	*2 or more*
Very Commited	103	95	118
Less Commited	67	72	66
Seekers	55	60	60
Non Relig.	58	55	53
Total	68	70	74
(N)	(6,402)	(2,124)	(1,893)

do females. Even male volunteers in the labour force volunteer as many hours as do female volunteers outside the labour force. I can think of no convincing reason for this last set of differences, but there they are. Differences by sex and labour force status have minor and sometimes surprising consequences.

Anyone who has had children in Guides, sports programs, and the like will be less than surprised to learn from table 5.9 that volunteering is linked to having children. Volunteering rates rise from a 28% level for those without children to 35% for those with one child and 42% with two or more. Less predictable is the same table's finding that the difference between the Very Committed and Seekers (measured by Tau-c) is greatest for those with two or more children. My initial guess was that parental obligations would pressure Canadians of all levels of religiousness into volunteering and therefore diminish religiosity's impact. I was wrong. In fact, the volunteering rate of the Very Committed is 82% higher than the Non Religious rate for those without children and 109% higher for those with two or more children. In a similar vein, we see in table 5.10 that the median number of hours put in by Non Religious volunteers actually declines with having children, whereas the Very Committed put in more time when they have two or more children. The obvious qualifier that has to be made is that having children does not increase the hours the Very Committed spend volunteering as much as it does their volunteering rate. In short, the presence of children in a household increases the volunteering rates of Canadians, but religiosity's impact is substantial for those with and without children and is actually greatest for those with two or more children.

Differences by income and education level, or what we might more broadly define as class differences are charted in tables 5.11 to 5.14. On both these dimensions of inequality, volunteering is more common among Canadians who are more privileged. The differences are considerable. The volunteering rate doubles from 21% among the bottom 24% of Canadians with annual family incomes below $20,000 to a 44% rate among the top 15% of Canadians with incomes of $80,000 or more. Similarly, the 18% volunteering rate among those with less than high school rises to 48% for those with a university education. Social class has a major impact on volunteering.

It is equally evident that the Very Committed at every educational and income level are most likely to volunteer and the Non Religious are least likely to do so. The gap between the volunteering rates of the Very Committed and the Non Religious are greatest in what might be loosely described as the lower-middle class, by which I mean those whose education ended with a high school diploma or those with family incomes of $20,000 to $39,999 a year. Thereafter the differential between the Very Committed and the Non Religious shrinks, but there is still a striking 66% margin of difference between the volunteering rates of the Very Committed and Non Religious with a university education. For those with incomes over $80,000 a year, there is an even more impressive 77% differential. Family income and educational attainment clearly affect volunteering habits, but religious involvement has its own independent impact. It follows that the higher volunteering rates of the Very Committed cannot be explained away as being caused by education and economic forces, since the Very Committed volunteer much more frequently than other Canadians at all educational and income levels.

When it comes to the number of hours volunteered, I would draw four conclusions from tables 5.13 and 5.14. The first and most predictable is that Very Committed volunteers at all income and

Table 5.11
Percent volunteer by religiosity and family income (1997 NSVGP)

	<$20,000	$20,000– 39,999	$40,000– 59,999	$60,000– 79,999	$80,000 plus
Very Commited	33	44	55	51	64
Less Commited	23	33	34	43	52
Seekers	17	25	28	32	41
Non Relig.	17	20	28	30	36
Total	21	29	33	36	44
(N)	(4,266)	(4,829)	(3,802)	(2,185)	(1,976)
Tau-c	.12***	.19***	.17***	.16***	.21***

***P < .001   **P < .01   *P < .05

Table 5.12
Median number of hours annually volunteered by religiosity and family income
among volunteers (1997 NSVGP)

	<$20,000	$20,000– 39,999	$40,000– 59,999	$60,000– 79,999	$80,000 plus
Very Commited	80	103	107	118	99
Less Commited	55	63	65	60	88
Seekers	56	67	60	55	50
Non Relig.	68	43	56	60	64
Total	67	68	70	70	71
(N)	(2,077)	(2,856)	(2,495)	(1,502)	(1,489)

educational levels spend much more time volunteering than do the
Non Religious. Among volunteers with a university education, for
instance, the Very Committed devote 129 hours a year; the Non Religious spend a much lower 66 hours a year. Second, Very Committed
volunteers put in more hours as their incomes rise, peaking at 118
hours a year in the second highest income bracket of $60,000 to
$79,999 and then falling to 99 hours in the top bracket. In contrast,
rising incomes are linked to a slight decline in the number of hours
Non Religious volunteers spend. Third, Non Religious volunteers do
put in more hours with higher levels of education, but the increase
is very modest and is much less than the comparable increase by the
Very Committed with higher educational attainment. In other words,
with the exception of the very richest of Canadians, growing affluence and higher education prompt Very Committed volunteers to
give more back to their communities, but this dynamic does not exist
among the Non Religious. This generalization must, of course, be

Table 5.13
Percent volunteer by religiosity and education (1997 NSVGP)

	Less than High School	Completed High School	Post Secondary[1]	University[1]
Very Commited	28	51	54	66
Less Commited	20	34	40	49
Seekers	17	26	29	45
Non Relig.	12	22	28	40
Total	18	30	35	48
(N)	(4,327)	(3,034)	(6,604)	(3,093)
Tau-c	.12***	.20***	.18***	.20***

[1]Some or completed   ***$P < .001$ **$P < .01$ *$P < .05$

Table 5.14
Median number of hours annually volunteered by religiosity and education among volunteers (1997 NSVGP)

	Less than High School	Completed High School	Post Secondary[1]	University[1]
Very Commited	60	123	98	129
Less Commited	55	57	67	87
Seekers	54	48	58	65
Non Relig.	54	46	59	66
Total	55	60	70	84
(N)	(1,917)	(1,823)	(4,276)	(2,404)

[1]Some or completed

qualified by my earlier observation that the Non Religious, like the Very Committed, are more likely to volunteer as their income rises. Fourth, the impact of class on the volunteering patterns of Seekers is much closer to that of the Non Religious than of the Very Committed. Finally, as we have just seen with the percentage who volunteer, the gap between Very Committed and Non Religious volunteers in the hours they put in is greatest in the lower middle class and smallest among the least economically privileged and least educated. In short, with few exceptions, religiosity has a major and compounding impact on the volunteering habits of Canadians that extends across classes and educational levels.

Like so many other aspects of Canadian life, there are marked regional differences in Canadian volunteering patterns. In table 5.15 we can see that Quebec stands out as the region with by far the smallest corps of volunteers (22%). That distinction is party caused

Table 5.15
Percent volunteer by religiosity and region (1997 NSVGP)

	Atlantic	Quebec	Ontario	Man./Sask.	Alberta	B.C.
Very Commited	54	32	46	63	61	54
Less Commited	41	28	33	48	48	35
Seekers	28	17	29	34	39	30
Non Relig.	25	21	26	36	29	27
Total	36	22	32	43	40	32
(N)	(3,429)	(3,074)	(5,158)	(2,557)	(1,370)	(1,470)
V	.25 ***	.13***	.16***	.24***	.24***	.19***

***P < .001   **P < .01   *P < .05

by Quebec having fewer Very Committed than any other Canadian region (table 2.21). It is then compounded by the overwhelmingly Catholic face of the Committed in Quebec, since we have just seen (table 5.14) that Catholics volunteer much less frequently than do Protestants. However, religious forces are not the only ones at play. There is a distinctively Quebec-wide influence here that ensures that Quebecers of all religious inclinations, including Seekers and the Non Religious, have the lowest volunteering rates in Canada.

At the other end of the spectrum, volunteering is most widely practised in Manitoba and Saskatchewan (43%), closely followed by Alberta (40%). Again religious considerations help to explain the pattern, since Manitoba and Saskatchewan have very large numbers of Committed, very low percentages of Non Religious, and comparatively fewer Catholics (tables 2.21 and 2.22). Alberta has fewer Very Committed, but it has even fewer Catholics and hence more Protestants, who volunteer so much more frequently than Catholics do. Of course, as in Quebec, religion alone does not explain the popularity of volunteering in the Prairies, since the Less Committed, Seekers, and Non Religious all have higher volunteering rates than their counterparts in central and eastern Canada. Analysis along these lines might also be applied to the other Canadian regions, but others must take up the endeavour, as it leads me too far from my central concerns.

Table 5.15 demonstrates the recurring refrain that the Very Committed in every region are much more likely to volunteer than are the Non Religious. The usual corollary that the Non Religious volunteer less frequently than anyone else applies to three of Canada's five regions. However, that generalization does not hold in Quebec and Manitoba/Saskatchewan, where Seekers have even lower volunteering

Table 5.16
Median number of hours annually volunteered by religiosity and region among
volunteers (1997 NSVGP)

	Atlantic	Quebec	Ontario	Man./Sask.	Alberta	B.C.
Very Commited	104	96	90	104	121	104
Less Commited	52	66	65	80	56	67
Seekers	52	52	54	54	64	56
Non Relig.	60	49	56	46	59	56
Total	69	60	67	70	75	70
(N)	(2,146)	(1,479)	(3,168)	(1,777)	(926)	(923)

rates than the Non Religious, though the differences are quite small.
Only in Quebec is the overall impact of religiosity, measured by Tau-c,
markedly lower than anywhere else. Religiosity's diminished impact
in Quebec stems from the distinctively low rate of volunteering
among its Very Committed (32%) who are overwhelmingly Catholic,
since – as we have just noted above – Catholics have much lower
volunteering rates than do Protestants.

As for the hours put in by volunteers, table 5.16 makes it clear that
the Very Committed in every region devote far more hours to volunteering than do anyone else. Quebec again stands out for having the
lowest activity level among it volunteers. The major explanation
seems to be the comparatively low number of hours put in by its
Non Religious, since they are so numerous and Quebec's Very Committed volunteers put in almost as many hours as the Very Committed elsewhere in Canada. At the other end of the spectrum, Alberta's
volunteers are more active (75 hours) than are volunteers in any other
part of Canada. This is partly explained by their high proportion of
Conservative Protestants, but it is by no means the whole story since
Alberta's Seekers and Non Religious volunteers spend more time
volunteering than their equivalents in all other regions. None of the
other regional differences are particularly striking. Quebec is indisputably our most distinct region.

I could look at other social forces that might shape volunteering to
see how they interact with religiosity, but I have already examined
the major ones. Further analysis would not be very fruitful. Table 5.17
allows me to take an additional step by comparing the relative impact
of religiosity and other social forces on volunteering. To make the
assessment as complete as possible I have included three additional
factors that do not warrant separate consideration. Community size

Table 5.17
Logistic regression of volunteering on its social causes (1997 NSVGP)

	Odds Ratio
Religiosity	2.157***
Education	2.003***
Income	1.615***
Having Children (0-2+)	1.393***
Time Reside in Community	1.260***
Sex	1.187***
Employed or not	1.170***
Age	1.045***
Married (or not)	0.960***
Community Size	0.657***

Chi-square = 1441.455   DF = 10   ***P<.001

has a predictable but modest impact, with volunteering rates rising from 27% in our biggest cities to 36% in rural areas. Similarly, Canadians who have resided in their community for more than ten years are a bit more likely to volunteer (33%) than are those who have been in their communities for a year or less (27%). Marital status has an equally minor impact; the volunteering rate for married Canadians (33%) is only marginally higher than the 27% rate for the unmarried. For technical reasons, I cannot do regression analysis here but I can employ the similar statistical technique of logistic regression[10] which assesses the influence of each of the social forces I have examined while taking into account the impact of all others. I would stress the following conclusions. First, religiosity, measured by the size of its odds ratio, has the single largest impact on the likelihood that Canadians will volunteer. Second, education's role in fostering volunteering ranks so closely behind religiosity that the two might be regarded as almost equally powerful influences. Third, income is the next most powerful factor affecting the likelihood of volunteering, but income's impact is noticeably less than either religiosity or education. Fourth, another rung below in importance might be clustered a variety of forces ranging from the number of children we have to the amount of time we have resided in our communities. All other social forces have even less impact on volunteering rates. Religiousness or its lack is one of the principal influences on volunteering in Canada.

Tables 5.18 and 5.19 test the cynic's view that the higher volunteering rates of the Very Committed are largely directed inward, serving themselves or those close to them, and therefore doing little for the

Table 5.18
Volunteering by religiosity and type of volunteer organization (NSVGP 1997)

	N	Very Commited	Less Commited	Seeker	Non Relig.	Total	Tau-c
RELIGIOUS ORGANIZATIONS							
% Volunteered in religious bodies last year	(17,044)	26	8	1	0	7	.18***
% of volunteers volunteering in religious organizations	(10,419)	55	23	5	2	21	.47***
Mean hours volunteered per year by volunteers to religious bodies	(2,442)	153	70	36	41	131	N/a
Median hours volunteered per year by volunteers to religious bodies	(2,442)	76	36	16	21	60	N/a
% Of all hours volunteered in religious agencies	(2,442)	89	8	2	1	100	N/a
SECULAR ORGANIZATIONS							
% Volunteered in secular bodies last year	(17,044)	35	32	27	25	28	.08***
% Of volunteers volunteering in secular agencies	(10,419)	73	91	98	99	90	−.21***
Mean hours volunteered per year by volunteers in secular bodies	(9,300)	158	123	135	131	137	N/a
Median hours volunteered per year by volunteers in secular bodies	(9,300)	64	61	58	56	60	N/a
% Of all hours volunteered in secular agencies	(9,300)	27	13	27	33	100	N/a

***P < .001   **P < .01   *P < .05

Table 5.19
Volunteering by religion and type of voluntary organization among the committed
(NSVGP 1997)

	N	RC Quebec	RC RoC	Main. Prot.	Con. Prot.	V
Religious organizations						
% Volunteered in religious bodies last year	(6,485)	3	11	33	39	.35***
% of volunteers volunteering in religious organizations	(4,724)	9	29	57	66	.41***
Mean hours volunteered per year by volunteers to religious bodies	(4,724)	107	104	103	174	N/a
Median hours volunteered per year by volunteers to religious bodies	(4,724)	55	44	53	104	N/a
Secular organizations						
% Volunteered in secular bodies last year	(6,485)	28	34	44	38	.12***
% of volunteers volunteering in secular agencies	(4,724)	95	88	76	65	.27***
Mean hours volunteered per year by volunteers in secular bodies	(4,724)	188	141	131	136	N/a
Median hours volunteered per year by volunteers in secular bodies	(4,724)	67	62	71	52	N/a

***$P < .001$ **$P < .01$ *$P < .05$

common good. The NSVGP asked all respondents to identify the particular agencies, organizations, and groups in which they volunteered. Statistics Canada coded these responses into a 12-category international classification of non-profit organizations. Remember that only 31% volunteer; far fewer do so in any of the 12 types. Barring the immediately following paragraph, I have therefore collapsed these many small categories into a twofold distinction between religious and non-religious agencies to produce cell sizes of a sufficient size for statistically reliable estimates. Since quite a few volunteers are involved in more than one type of organization, readers should bear in mind that the sum in percentages of participants in religious and non-religious agencies is greater than the percentage for all voluntary organizations, which was recorded earlier in tables 5.3 and 5.4. The methodologically minded might also care to consult this footnote.[11]

More Canadians volunteer in cultural and recreational (especially sports) organizations than in any other (10%). Social services (for children, youth, families, the handicapped, the elderly, the poor, refugees, the homeless, etc.) attract the next largest segment of Canadians (9%). Organizations dealing with education and health are in turn supported by 6% and 5% of Canadians over age 18. A much smaller 2% of Canadians devote themselves to advocacy and political organizations, while only 1% volunteer in environmental activities and organizations with international concerns. Summing them all up, 28% of Canadians volunteer in one or more secular, non-religious organizations. Religious bodies, by contrast, draw upon a much more modest 7% of Canadians as volunteers. Put somewhat differently, Canadians in 1997 contributed 189 million hours of volunteering to religious agencies and 859 million hours to secular bodies.

It cannot come as much of a surprise to learn from table 5.18 that only 0.4% of the Non Religious and 2% of the volunteers in their ranks volunteer in religious bodies. Seniors clubs, food banks, and the like run by religious bodies occasionally, but only very occasionally, are supported by the voluntary labour of the Non Religious. It may come as more of a surprise that more of the Very Committed volunteer in secular bodies (35%) than they do in religious ones (26%). In fact, substantially more Very Committed volunteers are involved in secular agencies (73%) than they are in religious ones (55%). Even more telling are the figures indicating that volunteering in secular bodies is more widely practised by the Very Committed (35%) than by Seekers (27%) and the Non Religious (25%). Such figures surely refute the cynical assumption that the Very Committed only – or even mainly – serve their own.

Because the number of hours put in by volunteers is so badly skewed by a small number of hyperactive volunteers, I include both the mean and the median measures of the general tendency, described earlier for table 5.3. Broken down by religiosity, both measures tell a similar tale, though the median is the more revealing indicator. It is surely predictable that the median number of hours volunteers expend in religious bodies is much higher for the Very Committed (76) than the Less Committed (36), Seekers (16) and the Non Religious (21). Since hardly any Seekers or Non Religious are religious volunteers, the Committed are responsible for 97% of the 189 million hours volunteered in religious bodies. In the much larger secular arena, the median number of hours donated by Very Committed volunteers (64) is 18% higher than the 56 hours contributed by Non Religious volunteers. Again we must remember that there is a compounding effect at play here in that fewer Seekers and Non

Religious do any volunteering at all. The net result is that the Committed, who are 32% of all Canadians, are responsible for 40% of the 859 million hours volunteered in secular agencies. In contrast, the 39% of Canadians who are Non Religious account for 33% of all secular volunteering hours. Even in the secular world, the Committed more than pull their weight. The Non Religious fail to do so.

Table 5.19 reveals some striking differences between the major religious families. The Conservative Protestant tradition of high religious commitment is reflected in their 39% rate of volunteering in religious bodies, which is higher than the 33% rate of Mainline Protestants and all others who are Committed. The religious intensity of Conservative Protestants is further revealed in the median of 104 hours their volunteers devote to religious bodies, which is almost double the 53 hours put in by their Mainline Protestant counterparts. On the secular side, the Mainline Protestant tradition of social activism can be seen in their 44% rate of secular volunteering, which is greater than the 38% rate for Conservative Protestants, though not by a wide margin. The median of 71 hours that Mainline Protestant volunteers devote to secular agencies is also higher than any other sector of the Committed, including the Conservative Protestant volunteers who contribute a median of 52 hours a year. Mainline Protestants are clearly the leaders in the secular world. However, it is worth noting that the numbers we have just reviewed undermine stereotypes of Conservative Protestant disengagement from the secular world, since Conservative Protestants are actually more likely to volunteer in secular endeavours (38%) than are either Catholics (31%) or the Non Religious (25%).

On the Catholic side, what stands out is the incredibly low level of volunteering that even the Committed devote to their church. A tiny 3% of the Committed in Quebec volunteer their unpaid labour to their church. Catholic volunteering is almost four times as common in the rest of Canada, but this 11% who do are still volunteering at less than a third the rate of that occurring in Protestant churches. By this measure, the old tradition of clerical leadership and lay passivity is still deeply rooted in Canadian Catholicism. On the secular side, the 31% rate of volunteering for Catholics as a whole is lower than that of either Mainline Protestants (44%) or Conservative Protestants (38%), but the difference here is not of the same magnitude that we have just seen for religious volunteering. Catholics in Quebec are notably less involved in secular volunteering (28%) than Catholics in the rest of Canada (34%), who are within spitting distance of the Conservative Protestant rate. Nevertheless Catholics inside and outside Quebec both have secular volunteering rates that exceed those of the Non Religious, though Quebec Catholics do so only barely. Catholic volunteers in secular organizations across Canada also put in more hours than do either the Conservative Protestants or the Non Religious. Catholics concerned about their church are unlikely to derive much solace from these findings, but the NSVGP makes it clear that the Catholic reluctance to serve their church does not extend to the wider communities in which they reside. In this secular realm, Catholics volunteer at a rate and with an intensity that is roughly equally to the Canadian average and above that of the Non Religious.

We should not lose sight of the fact that the Very Committed are more likely to volunteer in secular organizations (35%) than in a religious one (26%). However, I here want to provide some sense of what is involved in volunteering at the local congregational level. The following is based on interview material I gathered while preparing a report on religion and volunteering for Volunteer Canada,[12] which I will also draw upon in the next segment on charitable giving. This involved visits to 24 local congregations and charitable agencies that represent nine different faith communities across the country. I cannot summarize this material in quantitative form, but there are three general findings that I would stress.

The first is that the majority of volunteers devote their time to either administrative activities or to specifically religious or ritual purposes. In the former category we can place all fund-raising efforts, financial management, repairs and physical maintenance, running of committees, and the general coordination of busy people with too many commitments. On the more specifically religious side are such matters as the staffing and implementing of an effective system of religious instruction, the preparing of the sanctuary, music, and the choir for services, and the incorporation of as many members as possible in entertaining and challenging services. All these varied activities are essential to the continued survival of the congregation and its religious environment, which, in turn, produce and sustain the Very Committed, who, the survey data tell us, volunteer so much more than other Canadians. Far from being irrelevant or extraneous, these everyday administrative and religious activities are the foundation upon which is built the voluntary and charitable outreach of the Very Committed.

The second point is that many of the congregations I visited are involved in various kinds of outreach programs that involve volunteers and are designed to reach out to the needy, the lonely, or the broken. The most common activity is the regular gathering of foodstuffs for local food banks, to which many local congregations across Canada are attached as formal members. Faith communities are a key element in this food bank network. A much smaller number of congregations use the kitchens in their church halls to prepare a weekly hot meal for the homeless or needy. In Scarborough, Ontario, for instance, a 200-family United Church congregation in 1997 distributed a hot meal once a week to about 60 refugees on social assistance, who were then housed in motels bordering this middle-class suburb. Another six local congregations of different denominations ran a similar program on a different night of the week, which they dubbed a "Caring Alliance." Many more congregations I encountered organize a team of volunteers who commit themselves to work a shift a week for a month or some longer period in one of the inner-city missions for the homeless. In Regina, for instance, the Roman Catholic Marion Centre produced about 150 hot lunches a day to a largely male clientele suffering from addictions and mental illness. Approximately 15 to 20 volunteers were relied on each day to prepare and serve the food. Periodically there were shortages, but I was told, "All we need to do is put out the word through the church bulletins. People are really anxious to volunteer and help." Less dramatically and more commonly, many congregations have organized groups of volunteers who visit elderly shut-ins or those in long-term care facilities. Other instances of outreach to the elderly, to immigrants, and to the needy could by cited, but those I have mentioned are the most common.

The last general point I want to stress is that those attending the major weekly service are regularly asked during a service to give to a charity, to volunteer, or to provide general support for a host of benevolent activities both inside and outside their particular faith group. Occasionally, when a member of the local congregation is actively involved, he or she will use five to ten minutes of the service to inform the congregation of what is being done and to seek support. At times, a display is set up in the foyer to the sanctuary, so that all attending may see the display when they enter or leave the service. Incidents of this sort occur infrequently, as clergy fear they would soon be inundated with requests that would disrupt the spiritual and worship purposes that underlie the weekly service. However, almost all congregations distribute weekly bulletins at their services, where the clergy are happy to include brief announcements and appeals from voluntary and charitable organizations. No doubt it is the regular encounter by the religiously active with appeals of this sort that helps to explain, at least in part, their distinctively high rates of volunteering.

One last theme that deserves attention is the question of motive, of why Canadians volunteer. The NSVGP asked those who volunteered whether they agreed or disagreed with seven possible reasons for volunteering. In analyzing the results, we must bear in mind that volunteers were allowed to choose as many of the motives as they wished. Volunteers were not required to choose only one motive or put them in a priority list. The results, enumerated in table 5.20, suggest four general conclusions.

First, 96% of volunteers agreed that they volunteer because it is "a cause in which you personally agree." With only slightly less unanimity, about 78% of volunteers say they volunteer because it gives them an opportunity to use their skills and experiences. On both these dimensions, the Committed, Seekers, and Non Religious do not differ in any noticeable or meaningful way. Second, at the other end of the spectrum, the two motives volunteers are least likely to admit to are that they volunteer because their friends do (24%) and because it improves their job opportunities (20%). Again, there is no difference between my religious categories in the impact of friends on their decision to volunteer, though the Very Committed (13%) are less likely than everyone else (24%) to say that improved job opportunities cause them to volunteer. The most we can conclude here is that the Very Committed are a little less likely to cite personal interest as a reason for their volunteering.

Third, between the highs and lows of the spectrum are the 68% who volunteered because they or someone they know has been personally affected by the cause the organization supports. There are also the 54% who do so in order to explore their own strengths. For the latter motive, religious involvement makes no appreciable difference, while slightly more of the Very Committed say they have been personally affected by the cause (72%) than do the inactive (63%). This small difference may be because the religious are more socially connected through their congregations than are the religiously inactive, but this speculation must be tempered by the small size of the difference and the lack of additional evidence.

Last and most important we find that the desire "to fulfil religious obligations or beliefs" motivates 65% of Very Committed volunteers and only 6% of the Non Religious. Far fewer of the Less Committed

Table 5.20
Motives for volunteering by religiosity among volunteers (NSVGP 1997)

	N	Very Commited	Less Commited	Seeker	Non Relig.	Total	Tau-c
Cause in which you believe	(10,421)	98	97	97	94	96	.03***
Use skills & experiences	(10,425)	79	78	78	77	78	.02
Personally effected by the cause	(10,408)	72	70	68	63	68	.08***
Explore own strengths	(10,405)	55	54	55	50	54	.05*
Fulfil religious obligations/beliefs	(10,423)	65	35	15	6	29	.52***
Friends volunteer	(10,426)	24	24	24	25	24	.01
Improve job opportunities	(10,427)	13	19	22	24	20	.10***

***P < .001   **P < .01   *P < .05

(35%) and Seekers (15%) say that religion prompted their volunteering. In other words, only religious considerations differentiate in a major way the Very Committed from other Canadians in the motivations that drive them to volunteer. I cannot here delve into the specific religious beliefs and obligations of Canada's many faith groups, but I did find a widespread conviction among those with whom I talked that religious faith calls for service to others. The following quote from a Mennonite Prairie pastor nicely conveys the religious motivations, or at least an idealized version of them, that prompt a spirit of volunteering: "We try to teach a philosophy of service and encourage service and give opportunities for service to the membership of the congregation. The expectation is that all members of the congregation will serve one way or another. The ministries happen through volunteers." That philosophy is not exclusively Christian or religious in character, but the NSVGP makes it abundantly clear that the Very Committed are much more likely than other Canadians to implement this ethic of service in their daily lives.

GIVING TO CHARITY

The great majority of Canadians (80%) say they have made a financial contribution over the last year to one or more charities or non-profit organizations. In table 5.21 we see that charitable giving is more widely practised by the Very Committed (91%) than it is by the Non Religious

Table 5.21
Charitable giving by religiosity (NSVGP 1997)

	N	Very Commited	Less Commited	Seeker	Non Relig.	Total	Tau-c
% Made charitable donation over the last year	(17,058)	91	88	83	70	80	.18***
Mean donation in dollars per donor	(14,842)	570	246	149	125	247	N/a
Mean donation in dollars by all Canadians	(17,058)	518	215	123	89	197	N/a
Median donation in dollars per donor	(14,842)	210	120	59	51	80	N/a
Median donation in dollars by all Canadians	(17,058)	186	97	40	22	50	N/a
% Of all money donated	(17,058)	51	14	18	18	100	N/a

***P < .001   **P < .01   *P < .05

(70%). The average or mean contribution by Very Committed donors ($570) is also a hefty three and a half times larger (356%) than the average contribution of Non Religious donors ($120). Even more revealing is the third line in the same table that calculates the mean contribution by all Canadians and therefore takes account of those who give nothing at all. By this standard, the mean donation of the Very Committed ($518) is almost five times (482%) higher than the $89 average contribution by the Non Religious. These are surely striking differences.

Charitable giving has a highly skewed distribution, which means in this case that that only 21% of Canadians actually give more than the national mean of $197. As I argued in the previous section, the median under these circumstances is the more revealing indicator of the "typical" donor right at the 50% mid-point between those who give least and most. For Canadians as a whole, including the 20% of us who give nothing at all, the median annual charitable donation is a much more modest $50. The median donations across all religious categories in table 5.21 are also much lower than their corresponding means. Nevertheless, the median donation for all of the Very Committed ($186) is more than eight times (830%) greater than the paltry $22 median donation by all Non Religious. The net result is that the 19% of Canadians who are Very Committed are responsible for 51% of all charitable giving. In contrast, the much larger 39% body of Non Religious Canadians generates only 18% of all charitable donations. Again, these are major differences.

Table 5.22
Charitable giving by religiosity (NSVGP 1997)

	N	RC Quebec	RC RoC	Main. Prot.	Con. Prot.	V
Whether made Charitable donation over the last year	(6,491)	92	89	93	91	.05**
Mean donation in dollars per donor	(6,159)	219	268	566	890	N/a
Mean donation in dollars by all Committed	(6,491)	201	239	526	810	N/a
Median donation in dollars per donor	(6,159)	83	155	265	345	N/a
Median donation in dollars by all Committed	(6,491)	71	135	228	266	N/a

***P < .001   **P < .01   *P < .05

Differences between the Committed in the three major Christian families are charted in table 5.22. I draw three principal conclusions. First, Conservative Protestants stand out as the superstars in charitable giving, though the magnitude of their edge depends on how we measure it. The mean donation by Conservative Protestant donors is a whopping $890, reduced, though not greatly, to a $810 mean donation by all Committed Protestants. These are much higher giving levels than their Mainline Protestant and Roman Catholic counterparts. When the median is our guide, Conservative Protestants still give more than anyone else, though the gap between them ($266) and Mainline Protestants ($225) is much reduced. Note that the median donation of all Conservative Protestants is 11 times greater than the $22 median donations by the Non Religious. Second, Mainline Protestants, no matter what standard we use, are strikingly generous charitable donors, especially when we compare them to Seekers and the Non Religious. Third, Roman Catholic giving levels lag far behind those of Protestants, no matter what measure we use. Catholics outside Quebec are almost twice as generous as Catholics in Quebec, who occupy a very distant last place within the ranks of the Committed. Nevertheless, the $71 median donation by Quebec Catholics is still notably higher than the average givings of Seekers ($40) and the Non Religious ($22).

In tables 5.23 to 5.27, I focus exclusively on median giving levels for all Canadians because it simplifies what follows. I also think it is the best single indictor of our overall willingness to give financially to others. Besides the aforementioned reasons for preferring the median over the mean, I think it is misleading to ignore those who

Table 5.23
Median annual charitable donation of all canadians by religiosity and age
(1997 NSVGP)

	Generation X (18–31)	Late Boomers (32–41)	Early Boomers (42–52)	Pre Boomers (52–64)	Pre-Boomers (65 plus)
Very Commited	91	195	238	165	193
Less Commited	52	88	110	130	110
Seekers	18	50	57	58	35
Non Relig.	8	35	38	42	23
Total	16	55	72	75	85
(N)	(3,840)	(4,325)	(3,237)	(2,774)	(2,882)

give nothing, which is what happens when we analyze giving levels of donors.

In table 5.23, charitable giving by all Canadians rises in every generation from a very modest $16 a year in Generation X to $85 a year for those in their retirement years. In every generation, the Very Committed give far more than the Non Religious. The gap is most marked among the young adults of Generation X and those in their retirement years. Among the latter, the median donation of the Very Committed ($193) is 739% higher than the $23 median donation of the Non Religious. However, the peak period for charitable giving in all four religious categories precedes the retirement years, when incomes and levels of charitable giving both fall.[13] It follows that the distinctively high giving of retired Canadians is caused by the greater generosity of the Very Committed and the higher levels of religiousness of older Canadians – and not by some tendency to give more to charity as death beckons.

For the Very Committed, it is early boomers who are their most generous donors with an average annual donation of $238. For everyone else, it is the subsequent pre-boomer, pre-retirement generation who are most generous. Though charitable giving diminishes in all religious categories as Canadians enter their retirement years, the decline from their peak giving years is much less pronounced for the Very Committed (19%) than it is for the Seekers (40%) and the Non Religious (45%).[14] Not only do the Very Committed give more at every stage in the life cycle, but they are also less influenced by the fluctuations in charitable giving that are associated with aging for other Canadians. In and of itself, high religious commitment makes a big difference.

Table 5.24 gives us some sense of how employment status and differences by sex or gender affect charitable giving. Overall, women

Table 5.24
Median annual charitable donation by religiosity, sex, and employment status*
age 25–60 (1997 NSVGP)

	Employed		Not Employed	
	Female	Male	Female	Male
Very Committed	219	225	155	100
Less Committed	120	85	83	70
Seekers	60	52	25	15
Non Religious	48	31	10	0
All Canadians	75	55	40	15
(N)	(4,928)	(4,621)	(1,668)	(590)

*Employed includes full-time and part-time; not employed are all others

give more to charity ($55) than do men ($41). This generalization holds for men and women who are employed and for those who are not, though the difference is more marked outside the labour force. Among the employed (full-time and part-time), the greater generosity of women is all the more remarkable because their median annual income (as recorded by the NSVGP) of $20,323 is a third less than the male income of $30,614. Only among the Very Committed who work do males give more than females, though the greater giving of these Very Committed men is still not commensurate with their higher incomes. Nevertheless, being Very Committed does cause employed men to live up to and even slightly exceed the more generous charitable habits of women. For no other set of male–female comparisons in table 5.24 does the last generalization apply. Beyond this salutary influence on employed males, the other key conclusion to be drawn from this table is that the Very Committed of both sexes, regardless of whether or not they are employed, give much more to charity than do Seekers and the Non Religious. When we look at the compounding influences of sex and employment status, religiosity's impact on charitable giving continues to stand out.

On the two class dimensions of family income and education, tables 5.25 and 5.26 make it clear that charitable giving rises as we look up the social class ladder. There is a clear linear relationship. Thus the $11 median charitable donation for Canadians with family incomes of less than $20,000 rises to $135 for those with family incomes of $80,000 or more. Similarly, the average charitable donation of $25 for those with less than a high school education increases to a $125 annual donation for Canadians with at least some university

Table 5.25
Median annual charitable donation of all canadians by religiosity and family income
(1997 NSVGP)

	<$20,000	$20,000–39,999	$40,000–59,999	$60,000–79,999	$80,000 plus
Very Commited	91	178	200	191	458
Less Commited	30	85	108	120	150
Seekers	10	30	47	69	126
Non Relig.	0	10	30	45	90
Total	11	38	56	75	135
(N)	(4,266)	(4,829)	(3,802)	(2,185)	(1,976)

Table 5.26
Medin annual charitable donation of all canadians by religiosity and education
(1997 NSVGP)

	Less than High School	Completed High School	Post Secondary*	University*
Very Commited	117	190	194	349
Less Commited	60	116	92	168
Seekers	20	47	42	80
Non Relig.	5	20	25	75
Total	25	46	50	125
(N)	(4,327)	(3,034)	(6,604)	(3,093)

*Some or completed

education. One might be inclined to conclude that rising privilege in Canada is linked to greater generosity, but Statistics Canada's general report on the release of the NSVGP effectively refutes that line of thinking. In fact, donors with lower incomes give a bigger percentage of their family incomes to charity than do the more privileged.[15]

The distinctively high level of charitable giving by the Very Committed cannot be attributed to greater privilege, since we have seen in chapter 2 that the Very Committed have incomes and educational attainments similar to other Canadians. At every income and education strata, the Very Committed give far more to charity than do the Less Committed, Seekers, and the Non Religious. Among upper-middle class Canadians with incomes of $60,000 to $79,999, the Very Committed give more than four times as much to charity ($191) as do the Non Religious ($45). Similarly, for those with a university education, the Very Committed's annual donation of $349 is more than four times higher than the Non Religious median of $75. As we have seen in so many other contexts, the Less Committed are far apart from the Very Committed in the amount they give to charity. Seekers also have a profile that is closer to that of the Non Religious than to anyone else. The examples I have just given of how the Very Committed and the Non Religious differ come from the privileged sectors of Canadian society. However, I want to stress that the gap between the Very Committed and the Non Religious is most pronounced at the bottom of the income and educational ladders. This gap steadily diminishes as Canadians grow more privileged. Thus, the 10-fold or greater differential between the Very Committed and the Non Religious in the bottom two income brackets falls to a more modest five-fold difference in the top bracket. Similar dynamics operate on the educational ladder. In other words, religiousness or its lack actually has its greatest impact on the amount of charitable donations by Canadians of humble background. Relatively, religiosity has less impact on privileged Canadians, though we should not underestimate or ignore the five-fold differential between the giving levels of the Very Committed and the Non Religious among the top 15% of Canadians with family incomes of $80,000 a year or more. Religiosity's impact is therefore substantial across all social classes.

When regional differences in charitable giving are examined, as is done in table 5.27, the highest median donations are found in Ontario ($69) and Manitoba/Saskatchewan ($68), with Alberta not far behind at $60. The fact that median annual incomes are higher in Ontario ($44,490) and Alberta ($40,570) than anywhere else (see table 5.28) helps to explain their leading role here. On the other hand, the comparatively high level of giving in Manitoba and Saskatchewan cannot be explained by their much more modest average income of $37,676, which is below the national average of $39,846 and ranks in fourth place for our six regions. Similarly, the far more meagre level of charitable giving in British Columbia ($42) cannot be explained in financial terms, since their median household income of $40,416 is above the national average and extremely close to Alberta's, where the average charitable donation is much higher ($60). The even lower median charitable donation of $30 in Quebec may be partly caused by their below-average incomes of $31,471, but the Atlantic region has an even lower median income of $30,290 and yet a much higher median charitable donation of $50. In short, regional economic disparities do not adequately or fully explain patterns of charitable giving.

Table 5.27
Median annual charitable donation of all canadians by religiosity and region
(1997 NSVGP)

	Atlantic	Quebec	Ontario	Man./Sask.	Alberta	B.C.
Very Commited	190	87	203	314	379	208
Less Commited	100	52	115	160	153	119
Seekers	29	24	56	40	50	40
Non Relig.	17	18	30	24	20	22
Total	50	30	69	68	60	42
(N)	(3,429)	(3,074)	(5,158)	(2,557)	(1,370)	(1,470)

Table 5.28
Mean and median annual household income of all Canadians by region (1997 NSVGP)

	Atlantic	Quebec	Ontario	Man./Sask.	Alberta	B.C.
Mean income	38,281	43,070	50,820	43,519	47,125	48,142
Median income	30,290	31,471	44,490	37,676	40,570	40,416
(N)	(3,510)	(3,164)	(5,270)	(2,640)	(1,411)	(1,513)

In every region of the country, we once more see that the Very Committed give much more to charity than do the Non Religious. The relatively low level of giving by Quebec's Very Committed is linked to their overwhelmingly Catholic allegiance, since Catholics give much less to charity than do Protestants (table 5.22). The low overall levels of charitable giving in Quebec and British Columbia must also be caused by their having the smallest percentages of Very Committed and the largest proportions of Non Religious in the country (table 2.21). However, Quebec's strikingly low level of charitable giving regardless of religiosity reminds us that religiosity alone cannot explain Quebec's singular ways. At the other end of the spectrum, Manitoba/Saskatchewan's distinction in having the largest body of Very Committed in the country again helps to explain their high level of charitable giving. On the other hand, the relatively high levels of overall charitable giving in Ontario and Alberta, especially among their Seekers, suggests that their economic privilege – and not their religiosity – is the cause. Religiosity is therefore not the sole cause of regional variations in charitable giving, but it is a major force.

Table 5.29 permits me to make a summary assessment of the relative importance of religiosity and all the other social forces just reviewed in determining how much we give to charity. This time,

Table 5.29
Multiple Regression of Charitable Giving on Social Forces (1997 NSVGP)

	Correlation (r)	Beta
Religiosity	0.360	0.336**
Household income	0.257	0.274**
Age	0.237	0.273**
Education	0.189	0.189**
Whether employed	0.006	0.049**
Community size	0.020	−0.019*
Time in Community	0.093	0.015*
Sex	0.004	0.012
Married or not	0.120	0.001

$R^2 = .293$ ***$P < .001$ **$P < .01$ *$P < .05$

I am able to use multiple regression. The statistically inclined may wish to consult this endnote.[16] Those less versed in statistics might wish to be reminded that the beta weights in the table measure the influence of the particular factor on charitable giving after taking account of or controlling for all the other factors or variables listed in table 5.29. The larger the beta weight, the bigger is the independent effect. The central, inescapable conclusion is that religiosity has the largest beta weight (0.336) and hence has the greatest independent impact on how much we Canadians give to charity. A notable notch lower are household income and age with virtually indentical beta weights of .274 and .273, which are then followed by education's even lower beta weight of .189. All the other potential forces have really very small beta weights, though the large size of the sample ensures that most are statistically significant. The one key qualifier that almost invariably happens in statistical exercises of this sort is that only about a quarter (29%) of the variance has been accounted for, though this is quite a high R^2 by the usual standards of survey research. In everyday language, this means that the social forces we have just reviewed do not allow us to predict with accuracy how much money any *individual* Canadian gives to charity. Given free will and the vagaries of the human condition, this is surely how it will always be. In the hierarchy of social forces that we can track, religiosity is the major determinant of charitable giving in Canada.

Patterns of charitable giving in religious and secular organizations are charted in table 5.30. As in table 5.29, I include a variety of indicators of giving levels to provide as complete a picture as possible,

Table 5.30
Charitable giving by religiosity and type of volunteer organization (1997 NSVGP)

	N	Very Commited	Less Commited	Seeker	Non Relig.	Total	Tau-c
RELIGIOUS ORGANIZATIONS							
% Made charitable donation over the last year	(17,058)	77	66	27	15	37	.52***
Mean donation in dollars per donor	(14,842)	409	146	39	18	127	N/a
Mean donation in dollars by all Canadians	(17,058)	372	128	32	13	102	N/a
Median donation in dollars per donor	(14,842)	145	49	0	0	0	N/a
Median donation in dollars by all Canadians	(17,058)	120	26	0	0	0	N/a
% Of all money donated to religious bodies	(17,058)	70	16	9	5	100	N/a
SECULAR ORGANIZATIONS							
% Made charitable donation over the last year	(17,058)	78	77	78	68	74	.10***
Mean donation in dollars per donor	(14,842)	158	95	106	103	115	N/a
Mean donation in dollars by all Canadians	(17,058)	143	83	88	73	92	N/a
Median donation in dollars per donor	(14,842)	41	35	40	40	40	N/a
Median donation in dollars by all Canadians	(17,058)	32	27	26	17	24	N/a
% Of all money donated to religious bodies	(17,058)	30	11	28	31	100	N/a

***P < .001   **P < .01   *P < .05

though I believe that the median donation by all Canadians is the best single indictor of our willingness to give to others.

When it comes to religious bodies, the mean donation of the Very Committed is an impressive $409, but that sum does not take account of the 23% of the Very Committed who give nothing and the small number of the Very Committed who give far more than anyone else. This is why the far more modest median donation of $120 by all the Very Committed is a much more accurate indicator of their typical behaviour. For the same reasons, the even more modest $26 median donation by all the Less Committed tells us more about their typical behaviour than does the mean donation of $146 by the 66% of the Less Committed who make a donation. About a quarter of Seekers (26%) and 15% of the Non Religious give to one or another religious organization or agency,[17] but we should not be surprised to learn that the median of all Canadians in both these categories is zero. The typical Seeker and Non Religious Canadian therefore gives absolutely nothing to religious bodies. In fact, 63% of Canadians, including the typical Canadian right at the 50% mid-point give nothing whatsoever to religious organizations. This is one more reason why I would describe Canada as a post-Christian secular society. The result is that the Committed as a whole provide 86% of the 2.3 billion dollars annually given by Canadians to religious organizations, which in turns amounts to about 51% of the estimated $4.51 billion given to charity in 1997.[18]

For the secular side that receives 2.2 billion dollars of donations a year, giving is again more common for the Very Committed (78%) than for the Non Religious (68%). Regardless of whether we use means or medians by donors or by all Canadians, the result is the same. The Very Committed give much more to religious bodies than they do to secular ones, but the Very Committed give more to these secular bodies than do the Non Religious or anyone else. I hasten to add that the median donation of all Canadians to secular agencies is a paltry $24 a year. The comparable donation by the Very Committed of $32 is equally unimpressive for a country as affluent as ours, but this meagre sum is almost twice the size of the $17 median donation by the Non Religious to secular affairs. The result, recorded in the bottom line of table 5.30 is that the 32% of Canadians who are Committed provide 41% of all the funds for secular charities and non-profit organizations. At the other end of religiosity's spectrum, the 39% of Canadians who are Non Religious generate 31% of charitable

Table 5.31
Charitable giving by religion and type of voluntary organization for the committed
(1997 NSVGP)

	N	RC Quebec	RC RoC	Main. Prot.	Con. Prot.	V
RELIGIOUS ORGANIZATIONS						
% Made charitable donation over the last year	(6,491)	68	71	75	80	.09***
Mean donation in dollars per donor	(6,159)	81	159	387	740	N/a
Mean donation in dollars by all Canadians	(6,491)	75	142	359	673	N/a
Median donation in dollars per donor	(6,159)	45	75	150	250	N/a
Median donation in dollars by all Canadians	(6,491)	30	50	125	193	N/a
SECULAR ORGANIZATIONS						
% Made charitable donation over the last year	(6,491)	77	81	86	75	.10***
Mean donation in dollars per donor	(6,159)	135	106	174	144	N/a
Mean donation in dollars by all Canadians	(6,491)	124	94	162	131	N/a
Median donation in dollars per donor	(6,159)	20	43	75	35	N/a
Median donation in dollars by all Canadians	(6,491)	18	31	65	25	N/a

***P < .001   **P < .01   *P < .05

giving to secular bodies. As in the world of volunteering, the Committed – above all the Very Committed – more than pull their weight. Once more, the Non Religious fail to do so.

When we confine our analysis to variations among Committed Christians, as is done in table 5.31, I would stress three broad conclusions that very much parallel my earlier observations on volunteering. First, in line with their tradition of secular activism, Mainline Protestants give more to secular charities (mean of $162 and median of $65) than anyone else by a considerable margin. In addition to the substantial amounts they give to their churches, the median Protestant donation to secular agencies is four times larger than the average giving of the Non Religious and more than double the average donation of Seekers.

Second, by whatever standard we employ, Conservative Protestants give far more to religious bodies than do the rest of the Committed. Even when we use the lowest estimate of median donation by all the Committed, the Conservative Protestant annual donation of $193 is 54% more than the Mainline Protestant median ($125) and almost four times greater than the $50 donation of all Roman Catholics. Conservative Protestants give far less to secular activities if the median is our guide ($25), though their mean of $131 is a little more respectable. Whether we use the median or the mean, Conservative Protestants give as much to secular activities as do Roman Catholics and they give much more than the Non Religious. Conservative Protestants primarily give to the religious world they know so intimately, but their donations to the secular world still exceed the norms of that secular world.

Last, I think it is worth emphasizing that the $50 annual median donation of Catholics outside Quebec and their even lower $30 donation in Quebec to what are presumably Catholic bodies stand in stark contrast to the much higher levels of giving by both Mainline ($125) and Conservative Protestants ($193) to their religious institutions. Affluence or its lack has very little to do with this state of affairs. As we saw in chapter 2 (table 2.28), Catholics outside Quebec have household incomes comparable to or higher than Protestants. Catholic incomes inside Quebec are about 13% lower than the Protestant average, but this small difference cannot account for the vastly lower giving levels of Quebec Catholics, and indeed all Catholics to Catholic agencies. When it comes to secular charities, the median Quebec Catholic donation ($18) is about the same as it is for the Non Religious, though the generosity of a small number of Catholic donors puts their mean donation to secular agencies ($124) well above the $73 average for the Non Religious. As for Catholics in the rest of Canada, both their mean and median donation to secular charities exceeds the generosity of the Non Religious. Thus it is the exceptionally low levels of giving by Catholics to their church that is really noteworthy.

The NSVGP, it may be recalled, calculated that 2.3 billion dollars, or 51% of all direct charitable giving in Canada went to religious bodies. However, the NSVGP cannot tell us how the money was spent in either the religious or secular sectors. I cannot provide a definitive answer to this intriguing question, but I have a few preliminary suggestions on the religious side, which came out of the interviews I conducted in 24 congregations and charitable agencies across the country for the aforementioned report I did for Volunteer Canada. I draw three general conclusions.

First, I cannot begin to do justice to the huge array of local, regional, and national bodies linked to any major faith group. To use but one example, Catholic Charities for the Archdiocese of Toronto coordinates and raises funds for 29 member agencies that serve the elderly, the handicapped, the homeless, youth, the poor, immigrants, and refugees. Through an annual campaign, the Archdiocese raises about $6,000,000 a year, which amounts to 13% of the total budget of the 29 agencies. The Catholic Children's Aid Society, with a budget of $43,000,000, is fully funded by the government, whereas Catholic Family Services of Toronto, with about 30,000 clients a year,[19] receives 90% of its $1,000,000 budget from Catholic charities. In between is Catholic Cross-Cultural Services, which serves some 15,000 immigrants a year of all faiths with a $250,000 subvention from Catholics Charities that amounts to about a third of its total budget. Similarly, the Conservative Protestant Scott Mission in Toronto provides a host of programs for the homeless, elderly, children, youths, and the needy in general with 70 full-time staff and about 1,000 volunteers. Over 98% of its approximately $4,000,000 budget is raised by direct charitable contributions from individuals and local congregations. The ability of this one Conservative Protestant agency to raise two-thirds of all charitable monies collected by Catholic Charities for the entire Toronto archdiocese confirms the NSVGP data that Conservative Protestants give far more to charity than do Catholics. As a third and final example, I would mention the United Church of Canada, which, at the national level, annually administers a budget of approximately $50,000,000. About 30% of this fund goes for programs beyond the local congregation that range from prison ministries, emergency relief, rural development, aid to overseas councils of churches, and justice advocacy in Canada and abroad.[20] However, it is generally agreed at head office that the approximately 4,000 United Church congregations across Canada raise and spend about ten times more money than the budget of the national office.

My second general finding is built on the mundane but by no means trivial observation that all the local congregations I visited devote a substantial proportion of their budgets to the care and upkeep of their physical plant. Apart from the sanctuary or place of worship, most congregations have a meeting hall with seating space for 100 or more, a kitchen, and several or more classes or meeting rooms. Not a few congregations have far more extensive physical facilities. When mortgage, heat, light, insurance, and repairs are added to the cost of a janitor and an administrator or secretary, somewhere between 25% to 40% of a typical congregation's budget is consumed. What I want to stress here is that these facilities provide a vast physical infrastructure across Canada, which is extensively used by far more than the members of the congregations. Boy Scouts, Girl Guides, Alcoholics Anonymous, daycares, seniors groups, literacy and sports programs, legal-aid, and a host of community groups were mentioned to me as regular users of congregational halls and meeting rooms. With the exception of a very few profit-making groups, congregations charge absolutely nothing for the use of their facilities, or, more commonly, they charge a nominal fee that might cover the heat and/or cleaning costs, but not the full costs of mortgage, maintenance, and the like. Faith communities therefore provide, subsidize, and maintain a major part of the physical plant that brings Canadians together and creates community, mutual aid, and civility.

The third conclusion I would stress is that the paid clergy in local congregations across Canada together constitute a small army of social workers and counsellors, whose services are used by far more than the inner core of the Very Committed, who provide the bulk of the clergy's salaries. According to the 1991 census, the 24,105 ministers of religion were almost half as numerous as the 61,135 social workers across the country.[21] The clergy I met estimate that they spend anywhere between 25% to 50% of their time in the liturgical or ritual activities of preparing for and conducting religious services. The usual round of services and sermons consumes much of their time, but they are also regularly called upon to perform baptisms, weddings, and funerals, which most Canadians, regardless of their current level of religious activity, still seek.[22] All these rituals now involve a substantial measure of counselling. Clergy are also regularly called upon to visit the sick and the elderly in hospital, at home, and in long-term care facilities. Less frequently but recurrently they are called upon for help at times of crisis when a marriage is failing, a teenager is beyond control, a loved one dies, or a family breadwinner loses his or her job. In addition, clergy are sometimes sought out for material or practical help when a transient asks for bus fare and a meal to see him on his way, a single mother cannot pay an electricity bill, or a widow cannot understand why her government pension has been cut. These are all delicate, time-consuming activities that, to quote one cleric, "are part of a day's work that get lost." Less dramatic but equally time consuming are the many demands on the clergy to serve on the local committees of the Red Cross, the Girl Guides, the hospital, the school board, and the hockey association. In sum, the clergy, who are financially supported by their congregations, are

Table 5.32
Motives for charitable giving by religiosity (1997 NSVGP)

	N	Very Commited	Less Commited	Seeker	Non Relig.	Total	Tau-c
Feel compassion for people in need	(14,744)	95	94	96	94	95	.01*
Help a cause in which believe	(14,744)	95	92	94	90	93	.04 ***
Have been or know someone affected by the cause	(14,741)	69	70	69	60	66	.08 ***
Feel owe something to community	(14,720)	70	58	59	51	59	.15 ***
To fulfil religious obligations	(14,741)	74	53	23	11	34	.53 ***
For an income tax credit	(14,741)	15	13	9	10	11	.04 ***

***P < .001   **P < .01   *P < .05

called upon in a variety of ways that strengthen the social fabric of the wider communities in which they reside. If all their various responsibilities were shouldered by secular, social work professionals, the additional financial burden on government would be large.

As I did in the previous section on volunteering, I want to conclude this section on charitable giving by analyzing the NSVGP questions asking donors whether they agreed or disagreed with six possible reasons for giving to charity. In analyzing the results, we must bear in mind that donors were permitted to select as many of the motives as they wished. Donors were not required to choose only one motive or put motives in a priority list. The results, enumerated in table 5.32, suggest four general conclusions.

First, over 90% of donors embrace the altruistic and humanistic explanations that they give to charity because they feel compassion for people in need and because they want to help a cause in which they personally believe. In overwhelmingly embracing these motives, the Committed, Seekers, and Non Religious do not appreciably differ. Technically, the differences are statistically significant, but a spread of 3% and 4% is so small that it deserves no more than passing mention. Second, only 11% of donors say they give because the government gives a credit on income taxes. Very Committed donors are slightly more likely to admit to this material consideration (15%) than are Non Religious donors (10%), though here too the difference is too small to matter. Third, approximately two-thirds of donors say their decision to give to charity was prompted by being personally affected by the cause the charity or organization supports. Non Religious donors are less likely to have been personally prompted in this way, but it would be unwise to attach much importance to a nine-point spread of this sort.

Finally, the two remaining motives reveal a sufficient magnitude of difference that they really do tell us something worthwhile. First, there is a 19-point spread between the 70% of Very Committed donors and the 51% of Non Religious donors who say they give to charity because "you feel you owe something to your community." It is surely worth noting that this attitudinal or motivational question is confirmed by all the earlier data showing that the Very Committed really do give more than the religiously inactive to secular as well as religious charities. Far more striking, though by now predictable, is the response of donors to the question of whether their charitable giving was driven by a desire to fulfil religious obligations or beliefs. Here there is a large 63-point spread between the 74% of Very Committed donors and the 11% of Non Religious donors who say religious considerations caused or motivated their giving. The inescapable conclusion is that religious motivations and high religious commitment have a profound impact on charitable giving.

In drawing together the various strands of this chapter, I would stress that Canadians are widely agreed that community involvement, volunteering, and support of charitable endeavours are all laudable activities that enrich the communities in which we live. In practice, a little less than half of us are involved in community organizations and about a third of us volunteer our time to one or another of these many community organisations. The likelihood of us volunteering and the hours we devote to it are both affected by our education levels, our family incomes, and the size of the communities in which we live, but religiosity continues to have an independent impact even after we control for these other, competing forces. In and of itself, religiousness or its lack is one of the principal causes of volunteering in Canada. Particularly striking are the NSVGP findings that more of the Very Committed volunteer in secular agencies (35%) than do the Non Religious (25%). Only about one in five Canadians are Very Committed (19%), but they account for 29% of all volunteers and they are responsible for 38% of all the hours volunteered in Canada. Even in the secular world, the Very Committed more than pull their weight by contributing 27% of all hours volunteered. If all Canadians volunteered as much as the Very Committed do, the number of volunteers in Canada would rise from 7.5 million to 11.2 million. By the same logic, the total number of hours volunteered would double from 1.1 billion to 2.2 billion. If all emulated the Non Religious, Canadian volunteers would be reduced to 5.9 million and the total hours volunteered would fall to 0.8 billion.[23] Between the Very Committed and the Non Religious the gap is huge.

The Very Committed also give far more to charities and non-profit organizations than other Canadians do. Among the Committed, Conservative Protestants give more than anyone else, while Catholics give much less. Here too there are notable variations by household income, education, age, and the like, but the Very Committed in all these other categories give more than the Non Religious do. Regression analysis reveals that religiosity has a greater impact on charitable giving in Canada than any other social force. The 19% of Canadians who are Very Committed are responsible for 51% of all direct charitable donations. Conversely, the 39% of Canadians who are Non Religious generate only 18% of all charitable giving. Even in the non-religious, secular world, the Very Committed give a striking 88% more per capita than do the Non Religious. If all gave as the Very Committed do, the total value of direct donations to the charitable and non-profit sectors would almost triple from $4.5 billion to $11.8 billion. Total charitable donations would fall to $2 billion if all gave as the Non Religious do. Without the Very Committed, all Canadians and our network of charities and non-profit organizations would be much diminished.

6

Public Life and Social Values

Preceding chapters have focused on the intimate areas of our lives, starting with the inner world of our psychological state and then extending outwards to our relationships with our families, our friends, and the local communities in which we reside. This chapter now turns to the public domain by exploring how religiosity and religious tradition affect the involvement of Canadians in politics, their voting habits, and their views on government and political protest. Of necessity, the survey data I have been using has caused me to focus on individual Canadians rather the wider institutions in which we all live out our lives. That bias continues in this chapter as I mine the rich data from the Angus Reid and Bibby surveys on whether the Committed differ from other Canadians on policy issues and the political priorities they embrace. Only to a limited degree do these survey questions permit me to explore whether Christian churches are actively involved in speaking out on political and policy issues. The surveys do, however, allow me to assess whether Canadians approve of Christian churches playing a part in public debate over national goals. Data of this sort will therefore give us some sense of whether our avowed multiculturalism embraces religious as well as secular cultural diversity.

INTEREST AND INVOLVEMENT IN POLITICAL LIFE

Neil Nevitte's penetrating analysis of the World Values Surveys (wvs) shows that Canadians have become more interested in politics in recent years. We are also more likely to discuss political matters with our friends than we were in 1980. Though similar developments are found in most postindustrial or postmodern societies, Nevitte further tells us that Canadians are more interested in politics than are either Americans or Europeans.[1] The crucial qualifier, to which Nevitte pays insufficient attention, is that almost half of the Canadians (42%) in the 1990 WVS said they were "not very" or "not at all" interested in politics. An even larger 52% admitted that politics is not important in their lives. Similarly, only 19% said they frequently discussed political matters with their friends, while 29% admitted to never doing so; the majority (56%) did so no more than "occasionally." The political interest levels of Canadians may therefore be above the norm for advanced industrial societies, but our political interest is neither universal nor exceptionally deep.

The top row in table 6.1 indicates that politics is a bit more important to the Very Committed than to the Non Religious. However, that conclusion is undermined by the answers to the next two questions that reveal no difference – statistically or substantively – between the Committed, Seekers, and the Non Religious in the percentages who say they are interested in politics or discuss these matters with their friends. There is always the possibility that the older age structure of the Very Committed masks underlying real differences, but differences by religiosity on two of these first three questions remain small and statistically insignificant when comparisons are confined to younger Canadians. The results are partially summarized in this endnote for all the questions in table 6.1.[2] The most sensible conclusion at this point is that religiousness or its lack does not significantly affect overall levels of political interest one way or the other.

The next line in table 6.1 summarizes the frequency with which Canadians follow national news and current affairs. I list here the percentage claiming to do so daily because 88% of Canadians 18 years of age or older say they keep track of national news at least several times a week; only 6% admit they do so rarely or never. I must confess to an ingrained, though unsubstantiated suspicion that these high numbers exaggerate the percentage of Canadians who pay serious attention to the news. Fortunately, independent evidence is available to assess Canadian claims as to whether they vote, which are recorded in the next three lines of table 6.1. In November 1997, the NSVGP found 76% of Canadians claimed to have voted in the last federal election, but official polling data from the federal election in

Table 6.1
Involvement in politics by religiosity

	N	Very Committed	Less Committed	Seeker	Non Relig.	Total	Tau-c
% Say politics is very / rather important in their life[1]	(1,713)	54	44	50	44	48	.08**
% Very or somewhat interested in politics[1]	(1,711)	59	55	58	59	58	.01
% Frequently discuss political matters with friends[1]	(1,710)	20	19	19	19	19	.01
% Daily follow national news & current affairs[2]	(17,053)	74	67	69	62	67	.09***
% Voted in last federal election,[2]	(17,023)	82	81	75	72	76	.10***
% Member/participant in a political organization[2]	(17,051)	5	5	4	4	4	.01***
% Worked for a candidate or party in an election last 2 years,[3]	(2,953)	9	12	10	8	9	.02
% Contributed money to a candidate or party last 2 years,[3]	(2,949)	17	19	14	12	15	.05**
% Contacted a politician about something last 2 years;[3]	(2,953)	42	44	35	32	36	.10***
Attended a public meeting on town or school affairs last 2 years,[3]	(2,953)	41	52	37	36	40	.08***

[1]WVS 1990 [2]NSVGP 1997 [3]Reid, 1996 ***P < .001 **P < .01 *P < .05

June indicated that only 67% had done so.[3] Since this official figure is based on the permanent voters' list that fails to enumerate about 15% of all potential voters, the voter turnout rate was really about 57% in 1997.[4] A discrepancy of this magnitude between the self-reported voting data in the NSVGP (76%) and the hard evidence of the actual election (between 57 and 67%) is striking. This discrepancy is a timely reminder that survey questions about socially admirable attitudes and behaviours may well produce exaggerated results. Yet having once more raised this vital qualification to all the data examined here, I hasten to add that I can think of no good reason for thinking that the religiously committed are more prone to exaggeration than anyone else.

When it comes to differences by levels of religiousness, 74% of the Very Committed versus 62% of the Non Religious say they follow the national news on a daily basis. I should add that virtually identical results exist on related questions that tap how frequently Canadians follow international and local news. Once more age is a confounding factor because older Canadians are much more likely to be avid news followers and to vote. When age is considered, as it is in the table in endnote 1, there are no noteworthy differences by religiosity, either substantively or statistically, in the voting habits of Canadians and in their level of interest in current affairs. I would conclude that it is age rather than religiousness per se that accounts for both the greater attention of the Committed to current affairs and their higher voter turnout. We can also safely conclude that high religious involvement in no way distracts Canadians from secular affairs and civic responsibilities. This finding is one more useful corrective to the erroneous notion that high religiousness fosters passivity and political disinterest.

The remaining five rows in table 6.1 give us some sense of how many Canadians become personally involved in a range of political activities. On the first three dimensions, very few Canadians were members or participants in a political organization (4%),[5] worked for a candidate or party in an election (9%), or contributed financially to a candidate or party (15%) over the last two years. Religiousness or its lack has no discernible impact on these kinds of behaviours. Older Canadians are more likely to get involved in both activities, but religiosity's impact remains negligible at every age. Many more Canadians have contacted a politician (36%) or attended a public meeting (40%), though a majority of Canadians have done neither. On both of these issues, the level of political activity is actually greater for the Very Committed than for any of the other religious categories, including the Non Religious. The contrast is most marked on the question of contacting a politician, which I would regard as a better measure of political involvement, since attending a public meeting on town or school affairs confounds educational with political issues. On the more purely political question, 42% of the Very Committed as opposed to 32% of the Non Religious have stirred themselves to make personal contact with a politician. It should be acknowledged that the differences on these last two questions are by no means large, but both questions differ from all the other measures of political involvement in that they are not reduced into insignificance when account is taken of the older age structure of the Very Committed.[6] In fact, it is precisely in the age group of 30 to 49, where political activity of this type is common, that the contrast between the Very Committed and the Non Religious is as strong as ever. By this standard, the Very Committed are the most politically active of Canadians; the Non Religious are the least so.

Table 6.2 allows us to explore differences in political involvement by religious family. As always, the World Values Survey questions cannot be used because their religious affiliation question does not distinguish between Mainline and Conservative Protestant. I would stress three broad conclusions.

First, Quebec Catholics follow current affairs more avidly than anyone else and they have the highest voter turnout rate. They are also more likely than anyone else to work in an election, though only a small minority does so. On the other hand, they admit to the lowest level of political involvement when it comes to contacting politicians and attending public meetings. Depending on the criteria we use, Quebec Catholics are both the most and the least politically engaged sector of the Committed. I would lean to the latter interpretation because I think that personal political engagement is most directly tapped by attendance at public meetings and making contact with politicians. Second, Catholics in the rest of Canada occupy a middle ground in that they are less likely than Quebec Catholics to vote or follow the news, but they are much more likely to attend meetings and contact politicians. Overall, the political profile of Catholics in English-speaking Canada has more in common with Protestants than it does with their Quebec co-religionists. Third, and not unexpectedly, Mainline Protestants have a relatively high to medium-high ranking

Table 6.2
Involvement in politics by religion among the committed

	N	RC Quebec	RC RoC	Main. Prot.	Con. Prot.	V
% Daily follow national news & current affairs[1]	(6,488)	80	69	76	65	.12***
% Voted in last federal election[1]	(6,478)	95	80	91	69	.26***
% Member/participant in a political organization[1]	(6,487)	6	3	7	5	.08***
% Worked for a candidate or party in an election last 2 years[2]	(865)	12	9	14	7	.09
% Contributed money to a candidate or party last 2 years[2]	(863)	16	15	26	15	.12**
% Contacted a politician about something last 2 years[2]	(864)	25	49	42	49	.19***
Attended a public meeting on town or school affairs last 2 years[2]	(865)	37	49	52	39	.12**

[1]NSVGP 1997 [2]Reid, 1996 ***P < .001 **P < .01 *P < .05

at all levels of political involvement. Their concern with and involvement in the political process is consistently and notably above the national average, though Catholics in the rest of Canada are not far behind. Finally, Conservative Protestants, like Quebec Catholics, display rather contrary tendencies. Compared to the rest of the Committed, they are least likely to vote and be avid news followers, but they are most likely to have been in touch with a politician. There is a sense here of a political concern that is less than happy with the existing political process, though I would not want to put too much weight on what are often small relative differences. Whatever standard is employed, there is precious little in these figures to support stereotyped views of Conservative Protestant disengagement from politics, since their voting and news-following profiles are roughly comparable to the Non Religious, who are notably less likely to have contacted a politician.

CHRISTIAN CHURCHES AND RELIGIOUS VALUES IN POLITICS

Committed Christians now represent less than a third of all Canadians, but their minority status has done nothing to curb the outspokenness of their churches on a host of public matters. That tradition is most deeply entrenched in Mainline Protestantism, going back to the "social gospel" movement in the first decades of the twentieth century, to which I have already alluded. With its "enlarged conception of sin and salvation," the social gospel "insisted that social institutions must also be redeemed in order to create an environment in which the individual could be healed and renewed."[7] Concretely, this meant an emphasis on Christian service and social reform, ranging from the traditional concerns with sabbatarianism and temperance to efforts to implement women's suffrage, pensions, slum clearance, public health, child welfare, labour safety regulations, and arbitration in industrial disputes.[8] Support for the social gospel reached a peak in the years just before World War I. Thereafter, some of the most radical of the social gospellers left their churches to embrace secular socialism and to found the CCF party, but the Social Service Council of Canada, with Protestant church funding, continued to work for a variety of social welfare reforms throughout the 1920s.[9] Even in the 1930s, when the Depression prompted a renewed concern with personal salvation and religious revival,[10] the Evangelism and Social Service Committee of the newly founded United Church continued to promote "the standard social gospel remedy of Christian social service and an enlightened social conscience."[11] Anglicans, on the other hand, were much more constrained. When the Anglican laity at the General Synod in 1931 passed a motion of solidarity "with all who suffer" from "an imperfect social and industrial order," their bishops vetoed the motion.[12]

In the affluent post-war years of the 1950s and 1960s, the United Church's tradition as "the social conscience of the nation" widened and sharpened in its many resolutions calling for social justice. By the middle of the 1960s, it saw itself "not as part of the Canadian establishment, but as part of that establishment's sometimes loyal opposition."[13] So great was the corresponding Anglican metamorphosis that the *Globe and Mail* was moved to complain "The Anglican Church is now the NDP at prayer."[14] A similar transformation also occurred in the Catholic Church, prompted by "the bishops' growing awareness of the Third World's churches' struggle for popular liberation" and new "teaching emerging in the wake of the Second Vatican Council."[15] It would take far too much space to enumerate all the public pronouncements disseminated through the mass media and sent to the federal cabinet by these three churches in recent years. Some idea of their wide-ranging scope may be gained from the recent public statements by the Canadian Conference of Catholic Bishops on topics ranging from the remission of the debt of developing countries to sanctions against Iraq, the bombing of Kosovo, the dangers of deficit cutting, migrant workers, the Congo, Aboriginal land rights, and child poverty.[16] The Anglican and United churches, expressing their concern for oppressed people at home and abroad, have issued very similar public pronouncements.[17]

Baptists were initially ardent supporters of the social gospel, but that tradition had vanished by 1945 as conservative American evangelical values came to dominate their world.[18] This tendency to withdraw from modern society, to be politically and socially inactive was characteristic of the Conservative Protestant world until at least the end of the 1960s. The notable exception to this general rule were the Mennonites, who emerged after 1950 out of their ethnic enclave to embrace a variety of social service and politically progressive causes.[19] Far more typical were Pentecostals, whose major denomination, the Pentecostal Assemblies of Canada (PAOC), paid little or no attention to social involvement and public affairs until at least the middle of the 1970s.[20]

That inward-looking tradition began to change in the 1980s when Brian Stiller became the full-time executive director of the Evangelical Fellowship of Canada (EFC), founded in 1964.[21] In the 1990s, the EFC issued a steady stream of position papers for submission to federal and provincial governments, as well as the courts. "Abortion, euthanasia, homosexuality, Christian education, and other family-oriented matters were predictably at the top of the list of concerns."[22] In this endeavour, the EFC has come to share a new common ground with the Catholic Church in their conservative stance on abortion and gay rights, which is not embraced by Mainline Protestants. The EFC has also given voluble support to Aboriginal rights and the ecumenical Jubilee Initiative calling for a moratorium on third world debt.[23] Nevertheless, the EFC's emphasis on social justice issues is much less pronounced than that of the Roman Catholic and Mainline Protestant churches.

The three major branches of contemporary Christianity have differing political agendas, but all give forceful and public expression to their views. Less clear is whether government and politicians pay much attention to the public pronouncements of the churches. I suspect the churches tend to be ignored, though that conclusion is difficult to substantiate.[24] Government indifference is partly caused by the lack of a unified voice among the churches. It also stems from the fact that Canada in the 1990s is a post-Christian society, where the Committed amount to no more than a third of the population. The third possibility is that the rank and file of the Committed do not hear, heed, or condone the political pronouncements of the institutions that purport to represent them. To this last set of explanations I now turn.

I have no way of assessing how many of the laity are familiar with the public statements by the many commissions and administrative bodies of their churches, though I am inclined to think these views are not much known beyond a quite narrow inner circle. However, 60% or more of the Committed enumerated in table 6.3 said their clergy "speak out" on public issues in their "church or place of worship." The precise percentage varies according to the issue and the religious tradition to which they are attached. Abortion and sexual behaviour are most commonly addressed by the clergy in Conservative Protestant churches (78%) and in Roman Catholic parishes outside Quebec (81%). Both findings are consistent with the views of their churches. The much lower frequency of attention to these sexual matters in Mainline Protestant churches (43%) also reflects the liberality of that tradition. Less clear for me is why the Catholic clergy in Quebec (50%) are so much more reticent than Catholic clergy elsewhere to speak on the same matters.

On the two questions that most closely tap social gospel or social justice issues, the 66% of the Committed reporting that their clergy speak on welfare and unemployment issues rises to 81% for topics such as poverty and civil rights. This high number, especially for Catholics and Mainline Protestants, is a clear demonstration that the ideas promoted by head offices do filter through the system. Not surprisingly, fewer Conservative Protestants report their clergy pay heed to such matters, but the more striking conclusion is surely that more than two-thirds (71%) attend churches where their clergy do speak out on unemployment, poverty and the like. Data of this sort give little support to stereotypes portraying Conservative Protestant churches as unconcerned with social justice.

Only 16% report their clergy voice opinions on candidates and elections. While that figure rises to 27% of Conservative Protestants, more than two-thirds say their clergy do not influence them politically. That reticence should come as no surprise since government regulations forbid charities from endorsing political parties. Thus in the federal election of 2000, the Conservative Protestant "Focus on the Family" organization did not endorse any particular party,

Table 6.3
Views on the role of religion and Christians in politics by religion of the committed

	N	RC Quebec	RC RoC	Main. Prot.	Con. Prot.	V
% Agree the clergy in your place of worship speak out on abortion and sexual behaviour[1]	(850)	50	81	43	78	.35***
% Agree the clergy in your place of worship speak out on welfare and unemployment[1]	(849)	65	69	68	58	.09
% Agree the clergy in your place of worship speak out on social justice issues like poverty or civil rights[1]	(849)	85	87	76	71	.15***
% Agree the clergy in your church or place of worship speak out on candidates and elections[1]	(859)	10	15	15	27	.15***
% Agree ministers should stick to religion & not concern themselves with social, economic, & political issues[2]	(588)	42	34	29	19	.16*
% Say religion is very important to your political thinking (4–5 on 5-point scale)[1]	(853)	14	40	37	64	.32***
% Say religion is not at all important to your political thinking (1–2 on 5-point scale)[1]	(853)	69	34	36	16	.35***
% Agree it is essential that traditional Christian values play a major role in politics[1]	(856)	56	64	69	83	.19***
% Agree Christians should get involved in politics to protect their values[1]	(857)	52	63	60	74	.16***

[1]Reid 1996   [2]Bibby 1995   [3]Reid, 1993   ***P < .001   **P < .01   *P < .05

though Stockwell Day's social and religious conservatism made him their logical choice.[25] However, we will see shortly that Conservative Protestant voters do not massively support any particular party.

Polls by Gallup and Bibby since the 1960s suggest that Canadians have not agreed for many years about how involved churches and clergy should be in political, social, and economic matters. Fifty-two percent of Canadians in 1968 and 50% in 1983 endorsed the idea that "churches should keep out of social and political matters."[26] On the very similar question of whether "ministers should stick to religion and not concern themselves with social, economic, and political issues," Bibby's various surveys indicate that national support for the

idea has fluctuated, rising from 37% in 1975 to 49% in 1985, falling
to 41% in 1990, rising again to 47% in 1995, and dropping once more
to 44% in 2000.[27] If the Gallup and Bibby data are combined, one
might argue that Canadians have grown more open to the involvement of churches and clergy in politics, though trends based on different questions are always problematic. If we use Bibby's consistent
question since 1975, there seems to be a slowly growing national
reluctance to accept clerical involvement in politics. When the question is narrowed to whether Canadians approve of "religious leaders
being actively involved in influencing the decisions of political leaders," 67% voiced their opposition in a 1996 poll.[28] The apparent disparity between these last two numbers might be reconciled by
concluding that about half of all Canadians (53%) think the clergy
have a right to voice their views on political matters, but 67% think
the clergy should not be allowed to impose or dictate their views.
Less charitably, one might equally conclude that about half of Canadians think the clergy should "stick to religion" and two-thirds think
they have no right to participate in organized political debate.

The 32% of the Very Committed in 1975 claiming "ministers should
stick to religion" rose only slightly to 34% in 1995 (see table 6.4).
Bibby's data in table 6.3 further demonstrate that this general support
for clerical involvement in politics stretches across all the major religious families. Quebec Catholics were most likely to claim that clergy
should steer clear of politics (42%), but only 33% of Catholics elsewhere, 29% of Mainline Protestants, and 19% of Conservative Protestants agreed. There has therefore been a consistent and enduring two-
thirds majority of the Very Committed who support their clergy voicing opinions on social, economic, and political matters. For the Very
Committed under the age of fifty, an even more striking 79% endorse
their clergy's political participation. That broad consensus stands in
marked contrast to the growing body of Non Religious whose 43%
level of support in 1975 for clergy keeping out of politics rose to 57%
in 1995. Five years later, Bibby's latest survey found that a very similar
55% of non-attenders again agreed that the clergy should "stick to
religion." The Non Religious are far from fully agreed that ministers
should have no say on political and social matters, but there are signs
of an emerging consensus here outside the ranks of the Committed
that is also increasingly embraced by Seekers.

The remaining questions in tables 6.3 and 6.4 shift the focus from
the role of organized religion to the importance of religious values

Table 6.4
Views on the role of religion and Christians in politics by religiosity

	N	Very Commited	Less Commited	Seeker	Non Relig.	Total	Tau-c
% Agree ministers should stick to religion – not concern themselves with social, economic, & political issues 1975[1]	(1,836)	32	27	38	43	37	-.11**
% Agree ministers should stick to religion – not concern themselves with social, economic, & political issues 1995[2]	(1,647)	34	36	48	57	47	-.21***
% Say religion is very important to your political thinking (4–5 on 5-point scale)[3]	(2,912)	49	25	17	5	21	.34***
% Say religion is not at all important to your political thinking (1–2 on 5-point scale)[3]	(2,912)	30	51	59	86	62	-.47***
% Agree it is essential that traditional Christian values play a major role in politics[3]	(2,911)	74	51	49	24	45	.40***
% Agree Christians should get involved in politics to protect their values[3]	(2,891)	66	54	50	32	47	.28***

[1]Bibby 1975 [2]Bibby 1995 [3]Reid, 1996 ***P < .001 **P < .01 *P < .05

in politics. Here the focus is on whether religious faith affects the political decision making of individual Canadians and whether this is appropriate. Only 21% of Canadians say religion is important to their political thinking; almost three times as many Canadians (61%) claim it is not.[29] Not surprisingly, religion affects the political thinking of only 5% of the Non Religious. Similarly, very few Seekers (17%) regard religion as politically important, which demonstrates once more that their professed religiousness rarely has social consequences for them beyond their interior life. We also see the familiar pattern of the social ramifications of religious faith being notably less strong for the Less Committed than for the Very Committed. However, slightly less than half (49%) of even the Very Committed say their faith affects their political thinking, though only 30% actually deny their faith's impact. Quebec Catholics again stand out for having so few who regard their religion as politically consequential (14%). The same claim is made by less than half of Catholics outside Quebec (40%) and Mainline Protestants (37%). Only among Conservative Protestants do a solid majority (64%) identify a political dimension to their faith, though we should not ignore the substantial third that disagree. It is difficult to tell from a question like this whether the Committed reject specific pronouncements of their churches on issues from Iraq to abortion, while continuing to think that their personal faith should shape their political thinking. The other possibility is that there are a variety of political issues (such as Quebec separation and economic policy) that the Committed, like all Canadians, judge on largely secular, instrumental grounds. I will take up this theme in greater detail shortly, when I examine views on a variety of specific social issues. For the time being, I would simply conclude that the Committed are very divided on whether their religious faith affects their political thinking.

On the related question of whether Christian values ought to play a part in politics, the last two rows in table 6.4 indicate that a little over half are opposed. Opposition is most widespread among the Non Religious, with some two-thirds to three-quarters disagreeing. There is therefore less than widespread support in Canada for the multicultural ideal that diverse cultural traditions – at least of a religious nature – should be given free expression in our pluralistic world.

At the other end of the religiosity spectrum, 66% to 74% of the Very Committed think that Christians and Christian values respectively should play an active role in politics. As we have seen so often before,

Conservative Protestants are most widely supportive of political involvement (74 to 83%), while Quebec Catholics are least so (52 to 56%). Note that the Committed in all major religious families are much more likely to believe that their Christian values should be a part of political debate than they are to make the blanket claim that their faith is very important to their political thinking. Note further that the Very Committed give more support to the involvement of Christian values in politics (74%) than they do for Christians being directly or personally involved (66%). There is an obvious danger in reading too much into what are sometimes minor differences between questions in a survey. Nonetheless, I am inclined to see here an indication that the Committed seek recognition in politics of their distinctive values, at the same time that they are more reluctant to endorse overtly Christian participation that might imply imposing their point of view over others. There is an inherently fuzzy boundary in any pluralistic society between having the right to express fully one's cultural uniqueness, recognizing the same right in others, and reconciling these divergent views in our political process. The endeavour to resolve these conflicting principles lies at the heart of the often ambiguous and divided responses by the Committed to questions about whether they and their churches should be politically engaged. That nuanced point of view stands in marked contrast to the widespread rejection by the Non Religious of any place in politics for Christians and their values.

SUPPORT FOR POLITICAL PARTIES

For some years now, political scientists have produced a small stream of research reports indicating religion is a neglected but quite powerful predictor of party preference in federal elections.[30] Catholics, says Bibby, have historically allied themselves to the Liberals, whereas "Protestants and Nones" have tended " to line up with the Conservatives and NDP."[31] The 1996 Angus Reid survey, summarized in tables 6.5 and 6.6, only partially confirms these earlier findings. In trying to reconcile these differences, readers should recall that my measures of religiosity and affiliation to a religious tradition differ from those used in this earlier research.

When I first wrote this in early 2001, Chrétien and his Liberals had just handily won their third straight federal election since 1993. Liberal success is explained in part by their ability in 1996 to win the

Table 6.5
Federal voting preferences in percent by religiosity among decided voters (Reid 1996)

	Very Commited	Less Commited	Seeker	Non Relig.	Total
Liberal	57	60	56	52	55
Conservative	17	15	15	14	15
Reform	15	11	12	11	12
NDP	5	7	8	11	8
Bloc Quebecois	4	6	7	10	7
Other	3	1	2	3	2
Total	100%	100%	100%	100%	100%
N	(446)	(392)	(537)	(840)	(2,215)

P > .001   V = .08

Table 6.6
Federal voting preferences in percent by religion of committed decided voters (Reid, 1996)

	RC Quebec	RC RoC	Main. Prot.	Con. Prot.	Total
Liberal	60	69	57	41	59
Conservative	7	15	24	18	17
Reform	0	10	10	31	12
NDP	0	5	8	5	5
Bloc Quebecois	32	0	0	1	6
Other	2	1	1	4	2
Total	100	100	100	100	100
N	(101)	(225)	(197)	(141)	(664)

P > .001   V = .36

support of a majority of decided voters across the entire spectrum from the Very Committed (57%) to the Non Religious (52%).[32] I should add that the 25% of Canadians who were undecided (19%) or said they would not vote (6%) were distributed in very similar proportions at all levels of religiousness. These non-voters therefore do not affect the relative ranking of party preferences in table 6.5. Though support for the NDP was greater among the Non Religious (11%) than the Very Committed (5%), only a very small minority of Canadians at all levels of religiousness were backers of the nation's major left-wing party. Conversely, support for Canada's two right-wing parties, the Conservatives and Reform, was greater among the Very Committed (32%) than the Non Religious (25%), but here too the differences are far from large. There is therefore no more than a minor tendency for the Very

Committed to lean to the right and for the Non Religious to be more left leaning. I hasten to add that signs of a right-wing tilt may also be seen among the Non Religious and Canadians as a whole. At least in the 1990s, religiousness or its lack did not have any significant impact on the party preferences of Canadians.

When we narrow our focus to the Committed, there are rather more striking differences between the major Christian families. A full two-thirds of all Catholics were Liberal supporters in 1996; that support rose from 60% in Quebec to 69% of Catholics outside Quebec. The tiny 9% of Committed United Church members who supported the NDP in 1996 (8% for all Mainline Protestants) certainly undermines the claim by Lorne Calvert, NDP Premier of Saskatchewan in 2001, that "The NDP is the United Church at work."[33] On the other hand, stereotypes of Mainline Protestantism as a conservative bedrock receive little support from the 36% favouring the two conservative parties and the much larger 56% supporting the Liberals. Only among Conservative Protestants did a plurality – but not quite a majority – of 49% support the two conservative parties. Here too, conceptions of a monolithic Conservative Protestant vote are obviated by the 41% of them who supported the Liberals and the 5% who chose the NDP.

The emergence of Stockwell Day as leader of the Alliance Party in 2000, with his open avowal of his Conservative Protestant faith, again raised the possibility of that tradition having a distinctive impact on Canadian politics. Day certainly drew upon a network of Conservative Protestant churches in his campaign to succeed Preston Manning as leader[34] after the Reform party had transformed itself into the Canadian Alliance. However, if the 1996 Reid poll is our guide, Day would have had to look well beyond his Conservative Protestant roots for his party to have any appreciable following, since less than a third of Conservative Protestants (31%) were Reform supporters in 1996. In the build-up to the 2000 election, one poll found that Conservative Protestant support for the Alliance grew to 67%, but that support quickly fell to 32% in 2001,[35] a level virtually identical to the Conservative Protestant support for Alliance in 1996.

In the aftermath to the 2000 leadership election, Alliance was riven by controversy over Day's leadership and support for the party fell. After much acrimony, the Alliance membership voted in March 2000 by a 55% to 38% margin to replace Day with Stephen Harper as their new leader.[36] Significantly, Harper made a point of "separating religion from party politics" during the leadership contest, though he is reputed to be a "devout Christian."[37] The reasons are not hard to find. Even if all Committed Conservative Protestants voted for the Alliance, which seems unlikely, they would amount to no more than 6–9% of the Canadian electorate.[38] This is why Day's predecessor, Preston Manning, downplayed his own evangelical Conservative Protestant values while leader of Reform.[39] Manning's decision must surely have been influenced by the experience of the Christian Heritage Party (CHP), which openly stressed its Conservative Protestant allegiance. Both Reform and the CHP were founded in 1987, but Reform under Manning won two and a half million votes in 1997, whereas the CHP garnered only 29,000 votes.[40] A major party under a Conservative Protestant banner is therefore unlikely to emerge in Canada for the foreseeable future. For the very same reasons, it is very likely that the Alliance will continue to remain wary of identifying too closely with Conservative Protestantism.

CONFIDENCE IN GOVERNMENT, PROTEST POLITICS, AND CIVIC PERMISSIVENESS

Neil Nevitte in Canada and Ronald Inglehart in the United States both draw upon the World Values Survey (WVS) to argue that political attitudes in postmodern or advanced industrial societies like Canada have undergone a marked transformation in the last half century. The "new politics" are characterized by falling voter turnout, weakening party attachments, and diminishing confidence in public institutions.[41] Citizens are said to "hanker for newer modes of participation"[42] that involve increasing support for more direct forms of political protest and new political movements concerned with environmentalism, human rights, and the like. The other, darker side of the same trend is a growing civic permissiveness that tolerates people putting "their own interests before the public welfare, if they think they can get away with it."[43] I was brought up on the Lipset thesis that Canadians have always been more traditional, conservative, and deferential than Americans, but the WVS data repudiate this long-held view. In fact, both political protest and civic permissiveness in 1990 were more widely embraced in Canada than in either the United States or in Western Europe.[44] These political discontents cannot be explained by dissatisfaction with particular leaders or policies, because they are growing in all advanced industrial or postmodern

Table 6.7
Percentage who have high[1] confidence in secular institutions by religiosity (Reid, 1996)

	N	Very Commited	Less Commited	Seeker	Non Relig.	Total	Tau-c
The News Media	(2,943)	39	40	44	46	43	−.06**
Parliament	(2,909)	45	40	37	40	40	.03
The Prime Minister	(2,929)	56	55	48	48	51	.07***
RCMP	(2,935)	85	80	82	82	82	.02
All Secular	(2,869)	18	12	13	13	14	.03
All Secular Age 30–49	(1,376)	19	11	15	11	14	.04
Most (3/4) Secular	(2,869)	44	40	36	40	40	.02
Most (3/4) Secular** Age 30–49	(1,376)	49	41	39	36	40	.09**

[1]"A Great Deal" or "Quite a Lot"   ***P < .001   **P < .01   *P < .05

societies. Instead, Inglehart and Nevitte say the "new politics" are driven by a far more educated and economically secure citizenry, who feel little need for the reassurances of institutional authority and put a high value on self expression, especially when this central value puts them in conflict with bureaucratic hierarchies.

In the 1980s, the percentage of Canadians prepared to voice "high confidence" in government institutions (military, police, parliament, and civil service) fell from 37% in 1981 to 29% in 1990. High confidence in non-government institutions (churches, press, schools, and legal system) over the same period also dropped from 40% to 34%.[45] The overall decline in the 1980s is by no means large, but the absolute level of high confidence in Canadian institutions, particularly in 1990, is strikingly low. That conclusion is reinforced in table 6.7, which lists confidence levels in a variety of secular institutions in 1996 (I will deal with religious institutions in the next chapter). There we see that more than half of Canadians report low confidence levels of "not very much" or "none at all" in their news media, parliament, and prime minister. Only for law enforcement agencies such as the RCMP do a strong 82% claim "a great deal" or "quite a lot" of confidence. When all are added together, only 14% of Canadians have high confidence in all four secular institutions; even when the benchmark is lowered to three of four institutions it is still less than half of Canadians (40%) who claim high confidence.

With the conspicuous exception of the media, the Very Committed are slightly more likely than other Canadians to claim high confidence in the secular institutions enumerated in table 6.7. Discontent with

Table 6.8
Percentage who have high[1] confidence in secular institutions by religion of the committed (Reid, 1996)

	N	RC Quebec	RC RoC	Main. Prot.	Con. Prot.	V
The News Media	(860)	63	37	36	29	.24***
Parliament	(846)	49	39	51	32	.15***
The Prime Minister	(846)	53	60	61	45	.12**
RCMP	(859)	73	83	92	84	.18***
All Secular	(835)	27	13	16	9	.16***
All Secular Age 30–49	(383)	28	17	14	9	.16*
Most (3/4) Secular	(835)	45	40	51	34	.12**
Most (3/4) Secular Age 30–49	(383)	45	47	52	30	.15*

[1]"A Great Deal" or "Quite a Lot"   ***P < .001   **P < .01   *P < .05

the media may well reflect some frustration among the Very Committed with its secular nature and the tendency of television in particular to neglect mainstream Christianity and to focus on non-mainstream faiths when religious news is presented.[46] To separate out the possible impact of the older age structure of the Very Committed on their responses here, I have calculated overall secular confidence levels for those aged 30–49. Narrowed in this way, the tendency of the Very Committed to have higher confidence in secular institutions is actually more pronounced, though I must repeat that the differences are modest and must be set against a backdrop of generally low confidence levels in secular institutions. What can be said with greater certainty is that the Very Committed are no more distrustful than other Canadians of our secular institutions as a whole.

Differences in secular confidence levels between the four major Christian families, outlined in table 6.8, are rather more marked. I would draw two minor and one major conclusions. First, Quebec Catholics are most likely to profess confidence in all secular institutions, though of course the majority does not do so. Why they profess such relatively high levels of confidence in Parliament and the prime minister is a conundrum I cannot begin to address here. Second, as we have seen in other areas, Catholics in the rest of Canada and Mainline Protestants have broadly similar levels of confidence in Canada's secular institutions. These two are very much the middle-of-the-road mainstream of Canada's Committed Christians. Where they differ most notably from Canadians beyond the ranks of the Committed is in their lower levels of confidence in the media.

Third and most striking, Conservative Protestants stand out for being the religious sector that is most disgruntled with Canada's secular institutions. This extends not only to the mass media but also to their relatively low confidence in Parliament and the prime minister, which stands at levels below those of even the Non Religious. The low confidence of Conservative Protestants in secular institutions stems from their belief that there is little political tolerance for their religious views in public life. During the 2000 federal election, for instance, the Evangelical Fellowship of Canada issued a public letter complaining "Critical and ridiculing statements made by public officials and media promote intolerance and call into question the competence of persons of faith to hold public office ... In our pluralistic society there should be room for faith diversity."[47] Not all Canadians agree; we have just seen in table 6.4 that 53% of all Canadians and 68% of the Non Religious disagree with the assertion that "Christians should get involved in politics to protect their values." No complex issue is resolved by one questionnaire item, but the responses to this question do suggest that Conservative Protestants have some grounds for feeling marginal. Brian Stiller, a former President of the EFC, has perceptively observed that secular suspicion of a Conservative Protestant presence in the public arena is rooted in a fear that the agenda of the American religious right will be forced on Canadians. Stiller suggests the fear is unfounded because Conservative Protestants are such a small minority.[48] His conclusion is surely buttressed by the evidence we have just reviewed indicating that the Conservative Protestant vote is not only small but also quite dispersed across a spectrum of political parties. There remains, of course, the underlying question of whether Conservative Protestants actually embrace some sort of right-wing agenda. That issue will be addressed in the last section of this chapter, where the political values and priorities of the Committed are examined.

Tables 6.9 and 6.10 allow us to explore the types of political protests Canadians are prepared to either condone or condemn. Not surprisingly, well over 90% of Canadians voice their approval of organizing meetings and publishing materials when protesting against governments. Almost as many (87%) condone organized marches as a legitimate part of political protest. The much more assertive but still lawful activities of joining a boycott or attending a legal demonstration provoke more widespread condemnation (35 to 36%), but just under two-thirds say they have participated in such activities or

Table 6.9
When protesting against governments, percent who think people should be allowed to
perform various activities by religiosity (Bibby 1990)

	N	Very Commited	Less Commited	Seeker	Non Relig.	Total	Tau-c
Organize public meetings	(1,404)	93	95	98	99	97	−.05***
Publish materials	(1,397)	91	90	93	96	94	−.05**
Organize marches	(1,395)	78	90	88	92	87	−.10***
Set up blockades	(1,399)	13	12	18	19	16	−.06*
Damage Public property	(1,404)	0	2	2	2	2	−.01*
Possess weapons	(1,401)	0	1	1	3	2	−.02**

***P < .001   **P < .01   *P < .05

Table 6.10
Opposition to (% "would never do")[1] protest politics by religiosity (WVS 1990)

	N	Very Commited	Less Commited	Seeker	Non Relig.	Total	Tau-c
Join in a Boycott	(1,665)	47	39	35	23	35	.21***
Attend a Lawful Demonstration	(1,668)	46	37	40	27	36	.15***
Join an unofficial strike	(1,636)	79	71	66	52	65	.24***
Occupy a building illegally	(1,633)	87	83	76	66	76	.19***
All 4 protests	(1,577)	35	27	26	17	25	.15***
All 4 protests Age 30–49	(708)	32	21	16	11	18	.16***

[1]The remainder "have done" or "might do."   ***P < .001   **P < .01   *P < .05

might do so if the occasion arose. Opposition is far more widespread
when it comes to joining an unofficial strike (65%), occupying a building illegally (76%), or setting up a blockade (84%). Nevertheless, 16
to 35% of Canadians, depending on the issues, are prepared to
endorse illegal action in the course of political protest. These various
kinds of elite-challenging behaviours caused Nevitte to title his book
on recent political trends in Canada *The Decline of Deference*. Though
we are becoming an increasingly truculent nation, Bibby's data indicate that we remain almost unanimously opposed (98%) to potentially violent behaviour involving damaging public property or
possessing weapons.

As is so often the case, levels of religiousness affect opinions about
political protest, though religiosity's impact here very much depends
on the particular type of protest involved. On the least controversial

matters of organizing public meetings and publishing materials, the Very Committed are a little less likely than the Non Religious to endorse these behaviours, though the differences are very small and over 90% of the Very Committed see these activities as legitimate endeavours. The gap between the Very Committed and the Non Religious is more marked over the propriety of organized marches, though here too we should not ignore the 78% of the Very Committed who think marches ought to be allowed in political protest. At the other end of the protest scale, support for the setting up of blockades is less widespread for the Very Committed (13%) than the Non Religious (19%), but the more compelling conclusion is surely that the difference is small. Over 80% at all levels of religiousness condemn such actions. Then when it comes to acts of violence, Canadians' sweeping condemnation extends itself with virtually no variation from the Committed to Seekers and the Non Religious. In short, at both ends of the political protest spectrum religiosity's impact on political protest is very modest, though it is statistically significant.

Religiosity has a much greater influence at the middle of the range of political protest scenarios. The evidence is charted in table 6.10. For the clearly activist but lawful activity of joining a boycott, condemnation by the Very Committed (47%) is double the level for the Non Religious (23%). Though the Very Committed are clearly and quite evenly divided on the issue, a very similar pattern of marked differences by level of religiousness is evident on the similar issue of attending a legal demonstration. Disavowals of illegal forms of political protest are much more common among Canadians regardless of their religiosity, but there is a striking contrast between the 21% of the Very Committed and the 48% of the Non Religious who approve of joining an unofficial strike. Similar though slightly less dramatic differences can also be seen on the issue of occupying a building illegally. A rather more modest 35% of the Very Committed say they could never participate in any of the four protest activities just enumerated, but here too it is double the 17% level for the Non Religious. Moreover, when the potentially confounding influence of age[49] is much reduced in the last line of table 6.10 by confining our comparisons to those aged 30–49, religiosity's impact is actually enhanced. Among the middle-aged, disavowal of all these types of political protest is almost three times higher for the Very Committed (32%) than it is for the Non Religious (11%). Let me reiterate that high religiousness has no appreciable influence on the willingness of

Table 6.11
Civil permissiveness: Percent strongly agree[1] the following behaviours are not justified by religiosity (WVS 1990)

	N	Very Commited	Less Commited	Seeker	Non Relig.	Total	Tau-c
Claim government benefit to which not entitled	(1,698)	90	88	89	82	87	.07**
Avoiding a fare on public transport	(1,701)	88	82	84	76	82	.10***
Cheating on tax if you have the chance	(1,700)	88	81	82	70	79	.16***
Buying something you knew was stolen	(1,702)	93	91	89	81	87	.12***
Accepting a bribe	(1,693)	94	92	92	90	92	.04***
Lying in your own interest	(1,700)	78	74	76	59	70	.17***
All of the above	(1,656)	65	53	56	40	52	.22***
All of the above Age 30–49	(747)	63	52	60	40	51	.20***

[1]Score 1–3 on original 10-point scale   ***P < .001   **P < .01   *P < .05

Canadians to involve themselves in the non-aggressive forms of political protest involved in organizing meetings and disseminating their points of view. There is no evidence of passivity here. However, strong religious commitment does have a clear dampening impact on the willingness of Canadians to condone more assertive and aggressive forms of protest up to the outer limit of violent protest, which is condemned by all. There is a gentleness among the Very Committed that sets them apart from other Canadians. This should come as no surprise to anyone familiar with basic Christian teaching.

Table 6.11 leads us to the related issue of whether falling confidence in public institutions and rising levels of political protest are accompanied by a growth in civil permissiveness, or the willingness of Canadians to condone anti-social behaviours. Nevitte provides a very qualified answer. He notes that approval of a battery of anti-social behaviours grew from 1981 to 1990 in Canada, but the increase was far from large. Trends in other advanced industrial societies were also far more variable and inconsistent on these issues than those for protest politics and confidence in institutions.[50] My own measure of civil permissiveness is slightly different from Nevitte's,[51] but the data in table 6.11 make it clear that we have by no means fallen into some sort of laissez-faire swamp of anti-social anarchy. About fourth-fifths or more of Canadians are strongly agreed that it is never justified to illegally claim government benefits, avoid a fare on public transport, cheat on taxes, buy stolen goods, and accept a bribe. Only on the issue of lying in one's own interest are Canadians a bit more divided, though here too 70% voice their strong disapproval. Combining all six behaviours, half of us (52%) are strongly agreed that all six anti-social tendencies are never justified; another 22% indicate they might tolerate one of the six; only 26% condone two or more. With the less onerous standard of disapproval employed by Nevitte,[52] the percentages of Canadians condemning anti-social behaviour would be even higher.

Once more, religiosity makes a difference, affecting in this case attitudes to civil permissiveness. (Note that here and in the preceding discussion on political protest, the wvs does not allow me to explore differences by religious family.[53]) Across all six forms of anti-social behaviour, it is the Very Committed who are most likely to voice strong disapproval; the Non Religious are least likely to do so. Tau-c indicates that differences of opinion are most marked about lying in one's own interest and tax evasion; they are least so about accepting a bribe and claiming a government benefit to which one is not entitled. Overall, there is a cumulative effect, seen in a Tau-c of .22, whereby the gap between the condemnation levels of the Very Committed (65%) and the Non Religious (40%) for all six behaviours is greater than for any one item. Here too, civil permissiveness diminishes substantially with age, but confining analysis to the middle-aged (in the last line of table 6.11) reveals that religiosity alone continues to have about the same independent impact (Tau-c of .20),[54] as it does when age is not controlled. The key or core conclusion is that the Very Committed are more critical of anti-social behaviour than are other Canadians; the Non Religious are notably less so. This is the crucial counterpart to the just-noted evidence that high religiousness discourages more aggressive forms of political protest, while low religiousness has the opposite effect. The common thread underlying these findings on both protest and permissiveness is that religiosity is intimately linked to civility.

POLITICAL VALUES AND PRIORITIES

Readers may recall from the introductory chapter that Bibby has consistently argued that religion has little or no impact on the everyday life of Canadians, including social or political concerns with such matters as unemployment, the economy, child abuse, pollution, crime, and poverty. His evidence indicates that this generalization is as true of the religiously committed as it is of the uncommitted.[55] In the very different climate of the United States, a number of observers have described a state of "cultural wars" between religious liberals and the non religious on the one hand, and religious conservatives on the other hand. Though a number of recent empirical studies in the United States have called into question the notion that Conservative Protestants share a monolithic political agenda, few would deny that religious forces are an active element in the American political system.[56] We cannot, of course, assume that what is true of the United States is necessarily true of Canada. In an analysis of some Angus Reid polls that I also use, Sam Reimer has shown that Canadian and American evangelicals share similar religious beliefs, but Canadians evangelicals are more tolerant on racial, moral, and political issues.[57] This is surely welcome news for those who fear an American-style Conservative Protestant political agenda in Canada.

In what follows, I concentrate on how religiousness affects political views here in Canada. As I wend through a thicket of data, readers might like to know that I find more support for Bibby's thesis in this public, political realm than I do in the more intimate spheres of family, friends, and local community. Nevertheless, I believe there are some key ways in which the religiously committed differ amongst themselves and when compared to other Canadians. As always, the differing conclusions that Bibby and I sometimes draw are rooted in the different ways we define religiosity and membership in a religious tradition.

Some have argued that declining confidence in public institutions reflects a general turning away from big government as the limits of the modernizing, bureaucratic, and welfare state become ever more evident.[58] However polls suggest that Canadians are still much divided on the matter. Tables 6.12 and 6.13 summarize a variety of Canadian perceptions on the role of government in their lives. Almost half of Canadians (47%) agree "the less government the better," but slightly more than half take the opposite view that "governments should be involved in aspects of society." Similarly, at a time when governments across the country have been reining in their spending in the pursuit of balanced budgets, 55% of Canadians were claiming that we should put " a higher priority on health and social programs than on reducing the deficit." A much more striking 78% conclude "an emphasis on individual rights is making social life difficult." About half of all Canadians (49%) still think the Canadian political and economic system "is about the best there is," but that compares

Table 6.12
Views on government by religiosity

	N	Very Commited	Less Commited	Seeker	Non Relig.	Total	Tau-c
% Agree the less govt. the better Vs. Govt. should be involved in aspects of society[1]	(2,885)	50	46	43	47	47	.02
% Agree govt. should place a higher priority on health /social programs Vs reducing the deficit[1]	(1.423)	58	54	57	52	55	.05
% Agree an overemphasis on individual rights is making social life difficult[2]	(1,626)	86	75	83	72	78	.12***
% Agree overemphasis on individual rights is making social life difficult Age 30-49[2]	(599)	83	66	80	72	75	.06

[1]Reid 1996   [2]Bibby 1995   ***P < .001   **P < .01   *P < .05

Table 6.13
Views on government by religion of the committed

	N	RC Quebec	RC RoC	Main. Prot.	Con. Prot.	V
% Agree the less govt. the better Vs. Govt. should be involved in aspects of society[1]	(848)	53	48	47	52	.05
% Agree the less govt. the better Vs. Govt. should be involved in aspects of society Age 30–49[1]	(387)	49	45	51	62	.11
% Agree govt. should place a higher priority on health/social programs Vs. reducing the deficit[1]	(408)	57	61	54	53	.06
% Agree govt. should place a higher priority on health/social programs Vs. reducing the deficit Age 25–54[1]	(242)	51	62	49	49	.12
% Agree overemphasis on individual rights is making social life difficult[2]	(585)	77	82	87	90	.12
% Agree overemphasis on individual rights is making social life difficult Age 30–49[2]	(166)	62	74	79	88	.21

[1]Reid 1996   [2]Bibby 1995   ***$P < .001$ **$P < .01$ *$P < .05$

unfavourably with the 65% making the same claim in 1975.[59] Together these responses suggest to me a widespread and growing fear that diminishing government influence threatens the quality of our social life.

Slightly more of the Very Committed favour less government and slightly more want a higher priority given to social programs than deficit cutting, but neither set of differences is statistically or substantively significant. Concern that rampant individualism threatens social life is more widely felt by the Very Committed (86%) than by the Non Religious (72%), but that difference shrinks for those aged 30–49. (Here and in the following tables I include comparisons among the middle-aged whenever age influences the overall finding, because the Very Committed tend to be older and the Non Religious younger than other Canadians). Adherents of the four major religious traditions tend to have broadly similar though deeply divided views on the role of government in their lives today. Most distinctive are the Conservative Protestants who are most likely to approve of less government and most worried that individual rights threaten social life. Quebec Catholics, on the other hand, are least worried that individualism threatens their social life, perhaps because they have greater confidence in their government. Since all these differences across religious families are slightly greater among the middle-aged, we can be all the more confident they are caused by religious differences, and not some underlying age factor. However, it is pointless to pursue the matter further since none of the differences are very large and all are statistically insignificant. When it comes to expectations of government, Bibby is right: religion does not make much of a difference.

Tables 6.14 and 6.15 tap a number of attitudes about the responsibilities Canadians feel toward the less advantaged at home and abroad. As a nation, the great majority of us (84%) claim "poor people have a right to an adequate income." Almost as many (77%) believe "the gap between the rich and the poor is growing." Public profession of compassion or concern for the poor is therefore widespread, though a slightly lower proportion (61%) is willing to endorse greater government expenditures "to fight hunger and poverty."

Here too, it looks as if religiosity does not appreciably affect concern for the poor. The Very Committed are a little bit more likely to acknowledge the poor's right to an adequate income, but they are fractionally less likely to make the harder commitment of contributing their taxes to the cause. Reflecting perhaps the social justice tradition now current in the Catholic Church, Catholics are most likely (81%) to say the gap between rich and poor is a significant problem. Interestingly, Mainline Protestants with their social gospel tradition are least likely to do so, though the differences are small and a solid two-third majority in all religious families acknowledge poverty's challenge. On the harder issue of committing taxes to fight poverty, it is Conservative Protestants who profess the greatest reluctance to commit more tax money to the poor. Note that Conservative Protestant relative distaste for spending taxes on the poor is most marked among the middle aged, where age's impact is reduced and the impact of religion presumably more marked. By this standard, Conservative Protestants show less compassion for the poor than anyone else. However, we must not forget the strong evidence in chapter 5 that Conservative Protestants give far more to charity than anyone else. We also saw that the donations of the Very Committed, even to secular charities, substantially exceed the average level for the Non Religious. What we see in table 6.15 is the Conservative Protestant distrust of government, and not much more. When it comes to actual acts of compassion, be it volunteering or giving to charity, it is the

Table 6.14
Views on the poor, poverty, and foreign aid by religiosity (Reid, 1996)

	N	Very Commited	Less Commited	Seeker	Non Relig.	Total	Tau-c
% Agree Poor people have a right to an adequate income[1]	(1,618)	89	84	87	80	84	.07**
% Agree the gap between rich & poor in this country is a significant problem[2]	(2,924)	77	75	79	78	77	.01
% Agree govt should spend more to fight hunger & poverty, even if higher taxes[2]	(2,923)	58	57	65	60	61	-.02
% Feel they have an important responsibility to help poor people in countries around the world[3]	(1,480)	80	76	66	51	65	.26***
% Feel they have an important responsibility to help poor people around the world Age 24-44[3]	(749)	75	74	71	52	65	.21***
% Prepared to pay higher taxes so the govt. could do more for poor in developing countries[3]	(1,465)	42	38	35	26	34	.14***
% Contributed money for poor people overseas[2]	(1,459)	59	42	22	26	34	.26***
% Contributed money for poor people overseas Age 25-44[2]	(723)	55	39	21	24	29	.19***

[1]Bibby 1995 [2]Reid 1996 [3]Reid 1994 ***P < .001 **P < .01 *P < .05

Table 6.15
Views on the poor, poverty, and foreign aid by religion of the committed

	N	RC Quebec	RC RoC	Main. Prot.	Con. Prot.	V
% Agree Poor people have a right to an adequate income[1]	(573)	93	88	91	89	.06
% Agree the gap between rich & poor in this country is a significant problem[2]	(855)	87	77	68	73	15
% Agree govt should spend more to fight hunger & poverty, even if higher taxes[2]	(856)	59	60	59	57	.02
% Agree govt should spend more to fight hunger & poverty, even if higher taxes Age 30–49[2]	(386)	57	63	60	47	.12
% Feel they have an important responsibility to help poor people around the world[3]	(427)	84	76	77	83	.08
% Feel they have an important responsibility to help poor people around the world Age 25–44[3]	(180)	80	59	79	93	.30**
% Prepared to pay higher taxes so the govt. could do more for poor in developing countries[3]	(418)	34	43	38	47	.09
% Prepared to pay higher taxes so the govt. could do more for poor in developing countries Age 25–44[3]	(177)	29	32	34	61	.25*
% Contributed money for poor people overseas in 1995[2]	(417)	43	49	61	66	.17**
% Contributed money for poor people overseas in 1995 Age 25–44[2]	(163)	43	42	49	60	.13

[1]Bibby 1995   [2]Reid 1996   [3]Reid 1994   ***P < .001   **P < .01   *P < .05

Very Committed, and the Conservative Protestants in particular, who lead the way.

Much the same conclusion emerges from the next set of questions on aid to the poor in developing countries. Canadians in general are less likely to voice concern for the needy abroad than for those at home, but religiousness or its lack has a much more marked impact on whether they feel "an important responsibility to poor people in countries around the world." A full 80% of the Very Committed and a much lower 51% of the Non Religious voice that opinion. Far fewer Canadians say they are willing to pay higher taxes "so the government could do more for the poor in developing countries," but there remains a marked, though reduced differential between the Very Committed and the Non Religious. On the critical question of how many have actually given money in the last year "to a charitable or voluntary organization to assist poor people overseas," there are more than twice as many donors among the Very Committed (59%) than among the Non Religious (26%). I fear I am being churlish, but I feel obliged to point out that Seekers who respond so positively on the attitudinal side of compassion are least likely to be actual donors. Once more, it is Conservative Protestants who are most likely to be donors (66%) and Quebec Catholics who are least likely (43%). In between are Catholics in the rest of Canada and Mainline Protestants whose corps of overseas donors is still about double the size of the donor pool of the Non Religious. Concern for the needy overseas is a distinctive and distinguishing trait of the religiously committed.

Tables 6.16 and 6.17 summarize the thinking of Canadians on a variety of current political or public issues ranging from legal matters to multiculturalism, gender equality, and the environment. Debates over gay rights, female clergy, and religion in the school system are left to the next chapter because they are controversies within the world of committed Christians in ways that the aforementioned issues are not. The topics covered in these two tables are not and could never be exhaustive, but they do represent a range of issues on which religious differences might be expected.

Despite a declining crime rate in recent years,[60] an overwhelming 87% of Canadians think we "do not deal harshly enough with criminals." Although the death penalty has not been exercised for some years, an almost equally large proportion of Canadians (82%) think it should be "in some instances." On both these issues, differences by level of religiousness are statistically and substantively insignificant. Differences across the four major religious traditions of committed Christians are also small and insignificant. One might, however, note that Conservative Protestants, who are so often portrayed as vengeful advocates of harsher justice, are no more bloodthirsty in their demands than other Canadians, including the Non Religious and Mainline Protestants with their liberal traditions.

Canada is distinguished by the large number of immigrants we have admitted for many years, the 17% or so who are immigrants today, and the vast cultural and racial diversity they bring with them.[61] The great majority of Canadians (79%) say "Canada's multicultural makeup is one of the best things about this country," though a question from Bibby's 1995 survey finds that we are roughly equally divided between those who think immigrants and their descendents

Table 6.16
Views on the courts, multiculturalism, gender and the environment by religiosity

	N	Very Committed	Less Committed	Seeker	Non Relig.	Total	Tau-c
% Agree courts do not deal harshly enough with criminals[1]	(1,659)	90	89	85	87	87	.02
% Agree death penalty should be exercised in some instances[1]	(1,659)	79	84	89	79	82	.02
% Agree Canada's multicultural makeup is one of the best things about this country[2]	(1,430)	82	83	80	76	79	.05*
% Approve of marriages between whites and visible minorities[1]	(1,534)	75	83	83	91	85	-.14***
% Approve of marriages between whites and visible minorities Age 30-49[1]	(593)	86	96	89	91	90	-.02
% Agree women who do the same work as men should receive the same pay[1]	(1,670)	96	100	98	98	98	-.01
& Agree married women should not be employed if husbands are capable of supporting them[1]	(1,664)	34	16	17	11	18	.18***
& Agree married women should not be employed if husbands capable of supporting them Age 30-49[1]	(619)	21	7	13	11	13	.05
% Women should take care of running their homes & leave running the country up to the men[1]	(1,665)	20	9	9	3	9	.13***
% Agree strict rules to protect environment are necessary, even if they raise prices or cost jobs[3]	(2,916)	71	75	73	78	75	-.06**
% Disagree it is mankind's right to use the earth and its resources as it suits us[4]	(1,458)	69	65	66	76	70	-.06*
% Disagree it is mankind's right to use the earth and its resources as it suits us Age 25-54[2]	(935)	74	65	64	76	70	.05

[1]Bibby 1995 [2]Reid 1993 [3]Reid 1996 ***P < .001 **P < .01 *P < .05

Table 6.17
Views on the courts, multiculturalism, gender and the environment by religion
of the committed

	N	RC Quebec	RC RoC	Main. Prot.	Con. Prot.	V
% Agree courts not deal harshly enough with criminals[1]	(591)	88	92	88	84	.08
% Agree Death penalty should be exercised in some instances[1]	(589)	79	86	81	82	.07
% Agree Canada's multicultural makeup is one of the best things about this country[2]	(426)	79	84	82	82	−.05
% Agree Canada's multicultural makeup is one of the best things about this country Age 25–54[2]	(235)	76	87	85	81	.11
% Approve of marriages between whites and visible minorities[1]	(520)	64	87	75	78	.21**
% Approve of marriages between whites & visible minorities Age 30–49[1]	(158)	96	92	86	84	.16
% Agree Women who do the same work as men should receive the same pay[1]	(594)	99	97	98	95	.08
& Agree Married women should not be employed if their husbands are capable of supporting them[1]	(690)	33	19	26	34	.14
& Agree Married women should not be employed if husbands capable of supporting them Age 30–49[1]	(172)	11	9	5	28	.24*
% Agree Women should take care of running their homes & leave running the country up to the men[1]	(589)	18	13	10	32	.19**
% Agree Women should take care of running their homes & leave – the country up to the men Age 30–49[1]	(168)	1	10	0	37	.42***
% Agree strict rules to protect environment are necessary, even if they raise prices or cost jobs[3]	(855)	59	73	81	69	.17***
% Disagree it is mankind's right to use the earth and its resources as it suits us[2]	(435)	47	70	83	64	.29***

[1]Bibby 1995   [2]Reid 1993   [3]Reid 1996   ***P < .001   **P < .01   *P < .05

should be encouraged to keep their customs (mosaic) and those who
think they should take on Canadian ways (melting pot). Table 6.16
indicates that the Very Committed are slightly more likely to support
multiculturalism than are the Non Religious. However, the difference
is really too minor to matter. Within the ranks of Committed Christians, Quebec Catholics are least likely to embrace multiculturalism.
This is undoubtedly linked to Quebecois nationalism that sees

multiculturalism as denigrating the special place of Quebec and francophones within Canada. Conservative Protestants, especially the
middle-aged, are a little less likely to embrace multiculturalism, but
here too these differences are a really quite small.

On the much more pointed question of whether one approves of
"marriage between whites and visible minorities"[62] or non-whites,
85% of Canadians say they do. The desire to appear politically correct
surely results in responses that underestimate the real level of racial
hostility in Canada, but I can think of no reason why this should be
more or less true of the Committed than anyone else. Overall, disapproval of marriages between whites and visible minorities is greater
among the Very Committed (25%) than among the Non Religious
(9%). However, we need to remember that the Very Committed tend
to be older than other Canadians, particularly the Non Religious. We
also need to bear in mind that opposition to marriages with visible
minorities rises from 4% for those under age 30 to 39% for those 65
or older. Thus, in the next line in table 6.16 comparing responses
among the middle-aged, the differences shrink into statistical insignificance, though the Very Committed remain a very little bit more
resistant to racial intermarriage. The initial starker differences are
therefore largely caused by a bias rooted in age rather than religion.
Among the middle-aged, Committed Protestants are a little more
likely to oppose racial intermarriage (16%) than are Committed Catholics (6%) or the Non Religious (9%), but these small differences with
such a slender sample sustain no firm conclusion. Since I came up
with virtually identical conclusions on the related issue of whether
Canadians "would rather have next door neighbours who are my
own colour," I have not bothered to present the numbers here. What
matters is the common conclusion – religion has no appreciable
impact on the racial and multicultural attitudes tapped here.

Turning to attitudes to gender equality (leaving the issue of female
clergy to the next chapter), there is now an almost universal consensus, unaffected by religiosity or religious tradition, that "women who
do the same work as men should receive the same pay." However,
there is a really striking difference between the 44% of the Very Committed and the 11% of the Non Religious who believe that "married
women should not be employed if their husbands are capable of
supporting them." The next line in table 6.16 reveals that this very
traditionalist view of the female role among so many of the Very
Committed is partially caused by having so many elderly in their

ranks. Support for that traditionalist view falls to 21% for the Very Committed who are middle-aged, though it is still double the endorsement level of the Non Religious in the same age bracket. Table 6.17 then demonstrates that the distinctive outlook of the Very Committed in middle age stems entirely from the 28% of Conservative Protestants of that age who think a woman's place is in the home. Support for that traditionalist view within all other branches of the Committed Christians in their middle age is extremely rare (between 5% and 11%) and at levels equal to or lower than that of the Non Religious. Precisely the same line of reasoning illuminates the comparable finding that 20% of the Very Committed and only 3% of the Non Religious think "women should take care of running their homes and leave the running of the country to the men." Among the middle-aged, a full third of Conservative Protestants (37%) embrace this subservient view of women's role in politics; only 5% of all other Committed Christians in middle age do so, which is almost at the minuscule level of the Non Religious (2%). We should not lose sight of the fact that solid majorities of even Conservative Protestants reject these traditionalist gender views. It nonetheless remains true that a significant minority of about a third of Conservative Protestants hold traditional views on the place of women inside and outside the home that defiantly set them apart from the Canadian mainstream. For all others, who make up the massive majority (81 to 84%[63]) of Committed Christians, their embrace of gender equality is overwhelming and on a par with the Non Religious.

On environmental issues about 70% of Canadians take a pro-environment stance on the two questions listed in tables 6.16 and 6.17. On the first question there is a statistically significant but really minor tendency for the Very Committed to be less likely than the Non Religious (71% vs. 78%) to agree that "strict rules to protect the environment are necessary, even if they raise prices or cut jobs." That small difference remains when we look at only the middle-aged. On the other question, the Very Committed again take a slightly less pro-environment stance, but here the difference disappears among the middle-aged. Within the Committed Christian world, Quebec Catholics are least sensitive to environmental issues and Mainline Protestants are most sensitive. I cannot discern a compelling reason for these findings, which are anyway too small to matter. On environmental matters, religiosity and religious tradition have no significant impact.

To conclude this section, I want to move beyond assessments of the importance of single issues to a sense of the political priorities of Canadians. In a world where we are often forced to choose between competing values, which ones do we hold most dear? One widely touted answer to that question is enshrined in the postmaterialism and postmodernization thesis of Inglehart, to which I have already referred. To recap, he argues that the unprecedented material security and prosperity after World War II have caused the citizens of advanced industrial societies to become less concerned with material security and social order and more concerned with autonomy, self expression, and quality of life.[64] The "new politics," described earlier, of shrinking confidence in public institutions and rising political protest is part of that transformation. Though only a minority (26%) of Canadians were pure postmaterialists in 1990, their numbers grew over the 1980s as the ranks of materialists fell.[65]

The 1996 Reid data in tables 6.18 and 6.19 build upon the insights of Inglehart and his colleagues, but the Reid battery of questions provides a more diverse conception of political priorities that is particularly useful in exploring religion's role in all this. The Reid pollsters asked Canadians to select the most important aim of the country over the next 10 years from two sets of three options presented in random order. From their two most important priorities, respondents were then asked to select the most important overall. Tables 6.18 and 6.19 combine the six possible choices of most important national aim or priority in three categories of my choosing. Those choosing "relationships" say that "raising moral standards" or "preserving and protecting the family" is the most important priority. Those opting for "security" selected either "maintaining law and order in the nation" or "building a healthy economy." Highly similar "security" items are used to identify "materialists" on Inglehart's postmaterialism scale. For want of a better word, "postmaterialists" are Canadians in the Reid survey who claim that "giving people more say in government" or "protecting the environment" is their prime priority. Again my two postmaterialist items closely parallel questions designed by Inglehart to tap concern for autonomy and quality of life issues, which are seen as the essential elements in the postmaterialist perspective.[66]

Almost half of all Canadians (47%) continue to see their primary concerns in life as centred on the building of a better economy (33%) or maintaining law and order (14%). In second place to those with

Table 6.18
Nation's most important aims over the next 10 years by religiosity (Reid 1996)

	Very Committed	Less Committed	Seekers	Non Religious	Total
Relationships (moral standards & family)	52	31	29	20	30
Security (law and order & a healthy economy)	34	52	45	53	47
Postmaterialism (more say in govt & the environment)	14	18	26	27	23
Total	100%	100%	100%	100%	100%
(N)	(574)	(489)	(717)	(1,078)	(2,858)

V = .19   P < = .001

Table 6.19
Nation's most important aims over the next 10 years by religion of the committed (Reid 1996)

	RC Quebec	RC RoC	Main. Prot.	Con. Prot.	Total
Relationships (moral standards & family)	37	40	34	65	42
Security (law and order & a healthy economy)	49	41	52	27	43
Postmaterialism (more say in govt & the environment)	15	19	15	8	15
Total	100%	100%	100%	100%	100%
(N)	(148)	(282)	(234)	(170)	(834)

V = .17   P < = .001

security or materialist goals are the 30% of us who stress the relationship issues of raising moral standards (9%) and preserving the family (21%). In third and last place are the postmaterialist values of giving people more say in government (11%) and protecting the environment (11%), which together are endorsed as primary priorities by 23% of all Canadians. Further breakdowns by age or generation (see this endnote[67]) show that the 30% endorsement of postmaterialist priorities among those born after the baby boom (age 18 to 30) is still less than it is for security goals (42%) and about the same as the 28% identifying relationships as their main concerns. Endorsement of postmaterialist values is less common among boomers (22%) and pre-boomers (18%), but that should not obscure the fact that less than a third (30%) of our youngest generation embrace postmaterialism as their first priority. Proclamations of a postmaterial or postmodern revolution appear premature.

Few should be surprised to learn that the Very Committed put a heavier stress on the importance of relationships (52%) than do the Less Committed (31%), Seekers (29%), and the Non Religious (20%). Conversely, the Very Committed emphasize security or material aims less commonly (34%) than anyone else. The Non Religious and Seekers attach greater importance to postmaterialist values than anyone, but both are still most likely by a wide margin to stress security as their prime concern. Endnote 67 demonstrates that these generalizations hold across generations. Since age is the only demographic factor notably differentiating the Very Committed from others, it is all the more certain that religiosity in and of itself really affects the national aims that Canadians regard as most important. Seekers, as we have come to expect, have a profile that is much closer to the Non Religious than to the Very Committed.

Among Committed Christians, Conservative Protestants exemplify in most exaggerated form the distinctive priorities of the Very Committed. Thus Conservative Protestants are most likely to endorse the importance of relationships (65%), and they are least likely to be concerned with security (27%) and postmaterial goals (8%). Adherents to the other three Christian families are more likely than the Non Religious to emphasis morality and family issues, but Catholics and Mainline Protestants are very much like the Non Religious in their pre-eminent concern with economic and legal security.

What Committed Christians of all stripes share in common is their relative lack of attention to postmaterialist priorities. We need to be clear about what this means. We have just seen in table 6.16 that the Committed differ little from other Canadians in their support for more rigorous environmental laws. We might also remember from chapter 3 (table 3.18) that the Committed are at least as likely as others to say they feel a serious responsibility to make the world a better place. wvs data contained in table 6.20 further demonstrate that the Very Committed do not differ from other Canadians in the relatively high approval levels they accord to the ecology, anti-nuclear, disarmament, and human rights movements. Thus the 77% of the Very Committed who approve of the disarmament movement is virtually identical to the 79% of the Non Religious who do so. As for the human rights movements at home and abroad, an even more striking 91% of the Committed voice their approval. In short, the

Table 6.20
Percentage who approve of new political movements (WVS, 1990)

	N	Very Commited	Less Commited	Seeker	Non Relig.	Total	Tau-c
Ecology movement	(1,675)	94	93	95	96	95	−.02
Anti-Nuclear energy movement	(1,636)	72	76	78	72	74	.01
Disarmament movement	(1,643)	77	79	83	79	79	.01
Human rights movement – home or abroad	(1,660)	91	96	94	95	94	.02

***P < .001   **P < .01   *P < .05

Committed are not politically passive or inattentive to quality-of-life issues. Where they do differ from other Canadians is in their ranking of national priorities. When asked to choose, the Committed – above all the Very Committed – give relatively low priority to postmaterialist priorities because they are much more likely than other Canadians to emphasize the need to improve relationships in families and communities. This, I think, is the central conclusion to be drawn from tables 6.18 and 6.19.

There are, of course, a variety of ways in which the political inclinations of the Very Committed have much in common with other Canadians. These commonalities range from their levels of political involvement, the type of political parties they support, their generally low trust of secular institutions, and their views on a host of issues ranging from big government to deficit cutting, capital punishment, multiculturalism, the environment, and gender equity. Only on this very last matter do a minority of Conservative Protestants really stand out. Secular non-religious values shape the political outlook of the Committed in a variety of ways. That said, there remain important political differences between the Very Committed and other Canadians. We have just seen that they are less likely to put a high priority on the materialist agenda of law, order, and a healthy economy. They are also singularly reluctant to attach great importance to the postmaterialist priorities of autonomy, personal development, and quality of life, though they are generally as supportive of progressive political causes as other Canadians. Where the Very Committed stand out most strongly is in the high priority they place on national aims that enhance family and moral standards. That conclusion is very much consistent with my earlier findings that the Very Committed are less likely to endorse confrontational forms of political protest and are notably more disapproving of anti-social behaviour. The common thread here is the distinctive importance that the Very Committed place on the quality of their relationships with others. This is not, of course, a new discovery. I will return to it in the conclusion.

7

Christians and Their Churches:
Beliefs, Attachments, and Controversies

This final substantive chapter turns inward to explore some of the major dynamics that shape the world of committed Christians. I now focus primarily on differences between the four major religious families of Quebec Catholics, Catholics in English-speaking Canada, Mainline Protestants, and Conservative Protestants. For obvious reasons, I am much less concerned with the Non Religious, though I will occasionally look at tables with breakdowns by religiosity to highlight how Seekers differ from the Committed. If Seekers, who profess to believe without belonging, really are the vanguard of a new form of religiousness, then we ought to know something about their beliefs and religious practices.

BELIEFS, FACTIONS, AND PRIORITIES

The survey data at my disposal cannot fully capture the diverse, richly textured worldviews of the many denominations in Canadian Christendom. Nevertheless, I believe it is possible to derive a basic sense of how rank-and-file committed Christians view a variety of beliefs central to their faith. Despite a huge drop in attendance levels at religious services since the 1960s, there has been no appreciable change in the 80% of Canadians who continue to say they believe in God.[1] Since so few deny God's existence, tables 7.1 and 7.2 sharpen the issue by focusing on those who say they definitely believe in God.

Table 7.1
Views on meaning in life, life after death, god, heaven, and hell by religiosity

	N	Very Commited	Less Commited	Seeker	Non Relig.	Total	Tau-c
% Definitely believe in God[1]	(1,608)	91	73	67	26	57	.57***
% Have an intense personal relationship with God[2]	(1,448)	88	62	55	7	45	.69***
% Strongly Agree have felt God's presence in my life[2]	(1,446)	76	51	37	6	36	.58***
% Believe (definitely & think so) have experienced God's presence[1]	(1,607)	80	59	41	15	41	.56***
% Felt in contact with something sacred or holy[2]	(1,443)	56	47	41	16	36	.34***
% Agree God is understanding and forgiving[2]	(1,402)	100	98	96	61	85	.35***
% Feel God is looking out for me personally[2]	(1,437)	96	85	82	27	65	.61***
% Agree God seems to be harsh and vindictive[3]	(1,252)	6	11	11	16	11	-.08***
% Definitely believe in life after death[1]	(1,619)	74	53	38	20	40	.45***
% Believe (definitely & think so) in life after death	(1,619)	91	79	77	51	70	.35***
% Definitely believe in heaven[1]	(1,640)	72	42	38	11	39	.53***
% Believe (definitely & think so) in heaven[1]	(1,640)	91	80	80	41	67	.46***
% Definitely believe in hell[1]	(1,618)	56	29	27	9	26	.37***
% Believe (definitely & think so) in hell[1]	(1,618)	76	55	57	26	48	.43***

[1]Bibby 1995   [2]Reid 1996   [3]Reid 1993   ***P < .001   **P < .01   *P < .05

Table 7.2
Views on meaning in life, life after death, god, heaven, and hell by religion of the committed

	N	RC Quebec	RC RoC	Main. Prot.	Con. Prot.	V
% Definitely believe in God[1]	(583)	92	80	80	96	.19***
% Have an intense personal relationship with God[2]	(413)	84	79	71	93	.20***
% Strongly Agree have felt God's presence in my life[2]	(414)	68	57	63	87	.22***
% Agree (strongly or moderately) have felt God's presence in my life[2]	(414)	89	88	86	96	.11
% Believe (definitely & think so) have experienced God's presence[1]	(571)	71	65	75	91	.20**
% Felt in contact with something sacred or holy[2]	(411)	39	49	53	67	.19**
% Agree God is understanding and forgiving[2]	(417)	99	99	99	100	.03
% Feel God is looking out for me personally[2]	(412)	93	92	87	95	.11
% Agree God seems to be harsh and vindictive[3]	(440)	7	10	6	8	.06
% Definitely believe in life after death[1]	(573)	68	62	62	85	.18**
% Believe (definitely & think so) in life after death	(573)	85	84	92	96	.09*
% Definitely believe in heaven[1]	(584)	58	60	64	91	.25***
% Believe (definitely & think so) in heaven[1]	(584)	82	87	91	99	.18**
% Definitely believe in hell[1]	(571)	30	42	43	83	.35***
% Believe (definitely & think so) in hell[1]	(571)	48	69	70	93	.31***

[1]Bibby 1995   [2]Reid 1996   [3]Reid 1993   ***$P < .001$ **$P < .01$ *$P < .05$

Substantially fewer Seekers (67%) than the Very Committed (91%) make this more categorical or definitive assertion. Not surprisingly, the Less Committed also voice a less robust faith. Far more perplexing are the 26% of the Non Religious who say they definitely believe in God.

I hasten to add that belief in God rises to 95% for Seekers (and to 98% of the Very Committed) when those who "think so" are added in. Only the more rigorous standard of certainty separates out Seekers, but that general conclusion is strengthened by all the other questions on God in the same table. Thus proclamations of "an intense personal relationship with God" are notably more common among the Very Committed (88%) than Seekers (55%). Similar differentials also exist on the related issues of strongly agreeing to "have felt God's presence in my life" (76% vs. 37%) and to simply affirming they "have experienced God's presence" (80% vs. 41%). The last question on "contact with something sacred or holy" is a much less traditional conception of the supernatural that might be regarded as more compatible with Seeker sensibilities. This less conventional definition does reduce the difference between the Very Committed and Seekers, but it does not make it disappear. Note further that less than half of Seekers (41%) say they have personal experience of the sacred or holy. As a general rule, Seekers are much less likely than the Very Committed to affirm the core or foundational premises of anyone with a religious outlook that they categorically believe in the existence of the supernatural and have personal experience of it.

Differences among Canada's four major Christian traditions are not nearly so marked, but a few conclusions are worth brief mention. First, Conservative Protestants are most likely to be categorical about their belief in God and say their faith is rooted in personal experience with God. Second, doubts over and estrangement from God are both more widespread among the rest of the Committed, but those who hold such views are very much a minority. Notions that Canada's mainstream churches are riddled with doubt and far from God receive little support here. Third, the greater willingness of the Committed to affirm their relationship with God than with the sacred or holy further demonstrates their preference for traditional language when speaking of their ultimate concern.

The next section in tables 7.1 and 7.2 show us that the Committed and Seekers hold a very benevolent conception of a God who is "understanding and forgiving" and "looking out for me personally." Hardly any think God is "harsh and vindictive." These generalizations extend with remarkable uniformity across the four major religious families. Old Testament notions of a vengeful, wrathful, and judgmental God are today embraced by very few.

The remaining questions in the same two tables tap levels of belief in life after death, heaven, and hell. Since the questions do not define their terms, we cannot be certain what people precisely mean when they say they do or do not believe in heaven, hell, or an afterlife. With this crucial qualification in mind, I draw the following conclusions. First, the identical 91% of the Very Committed who believe in life after death and heaven indicate that very few indeed are prepared to reject these orthodox beliefs. Second, Seekers are more than twice as likely as the Very Committed to express less than definite belief in life after death (62% vs. 26%) and heaven (62% vs. 28%), though clear majorities of Seekers say they "definitely" or "think" they agree on both matters. Uncertainty, doubt, or diffidence on these maters is markedly more prevalent among Seekers. Third, 20% or less of Catholics and Mainline Protestants say they do not believe in life after death or heaven, but substantial minorities deny that life after death (32% to 38%) and heaven (36% to 42%) definitely exist. Doubts over these two traditional beliefs in these mainstream churches are therefore much more widespread than is outright rejection. Fourth, doubts of this sort are much less common among Conservative Protestants. Fifth, both the Committed and Seekers are notably less likely to believe in hell than they are in heaven. I do not wish to overstate the case – two-thirds (68%) of the Committed definitely or think they believe in hell, though we do not know whether the hell they have in mind is experienced in this world or the next.[2] On the other hand, outside the Conservative Protestant world, definite belief in hell is claimed by less than half of Catholics (37%) and Mainline Protestants (43%); among Seekers it is only 27%. This unwillingness to believe categorically in hell is very much consistent with the just noted belief that God is forgiving, not harsh or vindictive. For the Committed rank and file today, it is the rewards of faith – not the punishments of hell – that they most fervently embrace and believe.

Tables 7.3 and 7.4 summarize a variety of questions about the Bible and the source of religious authority. Belief that the Bible is the "inspired word of God" is endorsed by the overwhelming majority of the Very Committed (94%) and almost as many Seekers (80%). Seekers may not be actively involved in institutional Christianity, but they obviously feel receptive to it. There is also strikingly high agreement among the Committed in all four religious families; the slightly higher level of dissent among Mainline Protestants (14%) is surely too small to matter. Disagreements do creep in over whether the Bible is to be "taken literally, word for word," though the views of the faithful recorded here have a strikingly conservative cast to them. In all, 57% of the Very Committed and 32% of Seekers endorse this literalist stance. Among Conservative Protestants, a really striking 82% say they interpret the Bible literally. Based on my experiences attending a Baptist church for several years, I am inclined to think – though I cannot prove – that many Conservative Protestants would choose the literalist option in a public poll because they see the Bible as so central to their faith, though they would not actually interpret it in a literally word-for-word fashion. In any case, far fewer Catholics

Table 7.3
The bible and religious authority by religiosity[1]

	N	Very Commited	Less Commited	Seeker	Non Relig.	Total	Tau-c
% Agree the Bible is the inspired word of God[2]	(2,767)	94	79	80	40	68	.46***
% Feel the Bible is God's word and is to be taken literally, word for word[2]	(2,815)	57	34	32	9	29	.39***
% Who know who denied Jesus three times[3]	(1,405)	81	59	37	36	49	.36***
% Who know what is the first book in the Old Testament[3]	(1,327)	85	72	56	57	64	.22***
% Who know what is the last book in the New Testament[3]	(1,295)	69	60	42	39	48	.25***
% Correct on all 3 knowledge questions[3]	(1,265)	61	40	20	22	32	.30***
% Agree my private beliefs about Christianity are more important than what is taught by any church[2]	(2,771)	66	79	78	76	75	.06**

[1]Not asked of Non Christians   [2]Reid 1996   [3]Bibby 1995   ***P < .001   **P < .01   *P < .05

Table 7.4
The bible and religious authority by religion of the committed

	N	RC Quebec	RC RoC	Main. Prot.	Con. Prot.	V
% Agree the Bible is the inspired word of God[1]	(859)	89	92	86	98	.15***
% Feel the Bible is God's word and is to be taken literally, word for word[1]	(854)	38	37	46	82	.33***
% Who know Peter denied Jesus three times[2]	(556)	76	72	77	84	.10
% Who know Genesis is the first book in the Old Testament[2]	(520)	83	63	93	98	.36***
% Who know the Book of Revelation is the last book in the New Testament[2]	(502)	74	43	70	88	.35***
% Correct on all 3 knowledge questions[2]	(489)	61	32	58	76	.32***
% Agree my private beliefs about Christianity are more important than what is taught by any church[1]	(845)	76	71	75	65	.09

[1]Reid 1996 [2]Bibby 1995 ***P < .001 **P < .01 *P < .05

and Mainline Protestants agree, though I remain struck by the substantial minorities of 37% to 46%[3] who do take this very conservative stance. I suspect far fewer of their clergy would agree. What comes through to me is the central importance that the Committed of all stripes continue to attach to their Bible as the divinely inspired source of their faith.

When it comes to actually knowing their Bible, 81% and 85% of the Very Committed are correct on the third and fourth questions listed in table 7.3; a less impressive 69% are correct on the last, slightly more difficult knowledge question. Taken together, we are down to 61% of the Very Committed who know the answers to all three of these very basic questions. The best one can say is that solid majorities do get each one right. Across religious families, Conservative Protestants are predictably most familiar with their Bible: 76% correctly answer all three questions. Catholics in Quebec and Mainline Protestants have similar levels of religious knowledge that are both about twice as high as they are for Catholics outside Quebec. Catholics in English-speaking Canada are such relative laggards, I suspect, for two very simple reasons. First, they lack the Sunday school tradition and Bible-centred liturgies of Protestants. Second, Catholic schools and the religious education they provide are almost universally available inside Quebec but much less so elsewhere.

Outside the world of the Committed, biblical knowledge is at predictably much lower levels, with about 20% being able to answer all three questions. For me the most striking finding is the rough equivalence of Seekers and the Non Religious. As is so often the case, Seekers profess much greater regard for the Bible than do the Non Religious, but the behavioural or concrete indicators of their actual knowledge have much more in common with the Non Religious than they do with the Committed.

Before moving on, we should not neglect the last row in tables 7.3 and 7.4 indicating that 66% of the Very Committed and 72% of all the Committed agree that "my private beliefs about Christianity are more important than what is taught by any church." Here, there is a broad-based 65% to 76% consensus across all four major religious families. It is undoubtedly rooted on the Protestant side in a long tradition emphasizing a personal and unmediated relationship with God, but it also surely stems from our cotemporary constellation of values that stresses autonomy, self-realization, and a general distrust of authority. Committed Christians today cherish their God and their Bible, but most believe that they – not their churches – are the final arbiters of their faith and its message.

Table 7.5 provides a vivid example of how Committed Christians today have come to believe that religious authority rests in themselves. The great creeds of all the major Christian denominations stress that Jesus Christ is the only Son of God and that salvation is through Him and through Him alone. However, all four of the questions summarized in table 7.5 indicate that a majority of the Committed rank and file disagree with Christianity's exclusivist stance. Thus three-quarters of Catholics inside and outside Quebec and 71% of Mainline Protestants agree "All the great religions in the world are equally good and true." Similarly, from another survey in another year, well over three-quarters of Catholics and Mainline Protestants reject the assertion that "people who do not accept Christ as their personal saviour can never go to heaven." Only Conservative Protestants support by a wide margin Christianity's exclusivist claim. However, a 66% majority of Conservative Protestants do take an ecumenical stance within Christianity that God does not care "which church you belong to." The net result, with the predictable exception of Conservative Protestants, is that it is now a minority of Catholics and Mainline Protestants, albeit a large minority, who endorse the traditional Christian conviction that "it is very important to encourage

Table 7.5
Other faiths and evangelism by religion of the committed

	N	RC Quebec	RC RoC	Main. Prot.	Con. Prot.	All Committed[1]	All Very Committed[1]	V
% Believe all the great religions in the world are equally good and true[2]	(1,047)	75	76	71	23	63	58	.41***
% Believe that people who do not accept Christ as their personal saviour can never go to heaven[3]	(412)	15	17	23	83	29	33	.53***
% Don't think God cares which church you belong to[4]	(403)	40	90	95	66	76	76	.51***
% Feel it is very important to encourage Non-Christians to become Christians[2]	(1,048)	43	38	47	85	51	64	.34***

[1]Not asked of Non Christians   [2]Reid 1996   [3]Reid 1993   [4]Reid 1994   ***P < .001   **P < .01   * P < .05

Non-Christians to become Christians." In our secular multicultural world, where respect for diversity is everywhere emphasized, most Committed Christians can no longer embrace the exclusivity of their ancestors.

I believe that differences within the Committed Christian world are most effectively captured by membership in one of the four broad religious families of Catholics inside and outside Quebec, Mainline Protestants, and Conservative Protestants. However, there have also long been factions, coalitions, or contending parties within each of the four major families that sometimes share common concerns across their denominational boundaries, though each particular faction is inevitably shaped by the denomination in which it is born and functions. In fact, I noted in chapter 2 that the very distinction between Mainline and Conservative Protestantism is rooted in a fundamental rift within Protestantism as a whole, whereby Conservatives tend to be evangelical, emphasizing the importance of the Bible, moral regeneration, personal conversion, and evangelism. Mainline or Liberal Protestantism, on the other hand, has stressed social gospel issues and the need to accommodate Christian thought and worship to contemporary circumstances. In recent years, dissident factions have emerged within Mainline churches such as the Essentials Movement, the Alpha Program, and the Prayer Book Society in Anglicanism, or the Community of Concern in the United Church.[4] These factions tend to be evangelical in tone, though their specific concerns range from the controversy over ordaining gay ministers in the United Church to charismatic renewal and liturgical change in the Anglican Church. Similarly, on the Catholic side the dominant faction's concern with social justice issues (see the previous chapter) has seen the emergence of a countervailing faction centred on the fight against abortion, but also extending more broadly to traditional views on belief, devotion, and sexual morality.[5] This book is simply not designed to outline in any detail the numerous factional disputes current in Christian churches. However, table 7.6 does provide some sense of three basic factions that cut across the four religious families of the Committed.

Table 7.6 indicates that 26% of the Committed and an even more striking 33% of the Very Committed consider themselves to be "an Evangelical Christian."[6] As I have noted before, we cannot be certain that all respondents understand *evangelical* in the same way. However, we should derive some reassurance from knowing that a much

Table 7.6
Evangelicals, fundamentalists, pentecostals and liberals: religious tradition by religion of the committed (Reid 1996)

	N	RC Quebec	RC RoC	Main. Prot.	Con. Prot.	All Committed[1]	All Very Committed[1]	V
% Consider self Evangelical	(1,000)	19	8	19	67	26	33	.49***
% Consider self Pentecostal/Charismatic	(1,000)	21	15	13	43	23	27	.26**
% Consider self a Liberal or Progressive	(1,000)	62	59	65	45	57	51	.14***

[1]Not asked of Non Christians   ***P < .001   **P < .01   *P < .05

Don't knows are here treated as not Evangelical, Pentecostal, Charismatic, or Liberal more complex, 10-item index of evangelicalism using behavioural and attitudinal indicators produces much the same result.[7] Not surprisingly, Conservative Protestants are most likely to define themselves as evangelical (67%), though we should not lose sight of the third who do not describe themselves as evangelicals, despite being part of a faith community that very much defines itself in these terms. About a fifth (19%) of Mainline Protestants are evangelicals, who rise to 27% of the Very Committed in their ranks. Evangelicals are also a surprising 12% minority of all Committed Catholics. For reasons that I have yet to discover, self-proclaimed evangelicals are much more prevalent among Quebec Catholics (19%) than Catholics in the rest of Canada (8%). Doubters might be interested to know that Grenville's more rigorous 10-point index reaches the virtually identical conclusion that 14% of Catholics are evangelical. Put in slightly different form, 49% of evangelicals are now affiliated to Catholic or Mainline Protestant churches. The evangelical tradition is therefore now a major force among Committed Christians that is diffused well beyond its Conservative Protestant base.

Pentecostalism is another distinctive movement that was initiated in California in 1906 and has since spread rapidly throughout the world. Its distinctiveness lies in its emotional, sometimes ecstatic traditions, which put great stress on "gifts of the spirit," most notably speaking in tongues, prophecy, and divine or faith healing. Above all it is a religion of the heart, which is part of the broader evangelical movement. Starting in the 1960s, a second Charismatic wave began to emerge, which practises the gifts of the spirit in a more muted style, tends to be more middle-class, and often – though not always- remains attached to Mainline Protestant and Catholic churches. By the middle of the 1980s, Pentecostals and Charismatics together were estimated to be about a fifth of all Christians worldwide.[8] Canada is no exception to this general trend; today 23% of all Committed Christians and 27% of the Very Committed say they are either Pentecostal or Charismatic.[9] Almost half (43%) of all Conservative Protestants make the same claim. However, like evangelicals, Pentecostals and Charismatics now have a strong presence outside their Conservative Protestant base, amounting to 18% of Catholics and 13% of Mainline Protestants. They too now have a major presence throughout contemporary Canadian Christianity.

The last faction consists of those who describe themselves as "liberal or progressive Christians." Despite the greater vitality of the Conservative Protestant world in recent years and the presence of substantial minorities of evangelicals within Catholic and Mainline Protestant churches, self-described liberals are still the largest single faction among Committed Christians. Liberals or progressives amount to 57% of the Committed and 52% of the inner core of the Very Committed. About 60 to 65% of Catholics and Mainline Protestants continue to describe themselves in these terms. Not only are about half (45%) of Conservative Protestants liberal or progressive, but the same is true of 50% of self-styled evangelicals. What we are seeing here is a complete shattering of the notion that there is a simple dichotomy between Conservative Protestantism and evangelicalism on the one hand and liberals, Catholics, and Mainline Protestants on the other. Allegiances are complex and crosscutting, insuring that evangelical, Pentecostal, and progressive factions are diffused among all the major religious traditions. This simple but essential conclusion is consistent with evidence from the previous chapter that differences in voting preferences and political values among the four major religious families vary in complex, often unexpected ways that cannot be reduced to some sort of right to left continuum.

This last conclusion is reinforced when we turn to table 7.7, which summarizes the religious priorities of the Committed. The first two questions in table 7.7 ask the rank and file of the Committed to choose between two clear options in their religious life. The two similar questions from different surveys are included to make it clear that they are not the product of one rogue survey. On the first one, the Committed are deeply divided, with 52% agreeing and 48% disagreeing that "it is more important to spread the world of God than it is to be active in social and political causes." When elsewhere confronted with a five-point scale on church priorities, more of the Committed emphasize "personal spirituality (37%) than they do social justice (19%). In this latter case, the Committed do favour the personal spirituality option, but not by a large or commanding margin; the majority (63%) are no so inclined. In fact, the biggest single group of the Committed (44%) sit firmly on the fence in this five-point scale, refusing to choose one option over the other. This conclusion applies with most force to Catholics and Mainline Protestants, whose religious convictions about the importance of faith and God in their lives are balanced by their social justice and social gospel traditions, described in the last chapter. This mainstream of approximately 75% to 80% of the Committed says that social justice and personal spirituality are both important priorities to be pursued in tandem.

Table 7.7
Justice, spirituality, evangelism: religious priorities by religion of the committed

	N	RC Quebec	RC RoC	Main. Prot.	Con. Prot.	All Committed	All Very Committed	V
% Agree it is more important to spread the word of God than it is to be active in social and political causes[1]	(434)	55	45	37	83	52	58	.31***
% Agree churches should concentrate on personal spirituality rather than social justice (1–2 on 5-point scale)[2]	(1,066)	33	31	33	59	37	41	.22***
% Agree churches should concentrate on social justice rather than personal spirituality (1–2 on 5-point scale)[2]	(1,066)	25	23	17	9	19	18	.15***
% Agree churches & religious organizations should spend more money on helping the poor[2]	(1,071)	77	87	76	88	82	83	.14***

[1]Reid 1993 [2]Reid 1996 ***P < .001 **P < .01 *P < .05

Conservative Protestants are the notable exceptions, with clear majorities favouring spreading the word of God (83%) and concentrating on personal spirituality (59%). That said, the bottom line in table 7.7 provides a much-needed corrective, showing that 88% of Conservative Protestants and 82% of the Committed as a whole say "churches and religious organizations should spend more money on helping the poor." There is a politically correct, "motherhood" tenor to this question that probably skews the answers in all religious traditions. Nevertheless, Conservative Protestants lead the pack at the progressive end when it comes to concern for the poor. Forced to choose, Conservative Protestants do not hesitate in affirming the primacy of religious or spiritual solutions to life's problems, but their commitment to providing material aid to the less advantaged is also deeply rooted.[10]

ATTACHMENTS: SPIRITUALITY, LOCAL CONGREGATIONS, AND CHURCHES

In the introductory chapter I mentioned how declining involvement in church services in recent decades has been accompanied by the growing popularity of spirituality as a new, privatized form of religious expression. I also noted in the second chapter the many signs of widespread interest in spirituality in Canada. These generalizations are certainly confirmed by Bibby's 1995 survey, in which 68% of Canadians said spirituality was important to them – only 57% made the same claim for religion. In tables 7.8 and 7.9, I draw upon his data to explore whether the Committed and Seekers differ in their sense of spirituality and in their interest in new forms of religious expression such as the New Age Movement.

Since Seekers say religion is important to them but they are not actively involved in a religious group, there is the implication that they have unmet religious needs. Putting aside the here irresolvable question of how and whether religious and spiritual needs differ, table 7.8 indicates that Seekers do not have a particularly acute spiritual hunger. Just over half say they have spiritual needs (58%); only about a third (35%) say spirituality is very important to them; and less than a fifth (18%) say their interest in spirituality has increased over the last five years. On all three counts, spiritual interest is far more widespread among the Very Committed. Similarly, for less conventional beliefs and practices, from belief in communion with the

Table 7.8
Involvement in spirituality and new age by religiosity

	N	Very Committed	Less Committed	Seeker	Non Relig.	Total	Tau-c
% Say spirituality is very important to them[1]	(1,653)	78	37	35	13	36	.52***
% Have spiritual needs[1]	(1,573)	79	66	58	30	52	.44***
% say there has been an increase in their interest in spirituality over last 5 years[1]	(1,608)	43	20	18	14	22	.22***
% Believe it is possible to communicate with the dead[1]	(1,584)	25	19	27	25	25	.02
% Believe they will be reincarnated[1]	(1,575)	19	31	32	24	26	.02
% Practice meditation using such techniques as sitting, breathing, or thinking in special ways[2]	(1,825)	6	6	5	13	8	-.05**
% Somewhat or very interested in New Age[1]	(1,625)	14	7	15	12	13	.00
% With spiritual needs who describe their spirituality in explicitly Christian terms	(734)	77	66	41	25	53	.47***

[1]Bibby 1995   [2]Bibby 1975   ***P < .001   **P < .01   *P < .05

Table 7.9
Involvement in spirituality and new age by religion of the committed

	N	RC Quebec	RC RoC	Main. Prot.	Con. Prot.	V
% Say spirituality is very important to them	(590)	46	64	65	89	.28***
% Have spiritual needs	(533)	70	68	79	91	.20**
% Had an increase in their interest in spirituality over last 5 years[1]	(572)	22	35	31	51	.20**
% Believe it is possible to communicate with the dead[1]	(560)	31	29	15	17	.17*
% Believe they will be reincarnated[1]	(554)	29	27	26	6	.19**
% Practice meditation techniques such as sitting, breathing, or thinking in special ways[2]	(700)	9	10	3	1	.14*
% Somewhat or very interested in New Age[1]*	(570)	28	7	6	3	.30***

[1]Bibby 1995   [2]Bibby 1975   ***P < .001   **P < .01   *P < .05

dead and reincarnation to the practice of meditation, the minority of Seekers with these interests are not much different from the equally low percentages among the Very Committed and Non Religious. Most tellingly, only 15% of Seekers say they are very or somewhat interested in New Age thought, which is the generic label for alternative religions today; 71% of Seekers say they have never even heard of the term. Even if Seekers are redefined as those who see spirituality as important yet are rarely or never involved in religious meetings, only 17% claim to be somewhat or very interested in New Age. Those looking for future religious or spiritual revival from unrequited Seekers had best think again.

Within the ranks of the Committed, Conservative Protestants display by far the highest levels of spirituality. About 90% say they have spiritual needs that are very important to them; half (51%) claim their interest in spirituality has grown over the last five years. The figures for Catholics and Mainline Protestants are less striking, but two-thirds or more say they have spiritual needs and 59% say these needs are very important to them. A full 90% of Catholics and Mainline Protestants define spirituality as very or somewhat important to them. Only when it comes to more unconventional beliefs and practices are there much lower levels of interest among the Committed, particularly Conservative Protestants, though Quebec Catholics profess an interest in New Age that exceeds everyone else, including Seekers. Such resounding concern with spirituality by the Committed, the much weaker interest of Seekers, and the pervasive lack of interest in New Age across the board reinforces for me the conclusion I drew in chapter 1 that there is little to be gained from portraying spirituality as separate from – on a par with, and yet antithetical to – religion.[11]

The next two tables, 7.10 and 7.11, allow me to explore a number of ways that Canadians might express their religious faith or commitment privately, without active participation in a church or faith community. From the very beginning, this book has been guided by the principle that involvement in a community is essential to religious commitment. That conviction has been vindicated, I think, by the recurring tendency of the Seekers, who believe without belonging, to behave in ways that align them much more closely with the Non Religious than the Committed. Nevertheless, it would be foolish to deny that private forms of religiousness are an integral part of religious life that are encouraged and nurtured in all faith traditions.

Even a majority of the Very Committed (55%) admit (or are not prepared to deny) that one does not "need to go to church in order to be a good Christian," though they are much divided on the issue, as 45% disagree. Not surprisingly, the vast majority of Seekers (92%) and Non Religious (96%) concur. Across the four religious families of the Committed, only a majority of Conservative Protestants (54%) reject that proposition, though only by a very small margin. Elsewhere, solid two-thirds to three-quarters of Catholics and Mainline Protestants affirm that going to church is not a prerequisite for being a good Christian. I am inclined to interpret this claim of the Committed as a symptom of modesty, sharpened by our multicultural climate that discourages any assertion that one way of life may be superior to any other. In and of itself attendance at religious services does not necessarily make people different, but we have seen in previous chapters that it often does.

When it comes to specific behavioural indicators of private religiousness, far more of the Very Committed (69%) than Seekers (11%) say they read the Bible or other religious material on at least a weekly basis. Praying weekly or more often outside formal religious services is also practised by more of the Very Committed (89%) than Seekers (53%), though in this case the difference is not as large. Many more Seekers pray than read religious literature. Among the Committed, Conservative Protestants are most likely to pursue their religion privately; Quebec Catholics are least likely to do so when it come to reading religious literature. I should add that the Less Committed are true to

Table 7.10
Personal or private indicators of religiousness by religiosity (Reid 1996)

	N	Very Commited	Less Commited	Seeker	Non Relig.	Total	Tau-c
% Don't think you need to go to church in order to be a good Christian	(2,914)	55	80	92	96	84	.31***
% Read the Bible or other religious material weekly or more often	(2,945)	69	24	11	2	22	.50***
% Pray weekly or more often outside of formal religious services	(2,934)	89	64	53	14	47	.63***
% Discuss spiritual issues at least monthly with family & friends outside a formal religious setting	(1,455)	80	56	37	19	42	.50***
% Discuss spiritual issues at least monthly with colleagues & acquaintances outside a formal religious setting	(1,458)	55	29	16	9	23	.36***

***P < .001   **P < .01   *P < .05

Table 7.11
Personal or private indicators of religiousness by religion of the committed (Reid 1996)

	N	RC Quebec	RC RoC	Main. Prot.	Con. Prot.	V
% Don't think you need to go to church in order to be a good Christian	(858)	68	68	74	46	.20***
% Read the Bible or other religious material weekly or more often	(865)	33	43	42	85	.36***
% Pray weekly or more often outside of formal religious services	(858)	78	79	69	93	.19***
% Discuss spiritual issues at least monthly with family & friends outside a formal religious setting	(418)	62	71	67	85	.17**
% Discuss spiritual issues at least monthly with colleagues & acquaintances outside a formal religious setting	(418)	43	40	35	69	.24***

***P < .001   **P < .01   *P < .05

form in their admission that they pray and read religious literature much less frequently than do the Very Committed.

Of course, both questions are flawed. In the former case, the primary emphasis on the Bible creates a traditional Christian bias that might discourage a positive response from Seekers engaged with unconventional spiritual literature, though the last part of the actual question does open up to that latter possibility. As for the question on prayer, I have always had the nagging concern that it does not adequately differentiate fleeting petitions to God to get one through the day from more focused efforts to set time aside for sustained prayer and spiritual reflection. All in all, I think reading religious literature is the better indicator of private religious activity because the act of reading is less ambiguous in its implication of a concerted effort. By this measure, privatized expressions of religiousness are strikingly weak among Seekers, though even weekly and daily prayers are far more commonly practiced by the Very Committed.

The last two questions in tables 7.10 and 7.11 tap more social forms of behaviour that nonetheless occur outside organized church settings. Only in this restricted and perhaps questionable sense are they indicators of individual or private commitment. When asked how often they discuss spiritual issues with family or friends outside a religious setting, far more of the Very Committed (80%) than Seekers (37%) say they do so at least monthly. As for discussing spiritual issues with colleagues and acquaintances, there is a similarly striking gap between the 55% of the Very Committed and the 16% of Seekers doing so at least monthly. On both counts, Conservative Protestants lead the way, as is consistent with their greater commitment to evangelism, charted in table 7.5. Nevertheless, Catholics and Mainline Protestants are far more likely than Seekers to say that they talk about their faith with family, friends, acquaintances, and colleagues outside formal religious settings. Seekers say that religion is important to them, but here too they are much less likely to manifest this assertion in their daily life.

For the remainder of this chapter I narrow my focus exclusively to the Committed. Table 7.12 summarizes a variety of survey questions that tap levels of involvement in the local congregations to which the Committed belong. The overall pattern is surely clear. Slightly more than half of the Committed say they are a member of a religious or church related group.[12] However, the level of that more intimate and intense involvement varies considerably across the four religious traditions. The key difference is a simple Catholic–Protestant one, with Catholics being notably less likely to belong to a particular church-related group. Since Catholic congregations tend to be larger than their Protestant counterparts,[13] the relatively lower degree of intimate involvement by Catholics is made all the greater. We have just seen that Conservative Protestants are more likely than Mainline Protestants to pray, read the Bible, and discuss spiritual matters. However, that greater private religiosity of Conservative Protestants does not extend to the social or public domain. By a variety of measures, Mainline and Conservative Protestants have broadly similar levels of involvement that cause a strikingly high 87% and 89% respectively to "feel they are an important part of the congregation" to which they are attached.

As a general rule, it is Quebec Catholics whose involvement with their local parish is most likely to be confined to their attendance at mass. That conclusion derives least support from the second line in table 7.12, but it is amply demonstrated in the other measures of involvement, from being in a small group to participating in social activities or feeling an important part of the congregation they attend. The exception comes from the Reid 1996 survey item on volunteering. However that Reid finding is not corroborated by the much larger, 1997 NSVGP survey by Statistics Canada in which I put greater trust because it is so explicitly focused on volunteering. The second NSVGP in 2000 also confirms that only a handful of Quebec Catholics volunteer

Table 7.12
Involvement in local congregation by religion of the committed

	N	RC Quebec	RC RoC	Main. Prot.	Con. Prot.	All Committed	All Very Committed	V
% Member of religious or church related groups[1]	(1,102)	25	37	66	63	53	55	.34***
% Volunteer in church related group[1]	(1,102)	23	27	55	55	39	48	.31***
% Volunteered in religious organizations last year[2]	(6,735)	3	11	33	39	19	26	.35***
% Served on committee in church related group[1]	(1,102)	14	16	39	37	26	33	.26***
% Involved in small group with church or religious group[1]	(472)	12	29	42	49	34	44	.29***
% Involved in social activities at or through the congregation they attend[3]	(410)	35	44	70	85	60	68	.38***
% Feel they are an important part of the congregation they attend[3]	(408)	61	84	87	89	82	88	.25***
% For whom most of their close friends belong to the congregation they attend[3]	(396)	46	24	17	45	30	35	.27***
% For whom more than half of their close friends belong to the congregation they attend[3]	(396)	46	24	17	45	30	35	.16*

[1]Reid 1996 [2]NSVGP 1997 [3]Reid 1994 ***P < .001 **P < .01 *P < .05

in religious bodies (6%), though the practice is far from widespread among Catholics in the rest of Canada (9%). We should also recall the dramatic evidence from table 5.31 that Quebec Catholics give much less annually to their church than do Catholics elsewhere, who in turn give much less than do Protestants. In short, all these varied indicators of volunteering, charitable giving, and social involvement with their parishes indicate that Quebec Catholics are much less attached to their local faith community than the Committed in the other three religious families.

The bottom line in table 7.12 adds one noteworthy qualification. Since the Committed regularly attend church services and frequently are much more involved, we might expect that most of their close friends would also be members of the congregations to which they are so attached. However, that is not actually the case. Large 45% to 46% minorities of Quebec Catholics and Conservative Protestants do say that most of their friends belong to the congregations they attend, but the majority deny this is so. As for Catholics in the rest of Canada and Mainline Protestants, less than a quarter draw most of their close friends from their local congregations. Overall, only 30% of the Committed and 35% of the Very Committed do so. Thus, the Committed are typically involved in their local faith communities in a variety of ways, but only about a third or less are socially confined to that world. The great majority maintain close personal ties with the outside world.

Table 7.13 provides an overview of how the Committed regard their churches. I am frankly surprised at how broadly positive and uncritical their professed views are. Over 90% of the Committed say their church "meets my spiritual needs very well;" an equally impressive proportion add that they "feel close or very close to their church or denomination." When it comes to receiving "a great deal or quite a bit of enjoyment from their religious group," a much lower 63% of the Committed respond positively, but that is largely caused by discontent on the part of the Less Committed; among the inner core of the Very Committed, a much more resounding 79% say they receive much joy from their faith community. With very few exceptions these highly positive opinions are endorsed in all the major religious families. Not surprisingly, Conservative Protestants, with their very high levels of personal and social commitment to their faith, are most likely to express their enjoyment. At the other end of the spectrum, Catholics outside Quebec do express notably less enjoyment from their church than anyone else, but that discontent is not apparent on

Table 7.13
Views on and confidence in organized religion by religion of the committed

	N	RC Quebec	RC RoC	Main. Prot.	Con. Prot.	All Committed	All Very Committed	V
% Look to the church for strong guidance on how to live my day to day life[1]	(435)	72	74	78	83	74	81	.09
% Agree the church I attend meets my spiritual needs very well[2]	(464)	94	91	90	92	91	96	.06
% Receive a great deal or quite a bit of enjoyment from their religious group[3]	(621)	67	46	66	86	64	79	.28
% Feel close or very close to their church or denomination[2]	(469)	94	89	86	95	90	96	.12
% Have a great deal/quite a lot of confidence in organized religion[4]	(1,094)	85	79	82	82	78	86	.06

[1]Reid 1994　[2]Reid 1993　[3]Bibby 1995　[4]Reid 1996　***P < .001　**P < .01　*P < .05

the other questions. Given the sharp disagreements that Catholics have with their church over a variety of sexual issues, to be examined shortly, I expected far deeper and far more widespread dissatisfaction from Catholics. It appears that the enjoyment and satisfaction of membership in a religious tradition are rooted more in the dynamics of local fellowship and shared faith than in agreement or disagreement on doctrinal matters.

A rather different take on the same theme may be derived from survey responses since 1980 on the confidence levels of Canadians in organized religion. Several Gallup polls since 1979 indicate that the 60% of Canadians who initially had a great deal or quite a lot of confidence in organized religion fell to 41% in 1993; in 1996 and 1997 confidence in the churches appeared to stabilize at 44%.[14] Table 7.14, covering roughly the same time span, but using other surveys, indicates that confidence in churches fell from 70% in 1980 to 52% in 1996 and 36% in 1995. Though I present these two most recent estimates as a reminder of how surveys can and do vary, I lean to the Reid 1996 estimate of 52% because its question precisely echoes the earlier questions used by the World Vales Survey. Perhaps Bibby's question on "the people in charge" evokes more negative responses than a generic question about confidence in the churches. In either case, there has been an appreciable decline in confidence in religious institutions that continued through the first half of the 1990s. Of course, readers should recall from the last chapter that there has been a general decline in confidence in public institutions brought on by higher educational levels and increased concern with autonomy and self-expression. To be specific, confidence in secular institutions fell by about 20% between 1980 and 1996, which is not much less than the 26% decline in confidence in religious bodies over the same period.[15] As Bibby rightly suggests, scandals over clerical abuse in these years may have contributed to the loss of confidence in churches, but there is clearly something more generic going on that affects all institutions.[16]

As for the Very Committed, their high 86% level of confidence in organized religion in 1996 shows very little variation by religious family and is consistent with the other very positive ratings of their churches shown in table 7.13. Despite a general decline in confidence in institutions, the Committed remain largely faithful adherents to their respective churches. Overt, vocal discontent from the Committed remains relatively rare.

Table 7.14
Confidence in organized religion by attendance

	N	Weekly	Monthly	Rarely	Never	Total	Tau-c
% Have a great deal / quite a lot of confidence in the church or organized religion 1996[1]	(2,940)	85	69	49	24	52	.51***
% Have a great deal / quite a bit of confidence in the people in charge of religious organizations 1995[2]	(1,663)	67	57	26	9	36	.45***
% Have a great deal / quite a lot of confidence in the church 1990[3]	(1,716)	90	87	60	33	64	.51***
% Have a great deal / quite a lot of confidence in the church, 1980[4]	(1,238)	93	85	64	31	70	.50***

[1]Reid 1996 [2]Bibby 1995 [3]WVS 1990 [4]WVS 1980 ***P < .001 **P < .01 *P < .05

CONTEMPORARY CHALLENGES:
EDUCATION, ABORIGINALS, AND SEXUALITY

This final section of the last substantive chapter analyzes the major challenges or controversies that Christians and their churches now confront. Please note that my necessarily brief comments cannot provide a full accounting on issues that are either on-going in nature or that still await thorough researching by others. Some of these issues do not impinge very greatly on the day-to-day life of their laity, but all evoke passion when debated. All are also likely to have a profound influence on the character, even the very survival, of Christians and their churches in years to come.

Debate over the role of religion in our school system has a long pedigree going back to Confederation, when the BNA Act stipulated that provinces joining Canada had to fund separate Roman Catholic schools if they were already in existence. That requirement reflected the power of organized Christianity in the middle of the 1800s. It also stemmed from the linguistic compact between Upper and Lower Canada, whereby anglophones in Quebec and francophones outside were to be assured constitutionally protected educational rights through this denominational system. A state-funded Catholic school system was eventually implemented in all provinces except British Columbia and Manitoba, but Catholic schools often received less financial support than state schools, which were generically Protestant in practice, if not in theory. Much later, even more partial provincial grants were extended to other religious schools in British Columbia, Alberta, Saskatchewan, Manitoba, and Quebec, which then permitted some support for Catholic schools in Manitoba and British Columbia. That basic system remained in place until recently, though there has always been considerable regional variation, as education is a provincial responsibility.[17]

In 1998, Newfoundland and Quebec, with the approval of the federal government, abolished their confessionally based educational systems, replacing them with state-run secular versions.[18] However these important developments do not auger any general dismantling of religiously based schooling in Canada. Moral and religious education will continue to be part of the required curriculum in Quebec schools.[19] In Ontario, after full funding was extended to its Catholic school system in 1985, a coalition of parents from a variety of faiths used the newly available equality provisions of the Charter of Rights and Freedoms to argue in the courts that the availability of full funding only for Catholic schools discriminated against all other faiths. In 1996, the Supreme Court ruled that Ontario had no obligation to provide funding for independent religious schools, though it recognised that Ontario, like other provinces, had the right to do so.[20] Then in 2001, the Conservative Ontario government introduced a system of tax credits for all independent schools that would undoubtedly have led to much growth, but the new Liberal government in the fall of 2003 introduced a bill to repeal the tax credit.[21] The latest statistics indicate that about 5% of Ontario students are in private schools. In Alberta and British Columbia, 9% of all students also attend private schools, which had been receiving for some time government grants at about half the level allocated for public schools.[22] About 70% of these private schools are estimated to be religiously based.[23]

Bibby's data in table 7.15 indicate that about 29% of all Canadians in 1995 had attended a parochial or church school; for those under age 30, it was still a healthy 24%. Despite the continued and possibly growing presence of religion-based schools outside Quebec, less than a quarter of Canadians in 1985 felt that government should fund "religious groups wishing to establish private schools." The great majority, including 67% of weekly attenders were opposed, including 60% of Catholics, who have most benefited from a confessional system. Though some evangelical or Conservative Protestant organizations have been particularly vocal in demanding their own state-funded, religion-based schools, their demand is not endorsed by over two-thirds of their rank and file. Primed in the right way, Canadians can be induced to voice greater support for separate religious schools.[24] However, I conclude from Bibby's generally neutral question that a solid majority of Canadians prefer to have the children of all faiths schooled together in a common, government-run system.

There remains, of course, the question of whether religion has a place in the state, non-confessional schools that most Canadians still attend. As I have not been able to find a thorough account for all ten provinces, Ontario must serve as an instructive example. From the beginning, the public school system had a generic Protestant ethos where permission was granted for daily recitations of the Lord's Prayer and Bible readings. In 1944 the general Protestant ethos was reinforced by the introduction into the curriculum of a regular program of religious education, though parents had the unconditional right to exempt their children from the program if they wished.

Table 7.15
Views on the role of religion in education by religiosity (Bibby)

	N	Very Commited	Less Commited	Seeker	Non Relig.	Total	Tau-c
% With at least some of their education in a church or parochial school (1995)	(1,610)	36	44	23	24	29	.12**
% Agree govt funding should be provided for all religious groups wishing to establish private schools (1985)[1]	(1,575)	33	27	21	13	23	.15***
% Agree it would be better not to have prayers said in public schools because not all Canadians have the same religious beliefs (1975)	(1,834)	22	29	39	70	43	.44***
% Agree it would be better not to have prayers said in public schools because not all Canadians have the same religious beliefs (1995)	(1,648)	23	25	40	69	46	.43***
% Agree public schools should offer courses in religion (1995)	(1,653)	73	74	59	36	55	.34***

[1]This question is cross-classified by frequency of attendance at religious services: weekly, monthly, rarely, or never

***P < .001   **P < .01   *P < .05

Table 7.16
Views on the role of religion in education by religion of the committed (Bibby)

	N	RC Quebec	RC RoC	Main. Prot.	Con. Prot.	V
% With at least some of their education in a church or parochial school (1995)	(573)	80	46	10	24	.54***
% Agree govt funding should be provided for all religious groups wishing to establish private schools (1985)	(627)	39	42	13	31	.27***
% Agree it would be better not to have prayers said in public schools because not all Canadians have the same religious beliefs (1975)	(700)	22	29	22	24	.07
% Agree it would be better not to have prayers said in public schools because not all Canadians have the same religious beliefs (1995)	(582)	25	21	22	11	.11
% Agree public schools should offer courses in religion (1995)	(588)	85	75	66	71	.16*

***P < .001   **P < .01   *P < .05

Detailed study guides were designed and introduced across the province, but the program fell "into desuetude by 1960 or so"[25] as more and more school boards exercised their right to opt out of the program in the face of parental opposition. Then, in 1969 the McKay Commission recommended the formal removal of the entire 1944 program, though the recommendation was never formally implemented because there was really no need to rescind what was already dead. Inaction of this sort was also "the least controversial action to take."[26] The McKay Commission had recommended that an optional course in world religions be offered to senior students as a substitute for the confessional teaching of the past, but less than 1% of senior students in 1980 took the course.[27]

There remained the old statutory provisions allowing for the Lord's Prayer and Bible readings, which were successfully challenged in court by a group of parents from Sudbury, who argued that the provisions discriminated against non-Christians. When the Ontario Court of Appeal in 1988 "ruled that the Education Act infringed upon freedom of religion and conscience as guaranteed by the Charter,"[28] the provincial government banished all religious instruction and expression throughout the Ontario school system. In 1998, the Supreme Court of Canada reinforced that legal decision when it refused to hear a lower court appeal by a group of Ontario parents from different faiths, who had been seeking the right to operate voluntary religious education programs in public schools.[29] Today, the Lord's Prayer is also legally prohibited in British Columbia, Manitoba, and Saskatchewan.[30] The education acts of Alberta and Nova Scotia still contain old provisions allowing for the use of the Lord's Prayer, but that right is rarely or never exercised in both provinces.[31] In Nova Scotia where I live, I gather that neither prayers nor religious instruction have been present since at least the 1960s. The courts therefore dealt the final blow, but Christianity's presence in the public school system had effectively disappeared as early as the middle of the 1960s.

Outside the courts and boards of education, survey data produce a rather more ambiguous picture. In table 7.15, we see that a little less than half of us think prayers should be excluded from public schools "because not all Canadians have the same religious beliefs." That percentage did not grow appreciably between 1975 and 1995. In fact, a small majority voiced their support for prayers in schools in both polls. There are therefore no signs of secular consensus on the matter, though we should not ignore the large minority in opposition. When it comes to offering courses in religion in schools, there is a very similar breakdown with 55% in favour and 45% opposed. Support for prayers and religious courses is predictably greatest among the Committed and least among the Non Religious, though we should not ignore the 36% of the Non Religious who think religion has some place in public schools. Had the question on religious courses differentiated between courses in comparative religion and those prompting a particular denomination's teachings, I suspect support for the former might have been higher. Even after the just mentioned court decisions in the late 1980s, the Ontario Ministry of Education was still prepared to admit that schools "may expose students to all religious views, but not impose a particular view."[32] However, efforts to introduce comparative courses in religion typically fail when humanists or the Non Religious voice their opposition.[33] Despite the many who feel that religion should have some place in schools, our public school system seems incapable of recognizing, explaining, or celebrating the religious traditions of Canadians. As we saw in the last chapter, Canadian multicultural ideas tend to stumble when we confront religious diversity.

Residential, denominationally based schools for Canada's First Nations or Aboriginals began to be phased out in the latter part of the 1960s. Initiated, funded, and ultimately supervised by the federal government, the 130 schools were administered by the Roman Catholic, Anglican, United, and Presbyterian churches. Almost all the schools had been closed by the middle of the 1970s, but the legacy of the residential schools continues to have a profound current impact on their former students and on the churches that ran them. In the late 1980s, and then accelerating in the 1990s, reports began to emerge of terrible cases of sexual abuse inflicted on children in the residential schools by their teachers and administrators. Though it is impossible to calculate precisely the overall level or frequency of sexual abuse, Miller's thorough and dispassionate research led him to conclude that "sexual abuse of children in these institutions was widespread and long standing."[34] The ensuing scandal prompted formal, public apologies to Aboriginals, starting with the United Church in 1986, the Oblates and Canadian Conference of Catholic Bishops in 1991, the Anglican Church in 1993, and the Presbyterians in 1994. The federal government was far slower to acknowledge its ultimate responsibility for the system, but it did so in 1998, voicing its apologies to those "who suffered this tragedy" that "should never have happened," and promising to establish a $350 million healing fund for Aboriginals.[35]

Tortured by old memories and faced with so many sweeping admissions of guilt, Aboriginals began to initiate civil lawsuits in ever-increasing numbers, demanding compensation for the abuse and suffering they had received at the hands of the government and the churches. From about 200 lawsuits in 1996, the number rose to 1,600 in late 1998,[36] to 7,600 in June of 2001,[37] and then to about 12,000 just a few months later in October, 2001. These rapidly rising claimants numbered in that year less than 15% of all still-living, former students.[38] It is therefore entirely possible that the number of litigants may grow substantially in the future.

Though only 5% of the cases had been settled by the end of 2002, the federal government had already paid out $47 million in claims.[39] Estimates of the final compensation package ranged from two to ten billion dollars in 2001.[40] Estimates at the higher end are based on the assumption that the courts will accept Aboriginal complaints of cultural genocide, emotional suffering, kidnapping, and forced confinement. The federal government insists that its legal liabilities are confined to proven cases of sexual and physical abuse, but that insistence has not deterred a recent $12.5 billion class-action lawsuit on behalf of all 90,000 residential school survivors, which demands compensation for "loss of language and culture," as well as physical and sexual abuse.[41] The number of successful claimants is also likely to grow even higher if the Supreme Court sustains a 2003 ruling by the Ontario Court of Appeal that the children of residential school attenders may join their parents in seeking damages for loss of language and culture.[42] To curb these potentially spiralling costs, the government in late 2002 proposed an expedited, out-of-court $1.7 billion settlement scheme that would be confined to those who could prove they had been a victim of sexual or physical abuse. Besides some questionable math in the estimate of the total cost, it is also less than clear whether the courts will offer compensation to plaintiffs who demand compensation for language and cultural losses. If this latest federal proposal is rejected, officials say the current, case-by-case court system will cost $2.3 billion in administrative costs alone and would take over 50 years.[43] In short, there are simply too many imponderables here to make a trustworthy assessment of the total cost of all these cases. All that can safely be said is that the financial cost is likely to be staggering.

According to Tony Merchant, whose Saskatchewan law office represented about half of all Aboriginal plaintiffs in 2000, the vast majority of his clients did not initially sue the churches, which were only brought in when counter-sued by the federal government.[44] The legal propriety of that federal action was greatly strengthened by a 1999 decision of the British Columbia Supreme Court, which said that the Anglican Church had a 60% responsibility (as against 40% for the government) for a lawsuit seeking damages for sexual abuse.[45] A year later, Donald Brenner, Chief Justice of the B.C. Supreme Court ruled that the United Church bore a 25% liability for damages of $410,000 awarded to six plaintiffs.[46] Both decisions are founded on the recent legal precedent of "vicarious liability" that has the endorsement of the Supreme Court. Vicarious liability means that an employer is responsible for the actions of an employee and may be required to pay damages, even when the employer did nothing wrong.[47] The four churches therefore became embroiled in every abuse lawsuit arising in schools that they formerly ran.

When negotiations floundered between government and the four churches, the government made a unilateral offer in the fall of 2001 to pay 70% of all liabilities, but this was rejected by the churches on the grounds that it might "drive them to financial ruin" without a set financial cap, which the government was unwilling to offer.[48]

Without a cap, church officials are understandably worried that their liability might be inflated by dubious complaints of sexual and physical abuse. When events occurred so long ago, eyewitnesses are rare, and when so much money is at stake, the possibility of dubious claims cannot be dismissed.[49]

Initially, the Anglican Church seemed to be most severely threatened. Eleven of its 30 dioceses were embroiled in the lawsuits of 2,200 claimants at the end of 2002.[50] In 2001, the small Diocese of Cariboo in northern British Columbia ceased to exist as a legal entity, its bishop retired, and its assets, mainly of church property, were placed in legal trust to await final court decisions in the Lytton case, where four former students had been awarded settlements of over $1 million dollars at this Anglican-run school.[51] At around the same time, Qu'Appelle diocese in Saskatchewan was in equally dire straits as it faced 350 lawsuits with funds to deal with no more than the first 50.[52] The other 19 dioceses were not directly involved in residential school lawsuits, but the General Synod, or national body of the Anglican Church, was named as a defendant in most lawsuits. So onerous were its legal responsibilities that there was serious talk of the General Synod being forced into bankruptcy. Had this occurred, 225 Aboriginal Anglican congregations, their 130 Aboriginal priests and deacons, and their four Aboriginal bishops in 2000 would have lost the $2.7 million annual subsidy the General Synod provided for northern communities.[53]

Faced with these combined pressures, the Anglican Church entered into separate negotiations with the federal government that resulted in an agreement in late 2002. To summarize very briefly a 53 page document of very technical language, the Anglican Church has agreed to pay liability up to a maximum of $25 million for cases of sexual and physical abuse that occurred in its schools. This agreement, which all 30 dioceses were obliged to ratify, ended Anglican involvement in all litigation and ensured that the monies raised by the Anglican Church would be awarded to the victims, and not their lawyers.[54] At the time the agreement was signed, 98% of the $5 million spent had gone to lawyers.[55] Though this agreement does not cover any future liability for language and cultural loss cases before the courts, defenders argued: 1) the legal foundation for such claims was very weak; 2) the government would bear the major cost in defending against them;[56] and 3) the most appropriate way to deal with cultural issues is through language and counselling programs in Aboriginal communities, rather than cash payments.[57] The Anglican Council of Indigenous Peoples subsequently rejected the agreement for failing to support the demand of Aboriginals that cultural and language losses deserve court mandated compensation.[58] More criticisms of the agreement may well emerge as it is implemented, but the agreement does appear to have secured the previously threatened institutional survival of the Anglican Church.

The situation is much less critical for the United Church because it has a larger pool of active members[59] and its 631[60] plaintiffs from United Church residential schools in 2001 were only about a third the number bringing lawsuits against the Anglican Church. With the Anglican agreement as our guide, we would expect that the United Church should be able to negotiate a liability cap of about $8 million with the federal government for charges of sexual and physical abuse. However, the United Church "has been vocal in its contention that the cultural loss … in residential schools has to be recognized in settlements with survivors."[61] This may well explain why they have not yet reached an agreement with the federal government. If this situation persists, the United Church will have to endure a very considerable cost that has already amounted, in 1999 alone, to $2.3 million in legal fees and an undisclosed amount in 22 out-of-court settlements.[62]

Presbyterians administered only two residential schools and face an even smaller 123 plaintiffs, of whom only "a few allege physical and/or sexual abuse."[63] Following closely the Anglican accord, Presbyterians have signed their own agreement that limits their liability for abuse to $1.3 million. Conservative Protestants are unaffected, since they never ran any residential school and do not face any lawsuits.

Roman Catholics, on the other hand, ran more schools than anyone else and faced lawsuits in 2001 from 6,381 plaintiffs, who were then a whopping 72% of all plaintiffs.[64] However, the Oblate order ran 57 of the 70 Catholic residential schools, most of them located in western Canada. The Oblates in 2000 were inundated with lawsuits from about 3,500 plaintiffs, who amounted to 81% of the then 4,110 plaintiffs making claims on the Catholic Church.[65] Not surprisingly, the six Oblate provinces were spending over $2 million a year for legal fees and face immanent bankruptcy.[66] The Oblates estimated that their liability could reach $90 million in Saskatchewan alone. Next door, in Manitoba they faced 2,000 claimants in 2000. They therefore proposed that they hand over all their assets, estimated to be worth "several million dollars," to the crown, in return for the crown assuming the order's remaining liability. The Oblates asked that they be allowed to put aside a small sum for the care of the 79 surviving Oblates whose average age was 72. The remaining Oblate assets would then be distributed to "legitimate victims."[67] Two years later, the Oblates of Manitoba sued for bankruptcy unable to deal with lawsuits estimated to amount to $270-million.[68] There were also reports that the Grandin Oblates of Alberta, who face another 1,200 lawsuits, were thinking of following "their Manitoba counterparts into bankruptcy."[69]

In earlier negotiations, Catholic representatives had argued that only specific dioceses or religious orders with contracts with the government should be liable in residential school lawsuits.[70] In the aftermath of the 2001 Anglican accord with the government, Msgr. Peter Schonenbach, then head of the Canadian Conference of Catholic Bishops, told the press that "there is no single corporate entity within the Catholic Church." Tellingly, Schonenbach suggested that Ottawa ought to seek compensation from "the Oblate missionaries and the Grey Nuns."[71]

If this strategy succeeds, it would place responsibility for about 80% of all Catholic lawsuits on the small and doomed Oblate order. There are estimated to be residential lawsuits against 20 of the Catholic Church's 71 dioceses,[72] but they are sufficiently reduced in number to be manageable, though they might well cause considerable stress here and there. It remains to be seen if the Catholic Church can sustain the legal stance that its many dioceses and orders are all legally separate from one another. Recent legal cases suggest it may be successful. In 2001, the Alberta Court of Appeal ruled that the Roman Catholic Church as a whole "is not a suable entity," though the Archdiocese and the Oblate Province of Grandin "remain in the lawsuit."[73] Next door, in Saskatchewan, a judge went even further, ruling that the government's attempt to name the Archdiocese as a defendant in an Oblate-run school was "devoid of merit."[74] Rulings like this may help to explain both the restrained response of the Catholic Church to the residential school controversy and the failure of the federal government to find a solution. Leaving aside the unanswerable question of how many abuse cases are legitimate, it appears the Catholic Church in Canada has found an effective means of avoiding collective responsibility for the approximately half of all abuse claimants who attended schools run by Oblates. Some may question whether this is morally acceptable or politically palatable.

A potentially far greater challenge for the Catholic Church is its shrinking, aging corpus of clergy. This is not a uniquely Canadian phenomenon. In the United States, the number of clergy is projected to decline 40% from 1965 to 2005, leaving the majority close to retirement.[75] Even in holy, Catholic, Ireland, the Archdiocese of Dublin is said to have had no new entrants to its seminaries in 1998.[76] I have not been able to locate up-to-date meaningful figures for all of Canada, but the available data all lead to the same conclusion. From the peak year of 1968, the number of diocesan clergy fell from 8,973 to 6,111 in 1993. That 32% decline in 25 years does not begin to reveal the magnitude of the crisis, since a whopping 42% in 1993 were aged 65 or older; another 27% were between 55 and 54 years, leaving just 31% below age 55 and only 9% under 40. By the year 2000, the 1995 report for the Canadian Conference of Catholic Bishops, from which I draw these numbers, estimates there would be "fewer than 3,000 diocesan priests under the age of 65."[77] In 1998, an even higher 60% of the 4,300 priests and brothers attached to religious orders were over age 65.[78] With the number of seminarians falling between 1988 and 1993, the haemorrhaging is likely to continue.[79] Thus the large Calgary diocese serving a nominal population of some 200,000 Catholics with 92 priests in 2000 expected to lose at least 30 of its priests over the next 10 years. The diocese was relying on 15 recently arrived priests from Poland and the Philippines, but the religious orders of Redemptorists, Scalabrini Fathers, Oblates, and Basilians, on which the diocese had long depended, were all pulling out. Only seven seminarians were in training locally.[80] Even an elite order like the Jesuits was forced to cut back on 16 of their projects in English-speaking Canada. They faced a deficit of $1 million, stock market losses, and a $7 million sexual abuse settlement with an Aboriginal community. Moreover, half of their 230 members were over age 65, no longer had their teaching salaries to draw upon, and sometimes needed "Jesuit-funded infirmary care."[81]

Since Vatican II in the early 1960s, reform-minded Catholics have sought to resolve the problem of declining vocations by proposing that priests be allowed to marry and women be admitted into the priesthood. In 1994 the Pope gave his answer saying, "The church has no authority whatsoever to confer priestly ordination on women." He stressed, "this judgement is to be definitively held by all the church's faithful," who should now stop talking about the whole matter.[82] In subsequent years bishops at Synods in Asia and Europe have raised

Table 7.17
Catholic views on married priests, women priests, divorce, and sexual abuse
(Reid 1993)

	Committed		Marginal		(N)	
	Quebec	RoC	Quebec	RoC	Quebec	RoC
% Agree that Roman Catholic priests should be allowed to marry	82	79	92	91	(266)	(263)
% Agree women should be able to become Catholic priests	80	74	87	80	(269)	(268)
% Agree the Catholic Church's requirements that all priests be celibate is one of the major reasons we have seen cases of sexual abuse by priests	57	69	73	76	(265)	(272)

the matter of married priests,[83] but the celibacy requirement still largely holds.[84] Despite petitions with millions of signatures from across the Western Catholic world,[85] there is no reason to believe the current Pope will change his strongly held views. The price he and his church pay is considerable. As can be seen in table 7.17, an impressive 80% of committed or active Catholics (attending at least monthly) agree that Catholic priests should be allowed to marry. An almost equally large majority (76%) feel women should be able to become priests. Note also that a little over half of all Committed Catholics think that celibacy "is one of the major reasons we have seen cases of sexual abuse by priests." In such a climate, where hardly any see the need for celibacy and quite a few think it is positively harmful, we should scarcely be surprised that so few men are prepared to enter a celibate priesthood. That conclusion is surely reinforced by another spate in 2002 of highly publicized accounts of priests sexually abusing children and juveniles in both Canada and the United States.

Across the country, dioceses struggle to amalgamate parishes and otherwise reorganize their shrinking human resources. In Edmonton's large Archdiocese, which covers roughly the land area of the United Kingdom, ambitious plans were introduced in 1998 to halve its 166 parishes, then served by only 79 priests. Even with the many closures and amalgamations, anticipated declines of clergy down to less than 50 would mean that most priests would have more laity for whom they would be responsible, typically in more than one church.[86] As their energy wanes with age and ill-health, more and more of their time must be devoted to liturgical activities of holding

mass, baptisms, weddings, and the like. Less and less of their time
can be devoted to pastoral counselling. Of necessity, parishes have
been turning to lay pastoral workers to run their affairs. The numbers
of lay workers grew from 1,938 to 3,075 in the brief five years between
1988 and 1993; presumably they are far more numerous today and
therefore outnumber all regular diocesan clergy. Over four-fifths of
these lay pastoral workers (83%) were women in 1993.[87] These are
surely revolutionary developments. In one case in 1998, a priest from
distant Edmonton made weekly visits to a parish in Hinton, Alberta
to administer mass. Otherwise the parish administrator was running
the affairs of the parish, along with her husband, who chaired the
parish council.[88] The Pope certainly did not intend events to unfold
this way, but his policies are surely at least partially responsible.[89]

Among Protestants, open or formal resistance to female clergy is
now most likely to be found in Conservative Protestant denominations, though they have a longer tradition of the occasionally noteworthy woman preacher. Sister Aimee Semple McPherson from
Ontario is the most striking example of this tradition. Founder of the
International Church of the Foursquare Gospel, Sister Aimee was a
twice-divorced, riveting evangelist whose powers to draw large
crowds enabled her to build the huge Angelus Temple in Los Angeles
(1923) and found a Bible College.[90] Far more typical are Atlantic
Baptists who have allowed the ordination of women since the 1940s,
but who had only 13 women among their 383 pastors in 1993.[91] On
the other hand, the Fellowship of Evangelical Baptist Churches in
Canada reiterated in 1997 that only men could be pastors,[92] and the
North American Baptist Conference did not ordain its first woman
until 1999.[93] Reluctance to ordain women has its theological roots in
a number of New Testament passages, particularly from St. Paul,
affirming female subordination to men. They also stem from a more
generic social conservatism manifested in table 6.16 in the last chapter, which indicates that about a third of Conservative Protestants
feel that men should be in charge of public life. The tensions between
the third who agree and the two-thirds who do not is nicely illus-
trated by a 1994 decision of the board of the Ontario Bible College
(OBC) to overturn an invitation to a woman to become it first ever
graduation speaker. Though the OBC had recently formulated a
gender policy saying, "women and men are called equally to serve
God," the board defended its decision on the grounds that a female
speaker might offend its "substantial conservative constituency" and

thereby lead to a loss of donations.[94] When social and theological conservatism combine, resistance to women clergy is strong.

Mainline Protestant churches eventually acceded to the principle of women clergy, though there was struggle and resistance in every denomination. Preceded by the United Church in 1936, Anglicans, Lutherans, and Presbyterians all allowed women clergy rather later in the 1970s. Since hard information on the current circumstances of women clergy is distressingly and surprisingly lacking for such a hot button issue in generally progressive churches, what follows is particularly sketchy. The ordination of six women priests in 1976 in the Anglican Church has been described as a "revolution from above," under the leadership of then-Primate Ted Scott. To mollify the dissidents, a conscience clause was inserted that left the final decision to each bishop and thus to each diocesan synod.[95] Initially, 37 of the 50 priests in the diocesan synod of British Columbia rejected female ordination, though a subsequent vote in 1986 did allow women priests.[96] I am told that the Diocese of Fredericton in New Brunswick was the last to make this decision in 1991. In 1980, Lois Wilson was elected as the first Moderator or head of the United Church,[97] but only 4% of all United Church clergy were female in 1978 – more than 40 years after the barrier was first broken.[98] Among Anglicans, the first female bishop, Victoria Matthews, was elected in 1994 and today three of the 43 bishops are female.[99] Change, therefore, has come recently and slowly in both these mainline denominations.

By the early 1980s, "nearly 50% of candidates for ministry" in the United Church were female.[100] I have no precise numbers for Canadian Anglicans, but the various sources I have checked are agreed that females equalled or outnumbered males in theological colleges in the 1990s, and possibly even earlier in the 1980s. Overall, there has been a huge upsurge since the 1970s in the percentage of women taking theological and ministerial training in all Mainline Protestant denominations in the United States and Britain, as well as in Canada.[101] However, the entrance of women into pastoral ministry or the running of congregations has proceeded much more slowly. By the end of 2000, 26% of ordained ministers in the United Church were female.[102] In the same year, women were 17% of active Anglican clergy.[103] This is a major transformation in a relatively short period of time, but it is far from gender parity.

There are two broad sets of explanations for the slow entry of so many trained female candidates into pastoral ministry. The first finds evidence of resistance to female clergy by the lay rank-and-file members of Protestant churches. Further evidence of gender discrimination is found in more women than men leaving pastoral ministry and women clergy earning less than males, even when they have the same qualifications and experience. However, research documenting these sorts of claims exists only in the United States.[104] Barring some anecdotal evidence of a glass ceiling,[105] this gender bias explanation has not been systematically assessed in Canada. It is possible that anti-female sentiments are at work, particularly among the elderly, who often serve on the committees of local congregations. On the other hand, we should not forget the evidence in table 6.16 that Mainline Protestants massively repudiate the notion that leadership should be a male preserve. We also ought to be wary of notions of systemic discrimination in the administrative structure of the Mainline Protestant churches. If anything the reverse is the case. At the 1997 General Council of the United Church, 70% of the lay commissioners and 54% of ministry commissioners were females. Both percentages were actually higher than their respective constituencies in the United Church as a whole. Similarly at the last Anglican General synod in 2001, 48% of the lay delegates were female because "gender parity is one of the principles the Church uses when choosing delegates."[106] If gender bias exists, we must look beyond head office for its source.

The second broad influence on the recruitment and promotion of women clergy is demographic in nature. There are two distinct elements here. First, the average age of Anglicans entering theological college between 1988 and 1998 in southern Ontario was 36 for men and 46 for women.[107] That is a considerable increase to the average age of ordination of 25 in the 1970s.[108] The older average entry age of women in particular may help to explain why few have risen to high rank. Being middle-aged may also create a variety of attachments to children and spouse that may hinder mobility to remote areas where entry-level clerical jobs tend to be more readily available.[109] Second, these have been trying times for anyone entering this profession, regardless of gender, since the potential pool of active members attending at least monthly fell by 35% among Anglicans and 39% in the United Church between 1985 and 2000.[110] This major contraction occurred in precisely the period when Anglican and United Church women were leaving theological colleges in unprecedented numbers.

Very recently, there have been reports here and there of clerical shortages arriving or soon arriving in Mainline Protestant churches, as early boomer clergy enter their retirement years.[111] The trend is too early and too undocumented to call with any certainty. We may therefore be entering a decisive new phase in the saga of women clergy, though these new opportunities will be tempered by the still shrinking number of Committed Mainline Protestants. Beyond these demographic impediments, there remains the fundamental reality that women outnumber men by a 57-to-43 margin in Mainline Protestant churches, which have large numbers of trained female aspirants to ministry. Given the further claim by Mainline Protestants and their churches that they are committed to gender equality, the rate at which they achieve this goal is a crucial test of their integrity and their capacity for renewal.

I have left to the very end the issue of homosexuality because it has emerged as a matter of public debate only relatively recently. Public attitudes and their attendant legislative expressions are still in a state of flux. In the 1960s, pollsters would have been unlikely to find many Canadians prepared to endorse either adultery or homosexuality, but only the homosexual act of sodomy was an indictable criminal offence. Though Trudeau's Liberal government had that statute removed in 1969, being gay was still ground for dismissal from the federal civil service.[112] Four years after the Charter of Rights and Freedoms was proclaimed, the federal government in 1986 announced its intention to add "sexual orientation" as a prohibited ground of discrimination in the Canadian Human Rights Act.[113] The federal government did not, in fact, pass the requisite legislation, Bill C-33, until 1996, but by that date seven of 10 provinces, including Ontario and Quebec had already enacted similar legislation.[114] In 1999, the Supreme Court ruled (*M.v H.*) that same-sex couples are entitled to spousal benefits, though here too Health Canada had three years earlier changed its definition of spouse to include gay partners.[115] Not long after, the federal government passed Bill C-23, which gave to gays and lesbians the same federal benefits enjoyed by heterosexual common-law couples.[116] Taken together, these various initiatives represent a major change in public policy that has extended an array of legal rights and protections to gays that they formerly did not possess.

Table 7.18 indicates that 68% of Canadians polled in 1996 were agreed that "homosexuals should have the same rights as other

Table 7.18
Views on homosexuality by religiosity

	N	Very Committed	Less Committed	Seeker	Non Relig.	Total	Tau-c
% Agree homosexuals should have the same rights as other Canadians[1]	(2,867)	55	68	67	76	68	-.15***
% Agree homosexuals should have the same rights as other Canadians (age 18–49)[1]	(2,026)	63	73	73	82	75	-.13***
% Believe 2 people of same sex having sex is always or almost always wrong 1975[2]	(1,808)	87	69	75	57	72	-.26***
% Believe 2 people of same sex having sex is always or almost always wrong 1995[3]	(1,632)	79	61	50	32	50	.40***
% Believe 2 people of same sex having sex is always or almost always wrong (Age 18–49)[3]	(707)	72	55	39	28	41	.33***
% Agree homosexuals should be eligible for ordination to be ministers or priests[3]	(1,605)	20	29	43	63	44	-.38***
% Agree homosexuals should be eligible for ordination to be ministers or priests (Age 18–49)[3]	(686)	22	32	51	67	51	-.37***

[1]Reid 1996   [2]Bibby 1975   [3]Bibby 1995   ***P < .001   **P < .01   *P < .05

Canadians." That percentage has not grown since a Bibby poll in 1980, though the two polls certainly confirm a solid, two-thirds level of support.[117] An even higher 76% of the Non Religious agree. Support for gay equity is notably lower among the Very Committed, who are almost equally divided between those for (55%) and against (45%). Though older Canadians are typically less open to gay rights, the many elderly among the Very Committed does not much influence their views on gay rights. As we can see in table 7.18, support for gay rights rises slightly to 63% for the Very Committed born after 1945, but the gap or spread between the Very Committed and the Non Religious remains about the same. Catholics and Mainline Protestants are less supportive of gay rights than the Non Religious, though the differences here are much less, especially for those under the age of 50. It is therefore Conservative Protestants who really stand out, with less than half willing to endorse equal rights for gays.

Unlike our largely unchanging views on gay rights, the percentage of Canadians who think gay sexuality is inherently wrong has fallen from 72% in 1975 to 50% in 1995. The transformation has been particularly marked among the Non Religious; by 1995 68% had come to believe that homosexuality is morally acceptable. There has been less movement in the same direction by the Very Committed, though the magnitude of the change does vary by religious family or tradition. Conservative Protestants have remained overwhelmingly (96% or more) convinced of homosexuality's sinfulness. On the other hand, the 89% of Mainline Protestants making that claim in 1975 fell to 68% in 1995 and was endorsed by an even lower 46% under the age of 50. Similar though less marked changes among Catholics inside and outside Quebec are also evident in table 7.19. A major change in thinking therefore seems to be underway for Catholics and Mainline Protestants, though I do not want to ignore the very substantial proportion of the Committed that differ from the Non Religious in their conviction that gay sexuality is wrong.

This pervasive conservatism of the laity is rooted in the universal and unquestioned teaching of all Christian Churches until recently that homosexuality is sinful or wrong. To this day, the Catholic Church insists that homosexual acts are "intrinsically disordered," though it is quick to add that a homosexual "tendency or inclination" is not itself a disorder. The church therefore "recognizes the dignity of all persons," including homosexuals, who "are precious in God's eyes."[118] While this teaching leaves open the possibility that a homosexually

Table 7.19
Views on gays by religion of the committed

	N	RC Quebec	RC RoC	Main. Prot.	Con. Prot.	V
% Agree homosexuals should have the same rights as other Canadians[1]	(832)	64	67	68	43	.18***
% Agree homosexuals should have the same rights as other Canadians (Age 18–49)[1]	(510)	72	76	80	45	.28***
% Believe 2 people of same sex having sex is always or almost always wrong 1975[2]	(698)	78	81	89	99	.17***
% Believe 2 people of same sex having sex is always or almost always wrong 1995[3]	(578)	67	67	68	97	.24***
% Believe 2 people of same sex having sex is always or almost always wrong (Age 18–49)[3]	(185)	58	57	46	96	.36***
% Agree homosexuals should be eligible for ordination to be ministers or priests[3]	(583)	20	22	38	11	.21***
% Agree homosexuals should be eligible for ordination to be ministers or priests (Age 18–49)[3]	(188)	27	25	59	12	.33***

[1]Reid 1996   [2]Bibby 1975   [3]Bibby 1995   ***P < .001   **P < .01   *P < .05

inclined celibate might become a priest,[119] about 80% of the Catholics surveyed in table 7.19 felt that homosexuals should not be eligible for ordination. The even lower percentage of Conservative Protestants (11%) who approve of homosexual clergy is rooted in their conviction that they are simply following "the teaching of the Scriptures that homosexual practice is unacceptable."[120] Thus debate over the ordination of homosexuals has largely been confined to Mainline Protestantism, where a substantial 38% minority in 1995 voiced agreement; for baby boomers and Generation Xers under the age of 50, that minority is transformed into a 59% majority.

Leading the way in this hotly contested debate was the United Church. As late as 1960, the General Council of the United Church had affirmed, "homosexuality was a sin against the self."[121] In the 1980s, various reports on homosexuality circulated, recommending a much more open attitude. At the 1988 General Council, after intense debate, the delegates from congregations from across the country voted by a three-to-one margin to accept "all persons regardless of sexual orientation" as "members of the United Church of Canada," making them eligible for ordination.[122] In the aftermath, about 4% of the membership, 70 clergy, and 60 congregations left in protest.[123]

Twelve years later, the General Council of 2000 explicitly repudiated its 1960 resolution on homosexuality. The General Council also asserted that lesbian, gay, and bisexual orientations are "gifts from God," and it called on the United Church to "affirm lesbian and gay partnerships, recognize them in church documentation and services of blessing, and actively work for their civil recognition."[124] The commissioners or delegates at the General Council would seem to be much more liberal on gay issues than their rank-and-file membership, though we should not forget the 59% of Mainline Protestants under 50 years of age who agree that homosexuals should be eligible for ordination. Only 13 local churches have declared themselves to be "Affirming Congregations" actively committed to welcoming gays.[125] There are also estimated to be no more than 27 clergy who openly describe themselves as gay or lesbian.[126] Given the small size of the gay community, that it to be expected. Nevertheless, a fundamental change has occurred in the United Church.

Lutherans have recently committed themselves in 1999 to becoming "a more inclusive place for gay and lesbian people." Their national convention also defeated a motion condemning " any sexual activity outside the boundaries of a heterosexual marriage,"[127] but that is as far as they have gone. Presbyterians, on the other hand, declared in 1994 that homosexuality is "not a Christian option." Two years later, their General Assembly voted by a "a wide margin" to overturn the decision of its Montreal Presbytery to accept the ordination of a practising gay minister who had the support of his local congregation, St. Andrew's, in Lachine, Quebec.[128] Despite minor portents of change, these recent experiences of the Lutheran and Presbyterian churches are a clear reminder that opposition to homosexuality is far from dead.

These competing tendencies for and against homosexuality are most clearly evident in the recent experience of the Anglican Church. In 1995 the General Synod "overwhelmingly passed a motion affirming the presence of gay men and lesbians in the church." When some tried to amend the motion with a proviso that the General Synod did not condone homosexual behaviour, the amendment was defeated.[129] Two years later at one of their national meetings, "a majority of the bishops called for an apology to gays and lesbians for the church's insensitivity and hostility."[130] However, the General Synod then and now abides by guidelines set down by the bishops in 1979, stipulating that celibate homosexuality is not an obstacle to ordination, while also insisting that practising gays and lesbians may not become priests. The guidelines also forbid the clergy to bless same-sex relationships on the grounds that even committed homosexual relationships must not be confused with marriage, which is confined to heterosexual relationships.[131] Underlying both rules is the premise that the only proper place for a sexual relationship is in marriage between male and female. Various motions have been introduced at recent national synods to reverse these two key provisions, but to date they have failed.

In 2002, a 63% majority at the synod of the Anglican Diocese of New Westminster, located in and around greater Vancouver, passed a motion asking the bishop to permit clergy to bless long-term homosexual relationships. Though Bishop Ingham actively supports extending gay rights in his church, he had refused to implement similar motions with smaller majorities in 1998 and 2001 on the grounds that the diocese was too divided on the matter.[132] This time he broke ranks with his fellow bishops, who had agreed by a two-to-one margin in 1997 that no bishop should seek an exemption from their ban on the blessing of gay relationships, if their diocese requested it.[133] Ingham stressed that the motion did not ask the church to recognize this blessing as a marriage.[134] He has also seen to it that the motion was "permissive not coercive," with a conscience clause allowing clergy and perishes to refuse to perform the blessing, if they wished.[135]

Despite Ingham's attempt to be conciliatory, the decision was quickly condemned by 13 of Ingham's fellow bishops and then by the Archbishop of Canterbury, the titular head of the worldwide Anglican community.[136] In a public statement, the House of Bishops admitted that they were "unable to speak with a unanimous voice," but the bishops asked Ingham to abide by the 1997 guidelines and to refrain from implementing the blessing until the whole issue could be addressed nationally at the 2004 General Synod. Ingham complied for almost a year, but in May of 2003 he authorized the blessing of same-sex marriages in six of his parishes, where blessings have since been conducted.[137] In protest, the Primates that head 14 of the 38 provinces in the world-wide Anglican Communion declared New Westminster to be in "a state of impaired communion."[138] When the American Episcopal Church elected and then confirmed Canon Gene Robinson, an openly gay man, as the Coadjutor Bishop of New Hampshire, the Archbishop of Canterbury felt obliged to call a special meeting of the Primates at which they expressed their "deep regret" over these recent actions in New Westminster and New Hampshire that "threaten the unity of our own Communion."[139] Equally intense is the storm of controversy that has erupted within the Diocese of New Westminster. In 2002, eight of the larger parishes in the diocese decided to withhold their diocesan contributions, putting a severe strain on the diocesan budget. The now 11 dissident parishes have also been involved in a well-publicized campaign to attach themselves to another bishop, which has in turn prompted fierce resistance from Ingham and endless administrative wrangling over a host of matters.[140] For the foreseeable future, Anglicans across Canada are likely to be embroiled in often acrimonious debate over same-sex marriages and gay issues in general.

When the federal government extended spousal benefits to same-sex couples in 1999, it tried to reassure those of a more conservative frame of mind by passing an amendment that marriage continues to mean "the lawful union of one man and one woman to the exclusion of all others."[141] Gays then turned to the courts, arguing that the current federal legislation confining marriage to heterosexual couples is in violation of Canada's Charter of Rights and Freedoms.[142] With the endorsement of the Canadian Human Rights Commission and the Law Commission of Canada,[143] gay couples in 2003 eventually won decisions in the higher courts in British Columbia and Ontario, granting them the legal right to civil marriages in both provinces. Since then, nine provinces have said they will accept "a planned federal law recognizing same-sex marriages."[144] To avoid future court challenges, the federal government has asked the Supreme Court to rule on the constitutionality of the draft legislation.[145] However, the federal government will eventually have to bring the legislation to a vote in a climate where the latest polls indicate that Canadians are evenly split between supporting (49%) and opposing (49%) same-sex marriages.[146] Much political wrangling may be anticipated, but the track record of the courts suggests that gays across Canada will soon have the legal right to marry.

There is also the possibility that disgruntled gays in their churches might petition the courts and human rights agencies to oblige the churches to overturn their prohibitions on ordaining homosexuals and marrying or blessing same-sex couples. The Evangelical Fellowship of Canada has been most outspoken in voicing fears of this possibility.[147] The EFC pointed with much satisfaction to the Vriend

Supreme Court decision of 1998, which stated that "sexual orientation rights cannot override the rights of Canadians to religious freedom."[148] In the 2003 judgment of the British Columbia Court of
Appeal that gays cannot be denied access to civil marriage, the judges
noted that their decision did not apply to religious marriages. Nothing in their decision, said the judges, undermines "the rights of religious groups to refuse to solemnize same-sex marriages that do not
accord with their religious beliefs."[149] In much the same vein, federal
officials insist that their draft legislation has been designed to ensure
that religious groups are "not forced to perform same-sex weddings."[150] However, given the repeated tendency of the courts to
create new laws over the last two decades, I think we cannot yet
dismiss the possibility of government regulation of churches in their
dealings with gays.[151]

That is the legal challenge that the churches confront, but it is not
the only challenge. Gays are likely to continue to demand full acceptance within Christian churches. The immediate prospects of change
are least likely in the Catholic Church, because its central policies are
set in the Vatican, which is not subject to the demands of its Canadian
laity. The high consensus among Conservative Protestants that homosexuality is sinful must deter gays from joining and makes change
in the short term all the more unlikely. The prospect of change is
therefore greatest in the Mainline Protestant churches where gays are
a vocal minority and the rank and file are deeply divided on how
Christians should respond to gays. This is an issue that is not going
to go away.

As the above combination of controversies is not easily summarized, I conclude this chapter by identifying very briefly a few key
findings from my earlier discussion of beliefs and attachments. First,
in our affluent, ego-centred world, very few of the Committed see
God as harsh and judging. Instead the vast majority think of God as
understanding, forgiving, and concerned about them as individuals.
Above all the Committed continue to affirm that they have and can
have a personal, enriching relationship with God. Other questions in
the game of survey research might elicit more distant and ethereal
conceptions of the divine, but the questions we have looked at make
it clear that Committed Christians retain a very traditional understanding of the God of their heritage. Second, in marked contrast,
few Christians today (barring Conservative Protestants) are prepared
to endorse the ancient credal doctrine that salvation is solely through

Christ. Christians affirm quite traditional notions of the Bible and Jesus,[149] but the ancient triumphalist tradition of Christian exclusivism no longer sits well with Committed Christians raised on the multicultural principles of tolerance and mutual respect.

Finally, despite a generally growing lack of confidence in public institutions, I am struck by how many Committed Christians continue say they are satisfied with the churches to which they belong. One might argue that what really matters is the discontent among the marginal and non-attenders that has driven them out of the churches. The test case here is surely the Catholic Church, which has so greatly suffered from much-publicized cases of clerical abuse and massive lay disagreement with its sexual policies. There must be some formerly active Catholics who fled in despair over any one of these various matters. However, we ought to recall that Committed Catholics are as discontented as inactive Catholics with their church's sexual policies, but large majorities continue to say that their spiritual needs are met and that they have confidence in their churches. The attachments Christians have to their churches are complex and less rooted in doctrinal assent than is commonly thought.

8

Conclusion

Enlightenment convictions that religion is backward, repressive, and destined for extinction have greatly influenced both the secularization theory of academics and the mindset of our secular elites in government, education, and the media. Those convictions have been buttressed by the recent dramatic fall in church attendance that occurred after 1945 when Canada emerged from its colonial, rural cocoon to become a modern or postmodern society with an array of secular institutions to shape and guide it. So intimately linked were these developments that few in the intellectual establishment questioned the inevitability or the advisability of Christianity's downward spiral. These assumptions that Christianity's decline is both inexorable and laudable provide the framework upon which I want to draw together my concluding comments about the state of Christians and their churches in Canada at the end of the second millennium. Though the assumption that Christianity's decline is inevitable has begun to be challenged inside and outside Canada, the latter notion that we are better off without Christianity has received far less attention, in large part because it is such a value-laden stance. Both intimately linked assumptions surely need to be examined if we are to understand the character of the world we inhabit today.

Among the many versions of the secularization theory reviewed in chapter 1, there is widespread acceptance of the differentiation thesis that industrialization, urbanization, and modernization have caused Christian churches in the Western world to lose much of their former institutional powers. In politics, education, the media, and the expanded welfare state, secular institutions have taken over many powers and responsibilities once exercised by the churches, leaving the churches and their clergy much diminished in social prestige and influence. Even the recent critics of other versions of secularization readily concede that differentiation has occurred on a massive scale. I see no point in summarizing here the Canadian experience of institutional secularization outlined in the first chapter, other than to note that the historians still have some work to do in English-speaking Canada charting the precise nature of the powers held by the churches before 1945. However, there seems little doubt that the churches had lost most of their public or institutional power by the 1960s, when secular elites were in full command of Canadian society. That same process came rather later to Quebec, but it swept through with a vengeance in the 1960s. Together the forces of delayed modernization and rising nationalism combined to overthrow the once all-powerful status of the Catholic Church as the institutional epicentre of Quebec society and guardian of Quebecois identity. Across Canada, this phalanx of secular institutions, above all in government, has defined the context over the last 40 years in which Christians have made their choices and lived out their lives.

In Europe and many other Western, post-industrial societies, the downward trend lines in church attendance rates have often been less impressive than some of the defenders of secularization would have us believe.[1] However, that generalization certainly does not apply to Canada. In the 1950s, some of the earliest Gallup polls we have put weekly attendance at somewhere between 54% and 61% of all Canadians. This means that Canadians had church attendance levels that were actually higher than those then current in the United States, which is so often touted as the prime example of a very modern state that has not undergone any decline in its overall levels of religious involvement. Barring a few dissenting voices, most observers claim that there has not been an appreciable decline in American attendance levels since the 1950s.[2] In marked contrast, Canadian attendance levels went into freefall after the 1950s, reaching a 20% weekly rate at the end of the 1990s, which is roughly a third of the attendance levels of Canadians some 40 years earlier. By any standard, this is a major contraction for such a short period of time. Even when we extend our ambit to embrace all who say they attend religious services or meetings at least monthly, then the percentage defined as religiously active in the late 1990s was still no more than a third of all Canadians. More than anything else, this is why I speak of Canada as a predominantly secular society.

Though I know of no one who would dispute the overall trend for Canada since the 1950s, Bibby, as I mentioned in the first chapter, has very recently argued that there are signs of "revitalization" in Canada's churches in the 1990s and much on-going general interest in religious matters, which suggest a possible "renaissance of religion in Canada." That empirical claim is buttressed by a more theoretical argument that humans are always driven to ask basic questions about the meaning and purpose of life that cannot be resolved by science, which "guarantees an ongoing place for religion in Canada."[3] I am a Christian convinced that my faith is uniquely compelling, but I cannot endorse the view that there is some sort of universal, immutable need in humans that guarantees future religious revival. I readily admit to personally thinking that my faith tradition is superior to a host of other meaning systems ranging from socialism to nationalism, or materialism, to name but a few, but I think it is simply wrong to think that everyone will come around to my or anyone else's point of view. Our capacity to choose, to prevaricate, to make bad choices, and to fail to do what we know is right ensures that nothing is certain other than these very basic human traits. This very same state of affairs also ensures that there is nothing inevitable about the future demise of religion in general or of any particular faith tradition. Since categorical predictions are inherently flawed, all we can safely do is look at prevailing trends at a given point in time, recognizing that they may change in the future.

Though I confine my comments here to church attendance trends, I should note that Bibby's data show that the percentage of Canadians who often think about the meaning of life, suffering, and life after death have actually shrunk since he first started his five-year surveys in 1975. Over the same time period, the percentages who admit they no longer think about such matters have also grown.[4] In the narrower and more recent period of the 1990s, the evidence I reviewed in chapter 2 showing that the totals number of the Committed fell by only 6% might suggest that the decline of previous decades has slowed, but that conclusion is not sustained by the much larger 15% contraction of the Very Committed over the same time frame. We also ought to compare both figures with the 15% growth in the 1990s of all Canadians and the even more striking 135% growth in the number of the Non Religious. Both relatively and absolutely, the number of the Committed, and above all the Very Committed, continued to decline throughout the 1990s.

Let me be clear – these trends do not mean that the Committed are about to disappear any time soon. When we look at Generation X, who were 18 to 31 years of age in 1997, 22% of them described themselves as Committed and 11% said they were Very Committed, which means that they attended religious services or meeting at least weekly and defined themselves as very or somewhat religious. These are, I think, quite rigorous standards of commitment, since we are dealing with an era and an age group in which social pressures to be religious are minimal. If we use the broader and looser definition of the Committed (those who attend at least monthly), then we may expect that about a fifth of Canadians will be identifiably religious into the foreseeable future. This is not an insignificant number or proportion of Canadians, though that 20% is still much reduced from the 32% of all Canadians who were Committed in 1997 and the 40% who were Committed in 1990.[5]

Of course, the future prospects of the Committed are very much dependent upon the particular religious tradition or family to which they belong. Ironically, the tradition in most serious trouble at present is the one that was historically the strongest, namely the Catholic community in Quebec. Within the relatively short span of 15 years between 1985 and 2000, the number of Quebec Catholics attending at least monthly fell by 36%; within the core group of the Very Committed, their numbers were literally halved, dropping from 1,440,000 in 1985 to 721,000 in 2000. In the even narrower time frame of the 1990s, weekly attenders shrank by a whopping 37%. In the year 2000, only 14% of Quebecers attended religious services weekly; for Quebecers under the age of 35, weekly attenders drop to a minuscule 4%. The magnitude of the decline becomes all the more striking when we compare these numbers from 2000 with the 84% of Quebecers attending weekly in 1956. We should also recall that the median donation of Quebec Catholics to their church is a paltry $30, which is much lower than for any other religious family, including Catholics in the rest of Canada. To add to their woes, the number of priests has been declining more rapidly in Quebec than in the rest of Canada, its priests are older than elsewhere,[6] and the percentage of the Catholic Committed laity who volunteer their time and energy to their church

(3%) is much lower than in any other religious family. This is a tradition in deep trouble.

Contraction in the Mainline Protestant world has not been quite so severe, but here too it been very considerable. Overall, the number of Committed Mainline Protestants shrank by 32% between 1985 and 2000; among their Very Committed inner core, their numbers were reduced by a very similar 30%. These losses continued over the 1990s, when the number of Committed and Very Committed Mainline Protestants fell by almost identical 20% and 21% rates. By any standard, Mainline Protestantism's loss of a fifth of its active constituency in a 10-year span is a major blow. These trends are likely to continue into the future because Mainline Protestants shared in 1997 with Quebec Catholics the unenviable distinction of having so many members in their retirement years (34% and 35% respectively) and so few born after the baby boom (12% & 10%). Within the dwindling ranks of the Committed, Mainline Protestantism's 30% share of retirees falls to 15% in Generation X.

Unlike the Catholic Church in Quebec, Mainline Protestant churches have far more volunteers to draw upon and their committed faithful are much more generous donors. Despite some recent talk of possible clergy shortages in the future, they still have an abundant supply of trained clergy, especially when we consider the marked decline in the number of lay faithful in recent years. In short, the Mainline Protestant churches are well endowed with financial resources and an active cadre of lay leaders. Apart from their diminishing rank and file, the major problem they now confront is how to reorganize, rationalize, or downsize the extensive network of churches and clergy from an earlier era that reached into every community in English-speaking Canada. To use but one example, Committed United Church members fell by 39% between 1985 and 2000, but the 4,222 United Church churches in 1985 declined by only 513 or 12% over the same period. In the same time frame, the 2,018 clergy in local congregations declined by a tiny 3%. Very similar trends also occurred in the Anglican Church.[7] Sooner or later this big plant will have to be much reduced. In the process, a goodly number of communities across Canada will see their Mainline Protestant churches close, their clergy withdrawn, and their church buildings left to rot, converted to secular purposes, or handed over to other religious bodies. The process will be particularly marked in the Anglican and United churches, which have the most extensive networks in English-

speaking Canada. If Generation X is our guide, then Mainline Protestantism's 15% share of the Committed outside Quebec will eventually amount to only 4% of all Canadians in these nine provinces. I
cannot stress too much that we can never be certain how the future
will unfold, but these stark projections are what emerge from the
information we have.

If numbers alone were the only issue, then the prospects for Catholics outside Quebec would appear much better than those faced by
Catholics in Quebec and by Mainline Protestants. That applies particularly to their minuscule 1% decline between 1990 and 2000 for all
who attended at least monthly, though the inner core of weekly
attending Catholics – which I regard as the best indicator of the
health of any religious body – did contract by a more noticeable 12%.
Decline remains the dominant trend, but it is certainly of a gentler
sort. Catholicism's strength outside Quebec stems from its distinctive
ability to reach out to immigrants and to retain a higher percentage
of young people than all other branches of the Committed, bar Conservative Protestants, though the Non Religious and Canadians as a
whole are even more youthful.

However, these relative, if not absolute, strengths of the Catholic
Church outside Quebec are confounded by two, interrelated matters.
The first is that their levels of volunteering and financial giving are
both low by all but the abysmal standard of Quebec Catholics. Thus
the median contributions of Committed Catholics outside Quebec
was a meagre $50 a year in 1997, and only 11% of these religious
actives volunteered their time and labour to their church. That tradition becomes particularly problematic as the rapidly greying body of
clergy shrinks through retirements, mortality, and the presence of so
few young ordinands to replace them. Without a tradition or habit
of lay leadership and with its clerical leadership so aged and decimated, the Catholic Church – outside and inside Quebec – faces massive challenges to its very existence. It may be that a new Pope will
change his church's policies on celibacy and a male-only priesthood,
but we need to bear in mind that almost all the contenders have been
selected by the current Pope, who is so adamant in his commitment
to the status quo. The Church's problems are then compounded by
the stigma of a renewed spate of sexual abuse cases, the financial
costs of compensating the abuse victims, the potentially onerous costs
of resolving the residential school lawsuits, and last but by no means
least, the meagre amounts that Committed Catholics typically give

to their church. I hinted in the preceding chapter that a new kind of lay-led, local leadership with a strong female presence may be emerging here and there at the parish, grass-roots level, but my very preliminary research and the lack of any other assessments along these lines makes the future impossible to predict with any certainty. The Catholic Church may be able to resolve its constellation of pressing problems, though I am less than sanguine that its aging body of clergy are up to the task. Few can be heartened by the apparent inability of the Canadian Conference of Catholic Bishops to acknowledge, let alone address, the residential school issue and their rapidly shrinking corpus of clergy. Whatever happens, I have little doubt that the emergent body will be radically different from the Church we know today.

Conservative Protestants stand out as the sole religious family to have actually grown in recent years. Over the 1990s, the number of their committed monthly attenders grew by a solid 15%, though they experienced a much more modest 8% growth in the more revealing inner core of weekly attenders. These numbers, of course, need to be compared with the 16% growth of the total Canadian population over the decade, a 38% increase in non-attenders, and a more than doubling of those who say they do not have a religion. Despite their singular achievement of absolute growth, Conservative Protestants in this most recent decade were still shrinking relatively, especially when compared with the growing number of avowedly secular Canadians.

The distinctive dynamism of Conservative Protestants is evident in a variety of other ways that extend well beyond the many youth in their ranks and their ability to draw their members from a wide range of ethnic and racial groups. They are more likely than the member of any other religious family to say they pray and read religious literature on a regular basis. They are also most likely to belong to a small group in their church and to be active in their church's social activities. Volunteers in church activities are as prevalent among Mainline as Conservative Protestants, but the latter put in about twice as many hours as the volunteers from other traditions. In the same vein, they give far more to their churches than the rest of the Committed and they are much more likely to say they have discussed spiritual matters with family, friends, and colleagues outside of a church setting. This last trait no doubt helps to explain why converts from other religious traditions are far more common among Conservative Protestants (47%) than among either Catholics (7%) or

Mainline Protestants (17%). The crucial counterpart to that outreach is the equally high proportion of Conservative Protestants (46%) who drop out of that tradition as they move from childhood into their adult years. This revolving-door winnowing of the marginal in turn explains both Conservative Protestant vitality and their rather modest rates of growth.

As early as 1990, Conservative Protestants had come to outnumber their Mainline counterparts within the restricted confines of the Very Committed. By 2000, that edge had grown so that they almost outnumbered Mainliners among all the Committed; within the core constituency of the Very Committed, Conservative Protestants outnumbered Mainline adherents by a comfortable 25% to 17% margin. That historic transformation in Canadian Protestantism is likely to lead to an even more startling change in the future. Using the religious profile of all the Committed in Generation X as our window into the future, Catholics in English-speaking Canada remain our largest single religious family (44%), but their numerical predominance vis à vis Conservative Protestants (28%) is much reduced from historic levels. Then, when we narrow the focus to the Very Committed across all of Canada, Conservative Protestants in this youngest age group (41%) actually outnumber the 37% Catholic share. Outside Quebec, Conservative Protestantism's edge (45%) over Catholicism (34%) among the young is even more marked. Thus the composition of the Committed in Canada continues to evolve in sometimes dramatic and unexpected ways. As always, the key qualifier to these portents of the future is that they emerge out of an overall pattern of shrinkage or decline in the number and percentage of Canadians who are actively involved in a faith community. Religious revival may break out at any time, but there were no convincing signs of it in the 1990s.

There remains the possibility, raised in the first chapter, that Seekers, who say religion is important to them but are not involved in a faith community, are coming to replace the aging and shrinking body of church attenders. The broader implication of this line of reasoning is that religion in our postmodern world is changing rather than declining. Lest there be any doubt, I want to pull together here the three core reasons why I reject this school of thought. First, over the admittedly short span of the last 25 years in which I can track survey trends, the ranks of the Committed, above all the Very Committed, have fallen, but there has been no corresponding increase in the percentage of Canadians who designate themselves as Seekers. With only two exceptions from the many soundings, the Seeker percentage of all Canadians has fluctuated in a very narrow range between 24% and 29%. When we narrow our focus to the 1990s, we also find in the large NSVGP survey in 1997 that the Committed shrink quite dramatically from 50% of Canadians over age 65 to 22% in Generation X. However, the percentage of Seekers remains virtually unchanged in every generation (29% to 31%), dropping only slightly to 26% among Canadians in their retirement years. Whichever data we use, be it the generational numbers for the 1990s or the trends since 1975, it is clear that the shrinking ranks of the Committed are being replaced by growing numbers of Non Religious Canadians – and not by Seekers. It is religious decline – not transformation – that is the dominant trend.

Second, the last chapter provides a wide body of evidence, coming from the mouths of Seekers themselves, that the strength of their personal religious convictions and the frequency of their private devotional practices are much less than those claimed by the Very Committed. Compared to the Very Committed, Seekers are much less likely to say they definitely believe in God (67% vs. 91%) or to have an intense personal relationship with God (55% vs. 88%). They are also less likely to say that spirituality is very important to them (35% vs. 78%), that they have spiritual needs (58% vs. 79%), and that their interest in spirituality has grown in recent years (18% vs. 43%). Particularly revealing are Bibby's data indicating that only 15% of Seekers say they are interested in New Age, which is the dominant, generic label for new forms of religiousness with a decidedly non-Western flavour operating outside traditional Christianity; 71% of Seekers say they are not even familiar with the term. To this must be added the large number of surveys showing that the Seekers are less likely than the Very Committed to say they regularly pray (53% vs. 89%) or read religious literature (11% vs. 69%). In short, if Seekers do represent the future of religion, then that is a future of diminished, superficial commitment.

That last conclusion is reinforced by the third general point I want to make about Seekers, namely that their professed faith or religious commitment rarely has discernible consequences for their daily life. Time and time again in previous chapters, we have seen that the profile of Seekers is very much closer to the Non Religious than it is to the Committed. That tendency can be seen in their professed satisfaction with life, their views on premarital and extramarital sex, their divorce rates, their involvement in community organizations, their volunteering habits, their levels of charitable giving, the importance of religion to their political thinking, and the importance they place on the political priorities of security and postmaterialism. Sometimes, when it comes to generalized expressions of concern for the poor, for relationships with others, or for thinking about the meaning of life, the Seekers occupy a more intermediate position between the Non Religious and the Committed. However, whenever the surveys pose more pointed questions about actual behaviour, be it giving to the poor overseas or choosing between the pursuit of riches versus a spiritual life, Seekers display their more typical pattern of emulating the Non Religious more than the Committed.

I fear the above has a mean-spirited tenor to it, but I think the general point needs to be made. With few exceptions, the professed religious commitment of Seekers appears to be confined to their interior life. Indeed, even their levels of happiness and life satisfaction are much the same as the avowedly Non Religious. Put somewhat differently, Seekers display an extreme version of the privatization process to which I alluded in the first chapter, whereby religion comes to have no consequences for daily life. That conclusion very much coincides with Bibby's long-held view that religion is "insignificant to everyday life."[8] I would simply qualify Bibby's indictment by saying it applies primarily to Seekers. This should come as no surprise. Without the shared rituals, joint projects, and reinforcements of communal life, commitment to any cause is surely weakened.

I must immediately acknowledge that there are some areas in life where high religious commitment does not appreciably differentiate the Committed from other Canadians in general and from the Non Religious in particular. Thus, we saw in chapter 3 that the Committed are very much like everyone else in the importance they attach to a variety of non-religious priorities ranging from self-fulfillment and freedom, to their careers, security, and being well respected. Given the very basic, generic character of these priorities – which the Committed and Non Religious may define in very different ways – I do not think that any clear conclusion can be drawn from the lack of differences in this domain.

Rather more revealing is the evidence from chapter 6 that Canadians, regardless of their level or type of religiousness, are very similar in their degree of political interest, their voting habits, their involvement in political organizations and campaigns, their lack of trust in secular institutions, and their willingness to support the ecology, anti-nuclear, disarmament, and human rights movements. Conservative Protestants are the one partial exception to that generalization, though their lower confidence in secular institutions ought to be set against their relatively high number in touch with a politician and their widespread conviction that they and their values should play a role in politics. Though they were more likely than other Canadians to vote for the Reform/Alliance Party, we ought to bear in mind that only a minority did so and even more cast their vote for the mainstream Liberals. We also need to recall that the Very Committed of all stripes, including Conservative Protestants, are slightly more likely than the Non Religious to say they have a "personal responsibility to make the world a better place." Conservative Protestant are therefore more likely than the rest of the Committed to voice dissatisfaction with the status quo in public life, but neither they nor any other branch of the Committed display any susceptibility to the stereotyped portraits of political apathy with which they have been so frequently charged. I have also long felt that there is not much evidence for the related common assumption that religious commitment causes an obsessive concern with the next world. I cannot prove this latter claim with the data at hand, but the evidence is surely compelling that the Committed are as engaged as other Canadians in the affairs of this world.

The surveys also indicate that levels of religiousness do not have any appreciable impact on the way Canadians think about quite a wide range of more specific policy issues in the political realm. We are all generally agreed that there is too big a gap between rich and poor; that the courts are too lenient in their treatment of criminals; that multiculturalism is a good thing; that racial intermarriages are perfectly acceptable; that women should be paid the same as men; and that we need more laws to protect the environment. We are much more divided on other matters, but here too there are no really striking differences between the Committed and the Non Religious when it comes to our thinking on the virtues of big government, the merits of expanded social programs, and whether we should pay higher taxes to fight hunger and poverty. One might want to argue that the generally tolerant and sometimes progressive views of most Canadians, regardless of how religious we are today, stem from our shared Christian heritage.[9] One could also argue that purely secular considerations have always heavily influenced the political choices we make. Yet however much we agree or disagree with these qualifications to the privatization thesis, we are still left with the conclusion that the Committed do not appreciably differ from the Non Religious on many matters in this public, political realm. This is important. However, we would be making a big mistake if we were to go on to conclude that religion is therefore toothless or inconsequential in all other social domains.

There are four broad areas of life where the Committed, above all the Very Committed, do display a very distinctive profile that sets them apart from other Canadians. First, we saw in chapter 3 that the Very Committed put a distinctively high value on the importance and quality of their relationships with others. Compared to the Non Religious, notably more of the Very Committed say they highly value a sense of belonging (69% vs. 53%), friendliness (80% vs. 63%) and kindness (85% vs. 71%). The Very Committed are even more likely to stress the importance of forgiveness (73% vs. 43%), generosity (71% vs. 42%), and concern for others (80% vs. 58%). Moreover, they are more inclined to disapprove of vengeance, to think we should forgive those who hurt us, and to believe that we ought to put our trust in others, even when we cannot be certain of reciprocation. This impressive, consistent, and cumulative set of differences suggests to me that the Very Committed are much more likely than other Canadians to be concerned with the welfare of others. I have not been concerned in this book with analyzing basic Christian teaching, but that concern for others is surely consistent with the fundamental Christian call to love one's neighbours. Though various secular moralities can and do preach the same virtues, it is the overwhelming Christian ranks of the Very Committed who most frequently and consistently endorse that ethic of forgiveness and concern for others.

If you believe as I do that it is deeds rather than words that ultimately matter, then the data I reviewed in chapter 4 on marriage, family, and friends add real weight to the claim that the Very Committed are different from other Canadians in important ways. Though most of us, regardless of how religious we are, say marriage and family are important to us, separation, divorce, and common-law relationships are much less frequent among the religiously active than the inactive. That commitment to marriage is also evident in admittedly attitudinal data showing that the Very Committed are much more likely than others to condemn pre-marital and extra-marital sex and to disapprove of children being raised in a home where the parents are not married. The Committed have certainly not been immune to the revolution in sexual mores and family rela-tionships that have swept through Canada and so many other nations since the 1960s. The attitudes of younger religious actives today would undoubtedly shock and horrify earlier generations, but the gap between the religiously active and inactive on so many of these matters is often actually more acute among the young than the old; rarely is it less so. Within this climate of growing liberality, religiousness continues to make a real difference.

Religiousness does not appreciably affect the percentage of Canadians saying they are in regular contact with relatives and friends. On the other hand, weekly attenders tell us that their net-work of friends and family outside their nuclear family with whom they feel close, which amounts to a combined average of 18 souls, is 50% larger than the average of 12 claimed by non-attenders. Again these are major differences, which, when combined with the greater stability of nuclear family life for the Committed, testify to the much more reliable and extensive network of intimates that high religious-ness produces. In a world where stable family relationships have been so corroded in recent years, these are scarce, valuable resources.

There can be little doubt that the presence or absence of religious commitment has its most profound impact on the ways in which Canadians relate to their local communities. Though we overwhelm-ingly agree that voluntary and charitable organizations are crucial to our collective well-being, only about a third of us actually volunteer in community organizations. Our median charitable donation of about $50 a year for the typical Canadian is also less than impressive, especially when we set it against the median family income at that time of around $40,000. The Very Committed could certainly be more generous with their time and money, but the 47% of them who vol-unteer is almost twice as high as the 25% of the Non Religious who do so. We also ought to recall that Very Committed volunteers devote far more hours to volunteering than their Non Religious counter-parts. As for charitable giving, the $186 median annual donation of the Very Committed towers above the meagre $22 donation of the Non Religious. The detailed analysis I conducted in chapter 5 further demonstrates that the markedly greater generosity of the Very Com-mitted remains after account is taken of how other social forces, (age, income, education, and the like) affect our volunteering and giving habits. The net result is that religiosity is one of the major social forces affecting the volunteering levels of Canadians and it is the most influ-ential factor bar none in determining how much we give to charity.

Religion's central role in shaping the quality of community life is strengthened by two further considerations that I would stress. First, even when we confine our focus to secular agencies, the Very Committed are still more generous than the Non Religious with their time and money. When we further restrict our focus to early boomers in order to eliminate the impact of the Very Committed's older age profile, their 45% rate of volunteering in the secular world remains much greater than the comparable 28% level for the Non Religious. We should therefore not be surprised to learn that the median $51 annual donation to secular charities by Very Committed early boomers is also significantly higher than the comparable $26 donation by the Non Religious. Taken together, these numbers make it clear that the generosity of the Very Committed cannot be dismissed as simply a selfish drive to serve their own. The Very Committed give generously to their own communities, but they also give to those outside their own world in ways that still set them apart from the Non Religious.

I think it is not sufficiently appreciated how central a role religious bodies play across the country in mobilizing an ethic of giving and in fostering civility or a concern for others. All the major denominations have specialized agencies that deal with foreign aid and disaster relief, or that provide a variety of services for the elderly, the homeless, and the hungry. Though some of these agencies are in financial partnership with government, all rely in significant ways on funds gathered through their church networks. Important as these various activities are, I want to stress here three rather more mundane but nonetheless vital ways in which local congregations strengthen our social fabric. First, congregations across the country build, maintain, and subsidize a vast physical plant of church halls and buildings that literally bring Canadians together through a wide variety of local community organizations. Second, the weekly round of meetings and services provides a regular forum for soliciting volunteers and informing those in attendance of a variety of worthy events and causes that they might support. Third, a considerable chunk of the time devoted to any congregation is caught up in preparing and holding the regular cycle of services, devotions, and religious instruction. These specifically religious activities appear to have no immediate practical benefit. However, that very secular point of view fails to recognize that the instilling and reinforcing of Christian values must lie behind the indisputable evidence from the surveys that the Committed, above all the Very Committed, really do give more to their communities than other Canadians. Without this network of churches and the faithful they nurture and guide, the social fabric of Canada would be much diminished.

I earlier mentioned that the political behaviours and values of the Committed rarely set them apart from other Canadians. However, there are two exceptions to that general rule that deserve brief mention, because they bring out so clearly how the Committed do differ from other Canadians. First we saw that the Very Committed are much more disapproving than other Canadians of anti-social behaviour and disruptive, confrontational politics. Second, when asked to choose between competing political priorities, the Very Committed are most likely to say their greatest national priorities are the raising of moral standards and the preservation of the family. These sorts of preferences have the whiff of a right-wing agenda that will undoubtedly raise the hackles of some. However I would remind readers that only a minority of the Committed support the Reform/Alliance party and fewer of the Very Committed than the Non Religious think that our first priority ought to be law, order, and a healthy economy. I see the singularity of the Very Committed in these two political domains as lying in the high value they place on caring, courteous relations with others, which I would define as a commitment to the value and virtue of civility.

That pre-eminent concern with civility is very much consistent with the distinctively high value the Very Committed place on forgiveness, generosity, and concern for others. It is also reflected in their singular commitment to the marriage bond, in their much larger network of family and friends, and in their distinctively high rates of volunteering and charitable giving. In both word and deed, a marked commitment to civility is the underlying value that sets the Very Committed apart from Canadians in general and from the Non Religious in particular. A qualified form of privatization might therefore be said to apply to our modern political world, but that certainly cannot be said of all these other important social domains I have just summarized, where religiousness or its lack continues to make a real difference. For the admittedly shrunken body of Canadians with high religious commitment, there is little to support the central tenet of privatization that religion has little or no impact on the daily life of its adherents.

Given the generally progressive values of the Committed and their clear record in serving others, it is surely regrettable that there is so much reluctance to recognize that Christians are an integral part of our culture. I am not one of those who lose sleep over the 1985 Supreme Court decision to abolish the Lord's Day Act because it unfairly privileged Christians.[10] Nor am I much bothered by recent attempt to have Christian prayers removed from the proceedings of municipal councils,[11] or by the failed 1999 attempt of Svend Robinson from the NDP to remove reference to God from Canada's constitution.[12] My own personal view is that we live in a secular world where there is little to be gained from trying to preserve the occasional symbol of an earlier era when the Christian character of the nation was an irrefutable premise. Times have changed. Far more serious, to my mind, is the emerging consensus among the growing ranks of the Non Religious that clergy should steer clear of social, economic, and political issues. I am also bothered by the much more widespread conviction among the Non Religious that Christians and their values are not legitimate participants in political life. That mindset is, of course, most clearly seen in the expelling of all religious practices and religious education from state schools. I do not think that schools should be involved in instilling commitment to a particular denomination or faith. However, I do think it is incumbent on the schools to instill respect, knowledge, tolerance, and understanding of the many religious traditions of Canadians. The current secular response of ignoring the religious traditions of Canadians is likely to promote ignorance and bigotry; it is certainly unlikely to combat these harmful outcomes. Above all else, the secular denial – or even denigration – of Canadian religious traditions is in flagrant violation of Canada's professed commitment to multiculturalism and the celebration of cultural diversity.

What then by way of summary should we make of the anti-religious Enlightenment heritage in Canada today? The powers of the churches have certainly declined mightily. Today our public political domain, most notably our public schools, no longer seems capable of recognizing, let alone affirming, our Christian religious diversity that is only likely to grow in the future. Since the 1950s, the percentage of Canadians actively involved in a faith community has fallen from a solid 60% majority of all Canadians to 20% or fewer today. In the more limited time frame since 1975 where my religiosity scale can be used, the ranks of the Committed have fallen, Seekers have undergone no appreciable growth, and the Non Religious have continued to grow in number and influence. High religious commitment continues to be a potent, positive force, but it is embraced by an ever smaller number of Canadians. Though religious revival may break out at any time, decline remained the dominant trend throughout the 1990s. If the expanding body of the Non Religious is our guide to the future, we may reasonably expect that life satisfaction will decline, concern for others will diminish, marriage will grow more fragile, family and friendship networks will shrink, volunteering will become less frequent, and we will grow ever less generous in our so very affluent world. In a word, our civility is threatened. If this is the victory that secularism and the Enlightenment have wrought, then we have no cause to celebrate.

Notes

CHAPTER ONE

1 Berger, *The Sacred Canopy*; Luckmann, *The Invisible Religion*; Martin, *A General Theory of Secularization*; Wilson, *Religion in Secular Society*.

2 Wilson, *Religion in Secular Society*, 14. Luckmann (*The Invisible Religion*, 29–40) would add that it is "church-orientated religion" that has undergone secularization. I will take up later Luckmann's thesis that privatized forms of religion continue to exist, despite secularization.

3 Martin, "The Secularisation Issue: Prospect and Retrospect," 465; Berger, "The Secularization of the World: A Global Overview," 204.

4 Stark, "Secularization: R.I.P." For a recent contrary view, see Bruce, *God is Dead*.

5 Stark, "Secularization: R.I.P," 252.

6 Martin, *A General theory of Secularization*, 3.

7 Wilson, "Reflections on a Many Sided Controversy," 200.

8 Luckmann, *The Invisible Religion*, 39.

9 Wilson, "Reflections on a Many Sided Controversy," 200.

10 Martin, "Sociology, Religion, and Secularization," 295.

11 Martin, *A General Theory of Secularization*, 14.

12 Ibid, 17.

13 Ibid, 21.

14 Chausse, "French Canada from Conquest to the 1840s," 71.

15 Ibid, 62.

16 Ibid, 76–105.

17 Perin, "French Speaking Canada From 1840," 203.

18 Baum, *The Church in Quebec*, 17.

19 Ibid, 19.

20 Ibid, 25.

21 Seljak, "Resisting the 'No Man's Land' of Private Religion," 135.

22 Murphy, "The English Speaking Colonies to 1854," 126.

23 Gauvreau, "Protestantism Transformed," 96–97.

24 Murphy, "The English Speaking Colonies to 1854," 162–186.

25 Marshall, *Secularizing the Faith*, 249–256.

26 Christie & Gauvreau, *A Full-Orbed Christianity*, 258.

27 Ibid, 248.

28 Grant, *The Church in the Canadian Era*, 202.

29 Ibid, 203. For a more extended analysis of the hierarchy's stance, see Appleby, *Responsible Parenthood*, 76–79 & 161–186.

30 Cuneo, *Catholics Against the Church*, 36.

31 Van Die, "Introduction." 14

32 Beyer, "Religious Vitality in Canada," 284.

33 Higgins, *The Muted Voice*.

34 See for instance, Rice, & Prince, *Changing Politics of Canadian Social Policy*, 51–84.

35 See Stark, "Secularization: R.I.P."

36 Inglehart, *Modernization and Postmodernization*, 281.

37 See for instance, Bruce, "The Pervasive World-View."

38 See Bruce, S., 1996. *Religion in the Modern World*, 129–168.

39 Martin, "The Secularisation Issue," 470.

40 Hadaway, Marler & Chaves, "What the Polls Don't Show." See also a variety of contending views in "A Symposium on Church Attendance in the United States."

41 As a counter to Stark's claim that church attendance has not fallen in most European countries ("Secularization: R.I.P.," 260), see Inglehart, *Modernization and Postmodernization*, 282.

42 Clarke, "English-Speaking Canada from 1854," 262.

43 Beyer, "Religious Vitality in Canada," 276.

44 Clarke, "English-Speaking Canada from 1854," 276.

45 Bibby, *Fragmented Gods*, 17.

46 These later figures are based on my own calculations from the 1956 Gallup poll, a copy of which was kindly given to me by Carleton University.

47 Noll, *A History of Christianity in the United States and Canada*. 548.

48 Grant, *The Church in the Canadian Era*, 160–163.

49 See Bibby, *Fragmented Gods*,11–45, and Bibby, *Unknown Gods*, 3–58.

50 Bibby, *Restless Gods*, 55–92.

51 Beyer, "Religious Vitality in Canada," 284–285.

52 Beckford, "Postmodernity, High Modernity, and New Modernity," 30.

53 Inglehart,. *Modernization and Postmodernization*, 32–45.

54 Stark, & Iannaccone, "A Supply-Side Reinterpretation of the Secularization of Europe."

55 Berger, *The Sacred Canopy*, 149–150.

56 Bibby, *Unknown Gods*, 185.

57 Bibby, *Fragmented Gods*, 111–136.

58 My conclusion that religious pluralism does not necessarily lead to either religious vitality or decline is strengthened by a recent review of a host of studies on this theme. See Voas, "Religious Pluralism and Participation."

59 Berger, *The Sacred Canopy*, 107–108.

60 Davie, *Religion in Modern Europe*, 9–11.

61 Davie, *Religion in Britain since 1945*, 12.

62 Inglehart, *Modernization and Postmodernization*, 45.

63 Inglehart & Baker, "Modernization, Cultural Change, and the Persistence of Traditional Values, 47.

64 Bibby, *Restless Gods*, 225.

65 Bibby, *Unknown Gods*, 177.

66 Davie, "Europe: the Exception that Proves the Rule?" 83.

67 Bellah et al., *Habits of the Heart*, 221.

68 Ibid, 246.

69 Wuthnow, R., 1998. *After Heaven*, 2, 168.

70 Berger, "Epistemological Modesty."

71 Emberley, *Divine Hunger*, 12.

72 Ibid, 16.

73 Ibid, 198–199, 242. These quotes come from Emberley's descriptions of Canadians involved in the New Age movement and in Eastern religions, which most closely approximate the interests of Seekers. Emberley also provides fascinating accounts of boomer encounters with the Orthodox Church, evangelicalism, the Toronto Blessing, and the modernist "tweakings" of Bill Phipps and the Jesus Seminar. What he does not do, as he is quick to admit, is trace those who remained in the Christian mainstream or who returned to it after falling away for a time. Ibid, 247.

74 Zinnbauer, Pargament, et al, "Religion and Spirituality: Unfuzzying the Fuzzy."

75 Wuthnow, *The Struggle for America's Soul*, 365.

76 Luckmann, *The Invisible Religion*, 99–102.

77 Bibby, *Fragmented Gods*, 1

78 Ibid, 62–85.

79 Ibid, 1–2.

80 Berger, *The Sacred Canopy*, 132–146.

81 Halman, Petersson, & Verweij, "The Religious Factor in Contemporary Society." See also Tamney & Johnson, "Consequential Religiosity in Modern Society."

82 Bibby, *Fragmented Gods*, 1.

83 Bibby, Hewitt, & Roof, "Religion and Identity," 241.

84 Bibby, *Restless Gods*, 213.

CHAPTER TWO

1 Statistics Canada, *Census of Canada 1981*.

2 Nazarene, Reformed, and Mennonite churches are also part of this Conservative Protestant tradition. Bibby, *Unknown Gods*, xx.

3 A substantial minority of Anglicans and members of the United Church are evangelicals, though the denominations as a whole are clearly liberal and hence mainline. Grenville, "The Awakened and the Spirit-Moved." Similarly, the Lutheran Church – Canada would best be described as conservative and evangelical, while the much larger Evangelical Lutheran Church of Canada is clearly liberal and in full communion with the Anglican Church. Pfrimmer, "A Lutheran Witness in Canadian Society," 136. Because the latter Lutheran body is twice the size of the former, I have put the undifferentiated Lutherans from surveys in the mainline camp.

4 The increase in the number of generic Protestants and Christians in the census has been meteoric, rising from 299,645 in 1981 to 1,329,655 in 2001. Since these years have also seen a very considerable decline in church attendance (to be charted shortly), I think it is fair to assume that a solid majority of these generic Christians were once members of Mainline Protestantism whose allegiance is in long-term decline.

5 Thus Bibby's surveys in 1990 and 1995 both estimated that 24% of all Canadians normally attended a religious service on a weekly basis. In 2000, his weekly attenders fell to 21% of Canadians (*Restless Gods*, 21).

6 Bibby's surveys in the 1990s do produce much lower estimates of those who never attend (17–18%), though his finding that 34% of Canadians in 1990 and 1995 attended monthly is very close to Statistics Canada's

numbers. There is therefore a broad consensus that only about a third of Canadians attend monthly. The other two-thirds, regardless of whether they attend rarely or never, surely are religiously inactive.

7 Bibby (*Unknown Gods*, 16) estimates that weekly attendance among early boomers rose from 12% in 1975 to 17% in 1985 and to 19% in 1990.

8 Estimates of weekly Conservative Protestant attendance ranged from 60% in 1993 to 51% in 1996.

9 Bibby, *Unknown Gods*, 23–29.

10 The narrowed focus in table 2.9 on the religiously active and the resulting reduction in sample obliges me to collapse the very small number of "other Christians", "non Christians" and "no religion" into a generic "other" category that is too internally diverse to tell us anything significant.

11 My conclusions differ from those of Bibby, who argues that Conservative Protestants have not been very successful recruiting from outside their own world and owe their vitality to their ability to retain the allegiance of their children. See Bibby & Brinkerhoff, M. "Circulation of the Saints 1966–1990." For a more recent statement, see his *Restless Gods*, 39–46. My analysis of Bibby's 1995 survey finds that 30% of Conservative Protestants today were raised outside the Conservative Protestant world. That 30% rate of outreach is noticeably less than 47% level in table 2.9 based on the 1993 Reid survey. Similarly, my analysis of Bibby's data indicate that 19% of Conservative Protestants in childhood moved out of that world as adults; again, this is lower than their 46% drop-out rate based on Reid in table 2.10. In short, I think Bibby's data provide some support for my revolving door thesis, but that support is clearly much weaker than the data I use from the 1993 Reid survey. Since the figures in tables 2.9 and 2.10 are based on a large 3,000 sample drawn by a respected polling company, the Reid data deserve serious consideration. More research, as is so often said in these situations, is obviously needed.

12 Trickey, "Canadians Value Spirituality."

13 Reverend Bill Phipps of the United Church is later cited as saying "today's off-the-shelf spirituality seems a little thin." *Globe and Mail*, 3 March 1999. This is a much more nuanced response than his comment in the *Vancouver Sun*.

14 "On a Higher Plane: Many Canadians are Turning Inward to Their Spiritual Selves." *Maclean's* 108, no. 52 (1996), 23.

15 Nemeth, M. et al, "God is Alive," 32.

16 "Is Jesus God? A Conversation with United Church Moderator Reverend Bill Phipps," *Ottawa Citizen*, 2 Nov. 1997.

17 Valpy, "Throwing Cold Water on the Fires of Hell."

18 See Roberts, *Religion in Sociological Perspective*, 13–20.

19 1993 Angus Reid Survey.

20 This 1% figure is confirmed in both the 1997 and 2000 NSVGP. In the 1993 Reid survey, 4% of the Less Committed attended weekly. In the 2000 NSVGP, weekly attenders were 6% of the Less Committed.

21 The atypically large size of the Less Committed in the October 1996 Reid survey is caused by its finding that 17% attended a religious service or meeting one to three times a month. I should stress that all the other Reid surveys, including one done in February 1996, put monthly attenders at between 8% and 12% of their respondents, with all but one of them in the narrower range of 10% to 12%. The NSVGP and recent General Social Surveys by Statistics Canada also place monthly attenders at between 10% and 14%. I once thought that the abnormally high estimate of monthly attenders from the Reid survey of October 1996 might have been caused by giving respondents the options of choosing "a few times a month" and "once a month," but Bibby follows the same procedure and produces estimates of monthly attenders consistent with everyone else. All the other surveys in the monthly range had only one option of "at least once a month or more." All this leads to the simple, statistically predictable conclusion that samples do vary in their estimates of population traits, with a minority of even well crafted surveys producing atypical results. I have included the October 1996 survey because it is such a striking reminder that survey results do vary. It is the general pattern – not single findings – that should be our prime concern. There is also much valuable data in the October 1996 survey on political and social issues that I want to use in later chapters.

22 The non-response rates in the 2000 NSVGP for the questions on religion (7.5%) and attendance (6.4%) are much higher than the comparable 2.5% and 2.4% non-response rates in 1997. On such key variables, this greater coverage and lesser ambiguity in the 1997 NSVGP is a real advantage. In addition, the 2000 NSVGP in its public form does not allow me to differentiate between Conservative and Mainline Protestants.

23 According to extensive polling by Environics, the values "of particular importance to boomers are: rejection of authority, rejection of order, control of destiny, pursuit of happiness to the detriment of duty, sexual permissiveness, and equality of the sexes." Adams, "Sex in the Snow," 22.

24 Similarly, though the question is slightly more restrictive, Reid's
    February 1996 survey indicated that only 17% of nominal adherents
    attending infrequently or less described themselves as a "formal
    member of a particular church or congregation."

25 Bibby, *Unknown Gods*, 10; Gee, "Gender Differences in Church
    Attendance in Canada."

26 The 1956 Gallup poll was based on a sample of 2,029. The subtleties of
    sampling were still being developed at this time. The next year the
    weekly attendance rates for Canada, Quebec, and British Columbia
    were 56%, 83%, and 25%. Thus the figures fluctuated substantially by
    year, but the relative standings of Quebec and British Columbia were
    unchanged.

27 Most crucially, these tables exclude a not insignificant 30% of "Other"
    Canadians who claimed more than one ethnicity or who were attached
    to an ethnic group deemed too small for separate enumeration. The
    varied and unknown ethnic allegiances of the "Others" make it mean-
    ingless to treat them as a unitary group and impossible to collapse
    them into other categories. There are also problems with the 20% who
    claimed a single "Canadian" ethnicity and who thereby confuse and
    underestimate the two largest ethnic affiliations of British and French.
    I have distributed these "Canadians" into the French and British cate-
    gories by the language in which they were interviewed. Mother tongue
    would have been a better variable to differentiate "Canadians," but
    neither mother tongue nor home language were asked in the NSVGP.
    Also included in the "French" category are the 13% of Canadians listed
    in the NSVGP as "Canadian and French." No "British and Canadian"
    category is available. I should also add that the "European" and "Visi-
    ble Minority" categories include only the largest ethnic groups in each
    category. Europeans are confined to Germans, Italians, Ukrainians,
    Dutch, Polish and Portuguese. Visible Minorities encompass Chinese,
    South Asians, and Blacks.

28 Average (Median) Annual Household Income by Religiosity:
    All Canadians & Canadians aged 40–59 (NSVGP 1997)

	Very Commit.	Less Commit.	Seekers	Non Religious	All Canadians	(N)
All Age 40–59	$47,615	$49,433	$49,086	$48,577	$49,034	(5,795)
All Ages	$35,127	$40,489	$40,117	$40,301	$39,980	(17,058)

29 The much needed weight variable in all the Statistics Canada surveys
    does two things. Besides adjusting for sampling error, it also estimates

the total number of Canadians over the age of 15 or 18 in the survey categories for the year the survey was taken. Thus even very small differences are invariably statistically significant because they are based on huge populations of many millions. In that situation, tests of statistical significance are meaningless. To make tests of significance meaningful, I have, with the guidance of others well versed in these matters, created a "fractional weight " for the Statistics Canada surveys that retains the original weight but recalibrates cell sizes to the original sample size. Of course, the large samples gathered by Statistics Canada mean that quite small differences are still deemed to be statistically significant when they are of little or no substantive significance.

CHAPTER THREE

1 See Beit-Hallahmi & Argyle, *The Psychology of Religious Behaviour, Belief and Experience*, 184–191; Ellison, "Introduction to Symposium; and Levin, & Chatters, "Research on Religion and Mental health."

2 Quoted in Batson et al., *Religion and the Individual*, 232.

3 Ibid, 259.

4 Ibid, 235–239.

5 Ellison, "Introduction to Symposium," 692. See also Beit-Hallahmi & Argyle, The Psychology of Religious Behaviour, 184–191; and Levin. & Chatters, "Research on Religion and Mental Health," 33–50. Batson and his colleagues (230–258) agree that mental health is linked to what they call "intrinsic" religiosity but not to "extrinsic" religiosity. The intrinsically religious take their faith seriously, regarding it as the master motive in their lives, while the extrinsically religious use religion for self-serving ends such as making friends. However, intrinsic religiousness correlates strongly with other measures of religiosity, such as frequency of attendance at services, whereas extrinsic religiosity does not. For this and a host of other technical reasons, some psychologists reject the extrinsic–intrinsic distinction. (See also Beit-Hallahmi & Argyle, *The Psychology of Religious Behaviour*, 43–46). I agree. What matters is that intrinsic religiosity, which Batson et al. clearly regard as the more authentic form of religiousness, is correlated with mental health.

6 Levin & Chatters, "Research on Religion and Mental Health," 38.

7 Ibid, 36.

8 Beit-Hallahmi & Argyle, *The Psychology of Religious Behaviour*, 187.

9 Levin & Chatters, "Research on Religion and Mental Health," 34

10 Beit-Hallahmi & Argyle, *The Psychology of Religious Behaviour*, 187.

11 Percent with Poor or Fair Health by Religiosity and Age (NSVGP, 1997)

	Generation X (18–31)	Boomers (32–51)	Pre Boomer I (52–64)	Pre Boomer II (65–74)	Pre Boomer III (75 plus)
Very Committed	6	11	23	23	23
Less Committed	4	12	24	24	39
Seekers	6	13	23	42	52
Non Religious	9	9	20	29	41
All Canadians*	7	11	22	29	38
(N)	(4,257)	(7,558)	(2,771)	(1,797)	(1,083)
Tau-c	−.03***	.03***	.02	−.09***	−.21***

***$P < .001$ **$P < .01$ *$P < .05$

12 Bibby, *Fragmented Gods*, 207.

13 Ibid, 105.

14 Gee & Veevers, "Religious Involvement and Life Satisfaction in Canada."

15 Clark, "Religious Observance: Marriage and Family."

16 Only on measures of mastery and self-esteem were there no significant differences. Frankel & Hewitt, "Religion and Well-Being among Canadian University Students."

17 Only 8% of Bibby's sample would admit to being "not too happy." On Reid's 7-point scale, the 45% rating themselves as 1–2 (extremely happy) may be compared to the 9% placing themselves 6–7 at the bottom end of the happiness range.

18 See Batson et al., *Religion and the Individual*, 287; & Frankel and Hewitt, "Religion and Well-Being among Canadian University Students," 70.

19 They found (*Religion and the Individual*, 287) "consistent evidence of a negative correlation with measures of general trait anxiety," which means the more religious tend to be less anxious than others.

20 The 4-point worry scale has a modest .16 negative correlation with household income.

21 Based on the Reid 1994 survey where extremely happy are those scoring 1–2 on a 7-point scale. If extremely happy is confined to those scoring 1, then 14% of Quebecers and 19% of all other Canadians rate themselves extremely happy.

22 Gallup Canada. *The Gallup Poll*, 55 no. 30 (1995).

23 Further detailed analysis of the data in tables 3.14 and 3.15 shows that these conclusions are not significantly altered by the older age structure of the Committed.

24 Here too, these conclusions still hold when account is taken of the older age structure of the Committed.

CHAPTER FOUR

1 Hobart, "Intimacy and Family Life," 150.
2 Bibby, *The Bibby Report*, 70.
3 Ibid, 65–69.
4 Reports of weekly or greater sexual activity fall from 65% of boomers (30–49 years) to a 44% rate for Canadians aged 50 to 65 and to an 18% level for Canadians 65 or older.
5 Richardson, "Divorce and Remarriage," 217 (1996).
6 Milan, "One Hundred Years of Families," 5.
7 Statistics Canada, *Vital Statistics Compendium 1996*; Statistics Canada, *The Daily*, 10 Dec. 2001.
8 Grindstaff, "The Baby Bust Revisited," 168–172.
9 Millan, "One Hundred Years of Families." 6.
10 Based on my calculations from the 1995 General Social Survey and McDaniel & Strike, *Family and Friends*.
11 Statistics Canada, *Canadian Families*.
12 Richardson, "Divorce and Remarriage." (2000).
13 Ibid.
14 Statistics Canada, *Vital Statistics Compendium, 1996*.
15 Statistics Canada, *The Daily*, 25 Nov. 1999.
16 Statistics Canada, *Vital Statistics Compendium, 1996*.
17 Richardson, "Divorce and Remarriage." (2000); Milan, "One Hundred Years of Families."
18 The widowed in this calculus are included with the still married as not having been separated or divorced.
19 Statistics Canada, *The Daily*, 14 Oct. 97.
20 Milan, "One Hundred Years of Families, "10.
21 Statistics Canada, *The Daily*, 14 Oct. 97; Milan, "One Hundred Years of Families," 10.
22 Statistics Canada, *The Daily*, 2 June 1998.
23 Garlarneau & Sturrock, *Family Income After Separation*, 7. The data are based on a 10% file of all taxpayers and their dependents in 1993 amounting to 2,083,590 individuals.
24 Statistics Canada, *The Daily*, 2 June 1998.
25 Galarneau & Sturrock, *Family Income After Separation*, 5. The separated after 5 years also include the divorced.
26 Picot, *Why Do Children Move Into and Out of Low Income*.
27 See Bourdais, Neil & Turcotte, "The Changing Face of Conjugal Relationships; Wu, "Premarital Cohabitation and the Timing of First Marriage"; Krishman, "Premarital Cohabitation and Marital Disruption."

28 Corak, *Death and Divorce.*

29 Frederick & Boyd, "The Impact of Family Structure on Completing High School."

30 The marital dissolution rate from the Reid and Bibby surveys is based on two simple questions that asked respondents whether they had ever been divorced and their current marital status. The GSS instead asked married respondents how their first marriage ended.

31 The Tau-c measure of the strength of a relationship assumes a linear relationship between the two variables, but Tau-c does not work very well in table 4.9 where the relationships tend to be curvilinear. This simply means that divorce is most common in the middle of the scale among Seekers and less common at the beginning and end of the scale for the Committed and Non Religious.

32 This was decided at the 1994 General conference. "Pentecostal Group Debates Remarriage," *Canadian Press Newswire*, 26 Aug. 1994. .

33 Heinrichs, K.. "Pentecostals Elect Woman to Executive."

34 Until 2001, approval by a diocesan Matrimonial Commission was required for divorced Anglicans wishing to remarry in their own church. Approval was typically granted if the local clergy were prepared to write to the Commission saying that the applicants were committed to a life-long second marriage that the priests were prepared to bless. The clergy were also subject to the same procedure. I am told that divorced and remarried clergy are by no means unknown in the Anglican Church of Canada. At the Anglican Church's General Synod in 2001, it was agreed to dissolve matrimonial commissions and leave all re-marriage decisions in the hands of the clergy. For that decision to be implemented, it needs to be ratified at the next General Synod in 2004. Portman, "Priests to Replace Marriage Commissions."

35 In technical language, differences in percentage separated or divorced by education produce a Tau-c of .07 for those aged 18–50. For the same age group, differences in percentage separated or divorced by attendance produce a Tau-c of -.17, which is more than double the Tau-c for education. This also applies to Tau-cs for each level of education listed in table 4.11.

36 The percentage who have ever lived common-law reaches 45% for those aged 25–29 and 30–34.

37 In Quebec in 1995, 24% of all families were common-law unions, which may be compared to the 9% rate for the rest of Canada. Statistics Canada, *Canadian Families.*

38 See footnote number 26 in this chapter for the various studies that confirm this link.

39 To be precise, the Tau-c measure of religiosity's impact on this question is still .11 for all under age 49 and .12 for the youngest age cohort of 18–29.

40 A reader of this book at the manuscript stage acknowledged that the traditional views of the Committed on sex outside marriage and working mothers are correlated with high religiosity, but she argued that the correlation is really caused by an underlying conservative mindset. Since other readers may think along the same line, I should make it clear why I disagree. First, I see little value in the tautological observation that a conservative mindset causes a particular conservative attitude. Secondly and more importantly, the notion that high religiosity is really caused by a conservative outlook on life is empirically refuted by much evidence we will later see in chapter 6 that the Committed are actually very progressive on many social issues. Since the Committed are conservative on some matters and progressive on others, high religiosity cannot be caused by a conservative mindset. Readers should also bear in mind's that chapter 2's detailed examination of the correlates of religiosity demonstrates that religiosity is a non-reducible variable that cannot be explained away as really being caused by underlying interests rooted in class, ethnicity, region, and the like. The one partial exception to that general rule is the tendency of the Very Committed to be older than other Canadians, but we have just seen that differences by religiosity remain when we confine our focus to the attitudes of younger Canadians on sexuality and working mothers. Thus I believe that religiosity has a marked impact on sexual attitudes and a much more modest influence on attitudes towards working mothers.

41 The gender gap is further diminished for Conservative Protestants under age 49. Here there is a minuscule difference between the 78% of them advising men and the 80% advising women to think of family before promotion.

42 The completed or total fertility rate is the number of children a woman can expect to have in her lifetime.

43 The NSVGP does not permit me to identify those in common-law unions.

44 When both partners work, it is the lesser amount of time that women are able to devote to childcare and housework that causes the male to female ratio to rise. The higher ratios are not caused by any increase in the time contributed by men.

45 When the analysis is confined to situations where males and females are both working full-time, I find the same contradictory set of tendencies in a slightly more magnified form.

46 Both male and female Quebec Catholics seem to devote less time to childcare than anyone else, though their male-to-female ratio is unremarkable. On the other hand, both sexes among Quebec Catholics seem to do more housework than do other religious actives. I am disinclined to read very much into such small and contrary findings.

47 Statistics Canada, *Census of Canada 1996*.

48 See table 2.10 and the attendant discussion in chapter 2.

49 Apart from the 71% of Canadians who say they are extremely or very confident they have a friend to call in an emergency, another 18% say they are fairly confident.

50 Even on the question of a loan from a friend, 27% admit to doubts; 13% say they are not very confident and 14% not at all confident.

CHAPTER FIVE

1 See Inglehart, *Modernization and Postmodernization*, 188–190."

2 Putnam, R, 1995. "Bowling Alone" & Paxton, "Is Social Capital Declining in the United States?"

3 Duchesne, "Giving Freely: Volunteers in Canada."

4 Statistics Canada, "National Survey of Giving, Volunteering, and Participating."

5 Statistics Canada, *Caring Canadians, Involved Canadians*, 14.

6 To be precise, on the 7-point scale used in this Reid survey, where 1 means "totally disagree" and 7 means "agree completely," 47% of Canadians rate themselves 5–7.

7 Curtis & Grabb, "Voluntary Association Membership in Fifteen Countries."

8 The NSVGP asked respondents if they had donated their unpaid labour during the previous 12 months to any group or organization. The NSVGP then went on to ask about volunteering in a wide range of specific organizations. Reid asked respondents whether they "do any voluntary work of any kind" for any of the 14 possible community associations in which they had just claimed membership. Thus both questions are detailed and prompt for possible volunteering in a variety of organizations.

9 Those in the labour force include all who are currently employed and those who are unemployed and looking for work.

10 To make the odds ratio on each independent variable comparable, readers should be aware that I have dichotomized all the independent variables.

11 Careful readers may note that the sum of hours volunteered in religious and non-religious organizations is slightly less than the total number of hours volunteered in table 5.3. The discrepancy stems from the questionnaire and coding design of Statistics Canada. Hours volunteered for specific types of organization were only recorded for a maximum of 3 organizations. Respondents were also asked how many additional hours they volunteered in other unspecified organizations. The latter information is included in the total number of hours volunteered.

12 Volunteer Canada and the Canadian Centre for Philanthropy, *Religion, Volunteering, and Religion: A Report.*

13 For all Canadians, median family income peaks at $49,417 in their early boomer years, falls to $39,178 for those aged 52–65, and drops again to $20, 222 in their retirement years.

14 For the Less Committed, there is a 15% decline in median charitable giving as they move from their peak giving years into retirement.

15 *Caring Canadians, Involved Canadians,* 16.

16 Because charitable giving is such a skewed ratio variable, I have run a log transformation on charitable giving to give it a normal distribution. The practice is common with financial data.

17 If anyone is troubled by the quite impressive mean and lower median donations by the minority of Seekers and the Non Religious who give to religious bodies, and who account for 14% of all monies given to religious bodies, they need only think of donations to the Salvation Army and a host of shelters and outreach programs for the poor and needy that are run by religious agencies.

18 The figures on total charitable giving and the percentage directed to religious bodies are obtained from *Caring Canadians, Involved Canadians,* 14, 19.

19 About 40% of the clients were estimated to be non-Catholics; only a minority were practising or Committed Catholics.

20 Another 30% of the national budget redistributes funds to needy local congregations and provides all congregations with literature, leadership training, and the like. The remainder of the budget is devoted to theological education, administrative expenses, and pensions.

21 Statistics Canada, *Employment Income by Occupation: 1991 Census.*

22 Bibby, *Fragmented Gods,* 108.

23 These calculations are based on the initial NSVGP estimates of the total number of volunteers in Canada and the total number of hours they volunteered. See *Caring Canadians, Involved Canadians,* 27.

CHAPTER SIX

1 Nevitte, *The Decline of Deference*, 52–54.

2 Involvement in Politics by Religiosity Age 30–49

	N	Very Commited	Less Commited	Seeker	Non Relig.	Total	Tau-c
% Say politics is very / quite important in their life[1]	(764)	42	43	47	47	45	–.05
% Very or somewhat interested in politics[1]	(764)	48	58	54	65	58	–.14**
% Frequently discuss political matters with friends[1]	(763)	17	21	18	22	20	–.04
% Daily follow national news & current affairs[2]	(7,704)	68	67	67	66	67	.01
% Voted in last federal election,[2]	(7,688)	76	78	77	75	76	.02
% Member/participant in a: political organization[2]	(7,703)	5	4	4	3	4	.01**
% Worked for a candidate or party in an election last 2 years,[3]	(1,396)	4	13	9	8	9	.00
% Contributed money to a candidate or party last 2 years,[3]	(1,395)	13	16	12	11	12	.03
% Contacted a politician about something last 2 years;[3]	(1,397)	45	48	37	35	39	.10**
Attended a public meeting on town or school affairs last 2 years,[3]	(1,397)	57	63	43	44	49	.14***

[1]WVS 1990   [2]NSVGP 1997   [3]Reid, 1996   ***P < .001   **P < .01   *P < .05

3 Elections Canada On-Line, "Past Elections."

4 Simpson, "So Who's Really Got Virtue on Their Side?"

5 That very low figure is confirmed by the NSVGP in 2000, which found that only 3% of Canadians were members or participants in a political organization.

6 See endnote 1 in this chapter for details.

7 Clarke, "English-Speaking Canada from 1854," 324.

8 Ibid, 329–334.

9 Christie & Gauvreau, *A Full-Orbed Christianity*, 198–223.

10 Ibid, 224–243.

11 Clarke, "English-Speaking Canada from 1854," 347.

12 Powles, "The Anglican Church and Canadian Culture," 20.

13 Lockhead, David, "The United Church of Canada and the Conscience of the Nation," 33. See also MacLeod, "The Cultural Transformation of the United Church of Canada," 30–33.

14 Powles, "The Anglican Church and Canadian Culture," 23.

15 Hewitt, "The Quest for the Just Society," 259.

16 See the lengthy list at the website of The Canadian Conference of Catholic Bishops (CCCB) <http://www.cccb.ca/english/default_e.htm>.

17 For Anglicans see <http://www.anglican.ca>. For the United Church see <http://www.uccan.org>.

18 Rawlyk, "The Champions of the Oppressed," 118.

19 These concerns ranged from the peace and war concerns of Plough-shares to refugee resettlement, disaster relief, Aboriginals, and prison inmates. Jansen, "Mennonites in Canada." 142–149.

20 Dawes, "The Pentecostal Assemblies of Canada," 157.

21 Stackhouse, *Canadian Evangelicalism in the Twentieth Century,* 164–172.

22 Stackhouse, J., "Bearing Witness," 117.

23 Ibid, 117–118. See also the extensive list of public policy statements at the EFC's website <http://www.efc-canada.com>.

24 This is Bibby's view. *Unknown Gods,* 60.

25 See the monthly newsletter during the 2000 election from Darrel Reid, President of Focus on the Family, Canada, in which much stress was placed on "family values" and opposition to gay marriages. The news-letter noted "Focus on the Family is a non-partisan, charitable organi-zation. We will not take sides in this election, or tell people for whom they should vote." Focus on the Family, "Newsletter."

26 Gallup Canada, *The Gallup Report,* 11 May 1983.

27 The 2000 estimate is from Bibby, *Restless Gods,* 190.

28 The poll was done by POLLARA with a sample of 1,410. *Vancouver Sun,* 22 Dec. 1996.

29 The remaining 18% were undecided or divided on the question saying religion was as important as it was unimportant in their political think-ing. To be precise, this 18% selected a response of 3, when asked to rate themselves on a scale from 1 to 5, where 1 = "not at all important" and 5 = "very important."

30 Mendelsohn & Nadeau, "The Religious Cleavage and the Media in Canada." Religion is measured as a dichotomous variable differentiating Catholic from Protestant without regard for level of religious commitment.

31 Bibby, *Fragmented Gods,* 193.

32 These are not rogue numbers. Three years earlier, just before the 1993 election, another Reid survey found lower overall support for Liberals (43% in 1993 vs. 55% in 1996), but Canadians at all levels of religiosity gave greater support to the Liberals than any other party.

33 He had formerly been a practising United Church minister. To be fair, he is reported to have made the comment in a joking manner. Specta-tor, "Cross anti-Christian Prejudice off the List of Alliance Excuses."

34 See "Political Winds Blow through Pews: Dangerous to Confuse Faith with Faction," *ChristianWeek*, 14 no. 6 (2000) and Heinrichs, "Fighting for the Alliance's Soul."

35 Hoover, "Ecumenism of the Trenches?"

36 See the Canadian Alliance website <http://www.canadianalliance.ca/index_e.cfm> (Accessed 1 May 2001).

37 Arnold, "Harper Day Battle on Religion."

38 The 6% is based on the 18% of all Committed Christians who are Conservative Protestants. The 9% figure is based on all Canadians who claim a Conservative Protestant allegiance.

39 Melnyk, "His Father's Mission"; Harrison, *Of Passionate Intensity*, 210.

40 Elections Canada On-Line, "Past Elections."

41 Nevitte, *The Decline of Deference*, 51. See also Inglehart, *Modernization and Postmodernization*, Ch. 10.

42 Nevitte, *The Decline of Deference*, 55.

43 Ibid, 95.

44 Ibid, 79–97.

45 Ibid, 56–60.

46 See for example the less than impartial report of the Fraser Institute, "Whose Ethics? Whose Religion?"

47 Evangelical Fellowship of Canada, "All Faiths Threatened by Criticism of Day's Beliefs."

48 Stiller is committed to "cultural pluralism" or the belief that diverse cultural groups ought to "live together in harmony without abandoning their right to speak openly about their beliefs. " He also acknowledges that the "reaction" of some evangelicals "to things we don't like has been emotional and abusive." Harvey, "Media Fear US-style religion."

49 Like confidence in institutions, there is a curvilinear relationship with age whereby willingness to protest rises from young adulthood to middle age and then slowly fall thereafter. Nevitte, *Decline of Deference*, 81–82.

50 Ibid, 94–97.

51 My version of the wvs does not allow me to use one of the question-naire items employed by Nevitte. I also use two items not employed by Nevitte. My 6-item summary measure of civil permissiveness has a Cronbach's alpha of .72, which is within the usual limit for the reliability of an index.

52 I measure strong agreement for saying behaviours are not justified as 1–3 on 10-point scale, rather than simply dichotomizing the scale, as Nevitte does.

53 Bibby's data on protest at the two ends of the spectrum (table 6.9) could have been broken down by religious family, but I have not done so because the differences are small and inconsequential. I suspect that the intermediate range of political protest tapped by the wvs would have produced more revealing differences, but the wvs does not allow me to differentiate between Mainline and Conservative Protestants.

54 For those under the age of 30, condemnation of all civil permissiveness falls to 37% from the 52% level of all Canadians. Tau-c for religiosity is reduced to .13 for those under age 30, but there remains a substantial gap between the 52% of the Very Committed and the 32% of the Non Religious who strongly agree that all forms of civil permissiveness should never be justified.

55 His most thorough treatment of political matters is in his first book; see Bibby, *Fragmented Gods*, 70–72. For a more recent statement, see Bibby, Hewitt, & Roof, "Religion and Identity." 241.

56 Davis & Robinson, "Religious Orthodoxy in American Society;" "Response to Davis and Robinson."

57 Reimer, "A Generic Evangelicalism?"

58 Inglehart, *Modernization and Postmodernization*, 28–30.

59 Derived from Bibby's Project Canada surveys in 1975 and 1995.

60 Evans, "Counting Crime."

61 See chapter 2's discussion of ethnicity and Isajiw, *Understanding Diversity.*

62 "Visible minority" is a government-inspired term to refer to all non-whites or non-Caucasians in Canada. The term may not be that widely known outside bureaucratic and academic circles, but it is preceded in Bibby's 1995 survey by a series of questions on whether approval is given to marriages between whites and blacks, whites and Asians etc, which provide a clear context to the summary question on visible minorities. The responses on specific non-white groups are also similar to those for visible minorities in general.

63 The nsvgp of 1997 puts Conservative Protestants at 21% of all Committed Christians. Bibby's 1995 survey produces an estimate of 16%.

64 Inglehart, *Modernization and Postmodernization*, 109–159.

65 Calculated from the 4-item postmaterialism scale in the WVS for Canada in 1981 and 1990. Over this decade, pure postmaterialists rose from 16% to 26% of Canadians; materialists fell from 22% to 12%. Thus the great majority (62% to 63%) of Canadians at both points in time had an in-between or mixed value orientation.

66 See the codebook for the WVS and the details of how the 4-item and 12-item postmaterialism scale is constructed at the website for The Inter-University Consortium for Political and Social Research, University of Michigan (Accessed 20 April 2001) http://www.icpsr.umich.edu/cgi/archive2.prl?num=2790&path=ICPSR.

67 Priorities by Religiosity and Generation, Reid 1996

	Very Commited	Less Commited	Seekers	Non Relig.	Total
GENERATION X (18–30)					
Relationships (morality & family)	55	33	26	22	28
Security (law and order & a healthy economy)	27	39	37	48	42
Postmaterialism (more say in govt. & the environment)	18	28	37	30	30
Total (V = .18 ***N = 670)	100%	100%	100%	100%	100%
BOOMERS (31–50)					
Relationships (morality & family)	53	34	31	21	31
Security (law and order & a healthy economy)	36	49	45	52	47
Postmaterialism (more say in govt & the environment)	11	16	24	27	22
Total (V = .18 ***N = 1344)	100%	100%	100%	100%	100%
PRE-BOOMERS (51+)					
Relationships (morality & family)	49	25	27	16	31
Security (law and order & a healthy economy)	36	63	53	61	52
Postmaterialism (more say in govt.& the environment)	14	11	20	24	18
Total (V = .22 ***N = 824)	100%	100%	100%	100%	100%

***P < .001   **P < .01   *P < .05

CHAPTER SEVEN

1 Bibby, *Unknown Gods*, 128.

2 For an example, see my comments in chapter 2 on the Pope's recent pronouncements on hell.

3 The disproportionate presence of elderly Canadians among the Committed affects these findings, but 30% of Catholics and 36% of Mainline Protestants who are boomers say they are literalists.

4 See Stiller, "Anglicans Consider Whether Centre Vanishing;" McAteer, "Alpha Grows in Spite of Controversy:" Koop, "Community of Concern Elects New Leader."

5 Cuneo, *Catholics Against the Church*, 148–184.

6 Though I normally exclude "don't know" responses from my analysis, I here include them with those who said they were not evangelical. Thus my estimate here is a conservative one. Excluding the "don't knows" would raise evangelicals to 36% of the Very Committed.

7 See Grenville, "The Awakened and the Spirit-Moved," 419–420. Grenville's scale indicates that 16% of Canadians are evangelical. The self-assessed indicator I employ suggests that about 12% of all Canadians are evangelical.

8 Barrett, D., "Statistics, Global."

9 Again, this is a conservative estimate that treats "don't know" responses as if they were not Pentecostal or Charismatic.

10 Bibby reaches much the same conclusion in *Restless Gods*, 188.

11 When the 52% of Canadians with spiritual needs in 1995 were asked to define their spirituality, Bibby found that about half (53%) used conventional, Christian terminology; the remaining 47% used a less conventional vocabulary (*Restless Gods*, 194–197). My analysis of his data shows that the Committed with spiritual needs were more likely to speak in conventional Christian terms (74%) than were Seekers (41%). Despite the clear tendencies here that cannot be surprising, I would place much greater stress on the fact that interest in spirituality, however described, is far more widespread and deeply felt by the Very Committed than by the Seekers.

12 Cramer's V, here as elsewhere, measures the magnitude of the difference between the four major religious families .

13 Bibby, *Restless Gods*, 209.

14 Gallup Canada, *The Gallup Poll*, 57 no. 27 (1997).

15 This is a rough and ready approximation comparing an index of confidence in 4 secular institutions from the 1981 wvs which are as closely matched as possible to the 4 secular institutions in my index of secular confidence in table 6.7.

16 Bibby, *Unknown Gods*, 75

17 See Sweet, *God in the Classroom*; and Blair, *The Policy and Practice of Religious Education*.

18 In Quebec, separate French and English school boards have recently replaced the old Protestant and Catholic boards. Smith, "Changes in Quebec Schools." See also Kelly, "Newfoundland: Living without Catholic Schools."

19 Smith, "Changes in Quebec Schools."

20 Sweet, *God in the Classroom*, 115.

21 *National Post*, 10 May 2001. The final tax credit of $3,500 planned for 2005 is about half the $7,015 per pupil operating cost in the public system in 2000. Federation of Independent Schools in Canada, "Provincial Funding of Independent Schools." Apart from very expensive and elite private schools, private schools of a religious nature are estimated to cost between $5,000 and $7,000 a child. Lewington, "Student Surge to Private Schools Unlikely." Blumfeld & Walfish, "Ontario Slaps its Minorities."

22 All data are from the web site of the aforementioned Federation of Independent Schools in Canada.

23 Sweet, *God in the Classroom*, 82

24 The Canadian Jewish Congress commissioned an Environics poll in Ontario indicating 54% agreement with the statement, "Ontario should fund all religion-based independent schools, given that it is constitutionally obliged to continue funding the Catholic system." Csillag, "Poll Finds 54% Support for Religious Schools."

25 Blair, *The Policy and Practice of Religious Education*, 19; For a more recent overview of the same years, see Gidney, & Miller, "The Christian Recessional in Ontario's Public Schools."

26 Blair, *The Policy and Practice of Religious Education*, 20

27 Ibid.

28 Sweet, *God in the Classroom*, 33.

29 Harvey, "Supreme Court Docket"

30 "Saskatoon Bans Lord's Prayer in Schools," *Toronto Star*, 28 June 1999.

31 Waytiuk, J., "Merry Christmas, Chnukah, Ramadan;" "Prayer Ruling Likely Won't Affect N.S," *Chronicle Herald*, 30 July 1999.

32 Sweet, *God in the Classroom*, 219.

33 Ibid, 220–222.

34 Miller, J.R., *Shingwauk's Vision*, 329.

35 Fenwick, "Residential School Update," 33; Miller, *Shingwauk's Vision*, 340.

36 Sillars, L., "Agree with Thine Adversary Quickly."

37 "Cabinet Clears Way for School Abuse Payouts," *National Post*, 8 June 2001.

38 Indian Residential Schools Resolution Canada, "Statistics."

39 By January 2003, 630 settlements had been reached with former students but only 21 had been resolved through the courts. The rest were all resolved by out-of-court settlements. Ibid.

40 "Abuse Suits May Hit $10B, Lawyer Says," *National Post*, 6 Feb. 2001.

41 Foot, "Natives Filed $12.5B Class Action." Shawn Tupper, Director of the Residential Schools Unit at the Department of Indian Affairs, says

the courts have not yet endorsed these broader charges. "Abuse Suits May Hit $10B, Lawyer Says," *National Post*, 6 Feb. 2001.

42 Makin, "Court Paves Way for Native Schools Lawsuit."

43 Some may question the government assumptions that total claimants for abuse will amount to 18,000, of whom 10,500 to 13,500 will eventually be deemed valid. Others may question the assumption of an average compensation of $75,000. See Bailey, "Native Abuse Claims to be Fast-Tracked" and Johnson, "Making the Gun Registry Look Good."

44 Blair, "Ottawa, Not Natives Behind Many Lawsuits."

45 Blair, "Church on Hook for Abuse."

46 This is a tiny fraction of the $5-million demanded by the plaintiffs. Mertl, "Compensation Decision Insults Native Abuse Victims."

47 See worried public statements by various churches on the 1999 decision of the Supreme Court on vicarious liability. Anglican Church of Canada, "Court Rulings Could Jeopardize Church Work;" Catholic Register, 21 June 1999; and United Church of Canada, "News Release on Vicarious Liability,"

48 The Canadian Conference of Catholic Bishops has been notably quiet in this public discussion. Apart from financial considerations, the Anglican and United churches have voiced concern over the failure of government to enact effective out-of-court settlements and to address "cultural" as well as sexual and physical abuse claims. See United Church of Canada, "Response to the Government Announcement on Residential Schools;" Valpy, Native Lawsuits Fuel Costly Bureaucracy;" Anglican Church of Canada, "Residential School Update #13."

49 In Nova Scotia, a subsequent legal investigation revealed "significant evidence" of "false and exaggerated claims" in a rushed compensation package for alleged abuse victims at the Shelbourne School for boys and a centre for girls in Truro. Fox, "Abuse-Redress Plan Flawed."

50 Anglican Church of Canada, "Towards a New Beginning,"

51 Valpy, "Lawsuits Spell End of Tiny B.C. Diocese."

52 O'Hara, J., "No Forgiving," 23.

53 Boyles, "Don't Blame the Churches;" Anglican Church of Canada, "Residential School Update #9."

54 See Anglican Church of Canada, "Towards a New Beginning" and its related links on the Anglican web page.

55 According to Archdeacon Boyle, General Secretary of the General Synod, at the special synod of the Diocese of Nova Scotia, which ratified the agreement in January, 2003.

56 If the Anglican Church is later held liable by the courts for cultural damage, the liability will be confined to the General Synod and will not apply to the dioceses. Anglican Church of Canada, "Towards a New Beginning."

57 In this vein and prior to the agreement, the General Synod's Healing and Reconciliation Fund has distributed since 1992 more than $1 million in grants to Aboriginal communities for healing programs. Ibid.

58 De Santis, S., "Church Reacts to Native Boycott."

59 According to the large NSVGP survey in 1997, the United Church had 645,757 active members over the age of 20 who attended at least monthly. The comparable figure for Anglicans was 411,460.

60 All numbers are from the Office of Indian Residential schools Resolution "Backgrounder."

61 Wilson, "Loosening the Residential School Logjam."

62 O'Hara, "No Forgiving," 23.

63 Presbyterian Church of Canada, "Residential Schools, Frequently Asked Questions."

64 Office of Indian Residential Schools Resolution, "Backgrounder."

65 O'Hara, "No Forgiving," 23; Babych, & Gonzalez, "Oblates Face Bankruptcy."

66 Ibid.

67 "Oblates Offer Their Assets in Exchange for Residential School Liability," *Canadian Press Newswire*, 12 July 2000.

68 Perault, "Historic Order Faces Bankruptcy."

69 Gonzalez, "Grandin Oblates Face Possible Bankruptcy."

70 Sr. Marie Zarowny, the Chair of the Catholic Organization's Task Group on Indian Residential Schools, describes as "unacceptable" Gray's argument "that the larger and more prosperous dioceses of the churches would help some smaller dioceses and orders that had been sued by victims directly." "Residential School Solutions, *Western Catholic Reporter,* 11 Feb. 2002.

71 Bailey, "Ottawa to Announce $25M Offer by Anglican Church." Suzanne Scorsone, "a spokeswoman for the Catholic Archdiocese of Toronto, said her church could not accept the Anglican "whole-church solution" that the government endorses. "She said it would be unjust to ask Catholics in Toronto to compensate a native person suing a Catholic organization in Western Canada." Foot, "Ottawa, Off-loading on Catholics."

72 "Churches Face Penance," *Canadian Press Newswire,* 31 Aug. 2000.

73 Anglican Church of Canada, "Residential School Update # 11."

74 "Sask Court Rules Church Cannot be Held Liable," *Canadian Press Newswire*, 25 Aug. 2001.

75 Over the same period, the Catholic laity is expected to grow by 65%. Chang, "Introduction: The Crisis is about Control," 2.

76 "APC Urged to Promote Priestly Vocations," *Western Catholic Reporter*, 26 April 1999.

77 Canadian Conference of Catholic Bishops, *Human Resources in the Catholic Church*, 11.

78 "The Greying of Canada's Sisters and Brothers," *Globe and Mail*, 23 Feb. 1999. Similarly and more recently, the Canadian Religious Conference estimated that its number would be halved by 2015; in that year only 10% would be under the age of 65. Babych, "Canadian Religious Conference Restructures."

79 Canadian Conference of Catholic Bishops, *Human Resources in the Catholic Church*.

80 Woodward, "Priest Shortage Threatens Parishes." For a similar story in next-door Saskatchewan, see Warwick, "Facing an Unprecedented Shortage of Priests."

81 Slobodian, "Jesuits Ending Funding to 16 Projects including Jesuit Centre."

82 "Pope's Refusal of Ordination to Women Stirs Quebec Catholics." *Canadian Press Newswire*, 14 July 1994.

83 *Catholic New Times*, 14 Nov. 1999 & 28 Nov. 1999.

84 When the Anglican Church in England accepted women as priests in 1992, some 500 dissident Anglican clergy were accepted into the Roman Catholic Church, despite being married. Some of these former Anglicans are still married and now running Catholic parishes in England, using the less than clear distinction that they are "priests-in-charge" and not "parish priests." Whitebloom, "Wedding Bells Ring for Catholic Priests."

85 Starting in Austria and Germany, the group, "We Are Church" solicited 2.5 million signatures seeking married and female priests. The documents were submitted to the Vatican, though a spokesperson admitted she was "not optimistic." *Catholic New Times*, 2 Nov. 1997.

86 Argan, "Parish Restructuring;" "Priest Shortage Leads to Closings," *The Christian Century*, 23–30 Dec. 1998.

87 Canadian Conference of Catholic Bishops, *Human Resources in the Catholic Church*, 5.

88 Argan, "Living the Priest Shortage."

89 Faced with an equally large decline in clergy in France, some dioceses have initiated a new system known as ADAP (Assemblees Dominicales

en l'Absence du Pretre), which "permits the celebration of the mass without a priest; responsibility is taken by the laity – and in 70 per cent of the parishes involved women play a crucial role in the proceedings." Davie, *Religion in Modern Europe*, 46.

90 Blumhofer, *Aimee Semple McPherson*.

91 Nason-Clark, "Gender Relations in Contemporary Christian Organizations", 226.

92 Daniels, D. "Women May Not Serve Officially as Pastors."

93 Heinricks, K. "Baptist Group Ordains First Female Pastor."

94 *Faith Today*, May/June, 1994.

95 Fletcher-Marsh, *Beyond the Walled Garden*, 124.

96 "A Challenge to Religious Freedom," *Western Report*, 10, no. 11 1995.

97 Lockhead, "The United Church and the Conscience of the Nation," 25.

98 Donnelly, "Still Unready For Women Clergy," 17.

99 De Santis. "Inroads by Women Fall short of Leadership Positions." In November 2003, the third female bishop, Susan Moxley, was elected suffragan bishop of the Diocese of Nova Scotia and Prince Edward Island.

100 Donnelly, "Still Unready For Women Clergy," 17.

101 Combined figures for Canada and the United States show that the female percentage of students listed by the Association of Theological Schools rose from 10% in 1978 to 34% in 1999. *Yearbook of American and Canadian Churches, 2001*, 369. At this time, females were 30% of entering students in "Catholic and evangelical institutions," and 50% in "mainline Protestant institutions." Nunley, "Study Says US Seminaries Should Raise Standards." The Church of England did not accept female clergy until 1992, but 43% of ordinands were female in 1999. *Church Times*, 10 Mar. 2000.

102 United Church of Canada, "Quick Facts."

103 Data provided by the Anglican Church of Canada Library, Toronto, 24 May 2002.

104 See Chang, "Female Clergy in the Contemporary Protestant Church."

105 De Santis, "Inroads by Women Fall Short of Leadership Positions."

106 Among the 117 clergy at the General Synod, 23% were women, which is a generous approximation to the 17% of all clergy who are women, though it is not gender parity. The 50:50 rule applies to all national committees. Communication from the General Secretary's Office, Anglican Church of Canada, 24 May 2002.

107 In the same article the United Church reports that 65% of its "ministers in training" had a prior career and an average age of 38, up from 29 in 1989. Csillig, "Autumn Vocations."

108 "A Changing Ministry," *Anglican Journal*, 119 no. 8 (1993).

109 "Too many Chiefs: Mainline Churches Ponder Their Excess Clergy." *Western Report*, 1 no. 22 1995.

110 These numbers are drawn from the 1985 General Social Survey and the 2000 NSVGP.

111 See "Clergy Crunch in Ottawa," *Anglican Journal*, 127 no. 3 (2001);" Todd, "Protestants Across Canada Join Roman Catholic Church in Clergy Shortage."

112 Equal Marriage for Same Sex Couples, "Evolution: 20th Century."

113 Evangelical Fellowship of Canada, Uncharted Waters," 1.

114 "Gays Gain Ground in Benefits," *Canadian Press Newswire*, 2 May 1996.

115 Ward, "Pension Committee to Debate Extending Same Sex Benefits."

116 Koop, "Same Sex Bill Threatens Marriage."

117 Bibby's surveys found that 70% of Canadians in 1980 and 68% in 1995 "agree homosexuals are entitled to the same rights as other Canadians."

118 Canadian Conference of Catholic Bishops, "The Catholic Church's Teaching on Homosexuality."

119 In a recent survey of Canadian seminarians, 75% described themselves as heterosexual; 13% said they were homosexual; 7% were bisexual; and 7% claimed they were unsure of their sexual orientation. The low 45% response rate in the survey casts some doubt on these findings, though a similar US survey had similar findings with 72% describing themselves as heterosexual. Rovers, "Clergy to the Right," 14. Of course, surveys of this type do not provide any insight into how many clergy or seminarians practice celibacy. For a recent review of various "estimates" of rates of homosexuality and celibacy in the Catholic Church, see Abbott, *A History of Celibacy*, 424–427.

120 Evangelical Fellowship of Canada, "Sexual Orientation."

121 Squires, "Homosexuality, Ordination, and the United Church," 338.

122 Ibid, 345.

123 When the 1988 decision was reaffirmed at the 1990 General Conference, about 100 of its 3,000 congregations formed a protest group that has since been dedicated to defending traditional views of sexuality and doctrine. Shepherd, "Unity Amidst Diversity," 5.

124 Betson, "United Church Promotes Homosexual Concerns."

125 United Church of Canada, "Gay and Lesbian Covenanting Services."

126 Bird, "In the Pews Life Goes On," 25.

127 These motions were made at the convention of The Evangelical Lutheran Church in Canada, and not its much more conservative, sister

denomination, the Lutheran Church – Canada. Portman, "Lutherans Want to be Welcoming to Gays."

128 "Gay Minister's Ordination Overturned," *Canadian Press Newswire,* 10 June 1996. Subsequently, St. Andrew's remained loyal to its gay pastor, Daryl Macdonald. It formally left the Presbyterian Church in Canada in 1998, though it still calls itself "St. Andrew's Presbyterian Church." In 1999, it held its own ordination service for MacDonald, which was attended by Presbyterian, Anglican, and United Church clergy. Shepherd, H., "Breakaway Congregation to Ordain Gay minister."

129 "Synod Struggles with Wording to Affirm Gays and Lesbians," *Anglican Journal,* 121 no. 7 (1995).

130 "Anglican bishops to Apologize to Gays," Canadian Press Newswire, 6 May 1997.

131 The House of Bishops reaffirmed these principles in 1997. Larmondin,"Bishops Issue Guidelines on Homosexuality." See also McAteer, "Bishops Vote Down Bill of Rights."

132 Larmondin, "New West Approves Same Sex Blessings."

133 Larmondin, "Bishops Issue Guidelines on Homosexuality."

134 Valpy, M., "Same-Sex Dispute Saddens Archbishop."

135 Stirk, "Same-Sex Blessings Split Synod."

136 Besides their doctrinal disagreements, the bishops and Archbishop both condemned New Westminster for failing to abide by the world-wide resolution of Anglicans at Lambeth in 1998 that refused to countenance gay marriages. Breaking with Lambeth and the expressed will of the Canadian Bishops as a whole, they contended, would only lead to disunity and schism. "Thirteen Anglican Bishops Respond to the Decision of the Diocese of New Westminster," Anglican News Service Canada, 17 June 2002. "Local Options Erode Communion, Carey Warns," Anglican Communion News Service, 16 Sept. 2002.

137 "Right of Blessing Authorized in Diocese of New Westminster," Anglican News Service Canada, 28 May 2003.

138 "Bishop Ingham Tells Same-Sex Blessing Critics: We Still Love You," Anglican New Service Canada, 28 May 2003.

139 "Statement by the Primates of the Anglican Communion Meeting in Lambeth, "Anglican New Service Canada, 16 October 2003.

140 Larmondin &. De Santis, "Same-Sex Decision Proves Costly;" Davidson, "New West Situation Simmers;" De Santis, "Dispute over Same-Sex Blessings Deepens over 'Illegal' Actions;" De Santis, "Yukon Bishop Faces Discipline."

141 Valpy, "Gays Claim First Legal Marriages."

142 Nichol, "Marriage Vows: Canada's Gays and Lesbians are Mounting a Strong Fight."

143 Equal Marriage for Same Sex Couples, "Equality – Timeline and Evolution of Marriage."

144 The British Columbia Court of Appeal lifted its one year suspension of their May decision after the Ontario Court of Appeal ruled in June that gays should have an immediate right to marry. Richards, "B.C. Joins Ontario in Embracing Same-Sex Marriage,"

145 LeBlanc, "Cauchon Pushes Same-Sex Marriage Bill."

146 This represents a slight decline from the 54% level of support for same-sex marriages in June. "Same-Sex Marriage: the Debate Enjoined." Ipsos-Reid, 8 August 2003.

147 This is why they opposed Bill C–33 (adding sexual orientation to the Human Rights Act as a legal ground for discrimination), while claiming that "homosexuals should have the same rights as everyone else in Canada." Evangelical Fellowship of Canada, "Uncharted Waters," 1.

148 Evangelical Fellowship of Canada, "The Vriend Decision."

149 As the *Globe and Mail* editorial in support of the BC decision pointed out, churches under this new ruling are under no more obligation to marry gays than they are "to marry every male-female couple that asks." "Give Same Sex Couples the Chance to Marry," *The Globe and Mail*, 3 May 2003.

150 LeBlanc, "Cauchon Pushes Same-Sex Marriage Bill."

151 In England, the Anglican Church is seeking exemption from recent, anti-discrimination legislation because it fears "bishops could be prosecuted if they refuse to ordain practicing homosexuals." Gay.com UK, "Church Demands Exemption From Anti-Gay Discrimination Legislation."

152 See my reference in chapter 2 to data from the 1993 Reid survey indicating substantial majorities of all Canadians agree that Jesus is "the divine son of God" and "was resurrected to eternal life." Agreement among the Committed is much higher.

CHAPTER EIGHT

1 Inglehart & Baker, "Modernization, Cultural Change, and the Persistence of Cultural Values," 46.

2 Roberts, *Religion in Sociological Perspective*, 351.

3 Bibby, *Restless Gods*, 94.

4 Bibby, *Restless Gods*, 133.

5 The 1997 estimate comes from the NSVGP. The 1990 figure is based on the WVS.

6 CCCB. *Human Resources in the Catholic Church in Canada*, 2, 8.

7 The number of monthly attenders fell by 35% , but the number of churches fell by 12% and the number of clergy in parish work actually grew by 8%.The latter numbers are for the years 1984 to 1999.

8 Bibby, *Fragmented Gods*, 1.

9 For an argument along these lines applied to the United States, see Demerath, "Cultural Victory and Organizational Defeat."

10 Emberley, *Divine Hunger*, 130.

11 "Some Councils Defy Court Ban," *Canadian Press Newswire*, 11 Jan. 2000.

12 "Svend Proposes, God Disposes," *British Columbia Report*, 10 no. 17 (1999).

Bibliography

Abbott, E. *A History of Celibacy.* Toronto: HarperCollins, 1999.

Adams, M. "Sex in the Snow: Deference is Dead in Canada." *Canadian Speeches,* 11 no. 4, 1997.

Anglican Church of Canada. "Residential School Update #13. 9 April 2002. 21 May 2002 http://anglican.ca/ministry/rs/reports/rsupdate13.html.

Anglican Church of Canada. "Towards a New Beginning." 30 Dec. 3002. 13 Jan. 2003 http://anglican.ca/ministries/rs/resources/towards.php.

Anglican Church of Canada. "Residential School Update #11." 16 Oct. 2001. 19 Jan. 2002 http://anglican.ca/ministry/rs/reports/rsupdate11.html.

Anglican Church of Canada. "Residential School Update #9." 30 Mar. 2001. 14 April 2001 http://anglican.ca/ministry/rs/reports/rsupdate9.html.

Anglican Church of Canada. "Court Rulings Could Jeopardize Church Work." 17 June 1999. 26 June 2002
http://www.anglican.ca/news/ans/ans.html?ansItem=1999–06–17_a.ans.

Anglican News Service Canada. "Statement by the Primates of the Anglican Communion Meeting in Lambeth." 16 October 2003. 18 October 2003. http://www.anglican.ca/news.

Anglican News Service Canada. "Bishop Ingham Tells Same-Sex Blessing Critics: We Still Love You." 28 May 2003. July 5 2003. http://anglican.ca/news.

Anglican News Service Canada. "Right of Blessing Authorized in Diocese of New Westminster." 28 May 2003. July 5 2003. http://www.anglican.ca/news.

Appleby, B. *Responsible Parenthood: Decriminalizing Contraception in Canada.* Toronto: University of Toronto, 1999.

Argan, G. "Parish Restructuring." *Western Catholic Reporter* 23 Nov. 1998.

Arnold, T. "Harper Day Battle on Religion." *National Post* 11 Feb. 2001.

Babych, A. "Canadian Religious Conference Restructures." *Western Catholic Reporter* 1 July 2002.

Babych, A., & R. Gonzalez. "Oblates Face Bankruptcy." *Western Catholic Reporter* 12 June 2000.

Bailey, S. "Ottawa to Announce $25M Offer by Anglican Church." *Canadian Press Newswire* 19 Nov. 2002.

Bailey, S. "Native Abuse Claims to be Fast-Tracked." *Canadian Press* 11 Nov. 2002.

Barrett, D. "Statistics, Global." In S. Burgess and G. McGee, eds. *Dictionary of Pentecostal and Charismatic Movements.* Grand Rapids, MI: Zondervan, 1988.

Batson, D. et al. *Religion and the Individual: A Social-Psychological Perspective.* Toronto: Oxford University Press, 1997.

Baum, G. *The Church in Quebec.* Ottawa: Novalis, 1991.

Beckford, J. "Postmodernity, High Modernity, and New Modernity: Three Concepts in Search of Religion." In K. Flanagan, ed. *Postmodernity, Sociology and Religion.* London: Macmillan, 1996.

Bellah, R. et al. *Habits of the Heart: Individualism and Commitment in American Life.* New York: Harper & Row, 1986.

Berger, P. "The Secularization of the World: A Global Overview." In P. Berger, ed. *The Desecularization of the World: Resurgent Religion and World Politics.* Grand Rapids, MI: W.B. Eerdmans, 1999.

Berger, P. "Epistemological Modesty: An Interview with Peter Berger," *Christian Century* 29 October 1997.

Berger, P. *The Sacred Canopy: Elements of a Sociological Theory of Religion.* New York: Doubleday, 1967.

Beit-Hallahmi, B. and M. Argyle. *The Psychology of Religious Behaviour, Belief and Experience.* New York: Routledge, 1997.

Betson, R. "United Church Promotes Homosexual Concerns." *ChristianWeek,* 14 no. 10 (2000).

Beyer, P. "Religious Vitality in Canada: The Complementarity of Religious Market and Secularisation Perspectives." *Journal for the Scientific Study of Religion* 36 no. 2 (1997).

Bibby, R. *Restless Gods: The Renaissance of Religion in Canada.* Toronto: Stoddart, 2002.

Bibby, R., W. Hewitt, and W.C. Roof. "Religion and Identity: The Canadian, American and Brazilian Cases." *International Journal of Comparative Sociology,* 39 no. 2 (1998).

Bibby, R. *The Bibby Report: Social Trends Canadian Style.* Toronto: Stoddart, 1995.

Bibby, R. and M. Brinkerhoff. "Circulation of the Saints 1966–1990: New Data, New Reflections." *Journal for the Scientific Study of Religion,* 33 no. 3 (1994).

Bibby. R. *Unknown Gods: The Ongoing Story of Religion in Canada.* Toronto: Stoddart, 1993.

Bibby, R. *Fragmented Gods: The Poverty and Potential of Religion in Canada.* Toronto: Irwin, 1987.

Bird, J. "In the Pews Life Goes On." *United Church Observer,* 61 no. 9 (1998).

Blair, A. *The Policy and Practice of Religious Education in Publicly Funded Elementary and Secondary Schools in Canada and Elsewhere.* Toronto: Ministry of Education, Ontario, 1986.

Blair, K. "Cariboo is 'Toast,' Synod is Told." *Anglican Journal,* 126 no. 9 (2000).

Blair, K. "Ottawa, Not Natives Behind Many Lawsuits." *Anglican Journal,* 126 no. 4 (2000).

Blair, K. "Church on Hook for Abuse." *Anglican Journal,* 125, no. 8 (1999).

Blumfeld, A. and I. Walfish, "Ontario Slaps its Minorities," *Globe and Mail,* 4 Dec. 2003.

Blumhofer, E. *Aimee Semple McPherson: Everybody's Sister.* Grand Rapids, MI: Eerdmans, 1993.

Bourdais, C., G. Neil, and P. Turcotte. "The Changing Face of Conjugal Relationships." *Canadian Social Trends* no. 59 (2000).

Boyles, J. "Don't Blame the Churches," *Globe and Mail,* 11 Sept. 2000.

Bruce, S. *God is Dead: Secularization in the West.* Oxford: Blackwell, 2002.

Bruce, S. "The Pervasive World-View: Religion in Pre-Modern Britain." *The British Journal of Sociology* 48:4 (1997).

Bruce, S. *Religion in the Modern World: From Cathedrals to Cults.* New York: Oxford University Press (1996).

Canadian Conference of Catholic Bishops. "The Catholic Church's Teaching on Homosexuality," 1997. 19 May 2003 http://www.cccb.ca/Backgrounders.htm?CD=&ID=80.

Canadian Conference of Catholic Bishops. *Human Resources in the Catholic Church in Canada 1993* (1995).

Chang, P. "Introduction: The Crisis is about Control: Consequences of Priestly Decline in the US Catholic Church." *Sociology of Religion* 59 no. 1 (1998).

Chang, P. "Female Clergy in the Contemporary Protestant Church." *Journal for the Scientific Study of Religion* 36:4 (1997).

Christie, Nancy and Michael Gauvreau, 1996. *A Full-Orbed Christianity: The Protestant Churches and Social Welfare in Canada, 1900–1940.* Montreal and Kingston: McGill-Queen's University Press, 1996.

Chausse, G. "French Canada from Conquest to the 1840s." In T. Murphy and R. Perrin, eds. *A Concise History of Christianity in Canada*. Toronto: Oxford University Press, 1996.

Clarke, B. "English-Speaking Canada from 1854." In T. Murphy and R. Perrin, eds. *A Concise History of Christianity in Canada*. Toronto: Oxford University Press, 1996.

Clark, W. "Religious Observance: Marriage and Family." *Canadian Social Trends* no. 50 (1998).

Corak, M. *Death and Divorce: The Long Term Consequences of Parental Loss on Adolescents*. Statistics Canada, Catalogue No: 11F0019, MPE no. 135, 1999.

Csillag, R. "Autumn Vocations," *Globe and Mail*, 26 Feb. 2001.

Csillag, R. "Poll Finds 54% Support for Religious Schools." *Canadian Jewish News* 30:3 (2000).

Cuneo, M. *Catholics Against the Church*. Toronto: Toronto University Press, 1994.

Curtis, J. and E. Grabb. "Voluntary Association Membership in Fifteen Countries: A Comparative Analysis." *American Sociological Review* 57 no. 1 (1992).

Daniels, D. "Women May Not Serve Officially as Pastors." *ChristianWeek* 11 no. 17 (1997).

Davidson, J. "New West Situation Simmers." *Anglican Journal* 129 no. 5 (2003).

Davidson, J. "Budget Hints at Reprieve." *Anglican Journal* 128 no. 1 (2001).

Davie, G. *Religion in Modern Europe: a Memory Mutates*. Oxford: Oxford University Press, 1999.

Davie, G. "Europe: the Exception that Proves the Rule?" In P. Berger, ed. *The Desecularization of the World: Resurgent Religion and World Politics*. Grand Rapids, MI: W.B. Eerdmans, 1999.

Davie, G. *Religion in Britain since 1945: Believing without Belonging*. Oxford: Blackwell, 1994.

Davis, N. and R. Robinson. "Religious Orthodoxy in American Society: The Myth of a Monolithic Camp." *Journal for the Scientific Study of Religion* 35 no. 3 (1996).

Dawes, W. "The Pentecostal Assemblies of Canada." In R. VanderVennen, ed. *Church and Canadian Culture*. Lanham: University Press of America, 1991.

Demerath III, N.J. "Cultural Victory and Organizational Defeat in the Paradoxical Decline of Liberal Protestantism." *Journal for the Scientific Study of Religion* 34 no. 4 (1995).

De Santis, S. "Dispute over Same-Sex Blessings Deepens over 'Illegal' Actions," *Anglican Journal*, 129 no. 8 (2003).

De Santis, S. "Yukon Bishop Faces Discipline," *Anglican Journal*, 129 no. 8 (2003).

De Santis, S. "Church Reacts to Native Boycott," *Anglican Journal* 129 no. 5 (2003).

De Santis, S. "Talks Proceed without Agreement," *Anglican Journal* 128 no. 44 (2002).

De Santis. S. "Inroads by Women Fall Short of Leadership Positions," *Anglican Journal* 127 no. 8 (2001).

De Santis, S. "Ottawa, Churches Discussing Financial Terms." *Anglican Journal* 127 no. 3 (2001).

De Santis, S. "Cost of Litigation Yields 2001 Deficit." *Anglican Journal,* 127 no. 01 (2001).

Donnelly, M. "Still Unready For Women Clergy," *Ecumenism* no. 73 (1984).

Duchesne, D. "Giving Freely: Volunteers in Canada." Statistics Canada, Labour Analytic Report No. 4, Catalogue No. 71–535, 1989.

Elections Canada On-Line, "Past Elections." 19 Dec. 2000 http://www.elections.ca/intro.asp?section=pas&document=index&lang=e&textonly=false.

Ellison, C. "Introduction to Symposium: Religion, Health, and Well-Being." *Journal for the Scientific Study of Religion* 37 no. 4 (1998).

Emberley, P. *Divine Hunger: Canadians on Spiritual Walkabout.* Toronto: HarperCollins, 2002.

Equal Marriage for Same Sex Couples, "Evolution: 20th Century." 15 May 2003 http://www.samesexmarriage.ca/evolution/20thcentury.html.

Equal Marriage for Same Sex Couples, "Equality – Timeline and Evolution of Marriage" 15 May 2003 http://www.samesexmarriage.ca/evolution/timeline.htm.

Evangelical Fellowship of Canada, "All Faiths Threatened by Criticism of Day's Beliefs." 21 Nov. 2000. 15 Mar. 2001 http://www.efc-canada.com/newsrel/policy/toler.htm.

Evangelical Fellowship of Canada, "The Vriend Decision." 2 April 1998. 23 Oct. 1999 http://www.evangelicalfellowship.ca/resources/resource_viewer.asp? Resource_ID=47.

Evangelical Fellowship of Canada, "Sexual Orientation." 15 May 2003 http://www.evangelicalfellowship.ca/social/issue_viewer.asp?Issue_Summary_ID=37.

Evangelical Fellowship of Canada, "Uncharted Waters: An Examination of the Federal Government's Plan to Include Sexual Orientation in the Human Rights Act of Canada," 1986. 14 May 2003 http://www.evangelicalfellowship.ca/resources/resource_viewer.asp?Resource_ID=80.

Evans, J. "Counting Crime." In R. Linden, ed. *Criminology: A Canadian Perspective,* 4th ed. Toronto: Harcourt Canada, 2001.

Federation of Independent Schools in Canada. "Provincial Funding of Independent Schools." 14 June, 2001
http://www.kingsu.ab.ca/~fisc/index.htm

Fenwick, F. "Residential School Update." *Law Now* 25 no. 3 (2001).

Fletcher-Marsh, W. *Beyond the Walled Garden: Anglican Women and the Priesthood*. Dundas, ON: Artemis Enterprises 1995. Quoted in a review by M. Powles in *Canadian Woman Studies* 17 no. 1 (1997): 124.

Focus on the Family, "Newsletter." Nov. 2000. 15 Jan. 2001
http://www.fotf.ca/resources/newsletters/CN1100.html.

Foot, R. "Ottawa, Off-loading on Catholics." *National Post* 27 Nov. 2002.

Foot, R. "Natives Filed $12.5B Class Action." *National Post* 4 Oct. 2002.

Foot, R. "Private Schools Must be Sold." *National Post* 24 May 2002.

Foot, R. "Ottawa Appeals Native Schools Ruling." *National Post* 11 Sept. 2001.

Foot, R. "Natives File $12.5B Class Action." *National Post* 4 Oct. 2002.

Fox, K. "Abuse-Redress Plan Flawed," *Globe and Mail* 1 Feb. 2002.

Frankel, B. and W.E. Hewitt. "Religion and Well-Being among Canadian University Students: The Role of Faith Groups on Campus." *Journal for the Scientific Study of Religion* 33 no. 1 (1994).

Fraser Institute. "Whose Ethics? Whose Religion? A Study of the Secular World of Secular News." *On Balance* 9 no. 1 (1996). 16 Feb. 2001
http://www.fraserinstitute.ca/publications/onbalance/1996/9-1.html.

Frederick, J.A. and M. Boyd. "The Impact of Family Structure on Completed High School." In *Canadian Social Trends* Vol. 3. Toronto: Thompson, 2000.

Gallup Canada. *The Gallup Poll* 57 no. 27 (1997).

Gallup Canada. *The Gallup Poll* 56 no. 78 (1996).

Gallup Canada. *The Gallup Poll* 55 no. 30 (1995).

Gallup Canada. *The Gallup Report*. 11 May 1983.

Garlarneau, D. and J. Sturrock. *Family Income After Separation*. Statistics Canada: Catalogue no. 13–588-MPB, no.5 (1997).

Gauvreau, M. "Protestantism Transformed: Personal Piety and the Evangelical Social Vision." In G Rawlyk, ed. *The Canadian Protestant Experience: 1760 to 1990*. Burlington, ON: Welch Publishing, 1990.

Gay.com UK. "Church Demands Exemption From Anti-Gay Discrimination Legislation." 18 Mar. 2003. 24 April 2003
http://uk.gay.com/headlines/3978.

Gee, E. "Gender Differences in Church Attendance in Canada: The Role of Labour Force Participation." *Review of Religious Research* 32 no. 3 (1991).

Gee, E. and J. Veevers. "Religious Involvement and Life Satisfaction in Canada." Sociological Analysis 51 no. 4 (1990).

Gidney, R. and W. Miller. "The Christian Recessional in Ontario's Public Schols." In M. Van Die, ed. *Religion in Public Life in Canada: Historical and Comparative Perspectives*. Toronto: University of Toronto Press, 2001.

Gonzalez, R. "Grandin Oblates Face Possible Bankruptcy." *Western Catholic Reporter*, 25 Mar. 2002.

Grant, John Webster. *The Church in the Canadian Era: The First Century of Confederation*. Toronto: McGraw-Hill, 1972.

Grenville, A. "The Awakened and the Spirit-Moved: The Religious Experiences of Canadian Evangelicals in the 1990s." In G. Rawlyk, ed. *Aspects of the Canadian Evangelical Experience*. Montreal and Kingston: McGill-Queen's University Press, 1997.

Grindstaff, C. "The Baby Bust Revisited." In C. Grindstaff and F. Trovato, eds. *Perspectives on Canada's Population: An Introduction to Concepts and Issues*. Toronto: Oxford University Press, 1994.

Hadaway, C., P. Marler, and M. Chaves. "What the Polls Don't Show: A Closer Look at US Church Attendance." *American Sociological Review* 58 no. 6 (1993).

Halman, L., T. Petersson, and J. Verweij. "The Religious Factor in Contemporary Society: The Differential Impact of Religion on the Private and Public Sphere in Comparative Perspective." *International Journal of Comparative Sociology* 40 no. 1 (1999).

Harrison, T. *Of Passionate Intensity: Right-Wing Populism and the Reform Party of Canada*. Toronto: University of Toronto Press, 1995.

Harvey, R. "Supreme Court Docket: End of the Road for Long Running Case." *ChristianWeek* 11 no. 22 (1998).

Harvey, R. "Media Fear US-style Religion." *Canadian Press Newswire* 22 Apr. 1997.

Heinrichs, K. "Fighting for the Alliance's Soul." *ChristianWeek* 14 no. 12 (2000).

Heinrichs, K. "Pentecostals Elect Woman to Executive." *ChristianWeek* 14 no. 11 (2000).

Heinrichs, K. "Baptist Group Ordains First Female Pastor." *ChristianWeek* 13 no. 6 (1999).

Hewitt, W. "The Quest for the Just Society: Canadian Catholicism in Transition." In W. Hewitt, ed. *The Sociology of Religion: A Canadian Focus*. Toronto: Butterworths, 1993.

Higgins, M. *The Muted Voice: Religion and the Media*. Ottawa: Novalis, 2000.

Hobart, C. "Intimacy and Family Life." In M. Baker, ed. *Families: Changing Trends in Canada*, 3rd ed. Toronto: McGraw Hill, 1996.

Hoover, Dennis. "Ecumenism of the Trenches? The Politics of Evangelical-Catholic Alliances in Canada and the United States." Colloquium on Cooperative Christianity, Atlantic Baptist University, Moncton, NB (April 2002).

Hunter, J. "Response to Davis and Robinson: Remembering Durkheim." *Journal for the Scientific Study of Religion* 35 no. 3 (1996).

Indian Residential Schools Resolution Canada. "Statistics." 19 Mar. 2003 http://www.irsr-rqpa.gc.ca/english/statistics.html.

Inglehart, R. and W. Baker. "Modernization, Cultural Change, and the Persistence of Traditional Values." *American Sociological Review* 65 no.1 (2000).

Inglehart, R. *Modernization and Postmodernization: Cultural, Economic, and Political Change in 43 Societies.* Princeton, NJ: Princeton University Press, 1997.

Ipsos-Reid. "Same Sex Marriage: the Debate Enjoined." 8 August 2003. 11 August 2003. http://www.ipsos-reid.com

Isajiw, W. *Understanding Diversity: Ethnicity and Race in the Canadian Context.* Toronto: Thompson, 1999.

Jansen, W. "Mennonites in Canada: Their Relations with and Effect on the Larger Society." In R. vanderVennen, ed. *Church and Canadian Culture.* Lanham: University Press of America, 1991.

Johnson, W. "Making the Gun Registry Look Good." *Globe and Mail* 16 Jan. 2003.

Kelly, K. "Newfoundland: Living without Catholic Schools." *Catholic New Times* 24 no. 7 (2000).

Koop, D. "Same Sex Bill Threatens Marriage." *ChristianWeek* 14 no. 4 (2000).

Koop, D. "Community of Concern Elects New Leader." *ChristianWeek* 13 no. 4 (1999).

Krishman, V. "Premarital Cohabitation and Marital Disruption." *Journal of Divorce and Remarriage* 28 no. 3–4 (1998).

Lamardin, L. "New West Approves Same Sex Blessings." *Anglican Journal* 128 no. 7 (2002).

Larmondin, L. and S. De Santis. "Same-Sex Decision Proves Costly." *Anglican Journal* 128 no. 7 (2002).

Larmondin, L. "Bishops Issue Guidelines on Homosexuality." *Anglican Journal* 123 no. 10 (1997).

LeBlanc, D. "Cauchon Pushes Same-Sex Marriage Bill," *Globe and Mail,* 18 July 2003.

Levin, J. and L. Chatters. "Research on Religion and Mental Health: An Overview of Empirical Findings and Theoretical Issues." In H. Koenig, ed. *Handbook of Religion and Mental Health.* San Diego, CA: Academic Press, 1998.

Lewington, J. "Student Surge to Private Schools Unlikely." *Globe and Mail* 11 May 2001.

Lockhead, D. "The United Church of Canada and the Conscience of the Nation." In R. vanderVennen, ed. *Church and Canadian Culture*. Lanham: University Press of America, 1991.

Luckmann, T. *The Invisible Religion: The Problem of Religion in Modern Society.* New York: Macmillan, 1967.

MacLeod, H. "The Cultural Transformation of the United Church of Canada." Paper presented at the Annual Meeting of the Canadian Sociology and Anthropology Association, 1981.

Makin, K. "Court Paves Way for Native Schools Lawsuit." *Globe and Mail* 28 Mar. 2003.

Marshall, D. *Secularizing the Faith: Canadian Protestant Clergy and the Crisis of Belief, 1850–1940*. Toronto: University of Toronto Press, 1992.

Martin, D. "Sociology, Religion, and Secularization: An Orientation." *Religion* 25 no. 4 (1995).

Martin, D. "The Secularisation Issue: Prospect and Retrospect." *British Journal of Sociology* 42 no. 3 (1991).

Martin, D. *A General Theory of Secularization*. Oxford: Blackwell, 1978.

McAteer, M. "Alpha Grows in Spite of Controversy." *Anglican Journal* 124 no. 6 (1998).

McAteer. M. "Bishops Vote Down Bill of Rights." *Anglican Journal* 124 no. 6 (1998).

McDaniel, S. and C. Strike. *Family and Friends*. General Social Survey Analysis Series No. 9, Statistics Canada, Catalogue no. 11–612E (1994).

Melnyk, G. "His Father's Mission: Preston Manning and the Christian Right." *The Canadian Forum* May 2000.

Mendelsohn, M. and R. Nadeau. "The Religious Cleavage and the Media in Canada." *Canadian Journal of Political Science* 30 no.1 (1997).

Mertl, S. "Compensation Decision Insults Native Abuse Victims." *The Chronicle-Herald* 14 July 2001.

Milan, A. "One Hundred Years of Families." *Canadian Social Trends* no. 56, 2000.

Miller, J. *Shingwauk's Vision: A History of Residential Schools*. Toronto: University of Toronto Press, 1996.

Murphy, T. "The English Speaking Colonies to 1854." In T. Murphy and R. Perrin, eds. *A Concise History of Christianity in Canada*. Toronto: Oxford University Press, 1996.

Nason-Clark, N. "Gender Relations in Contemporary Christian Organizations." In W.E. Hewitt, ed. *The Sociology of Religion: A Canadian Focus*. Toronto: Butterworths, 1993.

National Council of the Churches of Christ in the U.S.A. *Yearbook of American and Canadian Churches.* Nashville: Abingdon Press, 1973–2001.

Nemeth, M. et al. "God is Alive: Canada is a Nation of Believers." *Maclean's* 106 no. 4 (1993).

Nevitte, N. *The Decline of Deference: Canadian Value Change in Cross-national Perspective.* Peterborough, ON: Broadview, 1996.

Nichol. J. "Marriage Vows: Canada's Gays and Lesbians are Mounting a Strong Fight for the Legal Right to be Wed." *Macleans* 113 no. 52 (2001).

Noll, M. *A History of Christianity in the United States and Canada.* Grand Rapids, MI: W.B. Eerdmans, 1992.

Nunley, J. "Study Says US Seminaries Should Raise Standards," *Episcopal News Service* 12 April 2001. 22 Mar. 2002
http://www.ecusa.anglican.org/ens/2001–82.html.

Office of Indian Residential Schools Resolution. "Backgrounder." 1 Oct. 2001. 15 May 2002 http://www.ainc-inac.gc/ca/gs/sch/_e.html.

O'Hara, J. "No Forgiving: Canada's Largest Churches are Reeling Under Litigation." *MacLean's* 113 no. 25 (2000).

Paxton, P. "Is Social Capital Declining in the United States? A Multiple Indicator Assessment." *American Journal of Sociology* 105 no. 1 (1999).

Perault, L. "Historic Order Faces Bankruptcy." *National Post* 10 April 2002.

Perrin. R. "French Speaking Canada From 1840." In T. Murphy and R. Perrin, eds. *A Concise History of Christianity in Canada.* Toronto: Oxford University Press, 1996.

Pfrimmer, D. "A Lutheran Witness in Canadian Society." In R. vanderVennen, ed. *Church and Canadian Culture.* Lanham: University Press of America, 1991.

Picot, G. et al. *Why Do Children Move Into and Out of Low Income: Changing Labor Market Conditions or Marriage and Divorce.* Research Paper Series No.132. Statistics Canada (1999).

Portman, W. "Priests to Replace Marriage Commissions." *Anglican Journal* 127 no. 7 (2001).

Portman, W. "Lutherans Want to be Welcoming to Gays." *Anglican Journal* 125 no. 7 (1999).

Powles, C. "The Anglican Church and Canadian Culture." In R. vander-Vennen, ed. *Church and Canadian Culture.* Lanham: University Press of America, 1991.

Presbyterian Church of Canada. "Residential Schools, Frequently Asked Questions." 25 Mar. 2001.
http://www.presbyterian.ca/residentialschools/faq/html.

Putnam, R. "Bowling Alone: America's Declining Social Capital." *Journal of Democracy* 6 no. 1 (1995).

Rawlyk, G. "The Champions of the Oppressed: Canadian Baptists and Social, Political and Economic Realities." In R. vanderVennen, ed. *Church and Canadian Culture*. Lanham: University Press of America, 1991.

Reimer, S. "A Generic Evangelicalism? Comparing Evangelical Subcultures in Canada and the United States." In D. Lyons and M. Van Die, eds. *Rethinking Church, State & Modernity: Canada Between Europe and the USA*. Toronto: University of Toronto Press, 2000.

Rice, J. and M. Prince. *Changing Politics of Canadian Social Policy*. Toronto: University of Toronto Press, 2000.

Richards, G. "B.C. Joins Ontario in Embracing Same-Sex Marriage," *Globe and Mail*, 9 July 2003.

Richardson, C. "Divorce and Remarriage." In M. Baker, ed. *Families: Changing Trends in Canada*, 4th ed. Toronto: McGraw Hill, 2000.

Richardson, C. "Divorce and Remarriage." In M. Baker, ed. *Families: Changing Trends in Canada*, 3rd ed. Toronto: McGraw Hill, 1996.

Roberts, K. *Religion in Sociological Perspective*, 3rd ed. Wadsworth: Toronto, 1995.

Rovers, M. "Clergy to the Right: Social Factors and the Increasing Conservatism of Seminarians." *Grail* 11 no. 2 (1996).

Seljak, D. "Resisting the 'No Man's Land' of Private Religion: The Catholic Church and Public Politics in Quebec." In D. Lyon and M. Van Die, eds. *Rethinking Church, State, and Modernity: Canada Between Europe and America*. Toronto: University of Toronto Press, 2000.

Shepherd, H. "Breakaway Congregation to Ordain Gay Minister," *Canadian Press Newswire* 2 Feb. 1999.

Shepherd, L. "Unity Amidst Diversity? The Crisis over Homosexuality within the United Church of Canada." *Uniting Church Studies* 1 no. 2 (1995).

Sillars, L. "Agree with Thine Adversary Quickly." *British Columbia Report* 10 no. 1 (1998).

Simpson, J. "So Who's Really Got Virtue on Their Side?" *Globe and Mail* 10 Nov. 2000.

Slobodian L. "Jesuits Ending Funding to 16 Projects Including Jesuit Centre." *Catholic New Times* 9 Mar. 1997.

Smith, S. "Changes in Quebec Schools Create Opportunities." *ChristianWeek* 12 no. 10 (1998).

Spectator, N. "Cross Anti-Christian Prejudice off the List of Alliance Excuses." *Globe and Mail* 30 Jan. 2000.

Squires, A. "Homosexuality, Ordination, and the United Church of Canada." *Queen's Quarterly* 98 no. 2 (1991).

Stackhouse, J. "Bearing Witness: Christian Groups Engage Canadian Politics since the 1960s." In D. Lyons and M. Van Die, eds. *Rethinking Church, State*

& Modernity: Canada Between Europe and the USA. Toronto: University of
   Toronto Press, 2000.

Stackhouse, J. *Canadian Evangelicalism in the Twentieth Century: An Introduction
   to its Character.* Toronto: University of Toronto Press, 1993.

Stark, R. 1999. "Secularization: R.I.P." *Sociology of Religion* 60 no. 3 (1999).

Stark, R. and L. Iannaccone. "A Supply-side Reinterpretation of the Secularization of Europe." *Journal for the Scientific Study of Religion* 33 no. 3 (1994).

Statistics Canada. *The Daily* 10 Dec. 2001.

Statistics Canada. "National Survey of Giving, Volunteering, and Participating."
   The Daily 17 Aug. 2001.

Statistics Canada. *The Daily* 25 Nov. 1999

Statistics Canada. *Caring Canadians, Involved Canadians: Highlights from the
   1997 National Survey of Giving, Volunteering and Participating.* Catalogue
   no. 71–542-XIE (1998).

Statistics Canada. *The Daily* 2 June 98.

Statistics Canada. *Vital Statistics Compendium 1996.* Catalogue No. 84–214-
   XPE (1998).

Statistics Canada. *The Daily* 14 Oct. 1997.

Statistics Canada. *Canadian Families: Diversity and Change.* 15 June 2000
   http://www.statcan.ca/Daily/English/960619/d960619.htm#ART1 (1996).

Statistics Canada. *Census of Canada 1996.*

Statistics Canada. *Employment Income by Occupation: 1991. Census* Catalogue
   no. 93–332. (1993).

Statistics Canada. *Census of Canada 1981.* Catalogue no. 92–912 (1984).

Stiller, K. "Anglicans Consider Whether Centre Vanishing." *Anglican Journal*
   12 no. 10 (1998).

Stirk, F. "Same-Sex Blessings Split Synod." *ChristianWeek* 16 no. 7 (2002).

Sweet, L. *God in the Classroom.* Toronto: McClelland & Stewart, 1997.

Tamney, J. and S. Johnson. "Consequential Religiosity in Modern Society."
   Review of Religious Research 26 no. 4 (1985).

Todd, D. "Protestants Across Canada Join Roman Catholic Church in Clergy
   Shortage." *Canadian Press Newswire* 19 Aug. 2001.

Trickey, M. "Canadians Value Spirituality, Poll Indicates." *Vancouver Sun*
   22 Dec. 1997.

United Church of Canada. "Quick Facts." 2001. 15 May 2002
   http://www.uccan.org/ucc/quickfacts.htm.

United Church of Canada. "Response to the Government Announcement on
   Residential Schools." 30 Oct. 2001. 13 Dec. 2001
   http://www.uccan.org/airs/011030.htm.

United Church of Canada. "Gay and Lesbian Covenanting Services." 18 April 2001. 25 June 2001 http://www.uccan.org/marriage/glcs.htm.

United Church of Canada. "News Release on Vicarious Liability." 17 June 1999. 11 Jan. 2001 http://www.uccan.org/NewsRelease/990617.htm.

Valpy, M. "Same Sex Dispute Saddens Archbishop." *Globe and Mail* 19 June 2002.

Valpy, M. "Native Lawsuits Fuel Costly Bureaucracy." *Globe and Mail* 5 Mar. 2002.

Valpy, M. "Lawsuits Spell End of Tiny B.C. Diocese." *Globe and Mail* 29 Dec. 2001.

Valpy, M. "Gays Claim First Legal Marriages." *Globe and Mail* 15 Jan. 2001.

Valpy, M. "Throwing Cold Water on the Fires of Hell." *Globe and Mail* 29 July 1999.

Van Die, M. "Introduction." In M. Van Die, ed. *Religion and Public Life in Canada*. Toronto: University of Toronto Press, 2001.

Voas, D. et al. "Religious Pluralism and Participation: Why Previous Research is Wrong." *American Sociological Review* 67 no. 2 (1992).

Volunteer Canada and the Canadian Centre for Philanthropy. *Religion, Volunteering, and Religion: A Report* (1999).

Ward, M. "Pension Committee to Debate Extending Same Sex Benefits." *Anglican Journal* 125 no. 7 (1999).

Warwick, J. "Facing an Unprecedented Shortage of Priests." *Canadian Press Newswire* 12 Dec. 2000.

Waytiuk, J. "Merry Christmas, Chanukah, Ramadan." *Today's Parent* 16 no. 1 (2000).

Whitebloom, S. "Wedding Bells Ring for Catholic Priests." *Calgary Herald* 20 Nov. 1999.

Wilson, B. "Reflections on a Many Sided Controversy." In S. Bruce, ed. *"Religion and Modernization: Sociologists and Historians Debate the Secularization Thesis*. Oxford: Clarendon Press, 1992.

Wilson, B. *Religion in Secular Society*. Hammondsworth: Penguin, 1967.

Wilson, D. "Loosening the Residential School Logjam," *United Church Observer* Dec. 2002.

Woodward, J. "Priest Shortage Threatens Parishes." *Calgary Herald* 13 Feb. 2000.

Wu, Z. "Premarital Cohabitation and the Timing of First Marriage." *Canadian Review of Sociology and Anthropology* 36 no. 1 (1999).

Wuthnow, R. *After Heaven: Spirituality in America since the 1950s*. Berkeley, CA: University of California Press, 1998.

Wuthnow, R. *The Struggle for America's Soul: Evangelicals, Liberals, and Secularism*. Grand Rapids, MI: W.B. Eerdmans, 1989. Cited in L. Woodhead and P. Heelas, eds. *Religion in Modern Times: An Interpretative Anthology.* Oxford Blackwell, 2000.

Yearbook of American and Canadian Churches. Nashville: Abingdon Press, 1973–2001.

Zinnbauer, B., K. Pargament et al. "Religion and Spirituality: Unfuzzying the Fuzzy." *Journal for the Scientific Study of Religion* 36 no. 4 (1997).

Index